958   106392

Kwanten, L.
Imperial nomads.

DATE DUE

JAN 0 2 1996	
SR → San Anselmo	
Due Date: 2-19-98	
NOV 2 9 1998	
DEC 2 1 1998	
1-19-99	
JUN 0 7 2002	
DEC 2 2 2002	
MAR 1 8 2003	
AUG 1 3 2005	

GAYLORD   PRINTED IN U.S.A.

Imperial
Nomads

IMPERIAL

Luc Kwanten

A History
of Central Asia,
500-1500

NOMADS

University of Pennsylvania Press / 1979

Design by Tracy Baldwin
Composition by Deputy Crown, Inc.
Printing and binding by Halliday Lithograph

Library of Congress Cataloging in Publication Data

Kwanten, Luc.
  Imperial nomads.

  Bibliography: p.
  Includes index.
  1. Asia, Central—History. 2. Mongols—
History. I. Title.
DS786.K93   958   78-53339
ISBN 0-8122-7750-3

To Susie

Contents

Contents

Contents

Maps and Illustrations

Preface

The need for a new, up-to-date introduction to the history of Central Asia, and of the Mongols in particular, has been felt for a long time, especially as the only acceptable scholarly work was written more than four decades ago. The absence of such an introduction has frustrated many a student of the area. The present volume was conceived while I was preparing my lectures in the Department of Uralic and Altaic Studies at Indiana University. Over the semesters, these lectures notes expanded slowly, and as a result of the enthusiastic support of Robert Erwin, director of the University of Pennsylvania Press, finally assumed their present form.

The history of Central Asia presents numerous difficulties to those interested in it. One of the principal hurdles to overcome, if not the most important one, is that its history has been recorded in a multitude of languages, and it is beyond the ability of any one historian to be familiar with all of them. Consequently, the historian finds himself in the uneasy situation of having to rely on translations, whose accuracy and completeness he is unable to verify personally. I have had to rely on translations from Persian, Arabic, and Armenian, among other languages, and although I have been able to seek the opinion of many scholars competent in these languages, this nevertheless constitutes a major handicap. It is compounded by the fact, as I have had occasion to point out elsewhere, that many primary sources have neither been translated nor examined; in fact, a complete catalogue of available source material does not exist—has not yet been attempted.

Let me illustrate this particular problem with one example. In the present volume, I present an interpretation of early Turkic-Chinese relations based on an analysis of economic data. This analysis shows that Turkic-Chinese relations were determined by Turkic economic requirements, which were based, in turn, on their relations with the Byzantine empire. However, even though it is known that extensive Turkic-Byzantine contacts existed, only a few scholarly articles have been devoted to them. In fact, primary sources in Byzantine Greek have never been examined for precise information regarding the nature of these relations, and especially not with regard to economic data. Although I studied classical Greek, Byzantine sources remain a closed book to me, and my analysis is based essentially on Chinese sources. Therefore, it is quite possible that detailed examination of the Byzantine sources will substantially modify and refine the interpretation I have given, and I hope that my interpretation will stimulate the curiosity of a Byzantine scholar.

The problems referred to above, however, are not the only difficulties that confront the student of Central Asian history. Unlike almost all other areas of historical research, Central Asian history has not moved beyond the romantic interpretation. It is still the history of charismatic personalities, epic combats, and rampages across the steppe's vast expanse. The romantic interpretation has obscured, if not completely ignored, the fact that Central Asia had a tradition of its own and that, as in other areas of the world, economic, social, and political developments were closely interwoven. By training, as well as inclination, I belong to the French historiographical school commonly known as the *Annales* School, and I have rejected the impressionistic approach to Central Asian history that is still quite common today. Thus, the present volume presents a more objective approach to the subject and provides a new interpretation that rejects pure chance as a causative historical factor. The work, however, is a general introduction to the subject, and as such I felt it inappropriate to encumber it with a detailed scholarly apparatus presenting all the evidence for an interpretation or a conclusion. I intend, however, to present this evidence in an appropriate form to my colleagues in the not too distant future.

A work of this type is, quite obviously, deeply indebted to the work of other scholars, both past and present. It is a pleasure, therefore, to acknowledge this indebtedness, and even though it is impossible to mention every scholar who has influenced me, a few stand out. In particular, I wish to acknowledge the influence exerted on me, through their published scholarly work and through discussions, of Denis Sinor, Hans Bielenstein, Francis W. Cleaves, Herbert Franke, Walther Heissig, and John A. Boyle. On the practical side, I wish to thank my research assistants, Janet Novey and Michael Walter, for their untiring efforts in meeting my often impossible demands. Thanks are also due to John McGuigan and Jane Barry, my editors. Finally, a special word of gratitude to two people: Denis Sinor, chairman of the Department of Uralic and Altaic Studies, for so graciously indulging my urbanitis, and my wife, Susan, for reasons well known to her.

Chicago 1978

1

Introduction

For a long time Central Asia remained a neglected field of study, the domain of a few brilliant, eccentric scholars and a host of unenlightened amateurs. It is a field where misinformation is still more readily available than accurate documentation. During the last three decades there has been a remarkable change, and scholarly interest in the area has increased dramatically. Many reasons for this phenomenon could be advanced, but the driving force is the increased attention being given to comparative history: it now appears that the study of Central Asia in general, and of the Mongol empire in particular, is an important constituent element of integrative and comparative world history. A cursory glance at the history of the steppe empires clearly reveals this importance.

For those familiar with several major languages, a great number of highly specialized monographs and articles are available,[1] all of which require in addition a substantial knowledge of the region and its languages. When general works on Central Asia are considered, a serious dearth is immediately apparent. One is forced to rely on the work of the eminent French historian René Grousset, written more than three decades ago.[2] Although Grousset's work was a pioneering effort at the time it was written, it is now sadly and seriously outdated. Certainly Grousset cannot be blamed for not having incorporated the results of recent scholarly research into the many reprints and translations of his work. It must be pointed out, however, that the original work already suffered from a serious defect. Even though Grousset was an excellent writer and historian, his study was based entirely on secondary sources because he was unfamiliar with the area's principal languages. Thus, his work reflects the shortcomings of the material available to him.

Since the publication of Grousset's work, no attempt has been made to synthesize the results of modern research, or to use them with sources in the original languages. The present volume intends to do precisely that—to present to the nonspecialist an up-to-date, coherent, and, I hope, readable introduction to the fascinating history and civilization of Central Asia. To the specialist it offers a new interpretation, based upon an integrative approach, of the steppe's multifaceted history.

Many misconceptions about Central Asia exist, and one of the more common ones is that the area is a single, uniform topographic entity. In fact, Central Asia can be divided into four distinct regions. To the extreme north are the vast frozen marshes known as the tundra. South of this is the forested region, or taiga, which has two zones: the northern zone contains primarily coniferous trees; the southern, primarily deciduous ones. On its extreme southern reaches, the taiga permits agriculture in an area known as the black earth belt. From the taiga one reaches the steppe through a transition zone, the so-called wooded steppe. The steppe itself is a vast stretch of land, from the plains of Hungary to the Great Chinese Wall, suitable only for the growth of grasses. In its southern reaches it becomes a desert in which only a few oasitic regions permit agriculture. These four regions stretch out in belts over a huge area, from Hungary to China, from the Arctic Circle to the Persian plateaux. This area has one common physical feature—a cold and dry climate with enormous temperature variations nearly everywhere and less than six frost-free months a year.

Central Asia presents an environment hostile to the development of large human settlements. Only twentieth-century technology has permitted the creation of large towns in the tundra and taiga areas. The few ethnic groups that previously settled in these areas survived by means of the hunt, subsistence agriculture, and, in the extreme north, reindeer pastoralism; on account of the region's ecology, their numbers were always very small. Obviously the desert could support no society except settlements in the oasis areas, and here too, ecological conditions determined the size of the population. The only area suitable for the development of organized societies and states was the steppe itself and, to a more limited degree, the transition zone between the taiga and the steppe. On the steppe too, societal development was conditioned by ecological circumstances. In its natural state, the steppe is an enormous grazing land, suitable only for animal husbandry; hence, all steppe societies were of the pastoral-nomadic type. Some agriculture and hunting were practiced, for the most part on the steppe's fringes. The few sedentary states that existed, primarily in the desert oases, lived in close symbiotic relationship with the steppe, providing the pastoral nomads with agricultural products while the nomads provided them with animal products.

The steppe's staple product was the horse. Compared to the breeds of horses known in Western societies, the steppe horse is not a particularly beautiful animal. It is much smaller and stockier, and it has a thick neck, thick legs, a shaggy coat, and a disproportionately large head. What it lacks in beauty, however, it makes up for in resistance and endurance. A very sturdy animal, it can resist the extreme cold and the wide range of temperatures that prevail on the steppe, outlasting all other breeds, and it can subsist on almost any type of vegetal matter; it can even dig its food from under the snow. Its qualities were recognized in Western antiquity; Herodotus, describing the campaigns of Darius I (521–486 B.C.), stated that "the Scythian horse always put to flight the horses of the enemy."

The horse dominated all aspects of the steppe nomad's life. In steppe societies all the people were excellent horsemen and absolute masters of cavalry warfare. Their weapons and tactics were developed for maneuverability and efficiency on horseback. The steppe horsemen were thus the foremost archers of their time. Nearly seventeen hundred years after Herodotus, when the historians of the Chinese Ming dynasty attempted to explain the success of the Mongols, they wrote that "the Yüan arose in the northern areas. By nature they are good at riding and archery. Therefore, they took possession of the world through their advantage of bows and horses."[3] In the thirteenth century the Armenian historian Grigor of Akanc' wrote the history of the Mongol invasion of Armenia and entitled his work "History of the Nation of Archers."

Superior horsemanship and archery were combined with unique battle tactics to give the steppe nomad the military advantage over the soldier of the sedentary state. Because he was not encumbered by the impedimenta of war, the principal characteristics of the horseman's battle tactics were unpredictability and mobility. The technique of the hunt was clearly the source of the nomad's tactics. He never engaged in combat unless victory was almost inevitable. When confronted with a numerically superior force, which was nearly always the case, the steppe nomad avoided open combat as much as possible and attempted to lure the opponent into a trap. One of the most common tactics was for a small advance unit to feign withdrawal and draw the opponent into a long pursuit. When the latter was fatigued, the main steppe army moved in for the kill. Chinese, Persians, and generals of other nationalities through the ages complained bitterly about the wily and uncivilized ways of the steppe horseman, who refused to play by the rules of the art of war as determined by the sedentary, or so-called civilized, states. When a steppe state was powerful, a sedentary state could achieve a military victory only by a surprise attack.

Throughout its premodern history, the steppe's population was almost entirely of the Mongoloid race and the Altaic linguistic family. Only in the tundra, the desert oases, and a few isolated areas were other groups to be found, Paleoasiatic, Indo-European, and Uralic groups respectively. Most of the languages spoken on the steppe belonged to the Turkic group, followed in frequency by those of the Mongol and Tungusic groups, the latter primarily in present-day Manchuria. It appears that Turkic was for a long time the steppe's lingua franca. The steppe, however, was neither ethnically nor linquistically homogeneous. Deep cultural cleavages existed among the tribes inhabiting the steppe, and these cleavages, aggravated by political and economic differences, led to frequent conflicts. Indeed, warfare among the steppe tribes themselves and between the steppe tribes and sedentary states was a regular feature of steppe life. Peace was an uncommon phenomenon.

The Central Asian steppe was far from being merely an uncivilized and semi-arid region inhabited by nomadic barbarians solely concerned with rape and plunder. It was an area that fostered several major civilizations, though, because of their nomadic nature, these civilizations did not leave as many monuments, written or otherwise, as did the sedentary states. Nevertheless, their influence was felt by all the states that surrounded them, and, until the middle of the fifteenth century, they were a constant menace to the survival of the sedentary states. Militarily as well as politically, developments on the steppe had important consequences in such sedentary states as China and Persia. Until the beginning of modern times, a structured nomadic empire was always the strongest force for change on the Eurasian continent.

Although many nomadic states controlled substantial portions of the steppe, none was able to exert control simultaneously over both the nomadic and the sedentary zones of Eurasia. This task was left to the Mongol confederation, which, under the leadership of Chinggis-khan, established the world's largest continuous empire, extending from the plains of Russia to the China coast, from the Arctic reaches of Siberia to the sun-drenched Persian Gulf. From the beginning of the thirteenth century until the final decades of the fourteenth century, the known world was divided into two major parts—the Mongol empire and the European kingdoms. The Mongol conquest of sedentary states like China, Russia, and Persia resulted in profound changes in the traditional structures of these societies.

All too frequently, however, these nomadic empires, and especially the Mongol empire, are treated as if they were created *ex nihilo,* by accident, or by the wrath of God. Scholarly specialization on particular aspects of particular empires has obscured the fact that each one was built on the traditions of the previous empires, that there were common elements, other than their nomadic nature, in all of them. The principal common element was a historical tradition. When the Mongols created their empire, they were well aware of the history of the empires that had preceded them. Not only did they know what had brought these empires into existence, more importantly, they also knew what had led to their falls. Almost from the start, the Mongols took steps to assure their empire a longevity and a power not experienced by their predecessors.

One of the major difficulties in studying the history of Central Asian empires is that until the early eighth century none of them kept written records. With the creation of a script by the Turkic empire, the steppe people began to write their own history. Nevertheless, the native source material is very limited, barely enough to permit a rudimentary outline of the steppe's history, and then only beginning in the eighth century. It is possible, however, to trace the history of the steppe well back into antiquity, if one relies on the historical records of the sedentary states. This poses several serious methodological problems, for these sources are highly biased against the steppe nomad, which is not surprising given that these states were the steppe's perennial victims. Although the bias can be dealt with relatively easily, a major difficulty is created by the nature of the relations between the sedentary and the steppe worlds.[4] War was the predominant form of contact between them, and consequently most of the information contained in the sources deals with political and military affairs. Very little economic, social, and other information is available until late in the steppe's history when the steppe was unified by the Türks and the sedentary states were forced to obtain intelligence of this kind to counteract the Turkic threat. Another consequence of this situation is that more information is available about the heyday and the subsequent decline of a steppe empire than about its formation. Nevertheless, through a careful analysis of all the material available it is possible to elaborate a coherent picture of the steppe's historical development.

The nature of the material is not the sole problem that confronts the historian. The study of the steppe's history requires a knowledge of the languages of the principal sedentary states as well as their histories. Because the political center of the principal nomadic empires was the eastern steppe, the area that borders on China, a thorough familiarity not only with Chinese, but also with the peculiarities of Chinese historiography, is a prerequisite for the study of the nomadic empires. Chinese society was very history-conscious, but history always served a didactic and political purpose within the framework of Confucianism.[5] China viewed itself as the center of the world and as the world's most civilized nation; hence, a condescension dominated its perception of the steppe nomads and even led it to deny that the empires created by the nomads had any influence whatsoever on Chinese society.[6]

The Mongol empire was the culmination of a historical tradition that can be traced back to the Hsiung-nu empire, founded in the second century B.C. The Mongol empire was the most successful nomadic empire ever to be formed on the steppe, and hence the emphasis of the present volume is on its history. It is customarily divided into four primarily geographical subdivisions, and each of these is studied independently, with minimal, if any, reference to the other three, because of the nature of the available source material. An important consequence of this approach is that the differences between the subdivisions have been emphasized and their points in common are frequently glossed over. The specific differences between the subdivisions of the Mongol empire are important and cannot be denied, but, at the same time, it cannot be denied that there were important similarities, and, above all, a conceptual unity that existed almost until the empire's collapse.

As far as possible, this study will examine the Mongol empire as a coherent entity, not only its political history, but also its administrative, economic, and cultural structure. In contrast to many other general studies of the Mongols, the present one relies on primary sources and is not merely a synthesis of secondary material. In order to place the Mongol empire within a correct historical perspective, several chapters are devoted to the steppe empires that preceded the Chingizid empire. The steppe's historical traditions are traced from their first manifestation during the Hsiung-nu empire (209 B.C.–155 A.D.) through the formative years of the Mongol empire. Although attention is given to the western steppe, the emphasis is on the eastern steppe because the political center of nearly all steppe empires was located there, and, as a result, the nomadic empires had more contact with China than with any other sedentary state. This, combined with Chinese historical traditions, means that Chinese material contains the most abundant information on the steppe.

In antiquity, two empires dominated the steppe: the Scythian empire in the west and the Hsiung-nu empire in the east. Not enough is known about the two empires to enable one to form an accurate idea of the political and military situation on the steppe at that time. The history of the Hsiung-nu, however, is better documented than that of the Scythians, and consequently they are more important than the Scythians in an analysis of the structure of nomadic empires. Although it is limited, the information available permits the elaboration of the basic characteristics of a steppe empire, that is, those characteristics that all the nomadic empires up to and including the Mongols had in common. After the disappearance of the empires of antiquity, the steppe entered an unstructured period. Nomadic clans roamed its vast expanse, but no organized state appears to have come into existence. The first nomadic empire to succeed the Hsiung-nu was not formed until the fifth century, and it never enjoyed the importance the Hsiung-nu had known. The first attempts at empire building, roughly based on a Chinese model, did not last long. They were quickly succeeded by the formation of the Turkic empire and the unification of the steppe under its authority.

The Turkic people were the founders of the first major and relatively well documented steppe empire. They were also able to gain control over nearly the entire steppe. Their authority reached from the Great Wall of China to the Caspian Sea, and the existence of such a powerful empire had an impact on both the Chinese and Byzantine worlds. The sedentary world recognized the importance of the Turkic empire and the threat it posed to their security. Hence, more documentation is available, permitting a better evaluation of the processes of empire building and consolidation as well as an insight into the factors that caused the steppe empires to collapse. The Türks were the first nomads to create an administration of their own and the first for whom trade was an important economic factor. The importance of trade to the Türks and the reluctance of the Chinese in particular to engage in trade with them led to a high incidence of conflicts between the two empires. The Chinese, however, were successful in controlling the steppe and the steppe nomads only when internal steppe politics had drastically weakened the nomadic empire. Most of these internal tensions were a consequence of the absence of an adequate legal and legislative system, a defect that was remedied by the Mongols.

The collapse of the Turkic empire was followed by a long period of transition during which many Turkic tribes attempted to recreate their lost empire, although none of the states created during this period openly aimed at controlling the steppe in its entirety again. The restoration attempts took place not only on the steppe, where they led to the formation of the Uighur empires, but also in the surrounding sedentary areas. The main Turkic effort, hesitant at first, was concentrated in the Middle East, primarily Persia. There, at the beginning of the eleventh century, they were able to create the Saljuq empire, the first of many sedentary Turkic empires in the Middle East. While some Turkic tribes created sedentary Middle Eastern states and the Uighurs did the same on the central steppe, some minor tribes formed small nomadic kingdoms on the Russian steppe, in particular in the Volga-Don area.

During the Turkic Imperial period the western steppe had an important political role on account of trade requirements. However, simultaneously with the collapse of the Turkic empire, Chinese power went into a steep decline. The resulting power vacuum had important consequences: the western steppe's political role ceased, and it became, in essence, an area from which the Turkic Middle Eastern states drew their soldiery, while near the Chinese border several important border empires were formed, two of which empires in time came to be considered legitimate Chinese dynasties. Meanwhile the central steppe sank into a state of anarchy that lasted nearly two centuries.

This state of anarchy ended only when, late in the twelfth century, several tribes united to form the beginning of the Mongol confederation. Under the leadership of Temujin, the future Chinggis-khan, and drawing on the historical traditions of the steppe, the confederation expanded to become, quite rapidly, the most powerful force on the steppe. Once the confederation was solidly united behind its leader, it set out to conquer what had been the steppe's principal target for centuries: China. Eventually, the conquest led to control over practically the entire known world and the formation of the world's largest nomadic-sedentary empire ever.

When the Mongol empire collapsed, it was followed by a number of successor states, most located on the steppe and all having a mixed nomadic-sedentary structure. Some of these successor states, like the Timurids, had brief moments of glory, but none had anything close to an important historical role. The collapse of the Mongol empire meant the end of the steppe as a factor in world politics. The sedentary states, which had been occupied by the steppe nomads for well over a century, had acquired from them the techniques to resist aggression from the steppe. In a reversal of traditional roles, the sedentary states expanded into the steppe and in the end absorbed it completely. The steppe's decline is one of the most complex issues in the history of Central Asia. An examination of the causes, however, leads to the conclusion that if the Mongol empire was the culmination of a historical tradition, it also marked the end of the steppe's nomadic tradition: the Mongols were the last nomadic emperors.

2

The Formative
Years

The formation of an imperial tradition on the steppe, distinct from that prevalent in the sedentary states, began during the second century B.C. and was completed towards the end of the sixth century A.D. Although during this period the steppe witnessed the rise and fall of several empires and numerous kingdoms, all had one characteristic in common—the absence of a script in which to keep their own historical records.[1] The history of the steppe's formative period can be learned only through a careful examination of the records of the surrounding sedentary states. More often than not, relations between these states and the steppe were hostile, a fact clearly reflected in the historical sources, which refer primarily to political events, especially at times of war or tension; when peaceful relations existed, information becomes scarce and stereotyped. Political hostility was supplemented by cultural hostility, which led to the permanent negative portrayal of the steppe "barbarian."* If, moreover, it is recognized that the historical records of the sedentary states themselves are not abundant, it is easily understood that a coherent portrayal of Central Asian history during this period is an almost impossible task.

Nevertheless, it is possible to determine some of the constants of steppe history, which became more distinct as well as better documented as the Central Asian empires developed after the sixth century. Throughout the formative period, three constants can be noticed: first, the history of each empire appears to be cyclical; second, confederated states rather than homogeneous states were necessary for empire formation; and third, the empire's military power was disproportionate to its population. Each of the empires and kingdoms that existed during the eight-century-long formative period had its own distinct historical development. Nevertheless, their rises and collapses have these common characteristics in varying degrees.

The formation of a new empire or kingdom always occurred under the direction of a charismatic tribal chieftain who was capable of uniting divergent interests into a common cause and who was nearly always the best military leader within the tribal structure. Although hereditary rule existed in most of the states, it was neither a predominant nor an exclusive factor. Military and leadership qualities played the most important role in the selection of a ruler, and his position nearly always needed at least the tacit approval of the other chieftains. The charismatic nature of the leadership played an important role in the internal tensions of the state, and, nearly always, was one of the dominant factors in its decline. Challenges to the authority of the leader by other chieftains created centrifugal tendencies. When the charisma and therefore the power of the ruler declined, these centrifugal tendencies led to civil war, which in turn led to the breakup of the state's apparent unity. When a new state emerged from the turmoil, its leadership was once again in the hands of a charismatic military leader.

The movement for the creation of a new state appears to have been nearly always confined to a particular tribal unit. From there, through alliances, conquests, and threats of conquest, the size of the state increased. The distinction between empire and kingdom was basically one of territorial size. Ethnically, kingdoms appear to have been fairly homogeneous, with but a limited number of alliances with ethnically and linguistically related tribes; inherent in this is a limitation of territorial control. If the binding element in the kingdoms tended to be ethnic and linguistic unity, in the empires it was the charismatic personality and the military skill of the ruler. Furthermore, a necessary element in imperial unity was a com-

---

*The term *barbarian*, a translation of the Chinese *i*, is commonly used to refer, in general, to the people of Central Asia. The original meaning of *i* came close to the Greek *barbaroi*; thus, it was a generic designation for non-Chinese people. In time, and in most studies, the term has assumed an exclusively pejorative meaning. I use the term here as a matter of convention only, without adhering to its pejorative connotations.

munity of economic and political interests among the different tribes. The disappearance of such a community nearly always preceded the appearance of a challenge to the established authorities and was an equally important factor in an empire's disintegration.

The natural resources of the steppe were limited and could support only a relatively small population during the formative era and in the centuries following it. Although no figures are available, the evidence suggests that the steppe states had small populations, especially when compared with the sedentary states. For example, when the Avars penetrated Europe and founded their kingdom, both Turkic and Byzantine sources indicate that they numbered only 20,000.[2] Although the population of the steppe states was small, they nearly always presented the most serious threat to the security of the sedentary states. The strength of the nomad lay not in numbers but in his unsurpassed skills as a horseman and a warrior. Horses, the steppe's staple product, were available to the nomad in nearly unlimited numbers, whereas for the sedentary states they were frequently in short supply. The nomad thus possessed the advantage of mobility. An equally important element in the nomad's military superiority lay in the battle tactics used, which were based on hunting; until the end of the steppe as a political force, the nomad's military training was acquired in the hunt. The most common complaint uttered by opponents was that the nomad engaged in combat only when his chances of victory were the greatest; like the hunter, the nomad struck only when sure of success. Moreover, his mobility and guerilla tactics made it nearly impossible for the sedentary states to pursue and attack him on the steppe proper. The sedentary states were able to score victories over their nomadic foes only when they were able to stage a surprise attack. Nomadic states crumbled under military pressure only when attacked by other nomadic states.

The Steppe Unstructured

The history of the formative years of the steppe coincides, by and large, with the period of disorder that followed the collapse of China's first golden era, the Han dynasty (206 B.C.–220 A.D.). During the Han dynasty, the steppe was dominated by the Hsiung-nu empire, whose fate appears to have been closely tied to the history of the Han dynasty itself. This appearance, however, is a consequence of the fact that most of the information available on the Hsiung-nu is derived from the Chinese annals, whose information has been supplemented in the last few decades by major archeological discoveries in Noin-Ula and other places in Mongolia.[3]

The Hsiung-nu were not the first organized state on the steppe, for they appear to have built upon a pre-existing, but unknown, tradition. Only archeological evidence attests to the historical existence of earlier steppe civilizations,[4] but there were at least three such centers of civilization, and the evidence suggests a presence on the steppe several centuries before the Hsiung-nu. The first one was located in the Altai region and is named the Pazyryk culture after the place where the first tombs were opened in 1929. This and later finds revealed an advanced material culture never suspected to have existed on the steppe until well into the Christian era. The two other centers were located on the Yenissei River and are known as the Tagarsky and the Minusinsk cultures. The latter appears to have been the more important of the two, for it seems to have been a starting point of migrations and an area where different steppe cultures came into contact with each other. The relationship between these anonymous people and the Hsiung-nu is unknown.

The Hsiung-nu, a people speaking an Altaic language, dominated the steppe before the founding of the Han dynasty. Whether they were proto-Turkic or proto-Mongol, and whether or not they were related to the Huns of European history are still matters of heated debate among specialists, and it is unlikely that a satisfactory answer to these questions will ever be found. What is not in dispute is the fact that they are considered to be the first real steppe empire, contemporaneous with Chinese antiquity. During most of China's earliest history, they did not form a unified state.[5] Their empire building coincided with the unification of China under the Ch'in dynasty (221–207 B.C.). Founded about the year 210 B.C., the empire developed fully during the reign of its second ruler, Mao-tun (ca. 209–174 B.C.). The Hsiung-nu empire had the traits that were to be characteristic of all steppe empires until the advent of the Mongols. They clearly established that, even for a nomadic empire, land was of major importance. To Mao-tun is attributed the statement "Land is the basis of a nation."[6]

The relations between China and the Hsiung-nu were primarily of a hostile nature. The details of the numerous wars and treaties between the two antagonistic forces is outside the scope of the present account. It must be pointed out, however, that neither side was ever capable of gaining effective control over the other, but more often than not the advantage lay with the steppe nomads. Passive Chinese defense—the Great Wall—was ineffective and onerous; active defense—military campaigns deep into the steppe—had but a limited effect and that at a very high cost.

Thus, the Chinese were forced to develop a policy that dealt with the barbarian threat at a reasonable cost. After a long debate, a policy whose basic principle was appeasement was adopted. It was based on a set of assumptions, all of which reinforced the notion of the supremacy of Chinese institutions and culture and of their acceptability to the barbarians; the idea that the latter might not have had any need for Chinese culture was never entertained.[7] The policy had two important constituent elements: the *i-i chih-i,* "using barbarians to check barbarians," and *chi-mi,* "loose rein." The Chinese would not interfere with the barbarians unless they actually threatened China; they would use material inducements to draw the barbarians into the Chinese cultural realm and then absorb them; and, finally, they would destroy the barbarian confederation by dividing it. It is fair to state that the motto of Chinese foreign policy was "divide and conquer." Developed by the Han dynasty, it remained China's basic foreign policy until the twentieth century.

The policy proved to be successful. Dissensions among the Hsiung-nu tribes came to the fore in the years following Han Wu-ti's campaigns (140–87 B.C.). These campaigns had not been able to break Hsiung-nu power, but they had driven them away from the heartland of China, and war was confined to the *limes* of the Han empire, the Tarim basin and the Kansu corridor. When the ruler of the Hsiung-nu, Hu-han-yeh (58–31 B.C.), was challenged in his authority by his brother Chih-chih (56–36 B.C.), the Chinese government was given the opportunity to divide the Hsiung-nu. Hu-han-yeh needed Chinese protection to maintain his throne, an assistance the Chinese gladly provided. This resulted in a first division of the Hsiung-nu empire, into western and eastern branches. Very little is known about the first. The decline of the Former Han, which began shortly after the conflict between the two brothers, permitted a rise in power of the Hsiung-nu, as they were able to take advantage of the Chinese withdrawal from the steppe. By the time Wang Mang (9–25 A.D.) seized the throne and established his ephemeral dynasty, the Hsiung-nu were, once again, in control of the Tarim basin and major portions of the Kansu steppe.[8] Although Hsiung-nu power had decreased dramatically since the time of Mao-tun, China's power had declined even more.

In 25 A.D. a distant relative of the rulers of the Former Han dynasty (206 B.C.–8 A.D.) seized power in a coup d'état and proclaimed the rebirth of the Han dynasty. He adopted the reign title of Han Kuang-wu, and the dynasty he founded became known as the Later Han (25 A.D.–220 A.D.); it is one of the very few examples of a successful dynastic restoration in Chinese history.[9] Other than the restoration of imperial power, one of the problems requiring the immediate attention of the new emperor was the reopening of the Inner Asian trade routes, which, during the decline of the Former Han and the period of the Wang Mang usurpation, had come again under the control of the barbarian Hsiung-nu.

When Han Kuang-wu re-established the Han dynasty, he immediately took steps to reassert China's authority over the border regions. This reassertion was the work of three of the greatest generals in Chinese history. Ma Yüan (14 B.C.–49 A.D.) re-established Han control over the coastal areas and over portions of present-day North Vietnam. Pan Ch'ao (32 A.D.–102 A.D.) and Pan Yung (ca. 120 A.D.) re-established control over Turkestan and the Tarim basin in particular. Under Pan Ch'ao, Chinese Turkestan penetrated its farthest into Central Asian territory. In 97 A.D., he marched all the way to the Persian Gulf or the Black Sea before returning to China. Pan Ch'ao's campaigns reopened the so-called Silk Route, the main trade route between the Chinese and the Mediterranean worlds.[10]

The new Chinese penetration of the steppe had drastic consequences for the Hsiung-nu, whose power at the time was more apparent than real. Their internal dissensions, whose causes are not documented, resurfaced.

In 48 A.D., when a new ruler acceded to the throne, not all the tribes recognized him as their leader. This led to the division of the Eastern Hsiung-nu into northern and southern branches and virtually marked the end of their empire. The Northern Hsiung-nu established an empire roughly located in present-day Mongolia. The Chinese found an ally against them in another Central Asian tribe, then on the rise and favorably inclined towards the Chinese: the Hsien-pi. In 92 they inflicted a severe defeat on the Northern Hsiung-nu, and in 155 they eliminated the remnants of the Northern Hsiung-nu empire. The Hsien-pi, about whom very little is known, never formed a major empire and soon were completely sinicized.[11]

With the collapse of the Hsiung-nu empire, a long period of disorder and political instability began on the steppe proper and lasted until the beginning of the fifth century. Small Hsiung-nu kingdoms survived and occasionally raided Chinese territory. Little is known about them, however.

The relationship between the Hsiung-nu and the Huns who invaded Europe is a vexing problem. At the beginning of the fourth century, tribes that the Chinese called Hsiung-nu were still active on the Chinese border; in 311 they were able to sack the Chinese capital of Lo-yang, then in the hands of the Western Chin dynasty (266–316). It is not clear, however, whether these Hsiung-nu were descendants of the Northern or Southern branch. In a Sogdian letter referring to the sack of Lo-yang, they are referred to as "Huns." This establishes a tenuous relationship at best between the Hsiung-nu and the Huns.[12] What is known is that during the period in Chinese history called the Period of Disunion (316–589), several small dynasties were created by the alleged descendants of the Southern Hsiung-nu, none of which had an important historical role. Furthermore, most of these dynasties, although barbarian in origin, appear to have been almost completely sinicized.[13] Their scantily documented history no longer belongs to the history of the steppe, but to Chinese history.

The power vacuum created by the decline of the Hsiung-nu empire was not filled by any new group on the steppe. For a short while it permitted certain groups of Indo-European background to have a more important role in the Chinese annals. The two principal ones were the Wu-sun and the Kucha kingdom. Little is known about the Wu-sun except that they lived in what became known as Chinese Turkestan during the second century. It appears that they were identical with the people known to Strabo as the "Asioi" and that their language was related to Iranian. The Kucha kingdom, a sedentary state to the south of the Wu-sun, was founded at about the same time as the Former Han dynasty and survived until the sixth century. Its influence on the steppe was minimal, but it was important in Chinese intellectual and religious history, for it was one of the major areas responsible for the introduction of Buddhism into China in Han times.[14]

Whether or not the Hsiung-nu had a lasting influence on the steppe cannot be determined for lack of adequate information. It appears, however, that they developed a state structure that anticipated the one formed several centuries later by the Turkic tribes. At the head of the Hsiung-nu state was the *shan-yü,* or emperor, the predecessor of the Turkic *qaghan.* Like the latter, his appointment appears to have required the approval of the tribal chieftains. The Hsiung-nu elite seems to have been based on military prowess, a feature all the steppe empires were to have in common. Also found in an embryonic form was a community of economic and military interests. The available data, however, do not permit elaboration of this scanty outline of the structure of the Hsiung-nu empire.[15] In essence, the importance of the Hsiung-nu lies in the fact that their history was recorded, at least partially, by their primary enemy, the Chinese.

A Barbarian Dynasty in China

The power of the Later Han decreased precipitously during the second half of the second century. Although it was not formally abolished until the year 220, for all practical purposes it ceased to function in 190, when one of the generals fighting a major rebellion, known as the Yellow Turban Rebellion, seized the capital, deposed the emperor, and appointed one of his own. This action marked the beginning of a prolonged period of turmoil and territorial division in China that ended only in the later part of the sixth century. Many dynasties succeeded each other, each more ephemeral than the last. Warfare, rebellion, and banditry were the principal characteristics of this period, one of the darkest in China's history; an analogy is often made with the European Dark Ages.

A consequence of the turmoil was that many historical records of the period did not survive. The documents that did survive deal with events within Chinese territory; very little, if any, information is available about the steppe. Many tribes are referred to, but the scantiness of the information and the inconsistency of the names attributed to the tribes do not permit the formation of a comprehensive picture. By the beginning of the fourth century, the situation became somewhat clearer, in that China reflected a clear north-south division. During this period, which lasted until 589, North China witnessed the formation of several dynasties of barbarian origins; official Chinese historiography accounts for sixteen such dynasties. It was also during this period that a new ethnic group, the Tibetans, made their appearance on the Chinese political scene. It should be pointed out, however, that this identification is merely a matter of convention, based on later Chinese sources dealing with the Tibetan empire proper. It was one of these so-called Tibetan dynasties that attempted to consolidate the North. Fu Chien, its leader, temporarily succeeded in this effort, but when he planned a southward expansion he was defeated, in 383, at the Fei River, and his entire endeavor collapsed. The battle of the Fei River, whose importance is often exaggerated, traditionally marks the permanent division between the North and the South in Chinese history.[16]

It was around this time, too, that a new barbarian group, the T'o-pa, also known as the Tabghach, came forward. The contemporary Chinese records refer to the Tabghach as a branch of the Hsien-pi people. The confusion in Chinese sources dealing with the barbarians makes it impossible to take this statement at face value. Frequently the Tabghach are referred to as a Turkic people on the basis of remnants of their language that have survived in Chinese transcriptions. The linguistic techniques used to come to this conclusion, however, leave something to be desired. The most that can be said with certainty is that they had come from the steppe, were most likely of Altaic stock, and were successful in creating their own dynasty in North China, a dynasty known as the Northern Wei (386–534). Their success was such that their tribal name, Tabghach, was used by the people of Central Asia to designate North China.[17]

When the Tabghach created their dynasty and established full control over China, they retained in their state structure elements from the steppe. Several ethnic groups made up the dynasty's leading classes. Although statistics concerning this period must be treated carefully, nearly 40 percent of the elite was of barbarian origin, half of them being of Tabghach origin. The military aristocracy of the steppe was transferred easily to North China at a time when warfare was almost a permanent state of affairs. Accompanying the military aristocracy was the feudal administration of the state. The imposition of this system, and its acceptance by the native Chinese elite, was facilitated by the general return throughout China to feudal-type institutions. The feudalism introduced by the Tabghach made them the dominant social group in Northern Wei society. During the existence of the Northern Wei, nearly eight hundred and fifty appanages were awarded. Three quarters of these were in the hands of the Tabghach, and the remainder were divided among other ethnic groups.[18]

The actual administration of the state created by the Tabghach was in the hands of the Chinese elite and followed Confucian patterns. This is dramatically illustrated in the number of governors and censors appointed during the dynasty. Nearly twice as many Chinese were appointed to these important administrative positions as were Tabghach and other barbarians. The Tabghach, however, controlled all military posts, including those of military censors. It is clear that they viewed themselves as an aristocratic, military caste that stood above the rest of society and reaped the spoils of conquest.[19] The Northern Wei state was strictly centrally organized, and all the key positions within the central government were, and remained, in the hands of the Tabghach imperial family. Although the central administration was divided into a series of offices inspired by the Chinese model, the military nature of the Northern Wei state was reflected clearly within that structure, in most of its offices, as well as in its official titles. The only two purely Chinese institutions were the Ministry of Personnel and the Bureau of Historiography.[20]

The social stratification that developed among the Tabghach themselves led to a separation into two distinct social classes, which had little in common other than their ethnic origin. There were, on the one hand, the Tabghach imperial and associated families, and on the other hand, those Tabghach who had no function in the government of the Northern Wei state. The latter increasingly disassociated themselves from the state and resumed a nomadic existence. The Tabghach referred to in the records of the T'ang and Sung dynasties most likely were the descendants of the second group. While a substantial number of Tabghach returned to or at least maintained their steppe traditions, the elite underwent a slow but unmistakable sinicization. This process was markedly accelerated during the last two decades of the fifth century, when the emperors issued a series of edicts whose most obvious purpose was the identification of the Tabghach elite with Chinese culture.

The sinicization of the upper stratum of the Tabghach was progressive. It was completed and officialized during the reign of Emperor Hsiao-wen (471–499), who remodeled the institutions of the Northern Wei after the patterns existing in the Southern, that is, purely Chinese, dynasties. The first measures promulgated were the replacement of "barbarian" rituals by Chinese imperial rituals (in 480) and orders favoring interracial marriages (in 483). The three most important decrees were promulgated in 494, 495, and 496. The first was an important symbolic act, the transfer of the Northern Wei capital south to the former Chinese capital of Lo-yang.[21] The transfer created serious tensions among the Tabghach elite because many had important economic interests in the North, and it was a factor in the division of the Northern Wei four decades later. The second measure, more important in the long run, was the prohibition of the Tabghach language at the court in favor of Chinese. Severe penalties were imposed in order to enforce the decree. The final decree ordered the Tabghach elite to adopt Chinese surnames. The imperial family was henceforth referred to as "Yüan" rather than "T'o-pa."[22]

In the area of religion, however, the Tabghach did not follow a purely Chinese line. Rather than Confucianism, the Tabghach adopted Buddhism, albeit in its Chinese form, as their official religion, and became active propagators of their faith. By and large, however, even the adoption of Buddhism occurred within their assimilation policy. Indeed, the Period of Disunion, characterized by turmoil, warfare, and impermanence, was the time when Buddhism became firmly implanted in China and assumed the characteristics that distinguished it from its Indian original. To the scholar and the commoner alike, Buddhism provided an understanding of and an escape from the insecurity of daily existence that Confucianism could not.[23]

One of the major political consequences of the development of Chinese Buddhism was the formation of monastic institutions with their own hierarchies, which began to form a parallel authority to that of the rulers. This development eventually led to occasional persecutions of the faith. The first dynasty to react against the proliferation of monastic institutions and their independence from state authority was the Northern Wei. In 446 a serious persecution was ordered, but although many monasteries were destroyed and Buddhist books burned, the persecution did not have lasting consequences. Two decades later Buddhism was again flourishing and actively supported by the elite, a support that led to the creation of the famous Buddhist sculptures of the Yun-kang and Lung-men caves. In fact, during the Period of Disunion the arts flourished under the influence of Buddhism. From this viewpoint, it is one of the more interesting periods in Chinese history.[24]

The Northern Wei, begun as a "barbarian" dynasty, was by the beginning of the sixth century for all practical purposes a native Chinese dynasty. As such, it was drawn into the turmoil that led, in 581, to the reunification of China under the rule of the Sui dynasty (581–618), founded by Yang Chien, who is better known under his posthumous title of Sui Wen-ti (581–604). The Yang family had served, during the Period of Disunion, Tabghach and Hsien-pi rulers, and Yang Chien was married to a woman of "barbarian" origin. He became an important minister at the court of the Northern Chou dynasty (557–581), allied to the emperor through marriage ties. When the emperor died and the only successor was an infant, Yang Chien assumed the throne and began a long but successful campaign to reunify China. In the process, the territory that had once been under Tabghach control reverted to the Chinese.[25]

The Nomadic Empires

While the Tabghach identified themselves with the conquered society, on the steppe proper a new force made its appearance around the beginning of the fifth century: the Juan-juan. Very little is known about their ethnic and linguistic affiliation. The empire they formed covered, roughly, the territory between the watersheds of the Orkhon and Selenga rivers, the northern edge of the T'ien-shan Mountains, and the Ordos steppe. Even their real name is not known, for the name under which they became known to history was, in its multiple spelling variants, a Chinese pejorative term meaning the "wriggling worms."[26] They first appear in the historical records of the Northern Wei dynasty during the reign of the dynasty's founder, T'o-pa Kuei (386–409). At that time it was reported that a certain Shih-lun, a Juan-juan chieftain, had defeated and subjugated the Kao-ch'e people, who had a small kingdom in the Karashahr area. Later genealogies trace the Juan-juan to the Hsiung-nu and state that they were first mentioned around 277. The existing genealogies, however, are not in agreement with each other, and those of the Northern Wei clearly served a political purpose: to prove that the Juan-juan were a subject people.

The known political history of the Juan-juan is basically limited to the history of their military clashes with the Northern Wei. The wars between the Juan-juan and the Tabghach followed the traditional patterns of nomadic invasions, and frequently the Juan-juan emerged as the victors in these contests. To defend themselves, the Tabghach resorted first of all to a Chinese-style passive defense, a wall built on the border. The fortified border zone they erected was some five hundred miles long. This, however, proved inadequate, and they resorted to a more active defense: direct attacks on Juan-juan homelands and attempts at creating dissension among the Juan-juan clans. The first major attack took place in 425 and was conducted in the nomadic style of warfare. A light cavalry with a small supply train crossed the Gobi Desert, took the Juan-juan ruler, Ta-t'an (414–429), by surprise, and forced him to flee northwards. Building on this success, the Northern Wei emperor, T'ai-wu (424–451), began preparations for a massive and major attack, which was launched four years later. In the summer of 429, the Juan-juan were severely defeated; although Ta-t'an escaped capture, he apparently died shortly after the battle.

The Northern Wei, however, was confronted soon thereafter with the same problems the Han dynasty had had in its relations with the Hsiung-nu; neither a passive nor an active defense was particularly efficient, and both were onerous. Like the Han dynasty, the Northern Wei searched for allies on the steppe to conduct the war with the Juan-juan. Alliances were made with minor nomadic kingdoms such as those of the Wu-sun, the Kao-ch'e, and the Yüeh-pan on the eastern and western borders of the Juan-juan domain, but even after the Juan-juan were encircled, the threat of their attacks was not reduced. Two major campaigns launched by the Northern Wei in 438 and 443 were disastrous; in fact, they gave the Juan-juan the opportunity to take the offensive and regain control over some of the smaller states on their western borders.

During the following decades a continuous state of war existed, with the Northern Wei most frequently on the offensive. At the beginning of the reign of the Juan-juan emperor Yü-ch'eng (450–485), it appeared that he might recognize Tabghach overlordship. Nothing came of these plans, for in 452 the Northern Wei emperor was assassinated and his successor, Wen-ch'eng (452–465), again planned a military conquest of the Juan-juan. Although Wen-ch'eng was successful in several raids against his enemies, his attempts at their conquest failed. The years that followed another campaign in 470 were characterized by a relative peace on the eastern border of the Juan-juan empire. In contrast, the western border was in turmoil as the Juan-juan reasserted their control over the states of Karashahr and Khotan. Thus, the beginning of the sixth century saw the Juan-juan involved in conquests on their western border and subjected to Tabghach attacks on their eastern border.

If the campaigns of the Northern Wei created problems for the Juan-juan, they proved unable to break the military backbone of the steppe empire. Until the reign of Tou-lun (485–492), the Juan-juan appear to have presented a united force. If internal dissension existed, the sources do not reveal it, nor do they indicate that the Northern Wei was successful in creating dissension in the enemy camp. With the reign of Tou-lun, however, this situation began to change, marking the beginning of the decline of Juan-juan power, which was first manifested when Kao-ch'e regained its independence and which culminated in the destruction of the Juan-juan empire half a century later at the hands of a new force on the steppe, the Türks.

Tensions within the Juan-juan empire came to the fore when a military rivalry developed between Tou-lun and his uncle Na-kai. Whereas the former proved unable to score major military victories, the latter encountered success after success. As a consequence, he was apparently asked to become the new Juan-juan emperor. Na-kai declined, but accepted when Tou-lun met an untimely death in 492. Na-kai's reign, which lasted until 502, was marked by a series of defeats inflicted by the Northern Wei; other than that, not much is known about it. During the fourteen years that followed Na-kai's death, there was a quick succession of Juan-juan emperors; their names are known, but there is little information about them. During this period, however, there were reports of a Juan-juan uprising. By the year 520, when the new ruler was A-na-kuei, serious internal tensions existed within the Juan-juan empire. The Northern Wei emperor quickly exploited this situation to divide Juan-juan rule permanently. A-na-kuei's rule was challenged by his nephew P'o-lo-men, and he required assistance from the Northern Wei to maintain his throne. This led to a division of Juan-juan forces and permitted other ethnic groups to rise to power.

To assure Northern Wei support, A-na-kuei went to the court in Lo-yang and formally submitted to the Northern Wei emperor; subsequently, the latter supported him in his campaigns against P'o-lo-men. As peaceful entreaties failed to persuade P'o-lo-men to recognize A-na-kuei as the ruler, a full-scale military campaign was launched against him, apparently without success. A few years later, after a surprise attack, the Chinese captured P'o-lo-men and took him to Lo-yang, where he died under mysterious circumstances. The years that followed P'o-lo-men's death witnessed a tenuous friendship between the Northern Wei and the Juan-juan. At times the latter supported the Northern Wei against rebellious movements; at times they supported the rebels against the Northern Wei. Whatever the true nature of Juan-juan–Tabghach relations, during the reign of the Western Wei emperor Hsiao-wu (532–534), a marital alliance was established between the two states,[27] and it was renewed during the reign of Emperor Wen-ti (535–551); this time A-na-kuei's daughter was the bride. In the spring of 540, allegedly because of the ill-treatment his daughter had received, A-na-kuei invaded the territory of the Western Wei, but he withdrew shortly thereafter.

The year A-na-kuei invaded the Western Wei an event occurred that was to have important consequences for the Juan-juan empire several years later: the Western Wei agreed to an alliance with the Türks. Residing primarily in the Altai region, the Türks were a tributary people of the Juan-juan and were employed by them for metallurgical work. In the beginning of the sixth century, they had begun to assert their independence from the Juan-juan. Recognition by the Western Wei was an important step in the fulfillment of their goal. The exact nature of Juan-juan–Türk relations, however, is not well known. When the Türk chieftain Bumin requested a Juan-juan princess in marriage, he was refused on the grounds that no Juan-juan princess could marry a "blacksmith slave."[28] The refusal was used by Bumin as an excuse for an open rebellion. Early in 552, Bumin's and A-na-kuei's forces clashed to the north of the Huai-huang, and the Juan-juan army was utterly defeated. A-na-kuei committed suicide, and his death caused a formal split within the empire. A portion of the Juan-juan followed A-na-kuei's son, An-lo-chen, and submitted to the Western Wei. Another group adhered to a descendant of Tou-lun and attempted to continue the Juan-juan empire. Within the Juan-juan camp, however, serious dissension broke out, and the difficulties caused by the internal squabbling were aggravated by constant attacks by the Türks and their allies, the Ch'i-tan. In 555 and 556, the Türks inflicted a decisive defeat on the Juan-juan and established their own empire on the steppe, an act which was to have important consequences for the steppe as a whole.

While the Juan-juan dominated the central steppe (an area that corresponds more or less to the Mongolian People's Republic), the basin of the Oxus River, on the other end of the steppe, was dominated by the Hephtalites. For a long time a controversy existed within the scholarly community about the ethnic origin and linguistic affiliation of these people, and this controversy has not yet subsided. The Hephtalites were known to the Chinese and the Greeks alike, and, as is so often the case, it is difficult to reconcile the information available in these two sources; in addition, research on the Hephtalites cannot be done without knowledge of some long-extinct Indo-European languages. The scholarly difficulty originates not only in the conflicting information available, but also in the common assumption that Central Asia was inhabited solely by people of Uralo-Altaic origins.[29] Thus, it is usually stated that the Hephtalites were a Turkic people who had moved from the Altai mountain range, the cradle of Altaic civilization, to the basin of the Oxus River. This statement is based on a Chinese identification and on the occurrence of some Turkic titles among the Hephtalites. Chinese information about distant people, however, is not always reliable, and the Turkic titles appear to have been late borrowings. A careful examination of the available numismatic evidence, as well as some manuscript fragments, has shown conclusively that the Turkic hypothesis is invalid, and that the Hephtalites were a people of Indo-European origins whose language was Tocharian, an extinct Indo-European language belonging to its Indo-Iranian branch.[30]

The Hephtalites occupied a country commonly known as Bactria, roughly located in present-day Afghanistan, and maintained close relations with the Sassanian empire in Persia. In 371 they recognized the Persian emperor Shapur II as their suzerain and became the defenders of the *limes* of the powerful Persian empire. During the period that followed Shapur's death, the Hephtalites increasingly asserted their independence from Persia and even conquered other Persian tributary states, including the Indo-European state of Kidara. It was, however, during the reign of Yezdegerd I (399–421) that the Hephtalites made their first serious attempt to rid themselves of the Persian yoke. This effort was facilitated by serious dissension at Yezdegerd's court and by the war that had broken out between the Persians and a group of so-called Türks. During the reign of Yezdegerd II (438–457) the Hephtalites scored their first major victory against the Sassanian forces, at a time when the Persian empire's hegemony over its frontier zones was being challenged in the east and the west. With this victory the Hephtalites became an imperial power. Their power was consolidated in 484 when they routed a Persian force that had attempted to regain control over Bactria.[31]

The consolidation and the expansion of the Hephtalite empire was the work of King Ephdalanos, also called Hephtal III, who apparently reigned from 484 to 545. It was during his reign that the Hephtalite empire reached its maximum size, and according to the Chinese sources, exerted control over some thirty states covering almost all of Turkestan. It was at this time also that the Hephtalites began to entertain diplomatic relations with China. A first embassy arrived at the Chinese court in 516, and, with brief interruptions, a Hephtalite embassy arrived regularly until 558, the last year the Chinese annals mention such an embassy.

Hephtalite control over the region and intervention in Persian affairs continued well into the reign of Khosroes I, for Persian tribute payments did not cease until at least 545. Although Khosroes maintained excellent relations with the Hephtalites and was able to cease tribute payments without provoking retaliation, his intention was to destroy the Hephtalite empire. The opportunity to do so arose during the period from 563 to 567, when his enemies were involved in a war with the expanding Turkic empire, though it appears that the absence of a strong centralized government was the major factor in the disintegration of the Hephtalite empire. (If later sources, such as Firdowsi and Menandros, are to be believed, the *casus belli* was the assassination by the Hephtalites of a Turkic mission to Khosroes.) After 567, the Hephtalite territories to the north of the Oxus River came under control of the Türks, while the Persians, without much warfare, had gained full control over the areas to the south of the river. The Türks destroyed the Hephtalite empire, and Khosroes gained control over the south by giving asylum to the Hephtalite king Katoulphos. From that time on, the Türks were the major threat to the security of the Persian empire. Small Hephtalite kingdoms continued to exist, apparently until the eighth century, in present-day Afghanistan, especially the Kabul area.

Shortly after the destruction of the Juan-juan and the Hephtalite empires, a new people appeared on the borders of the Byzantine empire and were given asylum by Emperor Justinian in return for an attack on the Bulghars. These people were known as the Avars, and after their submission to Byzantine authority, around 562, they settled in the Dobrudja area, present-day Romania. The chronology of the destruction of the Juan-juan and the Hephtalites by the Türks and the appearance of the Avars a few years later has given rise to their identification frequently with the Juan-juan, and occasionally with the Hephtalites. The suggestion has been made that the three names covered one people.

Around 567 or 568, a Turkic mission arrived at the Byzantine court and protested against the granting of asylum to a people who were slaves of the Türks and had rebelled against them, a people over whom the Turkic ruler still claimed authority. The historian Theophylactus Simocattes devoted a long excursion to the history of the wars between the Avars and the Türks in which he stated that one group of defeated Avars fled to China and another group to Europe. His account, written at the end of the sixth century, does not clarify the origins of the Avars.

It is doubtful that the present sources will ever reveal the exact nature of the relationship between Juan-juan, Hephtalites, and Avars; it is not even certain that the difficult work of examining all the available sources would justify the results. By the time the Avars began to play a role in Lombard and Byzantine politics, the unchallenged force in Central Asia was the Turkic empire. Doubts about the origins of the Avars will remain. The solution offered in a recent study, which simply equated Juan-juan and Avars and then discussed Avar history and culture, is an unelegant and unscientific one.[32] Treating each as a separate entity seems to be a much more rational approach, even though such an approach leaves many questions unanswerable.

The Nomadic Kingdoms

While the steppe was dominated by the relatively large empires of the Juan-juan and the Hephtalites, the frontier areas of these empires were controlled by smaller kingdoms, mostly of Altaic origin. These kingdoms never played an important role in Central Asia's history even though they formed the buffer zone between the nomadic and the sedentary worlds. Their power was ephemeral, for it depended on the simultaneous weakening of the sedentary and nomadic states, a state of affairs which never existed for long. All that is known about these kingdoms are their names and a very incomplete listing of their kings. For a few, there are references in historical sources to their alliances with the sedentary states. Some, however, were important enough to have their own histories recorded by the surrounding states, at least in a fragmentary form. On the eastern steppe this was true of the T'u-yü-hun in particular, while on the western steppe the Sabirs, the Onogurs, and the Avars were the most important.

A people known as the T'u-yü-hun had apparently existed in the Kokonor area ever since the third century A.D., if the Chinese sources can be believed. The name of the tribe, allegedly of Hsien-pi origin, was given by the kingdom's third ruler, She-yen (ca. 330–352), in order to commemorate his grandfather, T'u-yü-hun. Not too much importance should be attached to the genealogies of the early T'u-yü-hun rulers, which were written in accordance with Chinese ritual texts. It was not until the beginning of the fifth century, after they had conquered the Western Ch'in (385–431) and the Hsia (407–431) dynasties and had made an alliance with the Northern Wei, that the T'u-yü-hun formed a moderately powerful kingdom. From that time on information becomes more reliable, even though nearly all the information deals with political matters important to China. The power of the T'u-yü-hun lay in the fact that they had gained control over the trade routes between China and Central Asia, China's supplier of horses.[33]

Where the T'u-yü-hun came from is not known. According to the Chinese annals they were descendants of the Hsien-pi in Liao-tung. Why they moved from this area to the distant Kokonor on the fringes of Tibet is never specifically stated. What is known is that, as with almost all other people of the steppe, the mainstay of the T'u-yü-hun state was horsebreeding. They were, however, not entirely nomadic: they possessed houses and walled villages, but apparently these were used solely as winter quarters, and most of the year was spent in tent camps searching for pasture and water. They also practiced some subsistence agriculture. The little that is known about their administrative structure, their social customs, and their legislation also places them within the steppe tradition. Although no solid evidence is available, it appears that the T'u-yü-hun, like other steppe states, were not a homogeneous state but a confederation of tribes with similar economic and political interests.

The power of the T'u-yü-hun was solidly established during the reign of Mu-li-yen (436–452), who was recognized as the legitimate ruler of the important frontier zone by the emperors of the Northern Wei and those of the Southern Sung (420–479) dynasties. If T'u-yü-hun relations with the Southern Sung and other southern Chinese states remained by and large cordial, relations with the Northern Wei soon reached a point of conflict. The primary reason for this was the Northern Wei's desire to control the Central Asian trade routes. War broke out in 444, and although the T'u-yü-hun were temporarily driven out of their territory, they returned in 446 and were the ultimate victors in the conflict. Indeed, while they were forced to withdraw from the Kokonor area, they established their suzerainty over some of the states of the Tarim basin; it has even been suggested that they penetrated as far as present-day Kabul in Afghanistan. Control over the Tarim basin gave the T'u-yü-hun complete control over the trade routes. Several times the Northern Wei unsuccessfully attempted to break the T'u-yü-hun monopoly. After the collapse of the Northern Wei, the power of the T'u-yü-hun increased. With the only challenger to its authority eliminated, the T'u-yü-hun territory became the principal foreign trade area for southern China and the eastern part of North China, especially the Western Wei dynasty. Relations, however, were not always peaceful, and trade missions frequently alternated with raiding parties.

The power of the T'u-yü-hun did not long survive the collapse of the Northern Wei. The decline began with the reunification of China during the reign of Sui Wen-ti and the almost simultaneous expansion of the Turkic empire, which had taken over a major portion of the horse and silk trades. Relations with China during the reign of Sui Wen-ti, who was primarily concerned with the reunification of China, were peaceful; the T'u-yü-hun ruler was even given a Chinese princess in marriage. The situation changed drastically with the accession to the throne of Sui Yang-ti, whose ambition was to re-establish China's authority over the Tarim basin. In alliance with certain Turkic tribes, who wanted control over the same area, Sui Yang-ti was able to force the T'u-yü-hun out of their territory and thus break their monopoly. The collapse of the Sui dynasty in turn permitted certain T'u-yü-hun groups to regain control over at least a portion of their former territory. After 617 the T'u-yü-hun domain was basically limited to the Kokonor area.

Control over the Tarim basin remained with the Türks and the Chinese of the T'ang dynasty.

The new T'u-yü-hun kingdom survived nearly half a century after the establishment of the T'ang dynasty. The T'ang actively pursued the expansionist policies of Sui Yang-ti, but penetrated the Tarim basin through the Kansu corridor rather than through the Kokonor area. Although the T'u-yü-hun were no longer a serious threat to Chinese interests and security, the T'ang nevertheless made sure that the unruly tribes in the Kokonor area were aware of its power. In 634 a military expedition was sent into the area and made an impressive show of force. From that time on, Chinese–T'u-yü-hun relations were peaceful. Meanwhile, however, a new force had arisen on the western borders of the T'u-yü-hun kingdom, and they were its first victims. The new force—the Tibetans—played a dominant role on China's borders for nearly two centuries. The first large-scale invasion of the Kokonor area by Tibetans took place in 660. Ignorant of the new power constellation, the Chinese emperor refused military aid to the T'u-yü-hun. This proved to be a major strategic and political blunder, for it opened not only the Tarim basin, but also China itself, to Tibetan penetration, and in the mid-eighth century, a Tibetan army occupied the Chinese capital, Ch'ang-an. The T'u-yü-hun kingdom did not survive the Tibetan advance, and by 670 it had ceased to exist. As an ethnic group, the T'u-yü-hun survived at least until the eleventh century, when they were absorbed into the mixed population of one of the Chinese Border Empires.

Though the T'u-yü-hun kingdom on the eastern borders of the steppe had a pivotal role in Chinese–Central Asian trade, the several small kingdoms of proto-Turkic origins on the western fringes of the steppe did not play an important historical role in Central Asia. Information on these kingdoms is scanty and often unreliable. They did not have a major cultural and political impact on the sedentary states that surrounded them, and on account of this have not been subjected to serious study. The most important of these kingdoms were those of the Sabirs, the Onogurs, and, finally, the Avars.

An ethnic group known as the Sabirs appeared for the first time in the fifth century on the fringes of the Eastern Roman Empire. It was reported by Byzantine historians that they were in conflict with other tribes and that they were driving the latter westwards; among their victims, the Onogurs are mentioned. The Sabirs settled in the area of the Caspian Sea and from there began to entertain diplomatic and commercial relations with the Byzantine empire. They were a fairly powerful state, for in 508 and again in 515 they thoroughly sacked Armenia and the Pontus region. In 527, after the establishment of a military alliance with Byzantium against the Persians, they were said to have fielded an army of some one hundred thousand men. When the Avars penetrated Europe, the Sabirs were forced to withdraw into the Caucasian steppe. From there they apparently migrated westwards to southern Russia, only to be absorbed by the Avar state. They are no longer mentioned in the sources after the ninth century.[34]

The Onogurs, pushed westwards by the movement of the Sabirs, appeared on the European scene at about the same time as the latter. They established themselves around the area of the Black Sea and united with the Bulghars, thus coming into conflict with Byzantium and its Avar allies. The Onogurs survived the conflicts that followed but apparently became a part of those people who, in the ninth century, laid the basis for the Magyar or Hungarian kingdom, the westernmost permanent penetration of Uralo-Altaic people.[35]

Of all the nomadic kingdoms on the western fringe of the Central Asian steppe (and there were many others besides the three mentioned), the Avar kingdom was unquestionably the most important.[36] For more than two centuries after their settlement in the Dobrudja area, the Avars were the most important state on the northern border of the Byzantine empire. Their position made them a buffer against the expansion of the Turkic empire on the steppe proper and by and large prevented the penetration of armies from the central steppe into Europe until well into the ninth century.

The Avars were not interested, at least during the sixth century, in the Byzantine empire itself. Shortly after their settlement in the Dobrudja area, they began a westward expansion of their domain at the expense of Slavic and Germanic tribes. They moved north of the Carpathian Mountains and from there into Thuringia. Allied with the Lombards, they destroyed and annexed the Gepid kingdom while the Lombards entered Italy. With their victory over the Gepid kingdom, the Avars had gained full control over the entire Carpathian area. By the end of the sixth century, Avar power appears to have reached its zenith.[37]

The decades that followed the destruction of the Gepid kingdom and the conquest of the Carpathian basin witnessed a continued expansion of Avar power throughout the Balkan Peninsula. One of the most important areas under their control, at least by 580, was the Dalmatian coast. At the beginning of the seventh century, it was clear that their ally, the Byzantine empire, could become their next victim. When the Byzantine emperor Heraclius (610–641) began his campaign against the Persians in 622, the Avars seized the opportunity to attack and lay siege to Constantinople. The Avar army, which included Bulghar and Slav elements, proved unable to breach the city's defenses. A vigorous counterattack, coupled with dissension within the ranks of the invaders, led to the complete failure of the enterprise. Not much is known about the years that followed the disastrous Byzantine campaign. It appears, however, that the Avars increasingly abandoned their nomadic customs, turned towards agriculture, and adopted Christianity. Avars are mentioned as a minor political force until well into the eighth century, after which they appear to have been completely absorbed by the heterogeneous population of the Balkan Peninsula.[38]

At the end of the formative period, the political orientation of the steppe had shifted neither to the west nor to the east. Within a few decades the minor nomadic states on the steppe's fringes had been absorbed by the expanding Turkic empire, and for several centuries after the Turkic empire's foundation the sedentary states were to be confronted with the threat of a nomadic invasion.

3

The Steppe Unified:
the Turkic Empire

The Türks were the first steppe people to keep their own historical records. Although these records are not numerous, enough are available to permit a more accurate examination of Central Asian history and political life than is possible for any preceding period. The autochthonous script that enabled them to keep such records is thus a landmark development, without precedent in the history of the steppe.

The script, known as "Runic Turkic" because of its resemblance to the script of the Germanic tribes,[1] was used during the later years of the Turkic empire. The only texts that have survived are early eighth-century inscriptions on stone found in the Orkhon region, the seat of Turkic imperial power, and hence known as the Orkhon inscriptions. In Chinese texts dealing with the spread of Buddhism among the Türks, there are a few tantalizing references to Turkic funerary inscriptions in a non-Chinese script which suggest that the Türks may have had a script nearly two centuries before the Orkhon inscriptions.[2] No Turkic texts, however, have ever been discovered, and the validity of these references remains in doubt. It is quite possible that the Chinese texts actually refer to the Sogdian script, which was familiar to the Chinese because many Sogdian merchants resided in their capital, and which later (in the ninth century) served as the basis for the development of the Uighur script.

The Orkhon inscriptions establish beyond any doubt that the Türks had a fully developed consciousness of their own history.

> When high above the blue sky and down below the brown earth had been created, betwixt the two were created the sons of men. And above the sons of men stood *my ancestors,* the kaghans Bumin and Ishtemi. Having become the masters of the Türk people, they installed and ruled its empire and fixed the law of the country. Many were their enemies in the four corners of the world, but leading campaigns against them, they subjugated and pacified many nations in the four corners of the world. They caused them to bow their heads and bend their knees. These were wise kaghans, these were valiant kaghans; all their officers were wise and valiant; the nobles, all of them, the entire people, were just. This was the reason why they were able to rule an empire so great, why governing the empire, they could uphold the law.[3]

The Orkhon inscriptions also show clearly that a history of Central Asia during the Turkic period can no longer be based solely on Chinese interpretations, as has been done traditionally. Because of the exclusive reliance on Chinese sources, it has been customary to divide the period of Turkic hegemony over the steppe into two distinct Turkic empires: the First Empire, created by Bumin and in existence from 552 until 583, and the Second, created by Qutluq Elterish, from 684 until 734. The century between these two empires has been roughly divided into two periods of fifty years each: the period of the Western and Eastern Khanates (583–630), and the period of disintegration, or, more appropriately, the period of Chinese hegemony.[4]

For the so-called Second Empire, the Orkhon inscriptions are *native* source material. When they are examined critically in conjunction with the material in Chinese, the "Second Empire" can be seen as a restoration of the "First Empire." Qutluq Elterish and his successors regarded themselves not only as the descendants of Bumin and Ishtemi, but also as the restorers of Turkic greatness. The century during which Turkic power was weak or almost nonexistent was viewed as a misfortune which *they had permitted* the *wily* Chinese to exploit.

> They [the Chinese] gave us gold, silver and silk in abundance. The words of the Chinese people have always been sweet and the materials of the Chinese people have always been soft . . . having heard these words, you unwise people went close to [the Chinese] and

were killed in great numbers. If you go towards those places, O Turkish people, you will die; if you stay in the land of Otuken, and send caravans from there, you will have no trouble.[5]

When the Turkic sources are examined in this manner, it becomes quite clear that the steppe had a history and tradition of its own, which was by and large free from Chinese influence. On the other hand, it cannot be denied that during the Turkic period, China was able to manipulate and even control portions of the steppe as it had never done before and as it was never to do again until the seventeenth century. Cursory examination gives the impression that China's foreign policy was successful because of its superior state system. The evidence, however, suggests that when the Chinese policies were successful, it was largely because a political vacuum existed on the steppe. As a rule, China's policies worked only when the "barbarians," for reasons of their own, were willing to accept Chinese over-lordship, or, as in the case of the Türks, when internal dissension made a united resistance against outside interference nearly impossible.

Whether the Türks recognized the absolute sovereignty of the Chinese emperor between the years 630 and 684, and whether Chinese control over the Turkic tribes was actual and absolute are matters that require further investigation. The sources, however, refer only to Chinese control of the steppe's sedentary, urban enclaves and almost never mention control over the steppe proper. It thus appears that even though Chinese armies were present on the steppe, they never exerted actual control over the majority of the Türks, that is, those who did not reside in cities. One important conclusion, however, can be drawn from a comparative examination of the Turkic and the Chinese sources—the latter must be treated with caution and cannot be used as the sole sources of information on the Turkic period.

The Origins of the Türks

The origins of the Türks, like those of nearly all Central Asian people, are shrouded in mystery and legend. The Turkic legends have been preserved in the Chinese annals, and, because of the extensive Sino-Turkic contacts, it is fair to assume that the Chinese version adequately represents a Turkic tradition.[6] The Chinese name for the Türks was *T'u-chüeh,* apparently derived from the name *Türküt,* which is commonly explained as a Mongol plural of the word *Türk.* While the meaning of *Türk* is well attested as "forceful, strong," the origin of the name and the alleged Mongol plural is a matter of dispute among Turkologists and, like many other problems, is far from solved.

According to the Chinese annals, the Türks were a special branch of the Hsiung-nu who had formed their own state to the north of the Hsiung-nu

Map 1
Eurasia
circa 750 A.D.

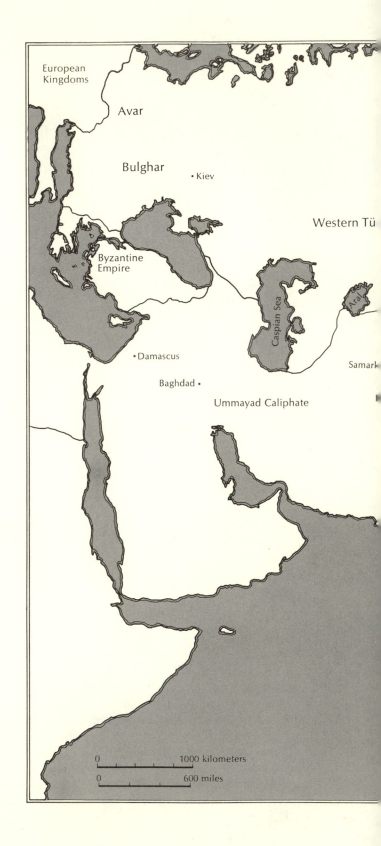

European
Kingdoms

Avar

Bulghar

• Kiev

Western Tü

Byzantine
Empire

Caspian Sea

Aral

•Damascus

Samark

Baghdad •

Ummayad Caliphate

0   1000 kilometers

0   600 miles

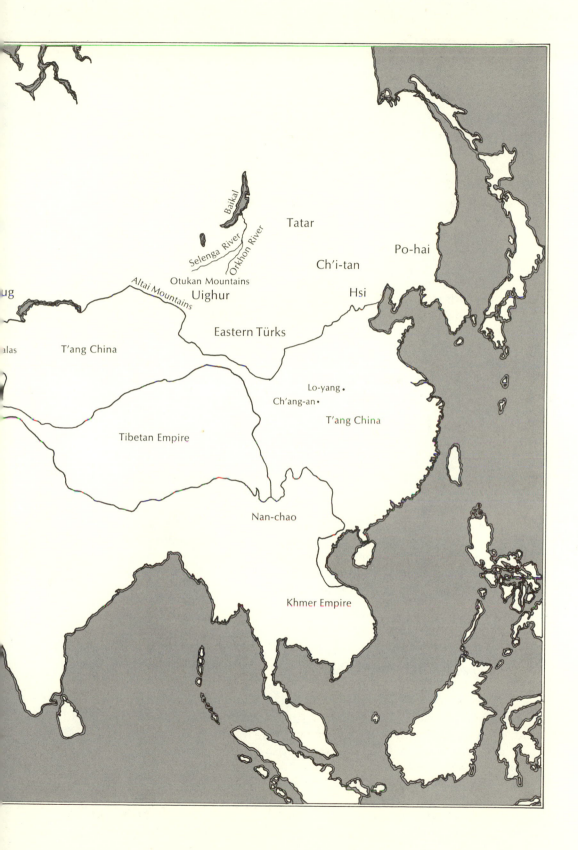

ug

Baikal

Tatar

Selenga River
Orkhon River

Po-hai

Ch'i-tan

Otukan Mountains

Altai Mountains
Uighur

Hsi

alas

Eastern Türks

T'ang China

Lo-yang •

Ch'ang-an •

T'ang China

Tibetan Empire

Nan-chao

Khmer Empire

empire. At an undetermined time, an unidentified enemy destroyed the tribe and killed all its people with the exception of a ten-year-old boy. Seized with compassion, the soldiers did not kill him; they merely cut off his feet and abandoned him in a bog, where the young boy was nourished back to health by a she-wolf. When he had recovered his health, the boy had intercourse with the wolf, who became pregnant just when the enemy ruler, having learned of the boy's survival, sent a party to kill him. What happened to the boy is not known, but the wolf fled to a hole in a mountain near Turfan where she gave birth to ten boys. Grown up, the boys married human women, multiplied, and went their separate ways after having adopted surnames. One of them assumed the name of A-shih-na and founded the line which, after several generations, gave rise to the Türks. The legends state that they were called *T'u-chüeh* because they lived in the Altai mountains, and that their overlords, the Juan-juan, gave them their word for helmet because the mountains looked like a helmet.[7] The Türks clearly believed in this legend, for they held pilgrimages to the cave of their ancestors.

The factual evidence about the origins of the Türks is very limited. They are first mentioned in the Chinese annals in the third century, but did not become a force to be reckoned with until the sixth. Their homeland was in the Altai mountain range. Soviet archeologists have found tomb sites in the Altai, but the state of the tombs, most of which have been robbed and abandoned, permits no formal conclusion.[8] The Türks were a subject people of the Juan-juan and worked for their rulers as blacksmiths and ironworkers. Travel accounts, in both Chinese and Greek, clearly refer to the importance of the metal industry among the Türks; the "Iron Gates" (apparently real structures) marked the borders of the Turkic empire. Turkic society, as far back as can be determined, was not purely nomadic, although it included pastoral nomads as well as farmers and blacksmiths. The Türks began to establish an urban base, the first in steppe history, and functioned around these settlements. It is possible to state that the Türks had reached a stage of "pastoral-urbanization."[9]

The Creation and Expansion of the Empire

The rise of the Turkic empire, typically of a steppe empire, revolved around a charismatic personality. The causes of Turkic unrest under Juan-juan rule are nowhere specified, but at least since the year 545 they had been attempting to rid themselves of this overlordship. The ascendancy of the Turkic people was the work of Bumin, the Türks' first emperor. How Bumin became the leader of the Turkic confederation is not known. The available information covers but a few years of his life, a period when he was already the uncontested leader of the Türks. The first important mention of Bumin occurs in the Chinese annals under the year 546. In that year he established friendly relations with the Western Wei dynasty, forming an alliance from which the Türks were to profit a few years later. Western Wei recognition, given in order to create a counterforce to the Juan-juan empire, provided the Türks with an important political tool. It was around the same time that Bumin engaged the Türks in the first documented expansion of their domain. His troops attacked and defeated the Ting-ling, most likely a Turkic tribe residing to the south of them, and incorporated them into their own state. It was after this victory that Bumin openly challenged Juan-juan overlordship by requesting a Juan-juan princess in marriage, an event discussed in the previous chapter. In 552, allied with forces from the Western Wei, Bumin destroyed the Juan-juan state. As a direct consequence of his victory, he became the uncontested ruler of the steppe.

Turkic victories over the Juan-juan, the Hephtalites, and several other smaller states and tribes concentrated control over the entire steppe in the hands of a single ethnic group for the first time. Bumin did not long survive his victory over the Juan-juan; he died at the end of 552 or the beginning of 553. As was customary, the empire he had created was divided among his descendants and his relatives. His son Muqan became the new *qaghan* and thus controlled the empire's political center, the eastern steppe.[10] Bumin's brother, Ishtemi, continued to exert control over the western steppe and to carry the title of *yabghu*, which roughly translates as "secondary ruler."

The reign of Muqan, which lasted until 572, witnessed a further expansion and consolidation of both eastern and western branches of the Turkic empire.[11] Muqan expanded the empire until it reached the borders of China. Among the major tribes he conquered were the Ch'i-tan, who played an important role in Chinese and Central Asian history several centuries later. Conquest of the Ch'i-tan meant that the Turkic empire reached almost to the gulf of Liaotung. Conquests in a southerly direction permitted Muqan to expand his domains to include Lake Baikal. Sino-Turkic relations, which had begun under Bumin, were continued, even though they assumed a more hostile orientation as the Türks sought to exploit dissensions within China. In 564 the Türks attacked the Northern Ch'i dynasty (550–557) and thoroughly looted the town of Chin-yang, present-day T'ai-yüan in Shensi province. Turkic attitudes toward China, however, reflected an interesting dichotomy; while they conducted wars and raids into China, they simultaneously maintained regular diplomatic relations, which during Muqan's reign even included the marriage of one of his daughters into the Western Wei.[12] Ishtemi ruled over the western Turkic domains until his death in 575 or 576, apparently without any antagonism toward Muqan.

Muqan died in 572 and was succeeded by Tsapar, apparently with Ishtemi's approval in spite of the fact that as the empire's elder statesman, he could have claimed the position of *qaghan*. Tsapar's reign marked the continuation of the power of the Türks on the Chinese border. China's policy consisted, in essence, in placating its powerful neighbor and sometime ally, even while it recorded all Turkic missions as tributary missions, that is, as vassals. Marital alliances and peaceful trade missions alternated with war. The Türks successfully appropriated the traditional Chinese policy by using Chinese against Chinese—the Northern Ch'i versus the Northern Chou—to promote their own political and economic interests.

Although Turkic power continued to be unchallenged by the sedentary states throughout Tsapar's reign, within the empire itself the first symptoms of centrifugal tendencies came to the fore. On the western steppe, Ishtemi had been succeeded by his son Tardu (576–603), who thus had become the new *yabghu*. Ambitious, he clearly was not satisfied with his secondary role in the empire and aspired to the position of *qaghan,* basing his claim in part on the apparent economic independence of the western steppe and on his ability to maintain his own armed forces. The *qaghan-yabghu* relationship, in which neither position was clearly defined, had not been a source of difficulty during the life of Ishtemi, as he accepted, without any known objections, the supremacy of the eastern steppe. However, if the *yabghu* was ambitious, as was the case with Tardu, and the *qaghan* complacent, as was the case with Tsapar, the duality held within it a source of conflict. Soon after his accession to the dignity of *yabghu,* Tardu made his position adamantly clear. He refused unequivocally to recognize Tsapar as *qaghan,* and, in his relations with Byzantium, presented himself as the sole ruler of the entire Turkic empire, as the *qaghan.*[13] Strangely, Tsapar took no steps to curb Tardu's ambitions and thus contributed to the difficulties that were to erupt after his death.

The year 581, the year of Tsapar's death, and, coincidentally, the year of China's reunification under the Sui dynasty, was of crucial importance in Turkic history, for it marked the beginning of a two-year period of strife that ended in the collapse of the empire's power. A dispute arose between two candidates for the position of *qaghan*—Tsapar's son An-lo and the latter's nephew T'a-lo-pin. T'a-lo-pin had the qualities necessary to be the *qaghan;* he was rejected, however, because of the low origins of his mother. An-lo became the *qaghan* but almost immediately abdicated in favor of T'a-lo-pin's brother, Ishpara. This occurred after relations between An-lo and T'a-lo-pin had become openly hostile; the latter had been sending missions to An-lo's court charged with the specific task of insulting him. An-lo retired from the political scene with the title *Second Qaghan,* while Ishpara attempted to mend fences with his brother by giving him the title *Apa Qaghan.* T'a-lo-pin's authority, however, was limited to his own clan, for his title and rank carried no appanage.

At the time of Tsapar's death, China was forcibly reunited by the founder of the Sui dynasty, Yang Chien, a powerful minister of the Northern Chou dynasty, which he had overthrown. Ishpara's wife had belonged to the Northern Chou, and she incited her husband to stage punitive raids on China. As China's defenses against penetration from the steppe were still in a state of disarray, these raids created serious problems for the new dynasty. Yang Chien, however, had no intention of allowing the Türks to continue raiding, and he made this abundantly clear in an edict issued in

583.[14] Not only did he issue a strong call to arms, but he also stated that China should take advantage of the Türks' proclivity to fight among themselves. That same year an open conflict arose between the Türks and the Chinese, and the latter defeated a force led by Ishpara.

Ishpara, apparently fearing a coup, staged a surprise attack on Apa Qaghan's camp, destroying his forces and forcing him to flee. Instead of seeking asylum in China, as had been the steppe custom, Apa Qaghan sought refuge with Tardu, the leader of the Western Türks. The break between the Eastern and the Western Türks became irreparable, especially since Ishpara had executed Apa Qaghan's mother. The years that followed witnessed a prolonged war between the two Turkic khanates, each of them seeking the intercession of China. Yang Chien, true to his word, did not intervene in favor of one or the other but used the situation to foment even more dissension among the Türks.

With Ishpara's attack on Apa Qaghan, the period commonly known as the First Turkic Empire came to an end. For the next fifty years, until 630, the steppe was divided into an Eastern and a Western Turkic Khanate, with the latter clearly dominating the political and military scene. In these wars the Eastern Khanate suffered the initial defeats and was forced to seek refuge with the Sui dynasty. Permission to enter Chinese territory was granted in 584. Subsequently Ishpara and his followers crossed the Gobi, hoping to return to the Orkhon but never realizing this dream. Ishpara and his successor, Ch'u-lo (587–588), carried on the war against Apa Qaghan and Tardu until Ch'u-lo was able to capture Apa Qaghan and execute him in 587.

The Sui dynasty exploited the situation as much as possible. Assistance to the Eastern Türks was viewed by the Chinese as being to their advantage, as it meant weakening Turkic power. The destruction of the Eastern Khanate would have resulted in a powerful united Turkic force on China's borders. The Chinese goal was the survival of both Turkic khanates, with the Eastern Khanate weakened enough to need Chinese support to survive; thus it would form a buffer between China and the powerful Western Khanate. China's traditional policy of "using barbarians to check barbarians" was again successful, but not until steppe politics had created the situation that permitted Chinese political intervention. The end of the first period in the history of the Turkic empire was entirely a consequence of steppe politics.

The years that followed Apa Qaghan's death witnessed a steady decline of the power of the Eastern Türks. Their survival hinged on Sui support, something the Chinese court was not likely to let them forget. In the meantime, the Western Türks were having problems of their own. Although Tardu presented himself as the sole Turkic emperor, at least to Byzantium, his authority was challenged by other tribes within his domains, in particular the Tölös. They rose in revolt against Tardu and forced him to flee to the Kokonor area, where he disappeared, never to be heard from again. The Western Khanate was not spared succession troubles, which permitted the Chinese to intervene once again. In 611 a grandson of Tardu, She-kuei, became the new ruler of the Western Türks, in part because the Chinese through intrigue had eliminated his only challenger. Although weakened, neither khanate gave up its claims to the glory and the domain of the unified Turkic empire.

At the dawn of the second decade of the seventh century, it appeared that the fortunes of the Turkic khanates would soon take a turn for the better. In 604 Yang Chien had been succeeded by his son, the notorious Yang-ti (604–619), who began in 611 a series of massive but disastrous campaigns against Korea. These campaigns, as well as his extravagant spending, broke the back of the Sui dynasty, and soon rebellions and dissent were running like wildfire throughout China. The Western Türks took advantage of the situation to rid themselves of Chinese influence, while the Eastern Türks began a political and, at times, military campaign to regain their former prominence. The fact that the Eastern Türks were vassals of the Sui dynasty did not constitute a barrier. Conditions had changed, and old alliances that were no longer in their interests ceased to exist.

The leader of the Eastern Türks at the time of the reign of Sui Yang-ti was Shih-pi (608–619). Shih-pi was quick to take advantage of the disorders within China and set out on a systematic campaign to regain control over the territories his predecessors had lost to China. As long as Shih-pi limited his activities to the steppe and the frontier zones, he did not have to fear a Chinese intervention. Sui Yang-ti's disastrous Korean campaigns precluded his intervention, and thus Shih-pi was successful in his endeavor.

In order to complete his achievement, Shih-pi needed to rid himself of Chinese overlordship. In 615 he attempted an invasion of the Sui domains, only to be forced to withdraw by the Sui general, Li Shih-min, later to be the T'ang emperor. When Li Shih-min and his father, Li Yüan, began their rebellion against the Sui emperor, Shih-pi switched his allegiance to the rebels. As the outcome of the rebellion was not immediately clear, for a while Shih-pi continued to send missions to the Sui court. He took, however, a military stand that did not threaten the rebellion in order to assure good will in case of a victory. Shih-pi apparently felt that even if the Sui emerged victorious, his forces would not be threatened. The coup took place in Ch'ang-an in 618, and Li Yüan became the first T'ang emperor.[15] Throughout the entire period, Shih-pi maintained a neutral but friendly attitude towards the rebels, while continuing his control over China's frontier zone. By the beginning of the T'ang dynasty, the Eastern Türks controlled nearly all of their old domains and, once again, were a threat to Chinese security.

Although the coup d'état perpetrated by Li Yüan and Li Shih-min was successful in eliminating the Sui dynasty, a ten-year-long campaign was necessary to consolidate the rule of the T'ang dynasty over China. Priority was given to internal matters; border affairs were neglected, thus providing the Türks with a unique opportunity to reassert themselves and make a clean break with the Chinese. Already in 619 the Türks felt strong enough to challenge the nascent dynasty, and they invaded China, threatening to seize its capital. The sudden death of Shih-pi, combined with a timely diplomatic intervention by the T'ang, temporarily removed the Turkic menace, but it again assumed ominous proportions during the reign of the Hsieh-li Qaghan, from 620 to 630, and seriously threatened the survival of the T'ang dynasty. Li Shih-min, who in 626 had assumed the throne with the title of T'ai-tsung, had no choice but to placate the Türks until political and economic conditions in China permitted a drastic intervention into the steppe proper.

Li Shih-min's plans to annihilate the power of the Eastern Türks as soon as realistically possible were facilitated by the Hsieh-li Qaghan's high-handed rule over subordinate tribes. In 627 rebellions against his rule broke out, and the rebels were able to inflict serious defeats on his forces. The Chinese court argued for intervention, but Li Shih-min prudently stalled until it became clear that the Hsieh-li Qaghan was in serious political and military difficulties as a consequence of the rebellion. Fierce fighting took place on the steppe throughout 629, with the Chinese observing from the sidelines and providing discreet assistance to the rebels. By the end of the year, it was clear to Li Shih-min that the time was ripe for intervention. In 630 Chinese forces penetrated the steppe, and early in the spring of that year they were able to capture the Hsieh-li Qaghan. The T'ang emperor appointed Hsieh-li's rival as *qaghan* while Hsieh-li was under house arrest in the Chinese capital, where he died in 634.

The capture and dethronement of the Hsieh-li Qaghan brought the power of the Eastern Türks to an end and made the domain of the Western Türks contiguous to the Chinese empire. The Western Türks were still powerful and posed a possible, if distant, threat to Chinese security. Since the founding of the T'ang dynasty, relations had been peaceful and the Western Turkic ruler more interested in the propagation of Buddhism than in military conquests. The Western Türks, however, were not to be spared the political turmoil that periodically shook the steppe. From 627 on, rebellions occurred. After the murder of the *yabghu* by the Qarluqs, a Turkic tribe, in 630, intense struggles developed over his succession. Li Shih-min took advantage of the situation to pursue a double goal: to eliminate the Western Türks as a political force and to regain control over the Turfan area, a territory once held by the Han dynasty. In two campaigns, the first in 639–640 and the second in 647–648, the T'ang emperor achieved this. T'ang control was extended even beyond the Turfan area, and the Türks were eliminated, at least temporarily, from the political stage.[16]

The years that followed Li Shih-min's victories were dark ones for the Türks; for nearly half a century they were under the direct control of the T'ang dynasty and its powerful armies. But the T'ang dynasty underwent a development similar to that of the Han dynasty. As time passed and the borders remained peaceful, the T'ang concentrated on its internal affairs. T'ang control over the border areas slackened, and soon the Türks saw the opportunity to recreate their empire, a dream which they had never completely abandoned. Under the leadership of the A-shih-te clan, the Türks rose against the Chinese in 679. The effort was premature and ill organized, and it failed; but it had given the impetus necessary for a Turkic restoration. In 683 Qutluq Elterish, aided by Tonyuquq, launched a well-organized attack against the Chinese. Every Chinese army sent against him was defeated. Four years and eleven wars later, the Türks were again free from Chinese overlordship. Qutluq Elterish's revolt marked the restoration of the Turkic empire, a period commonly known as the Second Turkic Empire.

The tasks confronting Qutluq Elterish and Tonyuquq after their victory over the Chinese were more complex than those that had confronted Bumin nearly two centuries earlier. At that time, the Türks were the only power on the steppe, and their ambitions had remained unchallenged. Qutluq Elterish was confronted not only with Chinese forces attempting to maintain their control, but also with Turkic federations, such as the Tölös and the Turgash, which were hostile to him and relatively friendly to China. Furthermore, the restored Turkic empire was challenged by two new forces: the Tibetans and the Arabs. Nevertheless, by the time of Qutluq Elterish's death in 691, the revived Turkic empire was solidly established on the eastern steppe.

His brother and successor, Qapaghan (691–716), brought it even further glory. Around 710 he achieved his most important success: he was able to force the Western Türks to recognize him as *qaghan*. Thus, the original Turkic empire was, in theory, restored. Qapaghan, however, made numerous enemies in the process, and in 716 he was lured into a trap by a minor Turkic group and decapitated. His head was presented to a Chinese envoy, a certain Ho Ling-ch'üan. The sudden and brutal death of Qapaghan and his alienation from friend and foe alike created a serious succession crisis that nearly brought the Turkic empire to an end. It was saved by the sons of Qutluq Elterish, in particular by Kül-tegin, who staged a coup and appointed his brother as the new *qaghan,* with the title of Bilge-qaghan. The coup was followed by a purge in which all of Qapaghan's relatives and many of his close associates lost their lives. The only survivor was the elder statesman Tonyuquq, then nearly seventy years old.

Under Kül-tegin and Bilge-qaghan, as far as can be determined from the Runic Turkic inscriptions, there was an attempt to consolidate the political and economic foundations of the empire, or at least of its eastern division. There are even indications that Bilge-qaghan's plans included the increased sedentarization of the Türks, for they apparently called for the construction of a walled city. Control over the western division appears to have been more nominal than real. They maintained more or less peaceful relations with China. Dissension among the Türks, however, had far from ceased, and latent resentment against the *qaghan* and opposition to his China policies precipitated the final crisis. Kül-tegin died in 731, and a few years later Bilge-qaghan was poisoned by one of his officials.[17] Although the poison was effective, Bilge-qaghan managed to execute the official and his entire family and to appoint his own son as his successor. In reality, however, the death of Bilge-qaghan marked the end of the Turkic empire, for almost immediately thereafter the appearance of unity, always tenuous at best, disappeared completely.

Two *qaghans* succeeded Bilge-qaghan, but neither had an important role. The first died shortly after his accession, apparently from a disease, and was succeeded by his younger brother Teng-li, still an infant. The regency was assumed by Teng-li's mother, which was unacceptable to many Türks. By 740 Teng-li and his mother were dead, and the Turkic domains were plunged into anarchy as attempts were made to gain control over the various tribes. The eventual victors, at least on the eastern steppe, were the Uighurs, a tribe not much different from the one that had founded the Turkic empire.

War
and Trade

In contrast to the earlier steppe empires, trade played an important role in the Turkic empire. Through their victory over the Juan-juan, the Türks had gained control over Central Asian trade routes and hence over the lucrative silk trade between China and Byzantium. The Türks had no intention either of abandoning the trade or of sharing it with other intermediaries. Since early Han times, nearly all of the Chinese silk shipped to the West passed through Persia, and thus it had become one of the trade's principal depots. The Türks, apparently quite well aware of the price differential between silk sold to Persian intermediaries and silk sold directly to Byzantium, at that time its principal consumer, felt that since they controlled the steppe, they could handle the trade without the Persians. Inevitably, this led to war between the Türks and the Sassanian empire. In order to create a viable monopoly, the Türks needed to be certain that the Byzantine empire was willing to purchase its silk directly from the Türks rather than via established routes. Consequently, Ishtemi sent embassies to Byzantium, the first one apparently in 567 or 568.

It is not quite clear whether the Türks obtained satisfaction immediately. What they learned, however, must have been both encouraging and disheartening. The Byzantine empire wanted nothing better than the cessation of commercial contacts with the Persians. It had attempted, apparently without success, to establish its own economic ties with China, but, at the same time, it had been experimenting rather successfully with the production of high-quality silk within the empire itself. It does not appear, however, that Byzantine production was sufficient for its needs, and thus the Türks were assured of a market for the silk supplies they obtained from China. The years that followed Ishtemi's first embassy witnessed a regular exchange between the two empires. It must be noted, however, that the Turkic missions strongly advocated war between Byzantium and Persia, a war which would be to the material benefit of the Türks alone. Thus, the Türks were indirectly responsible for the nearly twenty-year-long war between the

Greeks and the Persians. Notwithstanding the frequent exchange of embassies and the material benefits reaped by the Türks, Byzantine-Turkic relations were frequently tense, primarily because Byzantium readily granted asylum to the Türks' enemies, especially the Avars. That this was a major bone of contention was made quite clear by Tardu, Ishtemi's successor, who severely chastised the Byzantine envoy Valentinos when he came to the *yabghu*'s court simply to announce Tiberius's accession to the throne in 576.[18]

How the Türks operated the silk trade is, as yet, unknown. The western domains of the Turkic empire had the principal role in the sale of the silk, while the eastern domains acquired it from China. Hence, the requirements of the western domains had important repercussions in the eastern domains, in particular on Sino-Turkic relations. All too often these repercussions have been overlooked: although the sources frequently mention conflicts between the Türks and the Chinese,[19] no serious attempt has been made to analyze their causes. Most commonly, the wars are explained away as a mere expression of the "barbarian" nature of the steppe people. Because of the importance of trade to the Turkic empire, it is imperative to examine the relationship between war and trade in Turkic politics.[20] It then quickly becomes clear that the principal reasons for the numerous wars the Türks launched, on both their eastern and western frontiers, but especially on the former, were economic ones.

By and large, the Western nations were quite willing to trade with the Türks to satisfy their needs, and, furthermore, they were willing to do so on the basis of equality among states. China, on the other hand, had no particular need for any of the products the Türks could offer. The Türks, however, in order to fulfill the requirements of their Western clients, needed Chinese silk and were intent on obtaining it even though they had little to offer the Chinese. Sino-Turkic economic relations were further complicated by the existence of the so-called tribute system, a system of trade and diplomacy developed during the Han dynasty to deal with the Hsiung-nu, which advocated the supremacy of Chinese culture and Chinese political institutions. This meant that the Chinese viewed all trading items brought into China as tribute, that is, as tokens of respect toward China's cultural superiority, irrespective of the true nature of the foreign missions.[21] From the start, Chinese and Turkic concepts and requirements were irreconcilable and were to be a major source, if not the most important one, of conflict between the two empires.

The history of Sino-barbarian economic relations, however, reveals that China had a more realistic appraisal of the system's potential than the system's rhetoric suggests. Frequently, China was unable to prevent trade from being forced upon it, thus it found a means to accommodate these pressures in the border trade marts, where, on the principles of barter trade, "barbarian" products were exchanged for Chinese products. The guiding political idea behind this concession is clearly expressed in the Chinese records.

Our rulers when governing the Barbarians of the four directions, now used the method to treat them kindly in order to win their hearts and then they used the principle to control them by restraint. By this method they quieted the borderlands and calmed China; and thus, establishing barter trade, i.e. by the method of treating [the Barbarians] kindly and controlling [them], we retarded them. We have pursued this policy from the beginning of the Han period. Then we appointed the market places and enacted the laws concerning the [frontier] passes and markets. In this way, by bribes, we gained their confidence. Among [our] measures of defense this was one of the tactics to pacify the Barbarians.[22]

All trade was conducted by the government, and although some concessions were made, the Chinese court never lost sight of this fact. It determined the value of the goods. traded in return, a value more often determined by political than by economic considerations. The system suited the Chinese not only because it permitted them to control the foreigners, but also because they had no need for foreign products. The Chinese did want exotica, and the system satisfied that want excellently. The states surrounding China accepted this system voluntarily, as it presented certain advantages, the principal one being that the Chinese "gifts" often exceeded the value of the foreign "gifts." Even so, border raids occurred frequently; but their principal aim appears to have been the acquisition of more mundane goods, primarily agricultural products.

The rise to power of the Türks and their serious involvement in the silk trade profoundly affected the elaborate structure created by the Chinese. It does not appear that the Türks challenged the principle of the tribute mission, but only one of its more inconvenient aspects. The rate of exchange between foreign "gifts" and Chinese "gifts" was set by the whim, or the political needs, of the Chinese court and could not be predicted with any degree of certainty. To the Türks this was unacceptable because it imperiled their trading activities on their empire's western borders. Consequently, when the Türks began to present their "tribute" to the Chinese, they demanded specific gifts and specific quantities in return. To the Chinese this was a shocking innovation in their relations with Central Asia, and one against which they were powerless: before China's reunification under the Sui dynasty, no dynasty was in a position to resist a major Turkic invasion.[23]

The Turkic demands and the Chinese response to them bring into sharp focus the irreconcilable political and economic concepts held by the two states. A recent analysis of Sino-Turkic relations states that one of the reasons for the numerous conflicts was the failure on both sides to realize these conceptual differences.[24] As is shown by the history of T'ang-Turkic relations in particular, this appears not to have been the case. Both sides were well aware of their differences and of the economic realities. To the Chinese an open acknowledgment of this situation, and thus a potential lessening of tensions, was impossible because it would have invalidated

China's claim to cultural and political superiority. Hence, each empire used military power to force its concepts upon its opponent. The military advantage alternated between them; the victor's basic needs were satisfied at the other's expense.

The Structure of the Empire

The Chinese kept more information on the Türks than on any other foreign people up to that time. However, this information is neither more accurate nor less biased than that relating to earlier "barbarian" groups. With the exception of the elements directly related to Sino-Turkic political and military relations, the information in Chinese sources is scattered, and there was no attempt to verify its accuracy. Chinese social concepts were used to express Turkic concepts, without providing new definitions for the terms used and without consistency in their use. A careful examination of the available material, however, does permit the formation of a more than adequate perception of Turkic society and institutions, as well as of the weakness in them that resulted in the decline of Turkic power.[25]

On the basis of the scanty information available concerning the origins of the Türks and the apparent fact that the founding clan of the Turkic empire, the A-shih-na clan, traced its descent along the female line, Turkic society has frequently been described as matrilineal or matriarchal. The evidence for this statement is dubious, and it contradicts what is known about the Turkic empire at a later time for which more solid evidence is available; this later information clearly describes Turkic society as patrilineal and patriarchal. However, it should be pointed out that within nomadic societies on the steppe there existed an alternation between matrilineality-patrilineality and matriarchy-patriarchy. The alternation appears to have followed the fortunes of the nomadic group: when it was powerful, it was unquestionably patrilineal-patriarchal; when it was weak and its survival was threatened, it was matrilineal-matriarchal. To what degree this reflects an adaptation of society to the absence of adult males cannot be precisely determined, although most likely this was an important factor. Even at politically and economically favorable times, however, matrilineal influence could be important, although in fact only one example of this is available: that of Ta-lo-pin, who was passed over in the succession because of his mother's "low" origins.[26]

Turkic society as a whole can be divided into three principal groups. The most important one is the tribe, *pu-lo* in Chinese. This was subdivided into a number of clans, *hsing* in Chinese, which made up the second group. The third group was a subdivision of the clan and known as the "tent," *chang* in Chinese, that is, the household. The number of tents, *chang,* rather than the number of families, *chia,* was the normal way in which the

Chinese scribes enumerated the population of foreign groups. The exact meaning of *chang*, as opposed to *chia*, is not quite clear, but it appears to have covered an extended family. The clan was the most common social structure of all Central Asian nomadic societies, and the Türks were no exception. It appears to have incorporated the largest exogamous patrilineal kinship group.[27] However, it had no political power as such.

Political power was vested in the tribe, the basis of every organized nomadic group. The tribe could contain within it related as well as unrelated clans, and its formation was dependent on the political and economic fortunes of the tribal leader. No specific number of clans was required to form a tribe, and an organized state likewise did not require a specific number of tribes. Formation of either appears to have been a function of the nomadic economy, although here too the evidence is scanty. The need for a community of interests among tribes, such as was described in the previous chapter, is apparent in Turkic society, along with the weakness inherent in such an organization.

The founder of the Hsiung-nu empire had stated, several centuries earlier, that land was of crucial importance to a nomadic state. This clearly was the case for Turkic tribal society. In fact, two elements were essential to the survival of an organized tribal group: the tribal land and the tribal army, the latter to defend the former. The loss of the tribal homeland, even in cases were the tribal leader survived the attack, meant the destruction of the tribal organization that had existed up to the time of the attack. This is aptly illustrated by the fate of Ta-lo-pin, or Apa Qaghan. After Ishpara had attacked and destroyed his home base, Apa Qaghan continued to conduct war against him, but he had to do so with troops provided by Tardu. He was never able to revive his own tribe.

The importance of the land to the tribal group is also evidenced by the fact that when tribes were at odds with each other, a tribe could be destroyed if it lost all or substantial portions of its pasture land, even if it maintained its homeland in the narrow sense of the term. There existed an intimate relationship between the size of the pasture land, hence the size of the herds, and the power wielded by a particular tribe. It was the more prosperous tribes, that is, those who controlled the most pasture land, who were at the basis of an empire's formation.

The Turkic empire differed from the earlier nomadic empires in possessing a more structured political system as well as a more or less fixed geographic center of political and cultural primordiality. The leadership of the empire was in the hands of the *qaghan,* who was always a member of the tribe that had founded, or restored, the empire. The residence of the *qaghan* and the political-cultural center of the empire were identical: it was located near the Otuken Mountain in the Altai chain, the place where the Türks maintained a cult of their ancestors. It is clear that all the people who were an integral part of the Turkic empire believed in a common ancestry and that the focus of this cultic orientation was centered in the *qaghan* and distinctly political. Although the center was more or less fixed in the Otuken Mountain, it moved in accordance with the political and military requirements of the moment.[28]

As was stated earlier, the Turkic empire had a secondary leader and a secondary seat of power in the person of the *yabghu*. This dual kingship can be traced back to ancient times on the steppe, for it appears to have existed at the time of the Hsiung-nu empire. The *yabghu*'s domains were always the western regions of the empire, and he was always the brother of the *qaghan*, at least in theory. Except for the cultic role of the *qaghan*, however, neither function was clearly defined, and at times the *yabghu* was actually senior to the *qaghan*, although, in theory, all power was in the *qaghan*'s hands. Furthermore, there did not exist any method, other than warfare, to accommodate or deal with political or economic conflicts between the *qaghan* and the *yabghu*. Finally, although both positions were, according to custom, hereditary, there was no mechanism to guarantee the new *qaghan* or *yabghu*'s recognition by the rest of the empire's tribal aristocracy. In a society where military skills and charisma had a predominant role in leadership recognition, the absence of such a system opened the way to numerous challenges.

The Chinese sources state that the Türks had twenty-eight categories of officials, all with both military and civil functions. For most of them, however, only titles are given, not functions; and where functions were defined by the Chinese, caution must be exercised, because the descriptions are in terms of the Chinese administrative positions corresponding to those titles; it is a distinct possibility that the function of *qaghan* is a transference of the role of the Chinese emperor, although to what degree this is true cannot be determined as yet.[29] The politico-administrative structure of the Turkic empire was concentrated within its tribal armies, all of which, at least according to the Chinese sources, were under the overall command of the *qaghan*. In fact, authority was divided among the leadership of the Turkic aristocracy, and although the *qaghan* was an absolute ruler, decisions appear to have been made by consensus. There appears not to have existed any clearly defined command structure.

Little is known about the actual organization of the Turkic military forces. From the fate of the tribes defeated in internecine warfare, it can be determined that all able-bodied adult males were automatically part of the tribal forces. The latter were apparently arranged in units consisting of multiples of ten, a system later perfected by the Mongols, although the Türks did not strictly adhere to it. The size of the Turkic forces as a whole is unknown, but it does not appear to have been very large. The tactics used were those of traditional nomadic warfare, based primarily on swift surprise attacks; tactics appear not to have had a particular organizational form. The Chinese repeatedly stated that Turkic military capabilities were a function of the charismatic personality of the *qaghan*.[30]

There were tribes that were nominal vassals of the Chinese court but frequently asserted their independence from it; the court tolerated this because these tribes provided China with crucial military assistance. These Turkic forces, combined with regular Chinese forces and those drawn from the militia, participated in campaigns in Central Asia, against Korea, and even in the suppression of internal Chinese rebellions.[31] When the militia system decayed, they became one of the principal border defense forces. Overall command remained in Chinese hands until the middle years of the dynasty, when Chinese political strength deteriorated and foreigners began to command foreign and Chinese troops. This situation led to the growth of militarism, an important factor in the dynasty's collapse. The foreign forces at the service of China were described as "the claws and the teeth" of the empire. When the dynasty weakened, "the claws and teeth" showed a mind of their own and moved in, not to protect China, but to get a share of the spoils.[32]

The religion of the Türks at the time they defeated the Juan-juan and established their own empire was animistic, shamanistic, and included ancestor worship. The principal deities were heaven and the sun, on account of which tent openings were always directed toward the east. The two most important religious ceremonies were the annual pilgrimage to the place of ancestry and, at the beginning of summer, the offerings to the sky deity. Both ceremonies were presided over by the *qaghan*.

Even at this time, however, other peoples of Central Asian origin who had created their own dynasties in North China, in particular the Tabghach, had abandoned their own religious traditions in favor of Buddhism in its Chinese form. The North Chinese dynasties were also active propagators of Buddhism, and through them the Türks came into contact with the religion. When the Turkic empire expanded and incorporated regions like the Tarim basin, the Türks encountered people who were as active in the propagation of Buddhism as the North Chinese dynasties had been, albeit Buddhism in a form closer to the Indian original.

The date at which the Türks adopted Buddhism is not clear, but it appears to have been sometime between the middle of the sixth and the middle of the seventh centuries. During the reign of Muqan, the Türks were receptive toward Buddhism, but whether or not it was actually adopted by a substantial number of Türks or by Muqan himself is not known. One of the driving forces behind the attempt to convert the Türks was Yü-wen T'ai, a minister of the Western Wei and the founder of the Northern Chou dynasty, a devout Buddhist. On his instructions a temple for the Turkic *qaghan* was erected around 555, the commemorative inscription of which has survived.[33] During the reign of Muqan's successor, the emperor of the Northern Ch'i ordered the Chinese scholar Liu Shih-ch'ing, who apparently was familiar with Turkic, to prepare a translation into Turkic of the *Nirvāṇasūtra*, which was presented as a gift to the *qaghan*. Furthermore, there is evidence that monks from the Buddhist state of Khotan were involved in missionary activity among the Türks at about that time. It must be pointed out, however, that when the famous Chinese Buddhist traveler Hsüan-tsung wrote the account of his travels, very little mention of Turkic Buddhists was made, at least among the inhabitants of the oasis states.[34]

Although the exact date of Turkic conversion cannot be pinpointed, it seems evident that by the first quarter of the seventh century most of the Western Türks at least had adopted Buddhism. As was stated above, T'ung, the ruler of the Western Türks from 618 to 630, was not involved in the affairs of the Eastern Khanate but devoted his energies to the propagation of Buddhism until the Qarluq rebellion in 630 plunged the Western Khanate into chaos. Buddhism's important role in the Eastern Khanate is revealed clearly in Chinese sources, which show Tonyuquq's virulent opposition to the faith. He is reported to have stated, "Furthermore, the teachings of the Buddhist and Taoist temples bring people only kindness and complacency. This is not the road to the conduct of war nor to obtaining power."[35] In spite of Tonyuquq's efforts, however, Buddhism remained prevalent among the Türks, although, as will be shown in the next chapter, it suffered a temporary setback in favor of Manicheism when the Uighur empire was founded. Furthermore, after the battles on the Talas River in 751, a substantial number of Türks in the western regions became faithful adherents of Islam.

The Islamic Thrust
into the Empire

At about the time the T'ang dynasty established its hegemony over China and thus began China's second Golden Age, the Middle East was undergoing one of the most dramatic upheavals in history: the establishment and expansion of Islam. Founded by Muhammad (570–632) in present-day Saudi Arabia, the new religion expanded outside of the Arabian peninsula. In 633 began the *jihad,* the Islamic holy war, which brought Arabic rule throughout North Africa and Spain and witnessed the Arab conquest of the entire Middle East, including the Christian holy places. Among the Middle Eastern states attacked was the Sassanian empire, which crumbled rapidly before the onslaught. The last of the Sassanian emperors died in 651, the year the Arabs took Herat. By the end of 652, the Arab forces had conquered the Sassanian empire in its entirety, including Balkh and Khurassan. Thus, by the middle of the seventh century the Arabs, and with them Islam, had reached the steppe's western borders.

An Islamic thrust into the steppe proper, however, did not occur until the beginning of the eighth century,[36] during the administration of Qutaiba ibn-Muslim, the Ummayad governor of Khurassan (705–715). The regions beyond Khurassan were under the control of a vast array of smaller Turkic states, some of which were related to the Turkic imperial house. (For the sake of clarity, these were not discussed in the preceding pages.) It was these smaller states which were the targets of Qutaiba ibn-Muslim's expansion. In 705 Qutaiba launched his conquests of Transoxiana by attacking Tokharistan, the former Bactria, ruled by descendants of the *yabghu* of the Western Türks. The conquest of Tokharistan was followed by a three-year war against Bukhara, and by 712 Qutaiba controlled not only the latter city, but also Samarqand.

Qutaiba ibn-Muslim's conquests sent waves of panic throughout Transoxiana and Turkestan. The local Turkic rulers appealed to Qapaghan for aid, and Turkic imperial forces were dispatched, under the command of Kül-tegin. A major clash between Qutaiba ibn-Muslim and Kül-tegin occurred near Bukhara around 707, and Qutaiba's forces pushed the Turkic armies back into the steppe proper. War continued sporadically until 714, but the number of clashes appears to have been quite small. After 714 Qapaghan and Kül-tegin—in fact, the entire Turkic empire—concentrated on internal problems. Consequently, Qutaiba ibn-Muslim and the forces of Islam had a free hand in Transoxiana, whose inhabitants soon began to undergo conversion, often quite involuntarily, to the new religion.

While Qutaiba ibn-Muslim was establishing his authority in Transoxiana, the T'ang dynasty in China had undergone its first major political crisis. By 713, however, when the emperor Hsüan-tsung (713–755) ascended to the throne, the T'ang had regained its political stability and plans were made to revive the expansionist policies of Li Shih-min. The opportunity to do so was created by the weakening of the Turkic empire and by the campaigns of Qutaiba ibn-Muslim. Indeed, the local rulers of Transoxiana had appealed for help against the Arabs not only to Qapaghan, but also to the Chinese emperor. Hsüan-tsung did not provide them with military assistance but only with moral encouragement in the form of ranks and diplomas, possibly accompanied by some cash. He nevertheless used the appeals to establish Chinese "sovereignty" over an entire series of small states in the area, such as, for example, Gilgit, Kashmir, Wakhan, and Zabulistan.

It has been suggested that the principal reason for Hsüan-tsung's caution was his desire to avoid a major conflict with the Ummayads.[37] In fact, he was forced to remain passive by the expansionist policies of the Tibetan empire. Ever since its formation in the middle of the seventh century, the Tibetan empire had been at odds with China. Although China had been able to inflict defeats upon the Tibetans, it had not been able to gain a clear military victory. Hence, it would have been dangerous to send troops to distant Transoxiana, for the Tibetans could, at any time, cut off Chinese communication and supply lines.

During the early years of Hsüan-tsung's reign, in spite of the numerous appeals from Transoxiana, China expressed more interest in the states of the Pamir range, undoubtedly because these states were in a position to provide the Chinese with assistance against the Tibetans: the creation of a second front in the mountains and high plateaux of the Pamir and Hindu-kush would relieve Tibetan pressure on China's border. Chinese policies were successful, at least in part—some of the states went to war against the Tibetans, but were conquered. This finally induced the Chinese court to take a more active role throughout the entire area, and, in 747, Chinese troops under the command of the Korean general Kao Hsien-chih were sent to the Pamirs. Chinese troop movements were greatly facilitated by the fact that the Turkic empire had disintegrated by then. While Kao Hsien-chih successfully defeated the Tibetans in Gilgit and Baltistan, other Chinese forces attempted, not quite successfully, to extend Chinese hegemony over the central steppe.

Chinese intervention against Tibet in the Pamirs was to have dramatic and unexpected consequences for Central Asia. After his successful campaign in the Pamirs, Kao Hsien-chih apparently decided to make some personal profit while in the area. In 750 he intervened in the affairs of Tashkent, and although he had promised safe passage to the city's governor if he surrendered, Kao Hsien-chih had him killed and seized all his possessions while his troops thoroughly looted the city. Although the area was nominally subject to the Chinese emperor, it now turned for help to the recently established 'Abbasid Caliphate. 'Abu Muslim, the 'Abbasid governor for Khurassan, did not hesitate when he received the appeal for aid, but immediately sent an army against Kao Hsien-chih. An alliance was established between the 'Abbasid forces and the Tibetans, and soon joined by the Turkic Qarluqs, who had revolted against Kao Hsien-chih. In July 751 the allied forces and the Chinese clashed on the banks of the Talas River, and the Chinese forces were utterly routed. Within a few years, Turkestan had come under Tibetan control, where it stayed for nearly a century, and Transoxiana under 'Abbasid suzerainty.

The battle at the Talas River is a watershed not only in Chinese history, for it eliminated China permanently from Transoxiana, but also in the history of Central Asia. The Turkic states and the Turkic tribes that resided there became an integral part of the Islamic world and have remained so until the present. The Islamization of the area was completed around 850, when the ruler of Zabulistan, in present-day Afghanistan, converted to the faith of Muhammad. The Turkic world was thus divided into two areas, each of which underwent a distinctly different historical evolution. The western regions of the former Turkic empire, as will be detailed in the following chapter, became sedentary Islamic states, expanding into the Middle East proper, where they gave rise to empires such as that of the Saljuqs. The central and eastern domains of the Turkic empire remained within the steppe tradition and adopted the Buddhist faith. It was from these regions that the Mongols set out to conquer the world.

4

The Transition
Empires

The end of the Turkic empire came abruptly, only a few years after the death of Bilge-qaghan, when the Uighurs, a Turkic tribe, overthrew the existing leadership and established an empire of their own. The Uighur rising marked the end of even a symbolic unity among the various Turkic tribes. After it, the larger tribal coalitions created empires of their own and expanded into the Middle East and the Russian steppe. Only the Uighurs remained in Central Asia proper. The collapse of the Turkic empire marked the beginning of a long transition period that culminated in the formation of the Mongol empire and the reunification of the steppe under the Mongol aegis. The principal empires created during this period were those of the Uighurs, the Qaraqanids, the Saljuqs, and the Qwarezm-shahs. All underwent complete sedentarization and were separated from each other by nomadic frontier zones inhabited by Turkic tribes following traditional practices. These empires were ethnically more homogeneous than the Turkic empire had been, and they adopted the structured religions of the sedentary areas, which provided them with an institutional framework.

The Triad
of Uighur Empires

According to the Chinese sources, the Uighurs were distant descendants of the Hsiung-nu, and their immediate ancestors were the members of the tribal confederation of the Tölös. Little is known about the Tölös confederation except that it maintained friendly relations with the Chinese empire and was constantly at odds with the Turkic empire. The confederation disintegrated early in the seventh century and thus gave the Uighurs their first opportunity to establish themselves as an independent kingdom along the upper reaches of the Selenga River. The Chinese court recognized Uighur independence as early as 629, the year in which the Chinese records for the first time identify a tribute mission as having come from the Uighurs. Through a careful exploitation of internal tensions within the Turkic empire, the Uighurs, by 641, were able to exert control over a substantial portion of the eastern steppe. Apparently around this time they created a new confederation known as the "Nine Clans," the Toquz-Oghuz. At the beginning of the eighth century, however, the Uighurs, and the entire Toquz-Oghuz confederation, were once again under complete Turkic control.[1]

Although the Toquz-Oghuz confederation lost its independence, it did not disintegrate. It continued to pursue the goal of forming on the eastern steppe a completely independent state that through friendly relations with China would control that country's Central Asian trade. In the turmoil following the death of Bilge-qaghan, confederated tribes led by the Uighurs allied themselves with two other Turkic tribes, the Besmil and the Qarluq, and were able to destroy the remnants of the Turkic empire. They expanded westwards, pushing most of the Turkic Qarluq further into the western steppe.[2] The leader of the Uighurs at this time, and thus the founder of their empire, was K'o-li-pei-lo, whose reign title was Qutluq Bilge Kül Qaghan and who ruled from 744 until 747. His hegemony over the eastern steppe was recognized by the Chinese in 745, and they awarded him the honorific title of *Huai-jen qaghan*, "the qaghan concerned with goodness." Like K'o-li-pei-lo, the Uighurs adopted reign titles as Chinese emperors did; the titles they adopted asserted that the qaghan's authority was derived directly from heaven.[3]

The empire created by K'o-li-pei-lo, known as the Orkhon empire, was the first of a series of Uighur empires, some of which lasted until well into the thirteenth century. For nearly a century, until its defeat by the Qirghiz in 840, the Orkhon empire dominated the eastern and the south-central steppe. It had a city as its capital, the present-day Qara-Balghasun, and a distinctly mixed nomadic-sedentary structure. The Orkhon empire reached its apogee during the reign of I-ti-chien, also known as Mu-yu Qaghan (759–779).[4] It extended from the Altai to Lake Baikal.

The Uighurs established a relationship with the Chinese that was unique in Chinese–Central Asian history. It was based on the Uighur desire to maintain a political *status quo* in China, a desire unquestionably dictated by Uighur trade requirements and facilitated by the fact that China was militarily weak at the time. As a result, when rebellions shook the foundations of the T'ang dynasty, in particular the An Lu-shan rebellion (755–763), Uighur troops assisted the Chinese in recapturing the imperial cities of Ch'ang-an and Lo-yang, in 757 and 762 respectively. Their assistance, however, was a double-edged sword: as "compensation" they extensively looted both cities and forcefully requested the establishment of Uighur settlements in them. Militarily, the T'ang dynasty was in no position to prevent the plunder, and the settlements were avoided only after very large "gifts" had been offered to the Uighur ruler. In spite of these difficulties, the Chinese court was forced to continue to rely on Uighur military strength.

The Uighurs provided assistance to the Chinese not only in China, but also in the oasis states under nominal Chinese control. Their military operations were directed primarily against the Tibetans. The reign of Mu-yu Qaghan largely coincided with that of the Tibetan emperor Khri-srong-Ide-btsan (755–797), under whose leadership the Tibetan empire reached the summit of its power and expansion, including a two-week-long occupation of the T'ang capital, Ch'ang-an. The principal Tibetan expansion, however, was not into China proper but into the Kansu corridor and the Tarim basin: hence, into the steppe. In 790 the Tibetans conquered the oasis states, as well as the Uighur city of Beshbaliq; they controlled the Tarim basin until 822. One of the principal aims of the Tibetan expansion into the Kansu corridor was to cut off Chinese-Uighur contacts and to gain control over the trade between the two countries. Soon after the death of Khri-srong-Ide-btsan, however, the Uighurs were able to retake Beshbaliq, Qocho, Qarashahr, and Kucha, thus regaining control over the cotton and silk trade. After 822 they were instrumental in driving the Tibetans out of the Tarim basin entirely. These victories had more important consequences, in the long run, than simply the restoration of Uighur trade supremacy. They extended Turkic language and culture into the area and consolidated the penetration of other Turkic tribes there, at the expense of the original inhabitants, the Indo-European tribes.

Relations between the Uighurs and the Sogdians, whose original settlement was in the Samarqand and Bukhara area, was facilitated by their common interest in trade. Since at least the fourth century A.D., the Sogdians had played an important role in the Central Asian transit trade along the so-called Silk Road, which lay between the city of Sugdaq on the Caspian Sea and the city of Lou-lan (Kroirana in Sogdian) on China's extreme western border. The Sogdians had warehousing rights in many important cities throughout Asia, including the Chinese capital. They had never created a major empire of their own, however, but had nearly always recognized the suzerainty of other states. Thus, the Uighurs simply took over the Sogdian trading activities. The Sogdians themselves were gradually absorbed into the Turkic and the Iranian worlds.

Contact with the Sogdians profoundly affected Uighur life. The most important event in their relationship was the Uighurs' adoption of the Iranian religion of Manicheism, through the intermediary of the Sogdians. The conversion apparently took place in the old Chinese capital of Lo-yang during Mu-yu Qaghan's residence there between 762 and 763; upon his return to the Uighur capital he was accompanied by several Manicheian priests. Sogdians became the principal advisors to the Uighur ruler. The adoption of a higher, "organized" religion led to an increased sedentarization of the Uighur population, which drew them away from their ancestral mountains to the steppe plains. There they created walled cities, the first ever erected by a Central Asian people.[5] The Uighurs adopted a modified Sogdian script to replace the cumbersome Runic one. The Sogdians also transmitted many sedentary crafts to the Uighurs, the most important being agricultural techniques, especially those involving irrigation, which was necessary for desert oasis cultivation. Other introductions were multiple-storied brick construction and fresco painting.

The cultural life developed within the Uighur empire was the exception on the steppe. Militarily and politically, however, they remained clearly within the steppe's traditions, even though the Chinese sources, the principal ones for Uighur history, are not very clear with regard to the Orkhon empire's internal developments. As with other empires on the steppe, political difficulties started with the end of the second generation, in this case with the reign of Mu-yu Qaghan. The first serious internal political crisis in the Orkhon empire occurred when Mu-yu Qaghan was assassinated by his cousin and minister, Bagha Tarqan, who assumed the position of ruler. He was recognized by the Chinese court in 780 and reigned until 789, when he was succeeded by his son. By the turn of the century, succession problems had become serious. In 832 the disputes degenerated into open conflict and paralyzed the Uighur leadership.

The internal conflicts of the Orkhon empire were aggravated by several other factors. One of the most important was directly related to the cultural change the Uighurs had undergone since the foundation of their empire. They had abandoned the Otüken region and allowed other tribes to settle there while they themselves had withdrawn to the cities and the sedentary enclaves in the Turfan region. As a direct consequence of this shift, Uighur military strength had declined. Indirectly, China's military weakness was another factor in the decline of Uighur military preparedness, for a weak China presented no threat to the steppe.

The condition of the Orkhon empire in 832 inevitably attracted intervention by one of the many nomadic tribes on the steppe that had not abandoned the traditional raiding party as a means of increasing their wealth. The destruction of the first Uighur empire came in 840 from just such an expedition on the part of the Qirghiz, a Turkic tribe whose history is barely known,[6] whom the Uighurs themselves had allowed to settle in the Otüken region. The Qirghiz victory, however, did not result in the creation of a strong confederation or a new empire: once their victory was obtained and the loot collected, the loosely organized Qirghiz returned to the north and resumed their traditional nomadic practices.[7] The principal significance of their victory was that it closed the central steppe to the influence of the Uighurs and hence to the influence of sedentary civilizations. The area was not to play an important role again until the middle of the twelfth century.

The fate of the defeated Uighurs did not follow traditional patterns, either, for they were neither absorbed into the Qirghiz nor did they resume a nomadic lifestyle. The Orkhon empire had broken up into various clan alliances, each of which fled in a different direction. Some of them went to the west, where they entered into conflict with the Qarluq; some fled to China, where, in time, they settled in the extreme western parts of Kansu. By the middle of the ninth century, at least five Uighur kingdoms had come into existence. The three most important ones were those of Kan-chou, Sha-chou, and Qocho, centered respectively near present-day Chang-i-hsien, Tunhuang, and Turfan. A few other principalities came into existence in present-day Sinkiang province, and it is quite possible that a few more were established further west. At this point, however, information becomes scarce, for the T'ang dynasty in China had entered into a period of drastic decline, and such periods usually resulted in a total lack of interest in foreign affairs among Chinese historians. Almost simultaneously, the Tibetan empire collapsed, never to recover. It is quite possible, even though no solid evidence exists, that it was the sudden decline of these two major powers that permitted the survival of the Uighur kingdoms.

The Kan-chou kingdom had the most frequent contacts with China, and hence its history is somewhat better documented than those of the other two kingdoms. Nevertheless, the available information is still only episodic, and it is not known exactly when or by whom the Kan-chou kingdom was founded. What is clear is that by the beginning of the tenth century, it was the dominant force in extreme western Kansu. The Kan-chou Uighurs established themselves on Central Asia's principal trade routes and were soon in full control of the trade. They were bent on continuing friendly relations with China. The Chinese court, on the other hand, although confronted by nearly insurmountable internal difficulties, preferred to keep the Uighurs at a distance. It was not until the creation of the Later T'ang dynasty (923–936) that relations were resumed on a regular basis and trade and diplomatic exchanges were revived. The Uighurs became China's principal foreign traders, selling primarily horses, jade, and other precious materials and acquiring primarily silk in return.

In the past, China had been relatively successful in controlling trade with Central Asia, but during the Five Dynasties period, such control was impossible: the strength of the Uighurs and their presence in Chinese cities could have had disastrous consequences for China. Hence, the missions that came to China increased in size every year. When the Later Chou dynasty (951–

960) was founded, the imperial treasury had such an excess of jade that it had nearly lost its value. Trade had to be controlled to avoid bankruptcy of the imperial treasury, but at the same time, measures could not be taken that would antagonize the Uighurs. It was then that the Chinese court came up with an idea that can perhaps be described as the first official devaluation of a precious commodity. Until this time, the Uighurs had traded only with the Chinese court, which kept part of the items purchased for itself and sold the remainder to the upper classes. The emperor T'ai-tsu (951–954) of the Later Chou decided to abolish the court's intermediary role and allow the Uighurs to trade directly on the open market. As a result, jade prices declined by 70 to 80 percent. Since the idea was to make trade unattractive to the Uighurs, it seems fairly certain that this drastic decline can be attributed, in part, to the court's selling its excess jade at the same time, although our sources do not state this. How the Uighurs reacted is not known, nor is it known how they reacted to Emperor Shih-tsung's (954–960) total refusal to buy jade for the court.[8] Since Uighur missions continued to arrive, it is fair to assume that jade was not an important element in their economy.

Much less is known about the Sha-chou kingdom, located in and around present-day Tunhuang, in spite of the fact that Tunhuang had a large Chinese population;[9] in fact, the area remained under Chinese control until 911. Its ruler from about 890 until 911 was a certain Chang Ch'eng-feng, who had been appointed by the dying T'ang dynasty as the military governor of Sha-chou. His ambition was to create an empire of his own that would exert control over the Uighurs, including those of Kan-chou. Inevitably there was conflict between him and the Uighurs, and in 911 he was soundly defeated. This date can be taken as the beginning of the Sha-chou kingdom, even though local Chinese officials continued to exert a leadership role subject to Kan-chou's approval.

Throughout the Five Dynasties period, the Sha-chou kingdom was also known as the "Chin-shan Empire of the Western Han," thus claiming a Chinese allegiance, and was ruled by people of Chinese extraction, in contrast to Kan-chou, where the local Chinese apparently had no political role. In common with Kan-chou, it had a rapid turnover of rulers. Relations between the two kingdoms fluctuated between tenuous friendship and overt hostility, apparently as a result of each kingdom's claim of suzerainty over the other. At the time of the formation of the Sung dynasty (960–1279), relations were peaceful, and Kan-chou was recognized as the more important of the two. Sha-chou's acquiescence in Kan-chou's superiority was dictated by economic considerations, for Kan-chou was in a position to close the trade routes between Sha-chou and China. During the Sung dynasty, missions from Sha-chou arrived more or less regularly at the Chinese court. It appears that the Sung authorities viewed Sha-chou and Kan-chou as two separate, independent entities, with Kan-chou as the principal Uighur kingdom.[10]

The dynastic changes in China appear to have had no influence upon the

Uighurs, for after the creation of the Sung dynasty, Sino-Uighur relations continued on the same basis as before. The only major difference was the complete cessation of Uighur military assistance to the Chinese, reflecting the decreased importance of military matters as such to the Uighurs themselves. The focal point of Sino-Uighur relations throughout the Sung dynasty remained trade, although trade volume during the first forty years of the dynasty declined in comparison to the Five Dynasties period. It was revived for some twenty-five years after 996, and remained regular until the destruction of the Kan-chou kingdom in 1028 by the Tangut empire. The trade stagnation was unrelated to China's traditional hostile attitude; rather it was a direct consequence of the military difficulties the Sung dynasty, as well as the Uighurs, experienced at the hands of the Tangut and the Ch'i-tan, two peoples who had established their own empires on China's northern and western borders and whose history is discussed in the next chapter. For, in spite of the difficulties involved, trade remained important and lucrative,[11] and other tribes, in particular the Tangut, aspired to control it. As soon as it became evident that the Uighurs no longer represented a military threat, their trade monopoly was openly and successfully challenged.

Tangut interference with Sino-Uighur trade expanded from brigandage to full-fledged attacks by the end of the tenth century; their raids became so effective that they brought trade to a near standstill. A Chinese-Uighur agreement was worked out by which each state was to provide military escorts for the trade missions. While the Tangut state was forced to retrench at the beginning of the eleventh century as a result of economic conditions, the Ch'i-tan were seeking to expand their control over the central steppe, especially over Sha-chou. They obtained recognition in 1006, and, two years later, the Ch'i-tan penetrated the Kan-chou kingdom. Whether or not Kan-chou recognized the Ch'i-tan as its overlord is not known, but most likely it did. In 1016, however, the situation changed rapidly. The Eastern Tibetan bCon-kha kingdom seized control of the trade routes, and the Tangut resumed their expansionist policies. Unable to conquer the bCon-kha kingdom, the Tangut turned westwards, to the starting points of the trade routes, attacked both Kan-chou and Sha-chou, and conquered them. By 1036 the Tangut controlled all Uighur domains with the exception of the Qocho kingdom. They had gained control over the trade routes and would keep it until the Mongol conquest two centuries later.[12]

The Qocho kingdom, founded about 850, was an oasis state with its center near present-day Turfan. It was at the crossroads of the Iranian, Sinitic, and steppe cultures, but sufficiently distant from the principal states not to be drawn constantly into their quarrels and difficulties. A consequence of the relative isolation of Qocho, however, is that only fragmentary information is available about its political history. At some point, the Qocho kingdom expanded to include the city of Beshbaliq, and later, during the twelfth century, it became the Uighur kingdom's capital. The Qocho-Beshbaliq Uighurs are known to have had relatively friendly relations with the Chinese, the Ch'i-tan, and later the Jürchen. Most of their difficulties came neither from China nor the steppe, but from the Islamic states, in particular the Qaraqanids.

Only slightly more information about Qocho becomes available during the Mongol period. At the beginning of the thirteenth century, the Qocho-Beshbaliq Uighurs had come under the overlordship of the Naiman, a tribe at constant odds with the forces of Chinggis-khan. Defeated in 1204, the Naiman had moved westwards and desired absolute control over the Uighur domains. In 1209, in order to free his state from their overlordship, the Uighur ruler, Barchuq, voluntarily recognized Chinggis-khan as his overlord and received from the Mongol emperor the assistance he needed. After Chinggis-khan's division of the empire among his sons, the Uighur kingdom became a part of the Chaghatai Khanate. By the middle of the thirteenth century, the independent Uighur kingdom of Qocho-Beshbaliq had ceased to exist.

Uighur Civilization: A Steppe Anomaly

At the beginning of the twentieth century, numerous expeditions converged on the Turfan area, the territory of the former Qocho kingdom. The area was an archeological treasure trove: written materials, artifacts, clothing, and frescoes, representative of nearly all the people and regimes that once held sway over the area, were discovered in great numbers.[13] A large amount of Uighur material was among that recovered and carted away to distant libraries and museums. Because of these discoveries, more is known about Uighur cultural life than about its political history, yet only a glimpse of this civilization is provided, for many areas that had an important role in Uighur history have never been investigated. The exact location of the old town of Beshbaliq, for example, has not yet been determined. The glimpse provided, however, shows a dynamic, proselytizing culture that exerted an important influence on the Turko-Mongol societies that followed the end of the Uighur empire.

The importance of Manicheism in the development of Uighur civilization must not be underestimated. Not only did it provide the stimulus for Uighur sedentarization and urbanization, but, through the intermediary of the Sogdians, it gave the Uighars an easy-to-use script. Thus, through the influence of Manicheism, the Uighurs developed a literate civilization, the first ever on the steppe, and for a long time the only one.[14] Although they eventually abandoned the Manicheian faith, the script continued in use, and later it was in the Uighur script that the early records of the Mongol empire were kept. Uighur civilization came into full bloom when, after the collapse of the Orkhon empire, the majority of the Uighurs adopted Buddhism, a religion with an extensive literature in many languages. Buddhism was apparently more congenial to the Uighurs than Manicheism, for under its influence other art forms, in particular fresco painting and architecture, flourished.

The bulk of Uighur literature recovered by the archeological expeditions is of either a religious or a commercial nature. Few historical documents were recovered, unquestionably because the places where such documents were most likely to be found were never explored. Most of the religious material deals with Buddhism, but there are a few texts dealing with Manicheism and Nestorianism, a heretical Christian sect. Uighur Buddhism found its roots in China and in Khotan, an Indo-European state, and by and large belonged to the Mahayana school. It is commonly stated that Buddhist literature of Central Asia is merely a translation literature, but such a statement can be based only on an unfamiliarity with the languages. Many Uighur texts—so-called translations from Chinese, Khotanese, or Sanskrit originals—are in fact adaptations of these texts to Uighur tastes and concepts. Uighar scholars, however, did not limit themselves to adapting, but also wrote learned treatises, often in the form of introductions to Buddhist doctrinal texts. The commercial documents are more down-to-earth, including contracts, decrees, deeds, and the like. Although their value as literature is perforce limited, from them it is learned that many people were literate and that knowledge of foreign languages was not uncommon among Uighurs. It is hardly surprising, then, that the Uighurs became the scribes and secretaries of the Central Asian empires, in particular that of the Mongols. René Grousset is undoubtedly correct when he labels the Uighurs the "professors of culture" in Central Asia.[15]

The Uighur kingdoms were located at the crossroads between the Sinitic and the Iranian worlds. Consequently, their art and architecture came to reflect a peculiar syncretism of the principal characteristics of these two cultures. Furthermore, after Buddhism became the principal Uighur faith, elements of Indian Buddhist art, in particular the Gandhara style, were added. Most religious buildings reflected this influence and were often bilevel structures; private residences combined Chinese and Iranian characteristics and were usually built on a single level, with several rooms arranged around a patio. Art, primarily in the form of frescoes, was found almost exclusively in the religious buildings, representing Buddhist influences. The style of the Uighurs, however, was not a slavish imitation of a foreign model, but clearly a native creation. The Sinitic-Iranian syncretism was superimposed on art styles borrowed from Gandhara or Kucha. It is not uncommon to see a Gandhara-style Buddha with Sinitic facial features and clothing. Uighur representations of Buddhist saints, like the Chinese, are always fully clothed, whereas in the Gandhara style, at least one of the shoulders is naked.[16]

The archeological excavations have yielded a considerable number of artifacts that permit an evaluation of Uighur material culture. This evidence confirms beyond any doubt statements made by the Chinese that the Uighurs were a sedentary people who engaged only marginally in pastoral animal husbandry. It also reveals, however, that the Uighurs had not abandoned all the steppe's military traditions. Large quantities of weapons were discovered, and Uighur clothing was adapted to cavalry warfare. Even in more ceremonial dress, Chinese influence was minimal. In furniture, kitchen utensils, and the like, Uighurs differed remarkably from the Chinese; these materials reflect the traditional steppe customs adapted to a sedentary lifestyle.[17]

The recovered commercial documents provide tantalizing insights into economic and social practices of the time. Information dating from Mongol times suggests that women in the steppe empires had more rights and independence than their counterparts in the sedentary states. These indications are confirmed for the Uighur empire. Women were entitled to their own property and were free to manage and dispose of it as they saw fit. They were also entitled to act as guarantors in contracts, and were provided for in testamentary regulations. Possession of land or slaves, on the other hand, was not an individual matter but a family one. Upon the death of the head of the family, the land remained within the family and did not revert automatically to the ruler, who, in theory, owned all the land within his domain. The documents reveal an advanced legal system, especially in civil law. Among its provisions was the right to sue for damages when the terms of a contract were violated.[18]

The combination of the Uighur material with the Chinese permits a somewhat better perception of the Uighur state structure than was possible for the Turkic empire. It appears more organized than the Turkic system, with positions and functions somewhat better defined. Possibly this is a consequence of the relatively small size of the Uighur kingdoms. At the head of the state was the *qaghan,* in whom all authority was vested. The succession of the *qaghan* is not clear, simply because of inadequate chronological information, but it appears to have been patrilineal. The *qaghan* was assisted by a chancellor, whose functions are not known, who always appears as the second most important person in the state. Nevertheless, he was always subordinate to the *qaghan*; apparently the Uighurs were able to avoid the *qaghan-yabghu* conflict that had created so many difficulties for the Türks. At a lower level, there were a series of officials known as the *beg* and the *elchi,* concerned respectively with financial and secretarial matters, but more research into these functions is required.

The smallest division of Uighur society was the family. The smallest military-administrative division was the unit of ten; these units were grouped to create higher organizational forms, units of a hundred and a thousand. The Mongols apparently followed the Uighur example in this respect. It is not clear whether the Uighur unit of ten refers to households (as in the Mongol system) or individuals, but most likely it was the former.

Neither the process nor the chronology of the Uighur transformation from a nomadic society into a sedentary, literate one is known. It is clear, on the one hand, that they continued tendencies begun during the Turkic empire. The Türks had created a script, albeit a cumbersome one; and we

know of Bilge-qaghan's plans to build walled cities from the recorded protests against them. On the other hand, the influence of the Uighur civilization on later Turko-Mongol societies, although it cannot be measured
precisely, apparently was substantial. They had shown that it was possible
to be sedentarized and literate without abandoning political ambitions and
steppe traditions, in fact, that a symbiosis of steppe and sedentary life was
possible if a solid sedentary economic base was present. Nevertheless, at
their historical zenith, the Uighurs were an anomaly on the steppe.

Turkic Islamization:
Qarluq and Qaraqanids

A Turkic people known as the Qarluq nomadized to the east of Lake
Balkash throughout most of the Turkic empire's hegemony over the steppe.
They apparently were not a strongly united tribe, for on several occasions
some small groups submitted to the Chinese; some even joined the
Tibetans. In 745, together with the Uighurs and the Besmil, another Turkic
tribe, they participated in the overthrow of the Turkic empire. The Qarluq
did not belong to the Toquz-Oghuz confederation, however, and after the
creation of the Orkhon empire, they began to move westward. In 751 they
assisted Arab and Tibetan forces against the Chinese during the battle at the
Talas River. Although the Qarluq contribution to the battle does not appear
to have been substantial, it was symptomatic of their anti-Chinese attitude,
whose basic causes are unknown. A consequence of this sentiment, however, was to place the Qarluq at odds with the more powerful, pro-Chinese
Uighurs. The increasing tensions between them led the majority of the
Qarluq to move farther west, into the Tarim basin and beyond into Kasghar.
The westward movement of the Qarluq coincided with the apogee of the
Tibetan empire. During the reign of Khri-srong-lde-btsan (755–797), the
Tibetan empire expanded into the Tarim basin, pushing the Qarluq even
further westward,[19] and isolating them from both the Uighur and the
Chinese, thus inevitably decreasing the amount of available information on
the Qarluq.

The Qarluq established themselves on the Chu River, west of Lake Issiq-
qul and north of the T'ien-shan mountains, in a place which they called
Quz Ordu but which is better known by its later name of Balasaghun. It
appears that the Qarluq viewed this place as a temporary base, a "western
refuge" from both Tibetan and Uighur pressures.[20] As long as the Orkhon
empire continued to dominate the central steppe, Qarluq power was relatively limited. With the collapse of the Orkhon empire, however, they became the most powerful group on the western steppe. The Qarluq, like the
Qirghiz, did not attempt to build a strong empire of their own, nor did
they attempt an eastward return. The minor state they created was, in fact,
a continuation of the Turkic empire they had helped overthrow. They were
divided, territorially and politically, into an eastern and a western khanate.

The ruler of both khanates was allegedly a descendant of a distant branch of the clan that had founded the Turkic empire. Instead of assuming the title of *yabghu,* commonly associated with the western steppe, the ruler of the Qarluq called himself *qan* ("khan"), often preceded by the epithet *qara,* "black."

The westward movement of the Qarluq into the territories of classical Ferghana brought the Türks to the fringes of the Iranian world and into an area that was undergoing a slow conversion to Islam. It was in this region that, during the ninth century, the Qarluq consolidated their state. At the same time, Arab power in the Iranian world was declining. By the end of the eighth century, Arab rule over Samarqand and Bukhara had passed into the hands of the native Iranian, but Islamic, population. During the early part of the ninth century, Arab influence declined in eastern Persia, and in 875 the first Iranian Islamic dynasty—the Samanids (875–999)—was created.[21] Although the Samanids recognized the sovereignty of the 'Abbasid caliphs in Baghdad, their reign marked the renascence of a purely Persian tradition. Throughout most of the tenth century, the Samanid dynasty acted as a barrier against a further westward penetration, into Persia and Afghanistan, of the Turkic tribes from the steppe.

Most of the contacts between the Samanids and the Qarluq were of a commercial nature. Attempts at conquest on the part of the Samanids were limited to the capture of the town of Talas (Taraz) in 893. Nevertheless, the Persian dynasty had an important influence on the future of the Turkic tribes on the western steppe by converting them to the Islamic faith; the conversion begun after the campaigns of Qutaiba ibn-Muslim was completed on their initiative. Little is known about the actual conversion process. It appears to have been progressive and to have been brought about primarily through traders, though the Samanids did establish a "Great Mosque" in Talas after they conquered it. Conversion on a large scale began about the middle of the tenth century, when devout, but not very orthodox, dervishes began to preach in the Qarluq domains, and when a Samanid prince sought refuge among them. The key date seems to be 961, when a war erupted between the eastern and the western Qarluqs. The latter apparently were already Muslims at that time and were supported by the Samanids. They were victorious, and consequently the Eastern Khanate also adopted Islam. Reports to the 'Abbasid caliph in Baghdad speak of the conversion of some one hundred thousand Turkic "tents," an enormous number.[22]

During the last decade of the tenth century, Samanid authority over western Persia was on the decline. The causes of the decline are outside the scope of this volume, but its consequences were important for the future of the Türks on the western steppe. The collapse of the Samanids under the attack of two new Turkic empires, the Qaraqanids and the Ghaznavids, brought the Türks to the Oxus (Amu-darya), the traditional border between Persia and the steppe world, without a challenge from the Persian heartland. The formation of two Turkic empires on the fringes of the Iranian world opened it to Turkic penetration, which was accomplished by the middle of the eleventh century with the creation of the Saljuq empire, discussed below.

The Ghaznavid dynasty, so called because it had its capital in Ghazna in present-day Afghanistan, was founded by Abu Mansur Sebuk Tegin (d. 997), a native of Issiq-qul and a member of the Samanid Turkic slave guard. After accompanying his master to Ghazna, he became the Samanid governor there in 977. When summoned, in 994, to the aid of the Samanids in Khurassan, he rebelled and established his own dynasty, seizing control over Khurassan and all the Samanid provinces south of the Oxus.[23] Although there is no doubt that the Ghaznavid dynasty was of Turkic origins, the evidence for the relationship between the Ghaznavids and the Qarluqs is scanty, since only one source—the Persian geography *Hudud al-'alam*[24]—refers to it. The Ghaznavid center of power remained in Afghanistan, and this Turkic dynasty ceased to have any real influence on steppe affairs.

The Qarluq origin of the Qaraqanid state—in contrast to the Ghaznavid—is not in doubt: it was founded by the western Qarluq khanate. Traditionally, the first Qaraqanid ruler is considered to be Satuq Bughra Khan (d. 955?), who converted to Islam early in the tenth century and assumed the Muslim name of 'Abd al-Karim. The two main centers of his power were Talas and Kashghar.[25] The relations between Bughra Khan and the Samanids are not very well known, but it is unlikely that they were friendly in light of his reconquest of Talas. Open conflict between the Samanids and the Qaraqanids broke out under Bughra Khan's grandson, Bughra Khan Harun. Taking advantage of rebellions within the Samanid state, Harun invaded the country and in 992 occupied Bukhara, then the Samanid capital. It was this Qaraqanid invasion, coupled with the rebellions in Khurassan, that led to the creation of the Ghaznavid state and the final collapse of the Samanids. Although the last Samanid ruler, Is'mail al-Muntasir, valiantly attempted to expel the Qaraqanids, he failed. The Samanids were finally overthrown by Harun's nephew, Ilig Nasr b.'Ali, in 999. Two years later, the Qaraqanids and the Ghaznavids agreed on the Oxus as the boundary between their domains. In 1005 Is'mail al-Muntasir was assassinated while traveling through the Qara-qum desert towards the Persian heartland. However, Turkic penetration of the Oxus had been achieved, and the steppe nomads were at the gate to Persia.

Although the Qaraqanids had been converted to Islam and had become fervent Sunnis, they remained a typical steppe empire and by and large followed the traditions of the Turkic empire. In fact, there were two Qaraqanid states, an eastern and a western one. If the Turkic empire had difficulties with its dual kingship structure, the Qaraqanids did not create a simpler system; on the contrary, theirs was even more complex. Each Qaraqanid khanate had two rulers—a supreme khan, known as *arslan-qan* ("the lion khan"), and a secondary khan—and two capitals within each khanate, one for each khan.[26] The four capital cities of the Qaraqanid empire were Balasaghun, Kashghar, Samarqand, and Bukhara. Although in principle the eastern khanate was superior, this varied with each khan's personal strength, and more often than not, the real power was with the western khanate. Under these circumstances, it is not surprising that Qaraqanid history is riddled with fratricidal warfare. Other Turkic states—first the Ghaznavids, later the Saljuqs—were to use these wars to extend their control over Transoxiana. The Qaraqanids were never a major force, and they never seriously threatened Persia itself.

Turkic Dominance in Persia:
The Saljuq Empire

Persia, governed by native rulers throughout almost all its long history, came under the absolute control of a Turkic tribe, the Saljuq, in the eleventh century. For almost nine hundred years after the creation of the Saljuq empire, Persia remained under either Turkic or Mongol rule. The history of the Saljuq empire is an integral part of the history of the Middle East and even of European history, for it was against Saljuq dominance of the Holy Land that the early Crusades were directed; but it relates only marginally to the history of Central Asia or the steppe. Before the Saljuqs occupied Persia, they were a minor Turkic group nomadizing on the western steppe. Therefore, the following paragraphs provide but a brief outline of their history.[27]

While the Qarluq established their domains in the former territories of Ferghana and, for all practical purposes, never crossed the Oxus, further to the west, between the Aral and Caspian seas, were other Turkic nomadic groups known under the generic name of Oghuzz. The Oghuzz confederation was apparently formed after the collapse of the Turkic empire and extended westward into the Volga region. During the reign of the 'Abbasid caliph al-Ma'mum (813–833), it is mentioned by Islamic writers, who refer primarily to the groups that had occupied the Dihistan steppe. The history of the Oghuzz confederation is still relatively obscure.[28] At the end of the tenth century, its power center appears to have been located on the Syr-darya (Jaxartes), to the north of the Qaraqanid state and in the contact zone between the Islamic and non-Islamic worlds. Among the military commanders of the *Yabghu,* as the rulers of the Oghuzz were known, were a certain Duqaq and his son Saljuq. At the beginning of the eleventh century, a conflict broke out between the Saljuq clan and the *Yabghu;* the former were forced to flee towards Jand, where they converted to Islam.

In Jand, the Saljuqs established their independence from the Oghuzz. During the first decades of their independence, they were a typical steppe state, indiscriminately raiding and looting the sedentary areas, in particular Khurassan, where Ghaznavid power was on the wane. Although it appears that, at that time, the Saljuqs had no intention of creating a large sedentary empire of their own, the increasing weakness of the Ghaznavids made it nearly inevitable that the Saljuqs would gain full control over Khurassan.

The Ghaznavids attempted to protect their northern possessions, but they did not have a clear policy, alternating between attack and alliance. Although they were of Turkic origin, the Ghaznavids had adopted the full impedimenta of sedentary warfare, including elephants. Thus encumbered, and operating from fixed bases, their *strategy* proved totally ineffective. Consequently, many of the great cities, such as Nishapur, Merv, and Herat, voluntarily submitted to the marauding Saljuq troops rather than rely on the unpredictable Ghaznavid military forces. In 1040, near Dandanqan, a major clash between the Saljuqs and the Ghaznavids occurred. The latter were utterly routed, and the Saljuqs found themselves the rulers of Khurassan, a sedentary area, with an open road into central and western Persia, areas then in political turmoil.[29]

During their penetration of Khurassan, the Saljuqs were ruled by a triumvirate. Toghril Beg Muhammad, the grandson of Saljuq, was the most important of the three rulers and the only one who anticipated the formation of a sedentary empire. Shortly after the Dandanqan victory, he emerged as the principal Saljuq leader. Toghril's two major concerns were the consolidation of Saljuq rule and the establishment of relations with the 'Abbasid caliphs, for recognition by the caliph would establish the legitimacy of the Saljuqs. He was successful in both endeavors, primarily because he was able to take advantage of the political instability of the 'Abbasid domain. Toghril's efforts were crowned in 1058, when, for the second time in his career, he entered Baghdad, this time to be received by the Caliph al-Qa'in and given important honorific titles by him. During the years that followed his recognition by the caliph, Toghril campaigned in Iraq against the caliph's enemies, in the process extending Saljuq control throughout central and western Persia and making the Saljuqs a major power. In 1062 the Saljuqs ceased to be nomadic invaders of Persia when a marital alliance was established between the caliph's family and Toghril, a matter in which the caliph had not much choice. When Toghril died in 1063, nearly seventy years old, the Saljuq empire was solidly established. From a marauding band of nomads, the Saljuqs had become the first Turkic rulers of a major sedentary power.

Toghril's was the first of many contested successions within the Saljuq empire, contests that were reminiscent of those that had periodically shaken the Turkic empire. Although Toghril had designated his brother's son Sulaiman as the successor, it was Sulaiman's older brother, Alp-Arslan, and his vizier, Nizam al-Mulk, who emerged as the victors in the succession conflict. The reign of Alp-Arslan (1063–1072), followed by the reign of his son Malik-Shah (1072–1092), marked the zenith of Saljuq power. During Alp-Arslan's reign, Persia was solidly unified under the rule of the Saljuqs. Perennial internal strife came to an end, and there was a reflorescence of Persian cultural life and a revival of its economic prosperity.

Nevertheless, certain difficulties inherited from the Saljuq's steppe traditions remained. As was seen in the previous chapter, the Turkic empire was always confronted with problems when the *qaghan* was the junior of the *yabghu*. In a somewhat modified form this situation recurred during Alp-Arslan's reign. His succession was challenged by his uncle Qutlumush b. Arslan Is'rail, who based his challenge on seniority, claiming that "by right, the sultanate should come to me, because my father was the senior and leading member of the tribe."[30] After a battle in which he was defeated, Qutlumush died under mysterious circumstances. Malik-Shah also suffered such a challenge, in his case from his uncle Qavurt, who governed parts of Fars and Kirman. As Alp-Arslan's brother, Qavurt claimed the sultanate and went to war. He was defeated in a battle near Hamadan in 1073. This battle revealed the unreliability of the Turkic tribal armies, one of the two components of the Saljuq military forces, and afterwards the Saljuq sultans relied more on their professional army, composed primarily of Arabs and Kurds. Malik-Shah made peace with the sons of Qavurt and allowed them to continue to rule Kirman, thus giving rise to the Kirman Saljuqs. Once his rule was consolidated, Malik-Shah engaged in a series of military campaigns outside the borders of the Saljuq empire, campaigns against the Qaraqanids and the Ghaznavids, further extending the areas under direct Saljuq control.

Contributing to the continuity of the empire was the thirty-year-long vizierate of Abu 'Ali Hasan b. 'Ali Tusi (1047?–1092), better known under the honorific title bestowed upon him by Alp-Arslan, Nizam al-Mulk ("Order of the Realm"). Like many of the leading officials of the Saljuq empire, he had served the Ghaznavids before switching his allegiance to the Saljuqs. Throughout his vizierate, Nizam al-Mulk remained committed to the Ghazhavid ideal of state structure, which advocated the absolute despotism of the sultan. This ideal is most clearly expressed in his book, the *Siyasat-nama* ("Book of Government"), according to whose prescriptions he attempted to model his sovereigns and their rule,[31] with but limited success.

With the death of Malik-Shah a turbulent era in Saljuq history began. A war over the succession lasting more than a decade ended in 1105 with the death of the principal contender, Berk-Yaruq, the son of Malik-Shah, who was supported by the Nizamiyya, the followers and descendants of Nizam al-Mulk. In spite of the war, the empire held together, largely as a result of the astute policies of Malik-Shah and Nizam al-Mulk, policies that had been aimed at keeping the empire's frontiers in check. In hindsight, however, this war marked the beginning of the decline of Saljuq power and prestige. One of its consequences was a slow division of the empire. Berk-Yaruq was forced to concentrate his efforts in its western domains and leave the administration of Khurassan, where the Saljuqs had established their power, to Sanjar, his half brother.[32] In 1105 Berk-Yaruq was defeated by Sanjar's full brother Muhammad Tapar, who ruled until 1118. After that date the office of sultan remained, in theory, with the descendants of Muhammad in the western domains, but the position of elder and leading statesman, the *de facto* sultan, was held by Sanjar in Khurassan. The centrifugal forces that had been kept in check until that time were now given a free rein, and the Saljuq empire embarked on a precipitous decline.

While the western domains of the Saljuq empire were in constant turmoil, the eastern domains were for nearly fifty years under Sanjar's stable rule. In one sense, he was the last of the great Saljuq rulers. Although he was primarily concerned with the consolidation of his rule over Khurassan, he occasionally intervened in the affairs of the western domains, making Muhammad's successors his vassals. Soon, however, Sanjar was confronted with serious threats on his northern and eastern borders, the one coming from the formation of the Qwarezmian empire and the other from the arrival of a new force on the steppe, the Qaraqitai, Ch'i-tan refugees from North China.

The ruler of Qwarezm, 'Ala al-Din Atsiz, remained a nominal vassal of Sanjar until his death in 1156, but in reality pursued an independent course. Atsiz rebelled against Sanjar in 1138 and one year later captured Bukhara, only to be forced to surrender to Sanjar in 1141. Later that year, however, Sanjar suffered a crushing defeat at the hands of the Qaraqitai, thus enabling Qwarezm to continue its independent policies. The final difficulties for Sanjar came when the Ghuzz tribes in Khurassan began to rebel against him. While attempting to subdue these pastoral tribes, Sanjar was taken captive and remained one for three years. During that period, rule over Khurassan slipped into the hands of the emirs. Although Sanjar escaped from the Ghuzz in 1156, he was unable to reassert his authority. He died a year later, and with his death Saljuq control over the eastern regions of Persia ceased to exist.

During the last decades of his rule, preoccupied with his own eastern borders, Sanjar had no opportunity to intervene in the western domains of the Saljuq empire. There the disintegration process continued unabated; although there were still Saljuq sultans, they no longer held the reins of power. The area, for all intents and purposes, was divided into smaller principalities ruled by the Turkish atabegs, theoretically the teachers and advisors of the sultans. Several smaller dynasties came into existence, such as the Salghurids in Fars and the Eldiguzids and the Ahmadilis in northwestern Iran; all were absorbed by the Mongol conquest early in the thirteenth century. Saljuq control over Iraq and areas beyond was eliminated when the 'Abbasid caliph al-Muqtafi successfully asserted the secular rights of the caliphs. When al-Nasir (1180–1225) acceded to the honor, the 'Abbasid caliph was once again the most important figure in the eastern Islamic world. During the last decades of the twelfth century, the power of the Turkic people was again limited to the steppe frontier zones of the Iranian world.

The Twilight
of Turkic Power

While Saljuq power over the Iranian world disintegrated, Turkic hegemony on its eastern borders, especially in the area that today is Afghanistan, was also being challenged. With the rise and expansion of the Saljuqs, the Turkic Ghaznavids, who had ruled over Khurassan, had moved into Afghanistan and northern India and had ceased to have an influence on the affairs of the steppe. At the beginning of the twelfth century, during the reign of 'Ala al-Daula Mas'ud III (1099–1115), the Ghaznavids were on friendly terms with the Saljuqs; there even existed a marital alliance between Mas'ud III and Sanjar. The domains of the Ghaznavids and the Saljuqs were separated by a mountainous area in central Afghanistan known as Ghur. Very little is known about this area, the *terra incognita* of the Muslim geographers. It was ruled by a local dynasty, the Shansabani, and nominally it was under Ghaznavid suzerainty. The Ghurids had adopted Islam only during the eleventh century, primarily under the influence of the Ghaznavids.

The internal history of the Ghurids is not well documented.[33] It appears, however, that at the beginning of the twelfth century, these mountain tribes began to aspire to create their own empire. Under the leadership of their ruler, 'Izz al-Din Husain (1100–1146), they recognized the sovereignty of the Saljuqs, in particular of Sanjar, who in 1107–1108 had staged a punitive raid into Ghur. Husain's actions clearly indicated the weakness of the Ghaznavids, a weakness that was confirmed when Sanjar occupied Ghazna twice, in 1117 and 1136, and forced the Ghaznavids to recognize his sovereignty. In 1146 the Ghurid ruler 'Ala al-Din Husain (1146–1161) began to expand the Ghurid domains at the expense of the Ghaznavids. The Ghurid empire reached its apogee during the reigns of Ghiyath al-Din (1163–1203) and his brother Mu'izz al-Din Muhammad (1203–1206). During the reign of the latter, the Turkic Ghaznavid empire came to a formal end. He occupied Ghazna and made it the eastern capital of the Ghurid domain. In 1215 the Ghurids themselves were conquered by the last Turkic empire of the Iranian world, Qwarezm, and again sank into oblivion.

A major change on the Iranian frontier with the steppe had taken place during the second decade of the twelfth century when a new Altaic, but non-Turkic, people, namely the Qaraqitai, suddenly made their appearance in the area. They appeared in Transoxiana, where they created a new empire, after a long migration across the steppe from North China. They were remnants of the Ch'i-tan empire, whose history is discussed in the next chapter.[34] Under the leadership of Yeh-lü Ta-shih (1124–1143), the Qaraqitai eliminated the remainder of Qaraqanid authority and set up an empire that combined sedentary and nomadic characteristics. The outstanding feature of the new empire was that its rulers were non-Muslims with a strict policy of religious tolerance, thus contributing to a revival of other religions, among them Nestorianism.

The formation of an empire by the Qaraqitai and their imposition of sovereignty over the Qaraqanid khanates soon brought them into conflict with the Saljug empire. By 1137 the Qaraqitai controlled nearly the entire Syr-darya basin as far as Khojand. Taking advantage of internal difficulties in Samarqand, they penetrated the remainder of Transoxiana. Sanjar used their march on Samarqand as a *casus belli,* and in 1141, near Ushrusana on the Qatvin steppe, east of Samarqand, Saljuq and Qaraqitai forces clashed.

The Saljuq army suffered a total and humiliating defeat. The area beyond the Oxus was irrevocably lost to the Saljuq, but the defeat also signaled to other tribes in the area, especially those in Qwarezm, that Saljuq power had reached its end. "Infidel" control was restored over Muslim areas. It was, in fact, welcomed, for the Qaraqitai were tolerant and provided relief from the oppressive rule of the Saljuq governors.

The Qaraqitai rulers, known in Islamic sources as "Gur-khans," apparently had no intention of expanding their control beyond the territories they already occupied. However, during the last quarter of the twelfth century, they came into conflict with Qwarezm. Qwarezmian intervention in Qaraqitai affairs was facilitated by several changes within the Qaraqitai state. Their rule, especially their fiscal administration, had become more oppressive and regularly led to minor popular uprisings. Furthermore, the central cohesion of the Qaraqitai empire had been weakened by several prolonged female regencies that witnessed serious infighting for the position of Gur-khan. The beginning of the thirteenth century brought the arrival of the Mongol Naiman empire, a tribe defeated by Chinggis-khan, on the eastern border of the Qaraqitai empire. The Gur-khan attempted to push back the Naiman, but his efforts failed because of a Muslim uprising within his domains. The Naiman chieftain, Kuchluq, was then able to force the Qaraqitai to withdraw, and eventually he brought their empire to an end. This permitted the Qwarezmshahs to assert their authority over large portions of the Qaraqitai domain, an action accomplished after a bloodbath in Samarqand in 1212.

Qwarezm was a fertile area along the lower Oxus, to the north of Khurassan. Its principal center, developed during the tenth century, was the city of Gurganj. It had long been under local Iranian rule, first by the Afrigids of Kath, and, after 995, by the Ma'munid dynasty (995–1017). Since that time, its rulers had been known as the Qwarezmshahs. Under their rule, the area developed an apparently flourishing culture, of which not much is known today because of the destruction wrought by subsequent Turkic and Mongol invasions. In 1017 the entire area came under the control of the Ghaznavids, which lasted until the conquest of the area by the Oghuzz in 1041. After the Saljuq victory over the Oghuzz, it came under Saljuq control until the early decades of the twelfth century, when Saljuq power began its decline. The Saljuq administration over Qwarezm was in the hands of the Turkic dynasty of the Anush-tegin, nominal vassals of the Saljuqs.

The Qwarezmian governors began to assert their independence during the administration of 'Ala al-Din Atsiz (1127–1156), who was in fact the founder of the Great Qwarezmian Empire. Most of his administration was spent in consolidating the borders of the province and protecting it against the non-Islamic Turkic tribes on the steppe between the Aral and the Caspian seas, an activity that earned Atsiz the honorific of *ghazi*, "defender of the faith." He secured control over the Maqishlaq peninsula and asserted Qwarezmian authority over the Qipcaq steppe. Atsiz rebelled against

Sanjar, but at that time Saljuq forces were still too powerful. He died a vassal of the Saljuqs, but the basis for an independent Qwarezmian empire had been laid.[35]

During the years that followed Atsiz's death, his successor Il-Arslan (1156–1172) was a vassal of the Qaraqitai. Il-Arslan attempted to assert his independence from the Gur-khan and died in battle with the Qaraqitai, a battle provoked by the Qwarezmian reluctance to continue paying tribute to that now weakened state. His son and successor, 'Ala al-Din Tekish (1172–1200), finally established the independence of Qwarezm. He eliminated the Ghurids and established Qwarezmian control over Khurassan in its entirety. He was even successful in gaining some measure of control over western Iran. Although Tekish owed his throne to the Qaraqitai, since they had assisted him in eliminating his rivals, he raised the standard of the *jihad* against them. By the turn of the century, Qwarezmian authority was firmly established, although resented, throughout Transoxiana. Tekish was succeeded by his son, Qutb al-Din Muhammad (1200–1220), under whom the Qwarezmian empire reached its apogee.[36] Soon after his accession to the throne, however, he was confronted with the rise to power of the Mongols. As will be shown later, his careless policies provoked the wrath of Chinggis-khan and the total destruction of the Qwarezmian empire in 1220. This destruction left the Mongols with an open road into the politically disorganized Iranian world.

5

The Chinese
Border Empires

Tribes of different ethnic and linguistic origins had been settling on the Chinese border ever since the collapse of the Hsiung-nu and Tabghach empires. The number of such tribes increased with the expansion of the Tibetan empire, since many tribes sought protection from the Tibetans by settling in the frontier zone, which was considered to be within the Chinese sphere of influence. The survival of these smaller tribes had always depended on the maintenance of a precarious balance of power between China and the empires of Central Asia. The last quarter of the ninth century, however, witnessed the almost simultaneous decline of both Turkic and Chinese influence. With no outside force to fill the power vacuum, the major tribes of China's northern and northwestern borders began to create their own empires.

The period of the Chinese Border Empires, lasting from approximately 900 to 1200 A.D., is one of the most complex in the history of the steppe, and in Chinese history as well. Several empires coexisted and continually interacted not only among themselves, but with Central Asia, with China, and, late in the period, even with the Middle East. Information about them is found almost exclusively in Chinese sources. The enmity between the so-called barbarians and the Chinese (which had existed since the beginning of Chinese recorded history) has biased these sources. Orthodox Chinese historiography later paid only scant attention to the border empires, even though two of them became official and legitimate "Chinese" dynasties. Until quite recently, their study was considered beneath the dignity of many Chinese historians: they were, after all, barbarian, legitimized only by another barbarian group, the Mongols. Nevertheless, the study of these empires is of crucial importance if a full understanding is to be reached of the Sung, Ming, and Ch'ing dynasties in China,[1] and also of the developments on the steppe that led to the creation of the world's largest empire, that of the Mongols.

The Chinese Border Empires are those created by the Ch'i-tan, the Jürchen, and the Tangut. The Ch'i-tan and the Jürchen empires succeeded each other in North China. The Tangut empire, located roughly in present-day Kansu province and the Ning-hsia Autonomous Region, existed for nearly three centuries. In the early part of the period, several smaller kingdoms—for example the Po-hai and the bCon-kha kingdoms, located respectively near Korea and in Eastern Tibet—played more or less important roles on the international scene. These smaller kingdoms were, however, soon absorbed by their more powerful neighbors.

The ethnic and linguistic affiliation of the Jürchen is quite definitely established, which cannot be said for either the Ch'i-tan or the Tangut. Of the three groups that created border empires, only the Jürchen survived as a distinct group until well into the Ming dynasty.[2] Because this was so, many contemporary Chinese materials dealing with them survived; besides the official history compiled by the Mongol Yüan dynasty, we have a contemporary account by the Sung scholar Hsü Meng-hsin (1126–1207) entitled the *San-ch'ao pei-meng hui-pien* ("Collected Accounts of the Treaties with the North under Three Reigns"), which contains a chapter devoted solely to the Jürchen people. As a result, many modern studies have been devoted to the Jürchen.[3]

Linguistically, the Jürchen were a Tungusic people who originally lived to the east of the Sungari River and the Ch'ang-pai mountains. Their domain stretched eastwards to the ocean; to the south it bordered on the Yalu; to the west, on the territory of the Tungusic Po-hai people; and to the north, on the territory of the Shih-wei, possibly a Mongol people. The center of the original Jürchen domain was, most likely, the Alcuka River, a tributary of the Sungari. Alcuka is the Manchu name for the river and comes from the Jürchen *alchun*, "gold." It was the Chinese translation of this word, *Chin*, that the Jürchen used as their dynastic title.[4]

Unanimity on the Jürchen's Tungusic origins does not mean that there is agreement on which Tungusic tribe was the one identified in Sung and Ch'i-tan documents as the Jürchen. Hsü Meng-hsin, having stated that they were descendants of the legendary founder of the Korean Koryogo kingdom, traces them back to the period known in Chinese history as the Three Kingdoms (220–ca. 280 A.D.). He mentions names such as Wu-chi, Hei-shui, and Mo-ho. During the T'ang dynasty, in 748, a mission arrived from the Ju-che tribe, a tribe sometimes identified as the ancestor of the Jürchen, but about which nothing else is known.[5] Sorting out the multitude of names given by the Chinese to foreign peoples would be a long and difficult task, and it is doubtful whether the results would be worth the effort.

The original homeland of the Ch'i-tan was along the course of the Liao River, basically in present-day Liaoning and Jehol. Ch'i-tan legends state that they lived to the north of China between a sacred mountain (alternately called Ma-yu and Mu-yeh) and two rivers, one male and the other female. Around the sacred mountain lived the eight tribes that originally made up the Ch'i-tan nation. It is clear from a recent study devoted to the Ch'i-tan prior to the creation of their empire that they resided for centuries in parts of what is known as Manchuria and that their principal activities were hunting, fishing, and horse breeding.[6]

There is still no agreement as to the ethnic origins or the nature of the language of the Ch'i-tan. Their own legends about their origins are not very helpful, and the Chinese sources contain a confusing array of names that still awaits sorting out. Ch'i-tan stories mix elements of the dog-ancestor myth common to many Mongol-Turkic tribes, and the pig-ancestor myth, which can be traced back to the times of the Hsiung-nu.[7] It was during the reign of the Northern Wei dynasty (386–532 A.D.) that the tribes adopted the name Ch'i-tan. On the basis of their geographical location, they are most commonly described as a proto-Tungusic people. On the other hand, when a careful study is undertaken of their customs and legends, as well as of Ch'i-tan personal names and titles, they appear most closely related to the Turkic, possibly the Mongol, people. The study of the two other tribes that lived in the Ch'i-tan empire, the Hsi and the Shih-wei, does not help in solving the Ch'i-tan problem,[8] as scholars also dispute over whether these tribes were Turkic or proto-Mongol. The Ch'i-tan appeared as a loosely organized group around the time of China's reunification under the Sui dynasty (581–618) and remained so until the close of the T'ang dynasty.

Uncritical acceptance of Chinese source materials has led to the identification of the Tangut people and their language as Tibetan. In the Chinese sources, the inhabitants of the Kansu corridor appear under the name Tang-hsiang and are said to be descendants of the Western Ch'iang, commonly considered to be a proto-Tibetan tribe. Since Han times, the Tang-hsiang were said to have lived a seminomadic existence in the frontier zone between China and Tibet, more specifically, in Western Szechuan. When the Tibetan empire began its expansion, they were driven out of the area and, like many other foreign groups, sought refuge with the T'ang dynasty. The Chinese resettled this relatively small group in the area of the Great Bend of the Yellow River, near the Hsia prefecture. Not much is known about them until they appear in Sung documents as rulers of the independent state of Hsi Hsia.

This fails to explain how and when the inhabitants of Hsi Hsia became known as Tangut. The Mongol histories refer to them by this name, and it is commonly assumed that it is a Mongol plural derived from the Chinese name *Tang-hsiang*. However, the name *Tangut* occurs much earlier in Turkic sources, where it is mentioned for the first time in the Runic Orkhon inscription dedicated to Bilge-qaghan. The date on the inscription is 733. The name *Tangut* is mentioned several times in Mahmud al-Kashghari's famous *Diwan Lughat at-Turk* (ca. 1075), where, in fact, it forms part of an independent verse cycle. al-Kashghari, a Qaraqanid Türk working for the rulers of Baghdad, travelled among the Turkic people "throughout their cities and their steppes." His aim was to provide the rulers of Baghdad with a complete lexicon of Turkic dialects. In the *Diwan*, the Tangut are described as "a tribe of Turks, they dwell near China."[9]

The history of the Kansu corridor, the territory under Tangut control, indicates that although Chinese and Tibetans inhabited the area, there were also a great number of Turkic-speaking people, among them descendants of the Tabghach. In 1032 the Hsi Hsia ruler Li Yüan-hao claimed to be a descendant of the Tabghach of the Northern Wei. Because the Tang-hsiang clan to which he belonged was called *T'o-pa*, written with the same characters as the *T'o-pa* for Tabghach, it has been assumed that Li Yüan-hao used this homonymic similarity as a device to legitimate his own dynasty.

Most scholars remain convinced that the Tangut language is a member of the Sino-Tibetan linguistic family, although they are far from agreeing on the existence of such a linguistic group. Recent linguistic research indicates that there is a distinct possibility that Tangut is either a Turkic dialect or a language heavily influenced by a Turkic dialect.[10]

The Tangut state has been the least studied of the Border Empires. Its language cannot yet be read with any degree of ease, but there is more than enough material in Chinese to study its history. Unlike the empires of the Ch'i-tan and the Jürchen, the Tangut did not become an official Chinese dynasty, and consequently Hsi Hsia was relegated to the dustbin of history. In fact, the Sung documents and other contemporary sources reveal that their role in Chinese history was much more important than that of the Ch'i-tan. Sung policies regarding the border states, whether in the north or the south, but especially regarding the Ch'i-tan, were formulated in light of potential Tangut reactions.[11]

The Decline
of Chinese Power

The beginning of the eclipse of the T'ang is relatively easy to date. In 751 an alliance of the Islamic armies, the Tibetans, and the Turkic Qarluq defeated the once invincible T'ang armies on the famous banks of the Talas River. This not only pushed the Chinese forces back over the Pamirs, but also marked the beginning of the Islamization of the Turkic tribes. About a decade later, the Chinese had abandoned the entire Tarim basin to the expanding Tibetan empire. Only a few towns in the area, the best-known one being Tun-huang, were witness that the area had once been under Chinese rule.

The causes of the T'ang decline in power are not as easy to identify. During the second half of the eighth century, the military advantage undoubtedly was with the Tibetans. However, the reduction in their military capabilities was by no means the only reason for the decline of Chinese influence and control on the Central Asian steppe. The T'ang was confronted with serious political, social, and economic difficulties in China itself. Problems existed everywhere, and the capital, Ch'ang-an, began to lose touch with the provinces and the borders. Unable to cope directly with all the problems, the court delegated more and more authority to the provincial military governors, the *chieh-tu-shih*.[12] Most of the authority was given to the *chieh-tu-shih* on the northern and the western borders. Soon these governors began to act as semi-independent rulers. The power vested in them was enormous: it is estimated that nearly 70 percent of the T'ang armed forces, roughly half a million men, was under their direct control. In addition, the dynasty was confronted with the harsh reality that expansion and maintenance of conquered territories was an expensive proposition. As the court had to pay the salaries of the huge standing armies, taxation was increased to almost unbearable levels, and the population within China itself began to rebel. However, the main threat to the court and the dynasty came from the huge standing armies on the borders, many of which were made up of foreign mercenaries and even commanded by foreign generals. The central bureaucracy was clearly aware of the dangers inherent in this situation, but, despite repeated warnings, the emperor failed to recognize, or chose to ignore, these serious dangers.[13]

The principal *chieh-tu-shih* was a man of steppe origins, An Lu-shan. Obese and uncouth, An Lu-shan amused the court with his antics and became so popular that he was treated by the emperor's favorite consort, Yang Kuei-fei, as her own son.[14] Though his ministers repeatedly warned that An Lu-shan could not be trusted, the emperor ignored the warnings. The emperor's officials were right; An Lu-shan's behavior was but a cover for his real ambition—to seize the throne. The institutional crisis began in July 755. An Lu-shan requested that the Chinese generals on the borders be replaced by generals of foreign origins. Over the strong objections of his ministers, the emperor acquiesced to this request. An Lu-shan interpreted this as a sure indication of the court's trust in him as well as of its weakness. He began his rebellion on 17 December 755.[15]

The An Lu-shan rebellion shook the foundations of the empire. Quickly his forces overran North China, occupied the symbolically important city of Lo-yang, and began their march towards the T'ang capital. While the rebellion grew in intensity, the court was paralyzed by an intense personal drama whose principal character was the emperor's favorite, Yang Kuei-fei. Because she had been one of An Lu-shan's patrons, the court now clamored for her execution. The emperor was faced with painful choices:

loose his throne, loose his favorite, or loose everything. The emperor chose the second, but in the end still lost everything. On 14 June 756 he and his court left the capital, leaving Yang Kuei-fei behind. The next day representatives of the central government proceeded with her execution. A few days later, on or about the eighteenth, the troops of An Lu-shan occupied the capital. Less than a month later, Emperor Hsüan-tsung was dead. According to legend, he died of sorrow.[16]

The occupation of Ch'ang-an was the climax of the An Lu-shan rebellion. An Lu-shan was assassinated by his own men in January 757, but the new emperor, Su-tsung, was unable to take advantage of his death. The rebellion continued unabated, now under the command of the Chinese *chieh-tu-shih,* Shih Ssu-ming. During November and December of that year, the court was able to recapture the cities of Ch'ang-an and Lo-yang. The year 758 brought no relief to the beleaguered T'ang dynasty, as Shih Ssu-ming continued to gain momentum. In October 759 he occupied Lo-yang again and challenged the legitimacy of the T'ang dynasty by proclaiming his own reign title.[17] Once again, however, the court was saved by the assassin's sword. In April 761 Shih Ssu-ming was murdered. His death turned the tide for the T'ang, but it was not until February 763 that the entire rebellion was extinguished.

The court had survived the struggle, but its power had not remained unscathed. After the rebellion, the court was less in control than before it. In order to achieve victory, it had been forced to rely heavily on assistance provided by the Uighurs; it had even attempted to make an alliance with the Arabs. Reliance on foreigners made it hard to control them after the rebellion, thus worsening an already bad situation on the borders. Moreover, social and institutional changes that had been in the offing were accelerated by the rebellion. The militia system, once the basis for the dynasty's defense, collapsed and was replaced by exclusively professional, largely mercenary armies.[18] These armies were not under the actual control of the court, but under that of the military governors, who after the rebellion were more independent than before. For a century after the end of the An Lu-shan rebellion, the power and the authority of the T'ang emperor steadily declined. Real power was usurped by the eunuchs at the court and the military governors in the provinces. Two emperors, Hsien-tsung (805–820) and Ching-tsung (824–826), attempted to reverse the course of events, but were murdered by their eunuchs, who felt their interests threatened. After them no emperor challenged the authority of either the eunuchs, to whom they literally owed the throne, or the military governors.

As the ninth century entered its last quarter, the T'ang emperors were but figureheads for the court cliques. The final blow to the emperor's authority came in the form of a popular uprising that had started in drought-stricken Honan in 875. Its leader, Huang Ch'ao, a salt merchant after whom the rebellion was named, quickly turned popular discontent into a repeat performance of the An Lu-shan rebellion.[19] This time, however, the rebellion spread from the interior to the borders. It lasted until 884 and finished the disruption begun by An Lu-shan. Huang Ch'ao also occupied the T'ang capital of Ch'ang-an. Once again, non-Chinese forces from the steppe and from the border regions were the saviors of the dynasty. Chinese troops in alliance with Uighur, Tangut, and other Turkic forces defeated Huang Ch'ao just outside the capital. The rebel leader committed suicide, but the country continued to be plagued by both rebellions and the depredations of the "barbarian" allies of the court for another two years.

Officially, the T'ang dynasty had survived. In reality, however, it had ceased to exist; but no Chinese official was ready, militarily or otherwise, to create a new dynasty. Thus, the two decades that followed the end of the Huang Ch'ao rebellion witnessed a jostling for position and an ever-increasing fragmentation of the state. The formal end of the T'ang came in 907, when Chu Wen, the most important military governor in the north, put an end to the T'ang fiction and proclaimed his own dynasty. This was the beginning of what became known to the Chinese historians, and hence to us, as the Five Dynasties period (907–960). The name is misleading, for in reality there were fifteen dynasties, five of which were considered to be "official" by the historians of the succeeding Sung dynasty (960–1279).[20]

During the Five Dynasties period, China neither controlled nor was able to control the border areas, much less the Central Asian steppe. Actually, China lost ground to the foreigners. The process of reunifying China began in 959, when Chao Kuang-yin was appointed to head the armies of the Later Chou dynasty (951–960). Shortly afterwards, a new infant emperor was placed on the throne. In 960 K'ai-feng, the capital, witnessed a bloodless coup, and Chao Kuang-yin created the Sung dynasty. His reign, under the name of T'ai-tsu, and that of his successor, T'ai-tsung (976–998), witnessed this reunification. Neither emperor, however, was capable of recovering all the territories once held by the T'ang dynasty. To the north, the Ch'i-tan were firmly entrenched, even though they did not show open hostility. The passage to the oasis states, through the Kansu corridor, was blocked by the Tangut. They claimed independence and equality with the Chinese emperor, a notion which Sung T'ai-tsu refused to accept, but which the Tanguts forced upon his successors.

The founding of the Sung dynasty was rather unusual, and the dynasty itself came to occupy a unique position in Chinese history. Considered one of the most brilliant periods culturally, the Sung is regarded unanimously by historians of China as a militarily weak dynasty, even as a basically anti-military one.[21] This interpretation fits in nicely with the existing theories about Chinese history. The approach, however, focuses on limited aspects of the Sung military experience and fails to take into consideration all the difficulties confronting the Sung government, and hence to realize what options were realistically left to it. The Sung was surrounded by powerful and hostile states. Together these states posed a serious threat to China. For example, if an alliance had been developed (and several were attempted) between the Ch'i-tan, the Tangut, and the Eastern Tibetans, the Northern Sung (960–1127) would have been confronted with almost certain defeat in the event of war. It is not often noted that the situation on the southern and southwestern borders was not much better than that on the northern and northwestern borders. It is clear that the Sung had to develop means other than military to deal with so many potential enemies. War would only have resulted in deeper trouble and, furthermore, could have precipitated the rise of independent warlords, as had happened before in Chinese history.

The new technique developed by the Sung was diplomacy. Only isolated aspects of T'ang and Sung diplomatic history have been studied so far, an approach that has yielded interesting albeit unsatisfying results. However, serious examination of all the available evidence shows that Sung policy cannot be adequately understood without looking at the totality of inter-relationships, because policy towards each barbarian group was clearly conditioned by the actions and interactions of other barbarian groups (both north and south), by the Sung's own relations with each of these groups, and by policy decisions regarding the states of An-nam and Nan-ch'ao.[22] The key factor in diplomacy between 980 and 1210 was policy toward the Tangut, whether promulgated by the Sung, the Ch'i-tan, or the Jürchen.

As a result of its often precarious international situation, the Sung not only developed new political concepts, methods, and approaches; it also perceived its position in the world in quite a different light than the pre-ceding and, especially, the succeeding dynasties did. The Sung reverted, at least in its international dealings, to the political concepts of the Warring States period (403–221 B.C.). It perceived itself as a *kuo* rather than *t'ien-hsia*—a nation, albeit more civilized than its neighbors, not a world-dominating empire.[23]

The History of
the Ch'i-tan Empire

Sometime between the end of the Huang Ch'ao rebellion and the formal end of the T'ang dynasty, the Ch'i-tan were united into a single state. The man behind the unification was called A-pao-chi. Traditionally, he is sup-posed to have been born in 872, but not much is known about him before 902. In that year he suddenly appeared on the Chinese political scene when he staged a major raid into what is now Shensi province. Over the next five years, A-pao-chi was continually involved in wars against the Hsi, the Jürchen, and especially the Black-Cart Shih-wei tribes, in order to establish his authority throughout the area. By 907 A-pao-chi apparently felt confi-dent enough of his power to proclaim himself emperor of the Ch'i-tan on the first day of the first month (15 February).[24]

Although this date seems to have been fixed after the fact, it is unques-tionable that A-pao-chi considered himself emperor. To a very large degree, the fact that China was in no position to intervene in foreign affairs at this time allowed for the consolidation of Ch'i-tan rule: no powerful Chinese emperor would have permitted the formation of a "barbarian" empire in the north. The only serious military problem A-pao-chi faced came not from the Chinese, but from the other non-Chinese tribes living within his domain or just at its borders. A major portion of A-pao-chi's reign (he died in 926) was spent in reducing these tribes to submission. Some, like the Jürchen, never completely submitted to Ch'i-tan overlordship.

During these campaigns, A-pao-chi considerably expanded the size of his domain, both to the east and to the west. Most of the expansion was at the expense of the non-Chinese tribes,[25] but A-pao-chi also wanted to obtain some of China's fertile agricultural lands under his administration. Thus, raids were staged, and bits and pieces of Chinese territory were incorporated into his domain. Eventually the Ch'i-tan gained full control over what was known as the Sixteen Prefectures, the most important of which was the Yen prefecture, roughly present-day Peking. As a result of this southerly expansion, substantial numbers of Chinese—farmers as well as intellectuals—were incorporated into the Ch'i-tan domain. The expansion also induced several other tribes to recognize Ch'i-tan suzerainty willingly or unwillingly, as the Uighur tribes decided to do after A-pao-chi penetrated the Orkhon area in 924 and defaced the Bilge-qaghan inscription, adding one that proclaimed his glory.[26]

While expanding the domain under Ch'i-tan control, A-pao-chi did not neglect to consolidate the power he had gained. The most serious threat he had to face during his reign was assassination by his equally ambitious brothers and other relatives. Twice, in 911 and 916, they began rebellions. Family quarrels and rivalries between ethnic groups and political factions were a characteristic of the Ch'i-tan empire until its collapse.

During the reign of the second Ch'i-tan emperor, the second son of A-pao-chi, the empire was faced with its first serious crisis. In 929 the eldest of A-pao-chi's sons, Yeh-lü Pei, otherwise known as Jen-huang, fled into China, where he was welcomed with open arms by the Later T'ang dynasty (923–936) and given a high noble rank and one of the most important military commissions. After several defeats in the wars that followed, the Ch'i-tan finally emerged as the victors. Part of the spoils was an even larger chunk of Chinese territory. This further consolidated the Ch'i-tan power base, and they no longer tolerated any contempt on the part of Chinese emperors or their representatives. The Later Chin (936–947) found this out the hard way when its ruler objected, in forceful language, to being called a Ch'i-tan subordinate. The Ch'i-tan reply was force, and after a few initial setbacks, they thoroughly defeated the Later Chin, once again acquiring Chinese territory in the process.

The principal source of information on these years is the official history of the Ch'i-tan, compiled in Chinese almost two centuries after the empire was destroyed.[27] From it one learns that in 947 the Ch'i-tan adopted a Chinese dynastic name, *Liao*, after the Chinese name of the river that ran through their homeland. This is the name under which they became known to history, even though Ch'i-tan use of it was highly irregular. Contemporary Sung documents clearly show that the rulers alternated between *Liao* and *Ch'i-tan,* without ever making either name the permanent designation of their empire.

During the years between 950 and 960, the Ch'i-tan became involved with the warring factions within China. In 951 the ruler of the Later Han, an official dynasty, was murdered by Kuo Wei, who proclaimed his own dynasty, the Later Chou (951–960). In the city of T'ai-yüan, another dynasty was established under the name of Northern Han (951–979). The Later Chou and the Northern Han went to war in the year of their creation. The Northern Han ruler requested Ch'i-tan aid, and it was promptly given. Why the Ch'i-tan decided to support the Northern Han dynasty is not quite clear, but most likely it was an attempt to prevent the reunification of China: the Later Chou had demonstrated its intention to reunite China by beginning a relatively successful reconquest of the southern territories, and a united China could become a formidable threat to the survival of the Ch'i-tan empire. By the middle of 959, the Later Chou emperor had died and been replaced by an infant. Whatever reassurance the Ch'i-tan might have felt, however, did not last long. Early in 960, the Later Chou army staged a bloodless coup (rather rare in those days) and proclaimed its commander Chao K'uang-yin, as emperor. Chao K'uang-yin "reluctantly" accepted the throne and proclaimed the Sung dynasty, as well as his intention to reunite all territories that had once belonged to the T'ang. Conflict between the newly established Sung and the Ch'i-tan was inevitable.

For the next decade, however, there was no significant interaction between the Ch'i-tan and the Sung. The first Sung expedition was against the treacherous Northern Han. The need to consolidate its resources in the south, and the fact that the Northern Han were receiving assistance from the Ch'i-tan, induced the Sung to halt the campaign temporarily. It is unknown whether the Ch'i-tan planned to take advantage of the fact that the Sung were preoccupied militarily with their expeditions in the south, but it is known that the Ch'i-tan had serious problems to confront at home. In 969 the emperor was assassinated and replaced by his brother. In 970 the first Ch'i-tan–Tangut war took place. At the same time, the Jürchen on the empire's eastern border began a series of raids and rebellions against the Ch'i-tan. The empire survived these crises handily, but when it was again able to turn its attention to the Northern Han, it was too late. The Sung had consolidated its hold over the rich south and was now in the possession of the resources necessary to undertake a successful northern campaign. War began in 976. Two years later, having received precious little Ch'i-tan assistance, the Northern Han surrendered to the Sung and disappeared from history.[28]

Apparently the Sung interpreted the Ch'i-tan failure to assist the Northern Han as a sign of weakness and began to proceed with the reconquest of Chinese territory under Ch'i-tan control. The first expedition was unsuccessful, and the Sung decided to put off a full-scale attack until the western territories under the Tangut were brought back into the Chinese fold. While the Sung turned west, the Ch'i-tan turned east to deal once and for all with the vexing Jürchen problem. These unruly people were attempting to establish formal relations with the Sung, which, if successful, would endanger Ch'i-tan security. In 984, after a tenacious resistance, the Jürchen surrendered and were reduced, for all practical purposes, to a slave people. Even so, it was not until the first decade of the eleventh century that the Ch'i-tan were able to stop all Jürchen diplomatic intercourse with the Sung.

The remainder of the tenth century was marked by the momentous development of the Tangut empire. The Tangut ruler, Li Chi-p'eng, submitted to the Sung in 984, but the Sung rulers were unable to take possession of the Tangut domains. Immediately after the submission, the ruler's cousin Li Ch'i-ch'ien proclaimed his independence, and went to war to prove it. By 990, his power was solidly established, and the Ch'i-tan recognized him as the legitimate ruler of the Hsi Hsia country and established close, amicable relations with him.

Ch'i-tan recognition of the Tangut state was strictly self-serving. The existence on the Chinese western border of a powerful state that was a close ally of the Ch'i-tan made Sung intervention against the Ch'i-tan less likely. After 990 the balance of power had shifted decidedly to the advantage of the non-Chinese states. The Sung, confronted with the possibility of war on two fronts and serious difficulties in the south, adopted a policy of appeasement toward the Ch'i-tan.

The Sung's evident inability to contain the Tangut led the Ch'i-tan to formulate a strategy of consolidation of their existing hold over Chinese territories and further expansion into China. Whether consultations were held between the Ch'i-tan and the Tangut is not known, but events make it likely that they were. Whatever joint plans there may have been, they came to naught when Li Ch'i-ch'ien died of wounds received in battle in 1003 or 1004. Nevertheless, the Ch'i-tan, confident of its armies and wanting to take advantage of the situation before the Sung had an opportunity to regroup, launched an invasion of Chinese territory in September 1004.

The Chinese quickly realized that this was not just a barbarian raid but a well-planned invasion. Sung defensive actions were hampered by continuing uncertainties on the Tangut border and persistent problems on the southern frontier.[29] All available troops were thrown into battle, but a decision was made to attempt to negotiate an end to the war. Like the Sung, the Ch'i-tan did not want a prolonged war, to which all signs pointed; hence they also were willing to negotiate. All that was necessary was an excuse that would enable each side to state that the other had asked peace first.

The excuse was provided by a Chinese prisoner, then in high government service at the Ch'i-tan court, Wang Chi-chung. Wang wrote a memorial to the Sung emperor that was a masterpiece of diplomatic literature. It did precisely what it was supposed to do: permit each side to state that the initiative had come from the other side.[30] Thus began a series of lengthy, sometimes stormy, negotiations between the Ch'i-tan and the Sung court that led to the signing of the peace treaty of Shan-yüan in 1005.[31]

The treaty had five major provisions, all of them to the advantage of the Ch'i-tan; because of their military disadvantage—at least they thought so themselves—the Sung bought peace at a high price. Chinese territory in Ch'i-tan possession remained in Ch'i-tan hands; moreover, the Sung had to pay the Ch'i-tan annually 200,000 bolts of silk and 100,000 ounces of silver. The treaty, however, showed that military conflicts could be avoided through negotiations and compromise. As a consequence, for the remainder of the Ch'i-tan empire's existence, an uneasy peace existed between it and the Sung. Several times relations were severely strained, but they were never broken off. Except for some minor border skirmishes, the Sung and the Ch'i-tan lived in peace, not interfering in each other's affairs.

The treaty also regulated the movement of people and goods between the two states. It stated that neither side should interfere with the farmers on the borders or give political asylum to refugees from the other side. Ironically, the mastermind of the negotiations, Wang Chi-chung, was a victim of the interpretation given to this provision. He had hoped to be allowed to return to his native China, but he died seventeen years later, still in exile.

Economic relations between the two states also improved as a result of the treaty. Since 976 trade with the Ch'i-tan empire had been a government monopoly, and after 986 it had, for all practical purposes, ceased to exist. The treaty of Shan-yüan revived the monopoly trade. The major items traded by the Ch'i-tan to the Sung were horses and salt; in the opposite direction travelled silk and tea. As with every monopoly, there was a high incidence of smuggling: the numerous edicts issued by both empires indicate that it was a very common practice.

Only twice in the years following the Shan-yüan treaty were Sung–Ch'i-tan relations put under severe pressure. The first incident was directly related to the Tangut empire. The Tangut and the Sung had gone to war over the imperial title, and the Sung forces suffered disastrous defeat upon disastrous defeat. In 1040 the Ch'i-tan seized the opportunity and threatened to intervene on the slim pretext that they were the allies of the Tangut; hostilities almost ensued. The Sung immediately began negotiations. Once the Ch'i-tan had achieved what they really wanted—an increase of 100,000 bolts of silk and 100,000 ounces of silver in the annual payments—all war preparations ceased, and the Ch'i-tan even threatened the Tangut with war if they did not soon halt the fighting against the Sung. They did, though the Tangut army was in sight of the Chinese capital.

The Shan-yüan treaty had stated that existing military posts could be maintained and repaired, but did not define these terms. Under the pretext of maintaining and repairing existing posts, the Sung began to increase and improve substantially their northern border defenses. In 1074 this led to vigorous protests by the Ch'i-tan, backed up by a sizeable show of force.

Negotiations were held, and the creation of a buffer zone was agreed upon.

As an established empire, the Ch'i-tan lost the vigor and dash it had had during the reigns of its first emperors. On two occasions, in 1010 and 1012, it attempted to resume its expansion by conquering Korea, but success there was limited. Throughout the dynasty's existence there were problems in dealing with the subjected Po-hai and Jürchen peoples. A coalition, including Koreans, was formed under Po-hai leadership in 1029, and war was declared on the Ch'i-tan. The action was premature and came to naught. However, at the beginning of the twelfth century, the Jürchen living within the Ch'i-tan state reunited with those living to the north of it (the so-called Wild Jürchen). Apparently, the Ch'i-tan had no knowledge of this. When this new coalition rose in arms in 1114, the Ch'i-tan empire crumbled almost overnight.[32]

The History of the Jürchen Empire

After the founding of their empire, the Ch'i-tan considered themselves the overlords of the various Jürchen tribes. Throughout the ninth century, Ch'i-tan efforts to exert their suzerainty met with only limited success. Jürchen chieftains were able to maintain extensive diplomatic contacts with both Korea and Sung China. They continually switched their allegiance between the Ch'i-tan and the Koreans. The signing of the Shan-yüan agreement, in 1005, and the subsequent stabilization of the Sung–Ch'i-tan border allowed the Ch'i-tan to assert more vigorously their authority over Liao-tung. Several successful campaigns against Korea brought to an end the occasional Jürchen pledges of allegiance to the Korean rulers. After 1019 the Sung sources no longer mention the arrival of Jürchen missions. For the remainder of the eleventh century, the latter were under strict Ch'i-tan control.[33]

Ch'i-tan rule over the Jürchen was repressive. Continued exactions and abuses caused frequent uprisings; however, as the Jürchen lacked cohesion, the uprisings never threatened the stability of Ch'i-tan rule. During the reign of Yeh-lü Yen-hsi, the ninth of the Ch'i-tan rulers, whose temple name was T'ien-tsu (1101–1125), Ch'i-tan exactions reached unprecedented levels; eventually this led to a general uprising and the fall of the Ch'i-tan state. Jürchen and Sung records describe the reign of Yeh-lü Yen-hsi as one of extravagant spending, whose cost was particularly oppressive to the Jürchen; they had to provide the Ch'i-tan ruler with precious pearls that had to be gathered in winter, forcing people to break river ice, and, also at great cost, with special white-clawed grey falcons, the most prized variety and very rare. To obtain these birds, the Jürchen had to wage war against the coastal people. When the Ch'i-tan set up a regular military and administrative structure among the Jürchen, the tribes had to pay levies and present tribute to the officials assigned to the area, even to those merely passing through. The Ch'i-tan considered and treated the Jürchen as a less civilized group of barbarians, and Ch'i-tan officials had no qualms about exacting more tribute than was permitted or customary. These exactions frequently were beyond the means of an individual tribe. Envoys from the Ch'i-tan emperor were traditionally accommodated among the lower ranks of the Jürchen and provided with virgins. During the reign of Yeh-lü Yen-hsi, these envoys, indiscriminately and with increasing frequency, took women from the upper classes without inquiring about their marital status. Apparently it was this behavior that led the Jürchen to begin plotting rebellion against the Ch'i-tan. Overtones of revenge and racial hatred were quickly apparent.[34]

The rebellion began among the Wan-yen clan, a group of "civilized" Jürchen residing in the territory of the Wild Jürchen.[35] Tradition has it that the first chieftain of this clan was a man from the Korean kingdom of Silla. Into this clan too, around 1067, was born Akuta, the future founder of the Jürchen empire. Much of the material on Akuta's youth is of dubious historicity. All the symbolic characteristics of a future emperor—a future Chinese emperor—were ascribed to him. There are many stories, perhaps apocryphal, which describe Akuta's strong resentment against the Ch'i-tan, even before he began to exert control over the Wild Jürchen, and his search for an occasion to rid himself and his people from the oppressive Ch'i-tan yoke. According to one story, his anti–Ch'i-tan sentiments almost cost him his life. On a tribute mission to the Ch'i-tan court, he played a game of "Double Six," a kind of backgammon, with a Ch'i-tan nobleman. As the latter began to lose, he began to cheat. Thereupon, the outraged Akuta grabbed his scabbard and was about to put the Ch'i-tan to the sword when he was restrained by a companion. Although the emperor was advised to execute Akuta for his disrespectful behavior, he desired to show his magnanimity to the Jürchen people and spared him. References in this story to rebels—An Lu-shan, for example—cast serious doubt on its authenticity; it does, however, reflect accurately the nature of Ch'i-tan–Jürchen relations.

Sometime around 1100, Akuta began to organize the Wild Jürchen surrounding the Wan-yen clan. He got control over the neighboring tribes either through peaceful negotiations or by stealing their cattle and other means of livelihood to force them into submission. He maintained a strong anti–Ch'i-tan posture, and, through careful manipulation of similar sentiments among the other Jürchen tribes, he was able to consolidate his control over them. In the spring of 1112, Yeh-lü Yen-hsi went on the Ch'i-tan court's annual fishing trip to the Sungari River. As was also customary, the chieftains of the local tribes came to the emperor's camp, where they presented him with local products and entertained him with song and dance. When Akuta's turn came, he stubbornly refused either to sing or to dance. The emperor, offended, wanted to banish Akuta to a dangerous post on the border, but reversed his decision after a discussion with Hsiao Feng-hsien, his brother-in-law.[36] Returning to his own domains, Akuta was aware that the time had come for an open rebellion. For the next two years, he and his allies continued to expand their control over the Jürchen tribes and to prepare carefully for war against the Ch'i-tan.

The rebellion broke out in 1114. After lengthy preparations, the Jürchen had been waiting for an excuse to take up arms. The excuse was provided by Akuta's former ally, Ashu, the leader of the Ho-shih-lieh tribe, who had defected to the Ch'i-tan. Several entreaties for Ashu's surrender were made, but the Ch'i-tan ignored them. Consequently, the Jürchen attacked the town of Ning-chiang, present-day Wu-chia-shan, on the Sungari River. The Jürchen victory there led to risings among other tribes, and soon the Ch'i-tan forces were overwhelmed by an army whose soldiers were well prepared and determined to take revenge on their oppressors. The Ch'i-tan forces suffered defeat upon defeat, and in February 1115 the Ch'i-tan emperor made the first of several peace overtures to the Jürchen. Akuta, convinced of the superiority of his forces, made proposals that were completely unacceptable to the Ch'i-tan. The war continued, and the advantage was always with the rebels. During the years 1116 and 1117, it seemed all the more unlikely that the Ch'i-tan would be able to change the course of events. In May 1116, Jürchen troops captured the Ch'i-tan Eastern Capital and, in February 1117, the Ch'i-tan troops in the northeast surrendered without a fight.

Shortly after these events, Akuta was confident enough to proclaim himself emperor, and he adopted the dynastic title *Chin*. No direct challenge against Akuta's imperial proclamation came from either the Ch'i-tan or the Sung court. Instead, missions travelled back and forth between the Ch'i-tan and the Jürchen with the task of coming to a peaceful settlement of the war. Akuta demanded that the Ch'i-tan emperor recognize the Jürchen emperor as an older brother; that an annual tribute be paid; that the administration of three important districts be turned over to the Jürchen; that all Jürchen officials be released together with their emblems of office; that the Ch'i-tan court send a prince, a princess, an imperial son-in-law, and the sons of several high officials as hostages to the Jürchen court; and, last but not least, that the Ch'i-tan court turn over to the Jürchen all diplomatic correspondence between the Ch'i-tan, the Tangut, the Chinese, and the Koreans. Acceding to all these demands, and in particular to the last one, meant virtually agreeing to abolish the office of the Ch'i-tan emperor. Nevertheless, the Ch'i-tan did agree to turn over all the diplomatic documents requested by the Jürchen.[37]

It became clear, however, that the Jürchen were not intent on making peace with the Ch'i-tan but were out to conquer the entire Ch'i-tan realm. The years that followed were characterized by acrimonious exchanges and the continued advance of the Jürchen forces into the Ch'i-tan domains. By the beginning of 1121, Akuta and his forces had control over more than half of the Ch'i-tan empire and had begun preparations for a final attack on the Central and the Southern Capitals.[38] They were captured, respectively, during the first and the twelfth months of the fifth year *t'ien-fu* (21 January–18 February 1122, and 10 January–8 February 1123). The Ch'i-tan empire ceased to exist, but the last emperor, T'ien-tsu, was not captured until 1125, a year after Akuta's death. He was demoted to the rank of king, and after that nothing more is heard about him. Not all the Ch'i-tan, however, accepted the Jürchen conquest. A substantial number of them under the leadership of Yeh-lü Ta-shih began a long trek through the desert and the steppe and settled in Transoxiana. There they created a new Ch'i-tan empire, that of the Qaraqitai, known in Chinese as the Hsi Liao empire: the Western Ch'i-tan empire.

Although the primary aim of the Jürchen forces was the capture of the Ch'i-tan empire, they were also interested in gaining control over the Chinese territories held by the Ch'i-tan. When it became clear that the Ch'i-tan were unable to halt the Jürchen advance, the Sung began both military and diplomatic attempts to reconquer the lost Sixteen Prefectures.[39] The Sung, however, also wanted to regain control over territory lost to the Tangut. In the spring of 1115, the Sung informed the Ch'i-tan of the cancellation of the Shan-yüan agreement, and three Sung armies set out for the Tangut state. The Sung armies made military history of sorts. One army returned without engaging in combat; one scored a minor victory; and the third, the principal army, was totally destroyed. Under the influence of the powerful court eunuch T'ung Kuan, the Sung made another assault on the Tangut in 1119 with the same disastrous results. In fact, the Sung was lucky that the Tangut ruler, Li Ch'ien-shun, was not desirous of revenge.[40]

While the Sung was engaged in these disastrous campaigns, of which the Jürchen were certainly aware, the forces under Akuta's command began a slow southward movement in the direction of the Sixteen Prefectures. The Sung was as uncertain of Jürchen intentions as it was certain that its own military forces were unable to resist the advancing Jürchen troops; therefore, the Chinese court decided to use diplomatic means to achieve its territorial aims. In the spring of 1120, a mission under the leadership of Chao Liang-ssu was sent to Akuta's court. Its secret instructions were to arrange for a unified attack against the Ch'i-tan forces in the Sixteen Prefectures and the cessation of the annual payments to the Ch'i-tan.[41]

The Sung mission arrived at Akuta's camp, to the north of the Dolon-nor in Inner Mongolia, shortly after Akuta had conquered the Ch'i-tan Supreme Capital. From the start of the negotiations it was clear that Akuta had no serious intention either of launching a joint Jürchen-Sung campaign or of turning over the Sixteen Prefectures to the Sung without adequate compensation. The past performances of the Sung armies did not inspire confidence in a joint effort. Furthermore, the deliberately vague language used by the Sung was interpreted by Akuta as meaning that his forces alone were to recapture the Sixteen Prefectures. When Akuta claimed that the Jürchen were the rightful successors to the annual payments, the negotiations ended in an impasse. Jürchen distrust of both Sung intentions and military capabilities was reinforced when a Sung army attempting to dislodge a Ch'i-tan force from Yen (roughly present-day Peking) was defeated. From 1120 to 1123 there were more negotiations in an atmosphere of mistrust and misunderstanding. Occasionally, military clashes occurred between Sung and Jürchen forces within the Sixteen Prefectures; more frequently than not, they were to the disadvantage of the Sung. Finally, in 1123, a treaty between the two states was signed. The text clearly reflected the desire of each party: the Sung recovered the territories lost to the Ch'i-tan, and the Jürchen took the place of the Ch'i-tan as the beneficiaries of the annual Sung payments.[42]

The treaty of 1123, however, did not hold for very long. By the summer of 1124, it was clear to the Sung that the ambitions of the so far undefeated Jürchen were not limited to Ch'i-tan territory. By the end of that year, war was imminent, although ten tense months passed before the Jürchen launched their attack. During this period, panic took hold of the Sung government in K'ai-feng, leaving it in a state of hopeless confusion and disarray. Emperor Hui-tsung transmitted the throne to his son, but never formally abdicated. The notion of an "acting emperor," however, simply did not exist in China. Desperate efforts by courageous officials, such as Li Kang (1083–1143), to restore order were to no avail.[43]

The Jürchen attack, a pincer movement, began during the tenth month of 1125 (28 October–26 November). Their forces, under the command of Oripu, encountered no real resistance, and they were within a week's march of the panic-stricken capital, K'ai-feng, by the second month of 1126 (24 February–25 March). The Sung desperately needed time to evacuate the capital and were ready to agree to peace under any circumstances. Such an agreement, if it can be called that, was made in February 1126. It is interesting to note that only the Sung submitted an oath letter; the Jürchen clearly did not feel the need for such a document.[44] This "peace treaty" lasted less than one calendar year. Hostilities resumed in 1127, and after a short battle, the Jürchen forces entered K'ai-feng on 9 January 1127.

The Northern Sung, as it is commonly known, thus came to an inglorious end, and "barbarians" controlled China down to the Huai River, and thus the entire Yellow River drainage area. With the loss of North China, the Sung lost nearly all contact with Inner Asia, and this had grave consequences for our knowledge of the steppe and the new confederations being formed there during the twelfth century. The Sung established a temporary capital, which in time became a permanent one, in the city of Hangchow. After fruitless attempts by both sides to cross the Huai River, a real peace treaty was signed in 1141 by the Sung and the Jürchen. After the 1141 treaty, their relations can best be described as a hostile coexistence. The Jürchen devoted themselves to dealing with the internal political and administrative problems created by the acquisition of an enormous domain that, furthermore, contained a numerically dominant Chinese population. The Sung, known henceforth as the Southern Sung, also turned inward and entered one of China's most brilliant cultural periods.

The history of the Jürchen after they completed their conquests was not very different from that of the Ch'i-tan. Once the administration of the empire was settled, the Jürchen began to enjoy the spoils of victory. Not everyone, however, felt that he had received a fair share of the spoils. Intrigues and the formation of factions began soon after the death of Tsung-pi, the last of Akuta's commanders, in 1148. A new generation of Jürchen, many of whom had known neither the Ch'i-tan yoke nor the beginning of the conquests, came to power. The new emperor, Hui-tsung, was a cruel man, and discontent was soon expressed almost openly. The leading clique was that of Hsiao Yü, the commander of Ta-tung and a man from the Hsi tribe, and the Prince of Liang, better known as Hai-ling, who was a descendant of Akuta. These men and their followers staged a coup on 11 January 1150, assassinating the emperor in his bedroom. If the Jürchen conspirators hoped that Hai-ling would be more magnanimous than his predecessor, they soon discovered that they were worse off than before. Hai-ling's reign was one of the bloodiest and most repressive ever witnessed in China and Inner Asia.[45]

Having obtained the throne by means of a murderous plot, Hai-ling feared that he might lose his newly gained power in the same way. Therefore, he wiped out literally his entire family, as well as anyone else who could challenge or threaten him. For the remainder of his reign, dismissal from office for any reason meant a death sentence, not only for the official involved, but often for his associates as well. Hai-ling also intended to keep his military forces occupied and ambitiously planned to gain control first over the Southern Sung, then over the Tangut state. It is not known how the Tangut emperor reacted to this, but the Sung emperor, Kao-tsung, did everything possible to avoid alienating the irascible Hai-ling, and he adhered strictly to the terms of the 1141 peace agreement. A conflict, however, was inevitable. Hai-ling became more ruthless and tyrannical with every passing year until, in 1161, he decided to move his capital to K'ai-feng, and began massive preparations for an invasion of Southern China. The moving of the Jürchen capital, the impressive preparations, and Hai-ling's well-known ruthlessness combined to create a panic among the population of Hangchow. Preparations for an evacuation were begun long before a single Jürchen soldier had crossed the Huai. However, Hai-ling's massive mobilization effort required such enormous exactions to man and prepare the army that the limit of tolerance among Jürchen officials was finally reached. In the northern part of the empire, a plot led by the Prince of Ts'ao, Wu-lu, finally took shape. The conspirators found it easy to overthrow and kill Hai-ling. In the Jürchen Eastern Capital, Wu-lu simply proclaimed himself emperor and issued a new reign title. When the soldiers under Hai-ling heard of the proclamation, they rose against him, overran his tent, and killed him, together with several of his followers.

The reign of Wu-lu, known as Emperor Shih-tsung, lasted until 1189 and was a peaceful one. There was among the Sung what can be called a revanchist party, which wanted to regain the lost territories north of the Huai and even north of the Yellow River, and who viewed Shih-tsung's pacifism as a sign of weakness.[46] This party came to power in 1208, and in earnest attempted to regain China's territories to the north of the river. As before, this effort was futile. The Jürchen began plans for retaliatory action, but before those could be implemented they were confronted by a serious threat coming from the central steppe: the Mongols under the leadership of Chinggis-khan. The year was 1209.

It is not certain when the Jürchen began to have contacts with the Mongols, but it is likely that they first occurred during the reign of Shih-tsung. During the twelfth century, the Jürchen fought not only against the Southern Sung, but also against a new force that had arisen on the central steppe, namely the Tatars (not to be confused with the Tartars, the Mongols mentioned in thirteenth-century European documents). The Jürchen rulers sought, and found, an ally on the steppe in the person of Toghril-khan, the leader of the Kereyit tribe. Among the officers of Toghril-khan was a relatively unknown commander, Temujin, the future Chinggis-khan. At the time of the alliance between the Jürchen and the Kereyit against the Tatars, the Jürchen clearly did not see a major threat on the steppe, but viewed the elimination of the Tatars as preventing the formation of a powerful nomadic alliance, the avowed aim of the Tatars. In 1209, however, the situation changed drastically when the ambitious ruler of the Mongols, Chinggis-khan, forced the Tangut into allegiance to him. After that date, only the Ch'i-tan troops on the Jürchen northern borders, who were of very uncertain loyalty, stood between them and the Mongols. The onslaught began in 1211. The Ch'i-tan forces defected en masse to the Mongols, and the Jürchen forces were driven back. Three years later, the Mongols were in control of almost the entire northern half of the Jürchen empire. Chinggis-khan returned to the steppe, and the Mongol commander, Muqali, began a systematic campaign of consolidation. In 1220 his forces began to penetrate the remainder of the Jürchen empire but were diverted on account of a Tangut breach of alliance.

The death of Muqali in 1223, the death of Chinggis-khan three years later, and the two-year interval before the confirmation of the new Mongol emperor, Ogodei, gave the Jürchen the chance to regroup, but their hope of regaining control over a part of their lost territories was a vain one. Under the leadership of Ogodei, the Mongol North China campaign resumed in full force; and the Jürchen's valiant resistance proved totally inadequate when confronted with the well-trained and seasoned Mongol war machine. In 1234 the Jürchen empire was conquered and became a province of the developing Mongol empire. Those Jürchen officials who did not join the Mongols were easily absorbed into the North Chinese population.

The Sung dynasty, in the meantime, had observed the developments in the north with some apprehension, but also with some satisfaction. Many at the Chinese court saw in an alliance with the Mongols the possibility of regaining North China, at least up to the old Ch'i-tan borders. The Sung forces attacked the weakened Jürchen and, for a while, were able to regain the symbolically important cities of K'ai-feng and Lo-yang. Once again, however, Sung policy of an alliance with a "barbarian" invader backfired. Soon after the Mongols had liquidated the Jürchen Chin dynasty, they began to attack the territories once held by the Jürchen, but then under Sung control. The Sung found that instead of having a barbarian ally it could control, it was confronted with the most powerful military force, until modern times, ever to attack China.

The Tangut
Imperial Confederation

As was indicated above, Chinese sources considered them to have lived originally in Western Szechuan, but the Tangut had no historical role of any importance until about three centuries after their settlement around the Hsia prefecture, when they aided the T'ang dynasty during the Huang Ch'ao rebellion. Their leader at that time was named T'o-pa Szu-kung. Because of his defense of the T'ang capital, he was awarded the title of *chieh-tu-shih* and given the right to carry the imperial surname, Li. From then on, this was the name by which the Tangut leaders were generally known in Chinese history. After T'o-pa Szu-kung's defense of the T'ang, the Tangut did not appear again in the Chinese records until the 930s, at which time they were a fairly well-organized state that was continually intercepting the Uighur trade missions to the Chinese court. Tangut control over the trade routes was a serious threat to the military resources of the Sung dynasty, for it meant a reduction in the supply of horses. After 939 their raids became so serious that both the Chinese and the Uighurs began to look for alternate trade routes and were forced to have their missions accompanied by regular army units. T'o-pa Szu-kung's military success in China and the resulting recognition of his political authority by the Chinese apparently permitted him to organize the mixed population of the Kansu corridor into an independent state, the predecessor of the Tangut empire.[47]

For the next four centuries, the Tangut state was to play an important role in both Central Asian and East Asian history. Why the Chinese permitted the formation of a state in such a strategically crucial area cannot be answered. Probably the central government and the emperor had lost touch with the Kansu corridor as a result of the An Lu-shan rebellion.

The Sung attitude toward the area is instructive. Having defeated the Northern Han, the Sung emperor decided first to recover the Hsia and other prefectures rather than to attack the apparently more powerful Ch'i-tan. In 984 after the Sung armies' initial successes, Li Chi-p'eng, the Tangut ruler, recognized Sung suzerainty. However, his cousin, Li Chi-ch'ien, and the citizens of the Tangut state were unwilling to go along. Li Chi-ch'ien successfully "rebelled" against the Sung. By 990, after the Ch'i-tan–Tangut alliance, it was evident that the Sung would be unable to gain more than a toehold in the Kansu area. Nevertheless, their policy toward the Tangut was one of containment. It was as if they considered the Tangut problem no more than a temporary nuisance: Li Chi-ch'ien and his forces, which continually defeated the Sung, were described merely as rebels. The Sung appointed officials to administer the Tangut domain; they never left the Chinese capital, and it was impossible for them to assume their assigned duties.

Almost immediately after the Ch'i-tan–Tangut alliance, Li Chi-ch'ien began an expansionist campaign aimed at gaining control over the Chinese–Central Asian trade routes, thus consolidating the economic foundation of the Tangut state. The major thrust of the campaign was toward the predominantly Tibetan town of Hsi-liang-fu, then the capital of the Eastern Tibetan "Six Horn" federation, and towards the Uighur principalities of Kan-chou and Sha-chou. On the Chinese border there were only minor and diversionary skirmishes.

Li Chi-ch'ien's campaign was only partially successful, and he died in battle in 1004.[48] However, the campaign forced the Sung to commit military forces to the defense of their western borders. As has been shown, this situation was exploited by the Ch'i-tan, who subsequently consolidated their gains in the treaty of Shan-yüan in 1005. Although the Sung sources clearly show the role of the Tangut in the treaty—an important, if indirect, one— modern studies based on them do not even mention the Tangut as a factor in the events and negotiations leading to the signing of this agreement.

Official Chinese sources depict the reign of Li Chi-ch'ien's son and successor, Li Te-ming, as much more favorable towards China than it in fact was. The first decade of Li Te-ming's reign was characterized by relatively peaceful relations with the Sung; indeed, after Li Chi-ch'ien's expansion, the Tangut state was in need of a period of political, economic, and administrative consolidation. Furthermore, during the first five years of Li Te-ming's reign, the area was plagued by a serious drought and an ensuing famine. Nevertheless, the fact remained that the Sung was completely unable to gain control over any portion of the Tangut domain. As before, the Chinese court appointed officials to the area, and, as before, these officials never left the Chinese capital, K'ai-feng. Historical appearances at least were saved. In 1015 Li Te-ming conquered Hsi-liang-fu and destroyed the remnants of the Six Horn federation. Consequently the usual trade routes were closed to the Sung and its supply of horses was jeopardized. Only a reluctant alliance with the Eastern Tibetans of the bCon-kha federation (around present-day Kokonor) made trade with the Uighur principalities and Kucha a possibility.[49]

When Li Te-ming died, in 1032, the Tangut state was again confident of its strength. Anti-Chinese feelings as well as imperial ambitions reached a new height, culminating in the reign of Li Yüan-hao (1032–1048). Well before he succeeded his father, Li Yüan-hao must have made his expansionist ambitions known; upon his accession to the throne, all the surrounding states, including the Ch'i-tan, began to strengthen their border defenses. Almost immediately after he succeeded his father, Li Yüan-hao began a campaign to completely interrupt communication between the Sung and the Uighurs. His initial target was the bCon-kha federation, the end of the Sung's Central Asian supply line. After several unsuccessful attempts at conquest, he turned his attention to the Uighur principalities of Kan-chou and Sha-chou. By 1036 he had full control over them and was able to begin concentrating on China itself.[50]

Between Li Yüan-hao and the Sung court an acrimonious exchange had already developed over the Sung's adoption of a reign title that included part of Li Te-ming's personal name—a taboo word, according to the Chinese tradition, if Li Te-ming had been a Chinese ruler. Under the threat of an invasion, in 1034 the Sung agreed to abandon the title and adopt one that was not offensive to the Tangut ruler. That same year, however, Li Yüan-hao himself adopted a reign title deliberately chosen to offend the Chinese. Chinese entreaties went unanswered. In 1038, to add insult to injury, Li Yüan-hao proclaimed himself "Son of Heaven," a title that in the East Asian political sphere was strictly reserved for the ruler of China.[51] Furthermore, he challenged the legitimacy of the Sung by proclaiming himself a descendant of the Northern Wei, the dynasty founded a few centuries earlier by the Tabghach. War between the Tangut and the Sung became inevitable, and the outcome at first appeared favorable to the Chinese. The war, best described as the "Titular War," broke out in 1040. It was a disaster for the Sung, and by the summer of 1042 it appeared that the next victim of the Tangut invasion would be the Sung capital itself. Then, quite suddenly, the Tangut forces halted their advance. They had not suffered a single defeat, and yet they found themselves in a precarious situation.

Shortly after the war began, the Sung considered negotiating with the Ch'i-tan to persuade them to use their influence as allies of the Tangut to end the war. They believed the Ch'i-tan were not opposed to such an intervention: Li Yüan-hao when he adopted the title "Son of Heaven" had also rejected Ch'i-tan nominal overlordship. Instead, however, the Ch'i-tan threatened to join the Tangut in their war against the Sung. Only after the Sung agreed to increase the annual payments provided for by the Shan-yüan agreement did the Ch'i-tan forcefully intercede with the Tanguts. While negotiating with the Ch'i-tan, the Sung was also negotiating with Chio-ssu-lo, the ruler of the bCon-kha federation. Supported by the Sung, Chio-ssu-lo felt secure enough not to ally himself with Li Yüan-hao and to defy the Tangut state.[52]

Thus, that summer Li Yüan-hao was confronted with three hostile states. Powerful as the Tangut were, war on three fronts was militarily and logistically impossible. Hence, the Tangut ruler began to negotiate with the Sung, and in 1044 an agreement similar to the Shan-yüan treaty was entered into. Li Yüan-hao relinquished the title "Son of Heaven"; the Sung emperor recognized him as an older brother; and the Sung made annual payments in silk and silver to the Tangut.

After the signing of the Tangut-Sung peace agreement, there is a serious gap in our information about the Tangut state. Although a few Sung attacks on the Tangut are mentioned, the existence of this state was no longer the Sung's major preoccupation; hence, the amount of information recorded about it decreased substantially. Ch'i-tan sources are not more explicit. Apparently the Tangut again recognized Ch'i-tan suzerainty, and, until the end of the Ch'i-tan empire, relations between the two appear to have been rather amicable. Li Yüan-hao's death in 1048 clearly marked the end of a period in Tangut history. The state's expansion ceased, and attention turned from the borders to internal affairs and commercial relations with both the Sung and the Ch'i-tan. The only expansionist campaign was the conquest of the bCon-kha state in 1068.

During the first years of the Jürchen conquest of the Ch'i-tan empire, the Tangut remained on the sidelines and did not come to the defense of their erstwhile allies. The Jürchen conquest progressed with lightning speed, and it was clear that whatever action the Tangut undertook, the days of the Ch'i-tan empire were numbered. When armed struggle broke out between the Sung and the Jürchen, the Tangut also attacked the Jürchen, thus coming to the aid of their former enemies. They were defeated, however, and soon began peace negotiations with the Jürchen, which led to the signing of two treaties, one in 1117 and one in 1124. In the 1117 treaty, which has not yet received the attention it deserves, the Tangut agreed not to intervene in Jürchen-Chinese affairs. This freed the Jürchen from having to station any troops on the Tangut border and permitted them to use all available forces to finish the conquest of the remainder of the Ch'i-tan empire and occupy Chinese territory. The importance of this treaty in the subsequent Jürchen overthrow of the Northern Sung cannot be overestimated. The 1124 treaty, which covered subsequent Jürchen-Tangut relations, was signed when the Sung had already begun to evacuate the northern regions.[53]

From the few surviving Chinese documents of the Jürchen dynasty, it appears that Tangut-Jürchen relations after the 1124 treaty were essentially peaceful. Mention of the Tangut in documents of the Southern Sung is even scantier. Since its capital was then in Hangchow, it no longer bordered on the Tangut state and had but sporadic contact with the once-feared enemy. It is only with the rise and expansion of the Mongol empire, during the period from 1206 to 1227, that there is more ample documentation of Tangut history, because the state was the first victim of the expansionist policies of Chinggis-khan: when he contemplated an attack on North China, through the Kansu corridor—that is, directly through the Tangut state—lay the most expedient route for the Mongol attack; his only alternative was to attack China through the Gobi Desert. Hence the decision was made to conquer the Tangut state or force it to become a vassal of the Mongols.

The first Mongol attacks, probably nothing more than reconnaissance raids, occurred in 1206 and 1207. By themselves these attacks were relatively unimportant, but because they have been interpreted, quite erroneously, as an attack by Chinggis-khan on Tibet, they have received more consideration than they warrant. In the summer of 1209, however, the Mongols laid siege to the Tangut capital. The Tangut ruler, Li An-ch'üan, submitted to the Mongols rather than attempt a futile resistance against their superior forces. The Tangut surrender opened the road to China for the Mongols. A mere two years later, Chinggis-khan began the systematic conquest of the Jürchen domain.

The Tanguts provided substantial troops for the Mongol campaign in

North China, but they refused to provide Chinggis-khan with more troops when he began his western campaign. The refusal is commonly interpreted as the reason for Chinggis-khan's total destruction of the state in 1227. The facts, however, do not support such a conclusion. In 1220, two years after Chinggis-khan had left Mongolia for the Middle East, the Tanguts attempted to rid themselves of the Mongol yoke. In North China, the Jürchen had begun to turn the tide against the Mongol commander Muqali, and it appeared that they might actually remove the Mongols from the area. The Tanguts thereupon broke their alliance with the Mongols and joined forces with the Jürchen.[54]

This breach of alliance jeopardized the Mongol effort in North China. In the attempt to maintain the communication and supply lines between the North China front and Mongolia, Muqali lost his life in Tangut territory. Muqali died of an illness, not in battle, but his death and the Tangut treason were behind Chinggis-khan's decision to eradicate the Tangut state. The campaign against the Tangut began in the winter of 1225 and ended in August 1227 with the most thorough destruction ever executed by the Mongol forces. During the reign of Chinggis-khan's grandson, Qubilai, when the order was given to compile the official Chinese histories of the dynasties discussed in this chapter, it was decided that the Tangut state, Hsi Hsia, did not merit an independent history of its own: a chapter or two in the official histories of the Sung, the Ch'i-tan, and the Jürchen was deemed sufficient. The Mongols thus destroyed not only the physical Tangut state, but also its history.[55]

The Structure of the Ch'i-tan Empire

Prior to the rise of A-pao-chi and the subsequent formation of the Ch'i-tan empire, the tribes at the basis of this empire were only loosely organized. Each tribe was headed by a chieftain, and, in appearance, all chieftains had the same rank. During the pre-imperial period, the Ch'i-tan did not use the title *qaghan*, or any other Altaic title with a similar or related meaning. The absence of this title, which remains unexplained, is unusual because from the end of the seventh century until some time during the tenth, the Ch'i-tan used Turkic titles to differentiate offices and ranks. During the tenth century, with the increasing influence of Chinese practices, many of these Turkic titles were replaced with Chinese ones, even though a few of the old ones were retained.[56]

A-pao-chi was an empire builder. Not only did he found the empire and expand it; he also provided it with an administrative structure. The administration he created was an extremely complex one in that it combined Chinese and Ch'i-tan elements, and in that it kept the two elements relatively separate. The Chinese model used was the one set forth in the *Chenkuan cheng-yao*, which describes the administration of the T'ang empire at the peak of its expansion, the years between 627 and 649.[57] This work, compiled about 707, became the model for all the Border Empires, and also for the Yüan dynasty during the reign of Qubilai (1260–1294).

The adoption of the Chinese model did not mean, however, that the Ch'i-tan abandoned their tribal traditions. These were maintained and incorporated into the Chinese model, a process that accounts for the extreme complexity and unwieldiness of the Ch'i-tan administration. This was aggravated by the proclamation of racial laws creating two classes, Ch'i-tan and Chinese. Into the former were incorporated non–Ch'i-tan tribes that had not been exposed to Chinese influence; into the latter, people like the Po-hai, who had been exposed to Chinese influence. Each racial group had its own administration, the Ch'i-tan one being the more important.

This division apparently began in 947, when the empire was divided into two courts, Northern and Southern. The division reflected the distribution of the ethnic groups within the empire. The Ch'i-tan was the first steppe empire (excluding the Turkic empires of the Middle East, which were not typical) to contain large numbers of sedentary-agricultural people. The region under the Northern Court was inhabited by tribal, non-Chinese people, whereas Chinese and Chinese-assimilated people inhabited the area under the Southern Court. If at the beginning of the empire the division was primarily geographical, in time the geographical distinctions became blurred, and the division reflected merely ethnic differences: thus, for example, the Northern Court had authority over Ch'i-tan people living in the territory of the Southern Court, and, *mutatis mutandis,* the Southern Court had the same function.

The Northern Court ranked above the Southern, even though the latter had more people to administer. Each court had its own officialdom. To these officials was added a third category, autonomous but under the aegis of the Northern Court, which was responsible for the administration of the tribes on the Central Asian border. In addition to the dual division, there was a fivefold territorial division of the empire. These divisions, called the Five Capitals, were in essence five provinces. There was a substantial overlap between the fivefold territorial division and the dual administration, and this accelerated the transition to an ethnic rather than a central government. The Northern Court, representing the central government, was located in the Supreme Capital, in present-day northwestern Jehol, between the Shira-Muren and the Khinghan mountains. The Southern Court, the secondary administration, was located in the Southern Capital, roughly present-day Peking.

Until almost the end of their empire, the Ch'i-tan remained close to their ancestral traditions, or at least the symbols of these traditions. The traditional ruler of a steppe empire was an autocrat in the proper sense of the term. The Ch'i-tan rulers adhered to this tradition; they were not and did not intend to be Chinese emperors. Although they adopted a Chinese model, the Ch'i-tan rulers eliminated the institutional and bureaucratic limitations that restrained a Chinese emperor. At the Ch'i-tan court, steppe traditions were expressed in the enormous amount of time the emperor spent travelling throughout his domain and in the importance of the hunt.

Frequently the emperor was away from the Supreme Capital for well over sixty days at a time. During these prolonged absences, he was accompanied by a rump government, whose members were selected from the Northern Court. Another manifestation of ancestral tradition was the maintenance, throughout the existence of the Ch'i-tan empire, of two ceremonial calendars: the traditional Ch'i-tan calendar and the Chinese, the calendar of Confucian ritual. The latter was evidently used for political as well as legitimation purposes.[58]

The Ch'i-tan steppe traditions were, however, most clearly expressed in the empire's military structure. As in the Turkic empire, the backbone of the Ch'i-tan military forces was its cavalry. These elite troops were drawn from a social unit known as the *ordo*. The *ordo* was, in a strict sense, a military camp of considerable importance. It was a Turkic creation and appears in the Ch'i-tan political and social structure only around 922. Whether or not this was an institutionalization of a pre-existing practice cannot be determined.[59] The *ordo* troops were under the direct command of the emperor himself, who also commanded the so-called imperial troops, known under the name "Great Tents." These were guard units, numbering seven in all. One of them functioned as the actual bodyguard of the emperor and was called the "Claws and Teeth."[60] It was comparable to the *keshig,* or the Mongol imperial bodyguard, discussed in a later chapter.

Like its civil administration, the Ch'i-tan military structure was complex. The emperor had command over the army, but the clan of the empress possessed its own troops. These units, like those of the emperor himself, were essentially supratribal troops. A more tribal organization was found in the private armies of the Ch'i-tan nobles. These armies were personally attached to a single individual and yet were a constituent part of the empire's military structure. Imperial clansmen who did not belong to the imperial troops proper were organized in the *She-li* troops, a term whose meaning is unclear.[61] These four categories of military organizations formed the basic structure of the Ch'i-tan army. They were supplemented by the frontier garrisons and the militia, whose functions are not clear.

Excluding the supplementary forces, the strength of the Ch'i-tan army fluctuated between seventy-five thousand and one hundred ten thousand men. The small size of the Ch'i-tan army shows it to be directly within the tradition of the previous steppe armies, none of which numbered more than a hundred thousand men. This small army proved capable not only of holding off the much larger Sung armies, but of actually capturing important sections of Sung territory.[62]

When the Ch'i-tan army began its conquests, a high degree of mobility was no longer the guarantee of a successful cavalry attack. Chinese weaponry and strategies had been adapted to the steppe peoples' style of warfare. The Ch'i-tan introduced a twofold modification in steppe tactics. Because of the more spectacular conquests of the Mongols a few centuries later, the Ch'i-tan innovations have been largely overlooked, or erroneously attributed to Chinggis-khan. It is, however, fair to say that without these modifications, the Mongol conquests might not have been as successful. The major Ch'i-tan innovation in cavalry warfare was the organization of the mounted archers into several tightly disciplined units, each capable of acting on its own or in coordination with the others. These units had the mobility and the attack capability of the traditional steppe cavalry; in addition, they were able to execute intricate and coordinated battlefield maneuvers in which precise timing played a crucial role.

This was not the Ch'i-tan's only modification. Intricate cavalry tactics were useless against cities and in terrain crisscrossed by rivers, canals, and marshes, so they introduced a combination of cavalry and infantry troops. The Ch'i-tan, however, did not experiment with siege warfare. Later, when Chinggis-khan added this refinement to the arsenal of the nomadic warrior, the steppe army became almost invincible. The city wall and the moat, the traditional defenses of the sedentary people against the horsemen of the steppe, became ineffective.

Whereas the Ch'i-tan were quickly able to adapt their military and administrative structures to their new status as a semisedentary empire, the social structure changed only slowly and awkwardly. According to A-pao-chi's strict laws differentiating between Chinese and non-Chinese, the Chinese and the people assimilated to them occupied the lower ranks of the administrative and social structure. At the top of the social structure were the two imperial clans, the Yeh-lü and the Hsiao, respectively the clans of the emperor and the empress. Each clan was further divided into an upper and a lower lineage, and the upper lineage itself was divided into two lines. The family of the emperor belonged to the first of these lines (which was confusingly known as the "Five Divisions," and was itself subdivided into two branches). The direct descendants of A-pao-chi were known as the "Horizontal Tents"; the descendants of his brothers and his uncles were known as the "Three Patriarchal Households." The upper lineage of the clan of the empress, drawn primarily from the Hsi people, was divided into three distinct families. Through succeeding generations, these families provided not only the empress herself, but also the holders of the post of Great Minister of the North. This post was second in importance to that of emperor.[63]

The two imperial clans were closely tied by marriage alliances, and, in theory, intermarriage was the rule for the upper lineages. The evidence, however, shows that this rule was not strictly adhered to and that marriages were dominated by exo-endogamic practices. Contrary to what is stated in K. A. Wittfogel and Feng Chia-sheng's magisterial study, there is no clear-cut evidence showing a similarity between the Chinese extended kinship group and the Ch'i-tan clan-kin group.[64] Ch'i-tan kinship relations existed only up to the ninth generation. Neither clan membership nor lineage affiliation had a direct bearing upon power or wealth.

At the beginning of the empire, the use of the names *Yeh-lü* and *Hsiao* was restricted to the two imperial clans. In time these restrictions disappeared, and both names were bestowed not only on other Ch'i-tan lineages, but also on meritorious Chinese. The manner in which this transfer of names occurred makes it abundantly clear that the Ch'i-tan rulers were following honorific practices of the T'ang court. For reasons never clearly explained, the Ch'i-tan permitted members of former ruling families, even of enemy states like the Po-hai, to retain high ranks quite out of proportion to their actual power. In fact, these families were permitted to retain only the symbols of their former power: thus, the Po-hai king was allowed to continue calling himself king and even to hold court, although he had no power whatsoever over the Po-hai people.

Below the imperial clans were the lesser nobility and the commoners. The status of the lesser nobility can best be compared to that enjoyed by the scholar-official class in China. They occupied the key positions within the state's administration. Among the commoners, Ch'i-tan, non-Ch'i-tan, and Chinese all enjoyed roughly the same political and social status. In the case of the Chinese, however, in order to belong to the commoner class, they had to have submitted voluntarily to Ch'i-tan rule. In time, the few legal distinctions between these three groups became blurred.

Two other groups—the so-called *Yün-wei* families and the artisans—enjoyed a more privileged position than the bulk of the Chinese population within the empire. The Ch'i-tan, and later the Mongols, who followed their example, made it a practice to spare all the artisans when they captured a place and to put them to work for the emperor's court. The *Yün-wei* families were Chinese who had achieved prominence through trade. The Ch'i-tan empire, as a non-Confucian state, did not view merchants as a socially disreputable class; in fact, the opposite was true. Hence, entrepreneurs flourished in a manner unknown to most of traditional China. It must be pointed out, however, that most of the Chinese population, especially the peasantry, belonged to the slave class, and as such were tied permanently to the land.[65]

With the large number of Chinese living within the empire, it was inevitable that cultural contacts and transfers would occur. Not much can be said about them, however, for the Chinese historians have left a highly biased account; to judge from their statements, cultural transfer was strictly a one-way street, from the Chinese to the Ch'i-tan. This assertion is not substantiated by the history of previous Sino-barbarian contacts; hence, there is reason to question it in the case of the Ch'i-tan empire. The only solid evidence available tends to indicate that cultural transfer tended to be of a political and fashionable nature, finding its expression in the adoption of new nomenclature and luxury items. The only clear evidence of Chinese cultural influence is found in the modification of the Ch'i-tan judicial system, which was brought into line with that of the T'ang dynasty, and in burial customs. The evidence, however, is so scanty that a generalization is impossible.[66]

Unlike most of the steppe peoples, the Ch'i-tan did not receive the Buddhist doctrines from Uighur missionaries. Even though Ch'i-tan–Uighur relations existed, there is little evidence of Uighur influence. Buddhism in its Chinese form did become the official state religion, but whether the Ch'i-tan adopted Buddhism as their personal religion is open to question. Buddhism appears to have been practiced more by the Chinese in the empire than by the Ch'i-tan, and even though it was the state religion, many original tribal religious practices appear to have been maintained. Little is known about specific Ch'i-tan tribal beliefs because the Chinese sources, on whom we have to rely for information, glossed over the details.[67]

For centuries, the visible symbol of Chinese cultural dominance has been its written language. The founder of the Ch'i-tan empire sought to diminish Chinese influence through the promulgation of a Ch'i-tan script, and in 920, at the same time that anti-Chinese racial laws were promulgated, one was issued—the so-called large characters. A few years later, allegedly under Uighur influence,[68] the so-called small script was adopted. To what degree it was successful in reducing Chinese cultural influence is extremely difficult to assess. Very few Chinese texts in Ch'i-tan have survived, and for all practical purposes, it remains undeciphered. Bilingual Chinese–Ch'i-tan texts and texts in Chinese by inhabitants of the Ch'i-tan state, Chinese or otherwise, are also extremely rare. Most of our information is derived from documents written by Chinese officials of the Sung, hardly unbiased sources.[69]

For almost two centuries the Ch'i-tan were able to maintain their empire on China's northern border and to protect their own ethnic identity. By the middle of the eleventh century, therefore, Ch'i-tan society had achieved an uneasy accommodation with the Chinese living within the empire.

The Culture of the Tangut State

At present, information about the Tangut state is derived almost exclusively from Chinese sources devoted primarily to the political relations between the Tangut state and its neighbors. They provide only glimpses of the political structure, the administration, and the economy of the state. The little that is known is easily summarized.

As a state it was an unusual phenomenon. Traditionally, steppe confederations were made up of a number of different clans, but these clans almost always belonged to the same ethnic and linguistic stock. This certainly was not the case for the Tangut state. Even if the Chinese sources are correct in claiming that the Tangut were a Tibetan people, their state consisted not only of Tangut Tibetans, but also of Uighurs, Türks, T'u-yü-hun, Chinese, and a few others. When the names of Tangut officials mentioned in the Chinese sources are tabulated by ethnic group and by office, it appears that while the emperor was always a Tangut, for other offices ethnic origins were not taken into consideration.

Like the Ch'i-tan, the Tangut state combined two different and traditionally antagonistic economic systems, the sedentary and the nomadic. Animal husbandry was perhaps the most important part of the state's economy and was generally carried on in the areas furthest removed from the Chinese border. Closer to the border, agriculture was practiced. The bulk of the state's revenue, however, came from trade. The Chinese sources clearly stress the crucial importance of trade to the Tangut state, and economic boycott was frequently its means of exerting pressure. How this trade was organized and what the annual revenues were cannot be exactly determined.

Judging from the size of the Tangut armies, and from the size of their tribute to Chinggis-khan, the state was wealthy, and trade must have been very lucrative.[70]

Chinese sources give even less information about the political and administrative structure of the state. These is no doubt that the state was a confederation, consisting of different ethnic and linguistic groups, and that the confederation was dominated by a people known in Chinese as the Tang-hsiang. It is also known that Li Yüan-hao issued a set of administrative rules and regulations derived from the Chinese classics. For their state structure, the Tanguts thus followed a Confucian model. The T'ang codex *Chen-kuan cheng-yao,* probably translated into Tangut during the reign of Li Yüan-hao, had as important an influence on the Tangut administration as it did on the Ch'i-tan.

Like the Ch'i-tan, the Tangut developed their own script, distinct from the Chinese, and substantially more complex, in appearance at least, than either Chinese or Ch'i-tan. Although Li Yüan-hao is usually credited with the invention of the script, it was actually his father, Li Te-ming, who, using as his model the Ch'i-tan script and possibly also the Chinese, created a writing system unique to the Tangut state; Li Yüan-hao's contribution was the standardization of the characters used. Standardization, never undertaken by either the Ch'i-tan or the Jürchen, undoubtedly had an important role in the script's survival and widespread use. Why Li Te-ming chose to develop an ideographic script when two syllabic scripts—Uighur and Tibetan—were in common use within his empire will remain, for a long time to come, an unanswered question.[71]

It is unquestionable that the script was in ordinary use until the destruction of the state, and its intelligentsia, by Chinggis-khan in 1227. It should be pointed out, however, that on several occasions throughout the Mongol Yüan dynasty, the script was used for Buddhist documents. In 1302, long after the Tangut state had ceased to exist, the Yüan court ordered the publication of the Buddhist canon in the Tangut language and script. This edition numbered some 3,620 chapters, and a substantial section of it has survived. Why the Mongol emperor sponsored this publication, an expensive undertaking, remains one of the many unanswered and puzzling questions in Tangut history.[72]

In fact, the existence of a Tangut script and a Tangut literature remained unknown until the end of the nineteenth century. At the beginning of the twentieth century, the Russian explorer I. Kozlov discovered a library in the dead city of Qaraqoto. This discovery made it possible to state that the dominant element in Tangut culture was Buddhism. There existed a vast corpus of Buddhist literature, translations, and original commentaries. Later, Tangut art that was also clearly of a Buddhist nature was discovered. This, however, poses another interesting puzzle: why did the Tanguts, allegedly Tibetans, follow Chinese Buddhism in their translations and in their art? This is all the more intriguing when it is realized that one of Tibet's principal Buddhist centers was located within the Tangut state. Furthermore, neither translations from Tibetan nor Tibetan influence have as yet been discovered.

Thus, although it is known that the Tangut state had a flourishing intellectual life, other than describing the volume of the surviving documents and artifacts, not much can be said about it. For all practical purposes, it is still impossible to read Tangut materials. It is only with great difficulty and with the simultaneous use of Chinese originals that known translations can be read. It is expected, however, that access to the language will be provided in the not too distant future.[73]

The Structure of
the Jürchen State

The first question to be answered about the structure of the Jürchen Chin dynasty is whether or not the Jürchen were a nomadic people with a steppe tradition. The most common interpretation of their history is that they were. At the time of the conquest of the Ch'i-tan empire, one of the mainstays of the Jürchen military force, as well as of its economy, was horse breeding; their skill as horsemen helped them to conquer the Ch'i-tan. Furthermore, contemporary Chinese reports describe the Jürchen as possessing no permanent dwellings, only tents. The people of Northern Manchuria, however, maintained two types of residence: tents for the summer and solid dwellings for the winter. Archeological evidence suggests that well before their conquest of the Ch'i-tan, the Jürchen maintained not only fixed dwellings, but also walled villages. Moreover, they were engaged in agriculture and also in a form of animal husbandry totally unsuited to a nomadic existence— pig breeding.[74] Further back in time, the people assumed to be the ancestors of the Jürchen are described as living a seminomadic existence based on hunting and fishing. When horse breeding became a major economic activity is not known, but the most likely period is the middle of the tenth century. Thus, at the time of the conquest of the Ch'i-tan, the Jürchen were, at most, only a marginal steppe people. Their society, however, was in the process of becoming dominated by a horse-breeding economy, one of the principal characteristics of the steppe.

The social structure of the Jürchen prior to their conquest, insofar as can be determined, also reveals marginal steppe traditions. They were divided into clans, and each clan was further divided into a limited number of lineages. The clans and their lineages lived in precisely delineated areas and were identified by the name of the region in which they lived or by the name of a river. Each lineage occupied a specific town. The clans were patrilineal, headed by a chieftain whose authority was limited to military affairs; other matters were the subject of clan discussion and agreement.[75] Interclan marriage existed, but only between lineages of identical social status. There was a precisely delineated hierarchy among the different clans. The sources tend to indicate that, at least prior to the conquest and the rise of Akuta, the leading groups were in essence only *primus inter pares*. A few other traditions also created marginal steppe ties for the Jürchen: they practiced the levirate, a practice that persisted long after the conquest; and unlike the Chinese, for whom it was the color of mourning, the Jürchen considered white an auspicious color, as the Koreans and the Mongols did.[76]

The main connection with the steppe tradition, however, was the political structure of the Jürchen prior to the conquest of North China. Known under the general name of *bogile*,[77] it encompassed all aspects of Jürchen life. In some respects it resembled the *ordo* of the Türks, although our present data do not permit us to determine exactly to what degree. The basic division was the clan lineage headed by a chieftain called *po-shih*; however, he held this function only during military emergencies. The smallest political, hence military, division was the *muke*, a group of one hundred men drawn from three hundred households. Ten *muke* were grouped in a *minggan*, encompassing a thousand men. In case of need, ten *minggan* were grouped in a *temu* (ten thousand men). This structure shows a close resemblance to that of the Mongols.[78]

At the beginning of the conquest, the Jürchen incorporated Ch'i-tan, Po-hai, and Chinese into the *muke-minggan* system, that is, into divisions based on the Jürchen system which did not include Jürchen. The formation of Chinese and Po-hai *muke-minggan* was halted in 1124, whereas the Ch'i-tan *muke-minggan* continued in existence until 1161 or 1162. During that period, because of the exactions of Hai-ling, the Ch'i-tan rebelled against him. Hai-ling's successor, Shih-tsung, perceived the threat to state security and began to dissolve the Ch'i-tan *muke-minggan* and incorporate the Ch'i-tan into Jürchen ones. This not only increased the security of the state, but accelerated Ch'i-tan assimilation by the Jürchen.[79] Although after the conquest of North China the Jürchen Chin dynasty increasingly followed Chinese administrative practices, the basic political and administrative division for the Jürchen themselves remained the *muke-minggan*. In 1187 it formed the basis of a census, one of the four held during the dynasty, which determined that the Jürchen population was about 6.5 million, or about 14 percent of the total population.[80]

The conquest of North China and the incorporation of substantial numbers of Chinese were inevitably to have consequences for the political and administrative organization of the Jürchen state. One of the most notable consequences was greater social stratification. Not only did the conquest create a distinction between the conquerors and the conquered, but among the conquerors it led to the formation of a conquest elite. The notion of *primus inter pares* disappeared, not without some strain on the Jürchen social fabric. The only remnant of the deliberative assemblies was the Court Council, whose membership was restricted to the elite. During the early years of the empire, from 1124 until 1150, the Jürchen court essentially practiced three different administrative forms, which were determined by the ethnic affiliation of the people affected. On the one hand, the Jürchen had their own administration; on the other hand, Ch'i-tan and Sung institutions were allowed to continue functioning within their respective areas. The same period was the heyday of the imperial clansmen, for they occupied almost all of the political positions.[81]

The situation changed rather drastically during the reign of Hai-ling, and preconquest institutions were replaced systematically by Chinese bureaucratic practices. One of the purposes of Hai-ling's reforms was to enhance the power of the emperor. Simultaneous with the reforms was a definite, and apparently fairly deliberate, trend towards Sinicization. Before Hai-ling's coup, a substantial number of Jürchen had migrated towards the conquered Chinese territories, where they settled as soldier-farmers. Their settlements resembled the Chinese military colonies, but in the opposite direction: instead of being on the border, they were now in the interior, that is, in the conquered territories, helping the central government to police these areas.[82] The movement, however, was a spontaneous one, the Jürchen being attracted by the comparatively easier life in China. The predominance of Chinese domain over native domain was made official when Hai-ling moved the capital southwards.

One of Hai-ling's first administrative reforms was the abolition of the deliberative Court Council, replacing it with an imperial secretariat under the emperor's direct authority. This reform was an essential preliminary to the adoption of a Chinese administrative system. Modeled on both the T'ang and Sung administrations, it nevertheless placed the Jürchen in the most favored positions. The division of tasks followed conquest lines, however; the Jürchen occupied most of the military positions, but on the civil administrative level, the Chinese were dominant. Chinese traditions were emphasized by the introduction of complete examination systems, the traditional Chinese access to government function, including the *chin-shih,* or doctoral degree. Although it was used before Hai-ling, during his reign it became, for all practical purposes, the principal form of recruitment. Jürchen did participate in the system and through the use of a quota system were guaranteed proportionally higher representation. In absolute numbers, however, the Chinese were the dominant element.[83]

Thus, during Hai-ling's long administration, the Jürchen dynasty assumed all the trappings of a legitimate Chinese dynasty. Unlike the Ch'i-tan, who adopted Chinese forms reluctantly, the Jürchen adopted them voluntarily and eagerly. When Hai-ling was overthrown, the Sinicization of the Jürchen had assumed dramatic proportions.[84] His successor, Emperor Shih-tsung, recognized the potential for disaster in this trend and attempted to reverse it by promoting the use of the Jürchen language and the maintenance of Jürchen traditions. His program concentrated on the elite, the social group most affected by Sinicization. Shih-tsung issued strict orders, in 1164 and 1187, aimed at preserving the Jürchen nature of the state. Orders were given to translate all Chinese classics and selected historical works, among them the *Chen-kuan cheng-yao,* into Jürchen. The 1187 decree made it a serious offense, accompanied by serious penalties, for a Jürchen official to adopt a Chinese name or even to wear Chinese-style clothing. In the administration, too, Shih-tsung attempted to reverse the trend towards Chinese domination by actively promoting Jürchen. His reign, dominated by his commitment to a Jürchen revival, was unsuccessful in either stopping or slowing down the trend toward Sinicization; at its end, despite all his efforts, it appeared that the Jürchen were to undergo the same fate as the Hsien-pi, a people of

Turkic stock, several centuries earlier: complete absorption into the conquered population.[85]

That Sinicization was bound to be a problem had already been realized by the dynasty's founder, Akuta, in spite of the fact that he adopted Chinese forms of legitimacy—for example, his adoption of a Chinese title and proclamation as emperor *more sinico*. Because of the substantially larger population conquered by the Jürchen, Sinicization pressures on them were bound to be stronger than those on the Ch'i-tan. The major threat was cultural. Thus, like the Ch'i-tan and the Tangut rulers, Akuta had a native Jürchen script developed. Although several attempts were made to promote and enforce the use of the script, it never became popular. The entire literature in Jürchen is a translation literature. Even Shih-tsung's deliberate promotion of the script was not successful. Very little of what was written in Jürchen at that time has survived, and what has is not yet fully deciphered.[86] Of the three border empires, the Jürchen were unquestionably the least successful in developing their own script and in maintaining their own language and traditions.

By the late Chin period, that is, after 1191, when the ban on interracial marriage was lifted—the ban had been widely ignored—Chinese influence had permeated all aspects of cultural and intellectual life in the dynasty. Most works of that time that have survived, whether in art or literature, are Chinese in the strict sense of the term. Religious beliefs also assumed Chinese forms through the adoption of Chinese Buddhism and Taoism. It was only with regard to Confucianism that the Jürchen remained "barbarian": it was accepted only as the most practical form of statecraft. Nevertheless, by the time of the Mongol conquests, it appeared that even this attitude was about to change, for Jürchen rituals, although still practiced, had all but lost their meaning. When the Mongols attacked the Jürchen state, they did not attack a real border empire but a state that was slowly but surely transforming itself into a legitimate and authentic Chinese dynasty.

The Problem of Acculturation and Sinicization

The Border Empires were not the first point of contact between China and the steppe, but, to a large degree, the period of the Border Empires was the first time that substantial portions of China were occupied by steppe people. More than any other steppe groups, the Ch'i-tan, the Tangut, and the Jürchen form an integral part of Chinese political and social history, in spite of the fact that traditional scholarship, whether Chinese or not, often does not attach great importance to them. That traditional Chinese historians adopted such an attitude is, to a certain degree, comprehensible, but modern Western historians must not continue to adhere to these traditional Sinocentric interpretations without question, as has been often the case. Thus, the traditional interpretation of the inevitable cultural contacts between the so-called barbarians and the Chinese is that the latter always absorbed the former. This view has been espoused even by some of the more renowned historians of Sino-barbarian relations. Unquestionably China was the culturally and politically dominant force in both East and Central Asia, and the steppe people, deliberately as well as unconsciously, adopted certain Chinese cultural forms. However, the statement that the conquered—because they were culturally superior—always absorbed the conquerors is without foundation in fact. The traditional interpretation of Sino-barbarian relations, whether or not in a conquest situation, has not often been challenged, and it is still propounded in almost every textbook.[87] To continue to advance it without renewed investigation represents an unjustified rejection on the part of historians of the conclusions of social scientists.

Three concepts advanced by social scientists—acculturation, transculturation, and assimilation—need to be investigated before an adequate assessment of Sino-barbarian contacts can be made. The first was defined in 1935 by three American anthropologists as the study of "those phenomena which result when groups of individuals having different cultures come into continuous firsthand contact, with subsequent changes in the original cultural patterns of either or both groups."[88] Since the period dealt with in the present chapter basically covers conquest societies, it is equally important to examine *transculturation*, "the radical transformation of a people's culture under the impact of another culture."[89] In light of the traditional interpretation of Sino-barbarian relations, *assimilation* can be renamed *Sinicization*, recently defined by John W. Dardess as "a process . . . which involved not only the loss of national or linguistic identity, but also a most un-Confucian denial of the facts of ancestry."[90]

In Chinese and Central Asian history, studies of these phenomena have been largely limited to either the Manchu or the modern period.[91] Little research has been done on the periods before those, in particular on the period when cultural exchanges were the most active and well documented: the period of the Border Empires, followed by the Mongol period in China. The first serious challenge to the existing interpretation came from Karl A. Wittfogel and Feng Chia-sheng's magisterial study of the Ch'i-tan, published nearly a quarter of a century ago.[92] Since then, for all practical purposes the only new study is that by John W. Dardess on Mongol China; he introduces a concept which might prove to be more profitable than any of the three named above: *Confucianization*, "the adoption by outsiders, even Chinese outsiders, of a certain system of ethical and political behavior," a term he clearly contrasts throughout his work with *Sinicization*.[93]

Although much more research is needed before a formal statement can be made about the Border Empires, the preceding paragraphs permit some preliminary conclusions, which, I hope will serve as the basis for renewed investigation. In considering this problem, however, the Tangut have to be excluded, primarily because not enough is known about their cultural and social structures, and also because their vast literature cannot yet be read.

Transculturation between Chinese, Ch'i-tan, and Jürchen also appears not to apply to the Border Empires. The same, however, cannot be said of the other non-Chinese tribes living within the Ch'i-tan or the Jürchen state. The most evident example of transculturation is the Ch'i-tan treatment of the Po-hai people, a subject that has not yet received the attention of modern scholarship. Acculturative processes were clearly at work in both directions between the conquered and the conquerors. On account of the traditional interpretation of Sino-barbarian relations, a substantial amount is known about Chinese elements adopted by both Ch'i-tan and Jürchen; on the other hand, very little is known about what the Chinese adopted. Sufficient evidence, however, is available to permit one to state that acculturation was not a one-way process. The culturally superior group, the Chinese, did adopt barbarian elements: it is sufficient to compare Chinese society of the Border Empire period with its counterpart in the Sung dynasty.

The Ch'i-tan clearly never assumed a trend towards Sinicization and, throughout their reign, carefully avoided actions that could give rise to such a trend. The fact that they did not occupy vast sections of Chinese territory might have facilitated this policy. Ch'i-tan society did, however, undergo a limited amount of Confucianization; indeed, Confucianism was the only political theory for governing an empire available to them. The complexity of the Ch'i-tan administration clearly indicates that, with the exception of the Southern Court, Confucianism as such never assumed a dominating role in Ch'i-tan society.

Unlike the Ch'i-tan, the Jürchen not only underwent Confucianization but, by the middle of their reign, had begun an irresistible trend towards Sinicization.[94] This trend was recognized even by their contemporaries: when the Mongols conquered North China and divided the population of their Chinese domains into four categories, the Jürchen were placed in the same category as the native North Chinese. The only exception were those Jürchen who had never learned Chinese and who had but limited contacts with the Chinese, that is, those who lived in the northernmost areas of the Jürchen empire. It is these Jürchen who are mentioned in the annals of the Ming dynasty (1368–1644), not those of the Jürchen Chin dynasty. What happened to the latter is not known.

The traditional interpretation of Sino-barbarian relations during the period of the Border Empires is thus clearly not a valid one. It is also clear that enough evidence is available for serious investigation of the subject. Cultural exchanges went on in both directions, even during the reign of the Jürchen. An investigation of these problems will not only throw a new light on the so-called barbarian cultures, but will also provide for a more realistic evaluation of Chinese culture itself. The evaluation of the latter, whether done by a Chinese or a Western scholar, has been too Sinocentric. Unquestionably, China enjoyed a higher level of cultural achievement, but it was not isolated from its neighbors. From Han times on, there is evidence that China was subjected to outside cultural influences, and these were even stronger during the Sung dynasty, when China was never in a position to force its world view on recalcitrant powerful neighbors.

6

The Creation of
the Mongol Empire

The standard textbooks on the history of East Asia often contain but a paragraph or two on the Mongols, even though they ruled China for over a century. The few histories that are devoted specifically to the Mongols tend to emphasize exclusively the more sensational and military aspects of their reign. Rarely is any attention given to the historical traditions and power dynamics that led to the Mongols' rise to power and their subsequent conquest of the world. Therefore, it is quite easy to gain the impression that the Mongols were an isolated historical phenomenon who arose out of nowhere and, without any motivation whatsoever, systematically set out to plunder and destroy the sedentary states surrounding the steppe.

Recently a theory has been advanced that explains the rise of the Mongols in climatological terms: weather patterns changed, forcing the Mongols to unite and go forth to conquer in order to survive.[1] This revival of a deterministic interpretation of Mongol history ignores the history of the steppe and its frontier zones. Although it is not impossible, it is highly doubtful that a people weakened by adverse climatological conditions would have been able to create the world's largest empire. The commonest approach is to express bafflement at the phenomenon, or more simply, ignore the problem altogether. An explanation still occasionally used today is to consider the Mongols "God's Wrath." This image was created by Muslim historians at the time of the Mongol conquests. What was a plausible explanation for that period is no longer so today, and consequently, it has been rewritten in contemporary terms.

> The sudden outburst of aggressive energy among the Mongols in the early thirteenth century remains a psychological riddle. To use an analogy with the physical sciences, a sort of psychic explosion occurred.[2]

The Steppe
Before the Mongols

Although it is difficult to obtain detailed and accurate information about the political situation on the central steppe, patient examination of the existing material permits the formation of an adequate perspective. As was shown in Chapter 4, the destruction of the first Uighur empire in 840 by the Qirghiz was a major cataclysm. This conquest did not lead to the formation of a unified Qirghiz state, but to several states, two of which were properly Uighur. The first was made up of the principalities of Kan-chou and Sha-chou; the second was the Uighur kingdom of Qocho, in the Turfan basin near present-day Qara-qojo. As a political entity, the Qocho kingdom survived until about 1250. Its political history is not very well known, but this once-nomadic group, which turned to sedentary life quite early in its history, has left a great number of marvelous cultural relics. These remarkable monuments indicate a standard of living never before enjoyed on the central steppe.[3] Not much more is known about the political history of the Kan-chou and Sha-chou principalities. Although largely sedentarized, these Uighurs never achieved the cultural level of their brethren in Qocho. They were primarily involved in the transit trade between Central Asia and China. The rise of the Tangut state, which desired to control all the trade routes between Central Asia and China, soon brought them under direct Tangut control. By 1038 they had ceased to exist as independent principalities and were an integral part of the Tangut administrative structure.

The later Uighur empires, however, had no direct influence on the central steppe, the heartland of the Mongols. This was the area bounded by the Selenga, the Onon, the Kerulen, the Orkhon, and the Irtysh rivers, roughly present-day Mongolia. The collapse of the Turkic and Uighur empires did not mean the end of political activity on the steppe, but it was a period of disunion, of political strife and civil wars. It was the resulting power vacuum that permitted the creation of the Chinese Border Empires. Throughout the tenth and the eleventh centuries, the central steppe was encircled by more-established, semisedentary kingdoms—those of the Uighurs, the Tangut, and the Ch'i-tan. To a very large degree, it was on these border states that the attention of the sedentary states became focused. Consequently, little attention was paid to the central steppe.

The previous chapter clearly showed how China's access to Central Asia was completely cut off by the hostile states on its borders. As was described in Chapter 4, the small, primarily Turkic empires on the western edge of the steppe were preoccupied with their own intense rivalries and took little notice of the weakened nomadic states on the central steppe. It is against this historical background that the rise of the Mongols must be examined. Because no threat from the central steppe seemed imminent, the sedentary states did not pay much attention to it; hence, the Mongols' appearance on the historical scene was almost a complete surprise.[4]

Shortly after A-pao-chi established the Ch'i-tan empire, missions from the central steppe arrived at his court. Among the tribes represented were the Tsu-pu and the Ta-tan. The Ta-tan were the Tatars, who, under the Jürchen, were to have an important role. Who the Tsu-pu were has not been determined. At the time their mission arrived at the Ch'i-tan court, they apparently nomadized along the Kerulen; later they appear to have expanded their domain to include the Orkhon. Because they lived in what is considered the Mongol homeland, the possibility exists that they were, to some degree, ancestors of the Mongols. In the two-hundred-year history of the Ch'i-tan empire, some sixty peaceful Tsu-pu missions arrived at the Ch'i-tan court; most of the time, however, their relations with the Ch'i-tan were hostile. They continually raided the Ch'i-tan frontier zone, and apparently also attacked the Kan-chou and Sha-chou Uighurs and the Tangut. References to these campaigns in the sources are, however, vague, for they never posed a serious threat to the Ch'i-tan empire. What can be determined from the scattered references to the Tsu-pu during the period of Ch'i-tan ascendancy is that they did not form a united group; the Tsu-pu clans were constantly vying with each other for supremacy.[5]

Although their relations with the Tsu-pu appear to have been the principal contact between the Ch'i-tan and the Mongol heartland, the sources mention other tribes as well. In 1096 and 1097, the Ch'i-tan were involved in combat with a tribe called, in Chinese, the Mei-li-chi. Undoubtedly this refers to the Merkid tribe, which, during the twelfth century, nomadized along the lower Selenga. Jürchen annals refer to a tribe called the Kereyit, which nomadized to the north of the Merkid. On the basis of information contained in the Persian sources for Mongol history, the Kereyit can be identified, tentatively, with the Northern Tsu-pu mentioned in the Ch'i-tan annals. The Naiman also appear as a distinctly identifiable entity for the first time in the annals of the Jürchen. Finally, the official history of the Ch'i-tan, the Chinese *Liao shih*, mentions the arrival in 1084 of envoys of a distant country called Meng-ku. It is possible that this refers to the Mongols themselves, but there is no evidence other than this brief and, as usual, cryptic entry in the annals.[6]

With the advent of the Jürchen dynasty, more becomes known about the political activity on the steppe. An understanding of the entries in the Jürchen annals, however, can be obtained only by consulting the primary sources for the history of the Mongols themselves.[7] When all the scattered material is brought into a coherent whole, the image of a tremendous political upheaval on the steppe appears. What occurred during the Ch'i-tan became evident during the Jürchen. The many tribes—the Kereyit, the Naiman, the Merkid, and the Tatars, to mention only the most important ones—were trying to unify the steppe, each under its own leadership, of course, and to recreate a steppe empire within the existing traditions. During the twelfth century the driving force behind the attempt, and the tribe most likely to succeed had not the Jürchen intervened, was that of the Tatars, who nomadized between the southern reaches of the Kerulen and the Khinghan mountains. It is clear that both the Jürchen and the Tangut felt that the developments on the steppe represented a potential threat to them. Because the threat was perceived only as a potentiality, however, no action was taken until it was far too late.

When and how these attempts to recreate a unified steppe empire began are clouded in myth and legend, as well as by the subsequent embellishments by the Mongols themselves of Chinggis-khan's career. It appears that one of the leaders was a Mongol called Qaidu, a distant ancestor of Chinggis-khan, who achieved prominence when he defeated a rival tribe, the Jalair. His great-grandson, Qabul, entered into conflict with the Jürchen around 1147, when they began to establish diplomatic relations with the tribes on the steppe. Around 1161 the Jürchen launched a series of campaigns against what appear to have been Mongol tribes. The Jürchen did not win a major victory, but the frontier zone was rendered peaceful. Later, around 1167, the Tatars began to be successful in establishing their hegemony over the steppe. Their control, however, was fragile and enforced solely through continuous warfare. One of their challengers was the father of Chinggis-khan, Yesugei, whom the Tatars poisoned during a feast.

The Rise of Chinggis-khan

The rise to power of the Mongols is synonymous with the rise of Temujin, the future Chinggis-khan. The history of his youth is clouded in mystery and embellishments, as the only source at our disposal is the *Secret History of the Mongols*, a work compiled several years after his death and after the major conquests had been concluded. The *Secret History,* so called because, although in Mongol, it was written in Chinese characters, has to be handled with some care, for it is not a history in the traditional sense of the term, but rather a collection of genealogies, legends, and historical facts.[8] Nevertheless, the information contained in it provides us with a fairly accurate picture of Chinggis-khan's early years.[9]

As was indicated above, Temujin's father was Yesugei. He belonged to the clan of the Borjigid and was deeply involved in the attempts to unify the steppe. Among his principal enemies were the Tatars. Sometime around the middle of the twelfth century, while hunting along the Onon River, Yesugei spotted the Merkid chieftain Yeke-chiledu, who was bringing a girl called Hoghelun from the Olqunughut tribe to his camp in order to make her his bride. After a brief struggle, Yesugei and his brothers captured her, and he took her as his wife.[10] At about this time a *quriltai,* or assembly of nobles, was held in the Qorqonoq valley of the Onon. The leader of the Mongols, Ambaqai, had been killed by the Tatars, and a new leader had to be chosen. Qutula, a relative of Yesugei, was elected *khan,* or ruler, of the Mongols. The Mongols went to war with the Tatars. They were unsuccessful, however, in subduing them or in taking revenge for Ambaqai's murder. During these wars, Yesugei was living near Dalighan-boldaq, where Chinggis-khan was born sometime between 1155 and 1167. At the time of his birth, his father had captured the Tatar chieftains Temujin-uge and Qori-buqa. Yesugei's son was given the name of the Tatar Temujin, in accordance with the Turco-Mongol tradition that required that a newborn be given the name of the most important event that occurred just before his birth or that of the first object his mother saw after his birth. The newborn child was said to have had a blood clot the size of a knucklebone in the palm of his hand, a portent that he was destined for the career of a hero. Temujin had three brothers—Jochi-qasar, Qachighen-chehi, and Temuge-otchigin—a sister, Temulen, and two half-brothers, Bekter and Belgetei, whose mother was Yesugei's second wife and who belonged to the clan of the Tayicighud.

When Temujin was nine years old, his father set out with him to find him a bride from the clan of his mother, Hoghelun. On his way to the camp of the Olqunughut tribe, Yesugei encountered a chieftain of the Qonggirad tribe, Dei-sechen. The latter explained to him a dream in which, as a portent of the future strength of the Mongols, it was suggested that a marital alliance be established between the Qonggirad and the Borjigid. Yesugei agreed, and his son was promised to Dei-sechen's daughter Börte, who was one year his senior. As was the custom, Temujin remained with his future father-in-law. On his way back to his own camp, alone, Yesugei imprudently sat down for dinner with some Tatars. The latter recognized him and put poison in his food. Feeling ill, Yesugei asked that his son be sent for, a request that was granted. Three days later he was dead.

The death of such a powerful figure as Yesugei created serious apprehension among his followers, and led the other clans associated with him, in particular the Tayicighud, to abandon Hoghelun and her sons in the wilderness. With almost no resources, Hoghelun began the difficult task of raising her sons in the noble tradition to which they had been born. According to the *Secret History*, it was during this period that Temujin began to display the traits of character that were to make him the absolute emperor of the Mongols. Not long after the death of Yesugei, the Tayicighud discovered that his oldest son had survived in the wilderness in which he had been abandoned. Fearing vengeance, they attempted to capture him. His mother and his brothers, however, saw to it that he managed to escape into the thickets of Tergune Heights. After hiding for nine days, without food, Temujin came out, hoping that his enemies had left. Immediately they captured him. (If the *Secret History* is to be believed, this was the only strategic mistake made by Temujin in his whole life.) While the Tayicighud were celebrating his capture, however, he managed to escape. A man from the Suldus tribe, a tribe allied with the Tayicighud, helped him and supplied him with two arrows. With these meager weapons, Temujin began his ascent to power.[10]

Temujin's adolescence was hard, and spent in poverty. Nevertheless, he managed not only to survive under the harsh conditions of the steppe, but even to begin to form his own clique of followers. When he came of age, he married Börte, the Qonggirad girl his father had selected to be his wife. Probably realizing that, alone, they would never be able to recreate the powerful coalition his father had commanded, Temujin and his brothers decided to submit to Toghril-khan, the chief of the Kereyit. The Kereyit and the Tatars, bitter enemies, were the most powerful of the tribes on the steppe. Toghril-khan and Yesugei had once become blood brothers. Hence, according to custom, Toghril-khan had father-like obligations towards Temujin and his brothers.[11] Temujin obtained from Toghril-khan a promise that he would reunite his people, the Borjigid. Then he returned to his own camp, which at that time was located near the Burqan-qaldun. In the thickets and the marshes of this area, Temujin was able to escape the murderous attempts at revenge by his enemies, the Tayicighud and the Merkid. (The Burqan-qaldun later became one of the most venerated places in Mongol history.) Temujin escaped his pursuers, but his wife Börte was abducted by the Merkid.

Immediately after this attack, Temujin returned to Toghril-khan, and the latter repeated his promise that he would reunite the people of Yesugei. Apparently, during this meeting plans were made to attack the Merkid. Attacked by the combined forces of Temujin, Toghril-khan, and Jamuqa,[12] representing more than ten thousand men, the Merkid were forced to flee and to disperse throughout the steppe. Temujin recovered his wife, Börte.[13] The back of the Merkid alliance was broken, but the pursuit of the Merkid and their numerous allies continued. These wars were the real beginning of Temujin's ascent to power and of the formation of the Mongol confederation. The ascent, however, was not an easy one, and the most serious threat to Temujin's increasing authority came from his blood brother, Jamuqa. After the attacks on the Merkid, they made camp together for a year and a half. Then Jamuqa began to show signs of his own ambitions, which could not accept the presence of another strong personality, like Temujin. Jamuqa planned a coup when the camp was moved. As had happened many times before, Temujin, who had become suspicious of Jamuqa's intentions, sought his mother's advice. She suggested that they should pretend to move to the place Jamuqa had chosen, but that in reality they should continue their journey through the night. Thus Temujin avoided Jamuqa's trap. The latter, his ambitions now well known, joined Temujin's enemies.[14]

The years that followed this incident witnessed the formation of two major coalitions, one under the command of Jamuqa, the other under the banner of Temujin. The nominal leader of both, however, was still Toghril-khan, or Wang-khan, as he is sometimes called.[15] He was getting on in age, however, and was less and less capable of keeping in check the ambitions of both Jamuqa and Temujin. An armed conflict between the two contenders for control over the Mongols appeared inevitable.

The catalyst for this struggle proved to be the Naiman, a powerful tribe living to the west of the Kereyit. To the Naiman, the rise of the confederation under the command of Temujin, combined with the decline in Toghril-khan's authority, was a serious threat. Therefore, they attempted to make an alliance with the Onggut, a tribe living near the Great Wall of China, in order to attack Temujin on two fronts. Fortunately for Temujin, the Onggut refused to participate in this alliance, but instead informed him of the Naiman plans and threw in their lot with his forces. Jamuqa, however, joined with the Naiman and thus felt that a strong enough coalition existed to check Temujin's rising ambitions. Rather than wait to be attacked, Temujin took the initiative and caught Jamuqa and his allies by surprise. After a ferocious and valiant struggle, both the Naiman and Jamuqa were defeated.

Temujin emerged as the sole leader on the steppe. Only one possible contender to his authority remained, the aging Toghril-khan, and it was only a matter of time before he was eliminated in combat and Temujin controlled all of the steppe. The entire struggle apparently went unnoticed in the surrounding sedentary states. The chronology of these events is relatively unclear, and the whole matter is still disputed among specialists. There is, however, common agreement that the most important of the preceding actions took place between 1197 and 1206.

Two important events towards the end of this period can be dated with some precision. The first event, known as the Baljuna Covenant after the lake or marsh where it was made, apparently occurred in 1203. This covenant was sealed between Temujin and nineteen of his followers after a battle with Jamuqa. The account of the battle is deliberately vague, and it is not certain whether Temujin won or lost. What is clear is that the covenant created an unbreakable tie between Temujin and his followers, all of whom were given the most important assignments during the Mongols' conquest of the world. The historicity of this event, for a long time dismissed as a legend, has now been established beyond the shadow of a doubt.[16]

In the spring of 1206, a *quriltai* of all Mongols was held on the banks of the Onon, and Temujin was unanimously chosen as the supreme ruler of all the Mongols. On that occasion he was given the title under which he was to become feared and famous throughout the world: Chinggis-khan. Mongolists and others still argue over the meaning of the title as well as its linguistic origins. It can be translated as the "Supreme Ruler over the Ocean," or, in the definition given by the Persian historian Rashid al-Din, "Emperor of Emperors." With the *quriltai* of 1206 a new steppe empire had come into existence.

The Conquest of the World

It was clear that the newly established empire was not to be satisfied with exclusive control over the steppe, but, like the empires that had preceded it, wanted to exert its influence and control over the surrounding sedentary states. The desire for control was dictated not so much by political motivations as by economic conditions. Indeed, the sedentary states were the principal purchasers of the steppe's essential product, horses. They also provided the steppe nomads with agricultural products and luxury items, such as silk. Judging from the scant references to this trade in the Chinese sources, the balance of trade at the time of the *quriltai* was not in the nomads' favor. Following the tradition of earlier empires, Mongol attention focused on China, the cultural and economic beacon of Asia. For Chinggis-khan and his followers, *China* meant the Jürchen Chin dynasty. Political and economical justifications for an attack on the Jürchen would have been easy to come by; nevertheless, the justification that has survived puts the Mongol attack within the Confucian perspective of righteousness—clearly a later interpolation.[17]

Contrary to the common assumption, the nomadic horsemen did not just mount their horses and attack. They might have done so a thousand years before Chinggis-khan, but if they had persisted in using this technique, no nomadic empires would have come into being. An army, nomadic or otherwise, needs a logistics train, if only for the supply of fresh horses. When planning the attack on North China, Chinggis-khan had a choice between two possible attack routes. The first was the direct route through the Gobi Desert, which would have required a very important, thus vulnerable, logistics train, for not only horses would have to be supplied, but also food and (especially) water for man and beast alike. Furthermore, the history of T'ang-Turkic relations, and even that of relations between the Hsiung-nu and the Han, made it clear that the Gobi route, although the shortest, was the least desirable of all possible attack routes. The alternative was to proceed through the Kansu corridor. Although this was a much longer route and presented a few diplomatic problems, it clearly made it easier to obtain food and water.

This area was controlled by the Tangut, and before he could proceed with the attack against China through the Kansu corridor, Chinggis-khan had to obtain, voluntarily or otherwise, Tangut recognition of Mongol superiority, if not suzerainty. The first campaign the Mongols undertook as a united nation was thus against the Hsi Hsia empire, called *Qashin* in Mongol.

The First
Tangut-Mongol War

By the beginning of the thirteenth century, the Tangut state had lost much of the military strength it had possessed in the time of the Northern Sung, but it was still a formidable enemy. The first Mongol attack, which is probably better described as a massive offensive reconnaissance raid, was staged in 1207. Not many factual details are known about this raid except that it ended inconclusively and that the Tangut ruler, Li An-ch'üan, gave indications that he was willing to come to terms with the Mongols. The reason invoked by Chinggis-khan for his attack was that it was to punish the Tangut for their inhumane treatment almost a decade earlier of his erstwhile overlord and then enemy, Toghril-khan.[18] This can only have been interpreted by all parties as a mere self-serving excuse. The Tangut, more than any other nation in East Asia, realized the potential Mongol threat. They must have seen that their options were limited to resisting another attack, or, following their own historical traditions, to submitting to a superior force, even if it meant breaking a friendship treaty such as the one between them and the Jürchen.

The Tangut court's analysis of Chinggis-khan's intentions proved correct. In 1209 the Mongols attacked in force and laid siege to the Tangut capital. This was a drastic change in nomadic warfare—never before had a nomadic army, basically comprised of cavalry, used the military techniques of the sedentary states. City walls and moats suddenly ceased to be an adequate defense. On the other hand, it cannot be said that this first siege by nomads was a resounding success: at one point instead of flooding the city, the Mongols flooded their own encampment. Yet, it was a portent of things to come. The Tangut ruler, rather than risk the destruction of his state and of its capital, decided to formally recognize Mongol suzerainty. He offered to pay the Mongols a substantial annual tribute and to provide them with economic and military assistance. The Mongols were satisfied with this and withdrew without entering the Tangut capital. The road to China was now open. Chinggis-khan and his commanders must have begun preparations for the North China campaign almost immediately thereafter. Within the

Tangut state itself, Li An-ch'üan was forced to abdicate in favor of a distant relative, Li Tsun-hsü. His abdication occurred in December 1211, and he died less than a month later.

The standard interpretation of the Mongol campaign of 1207 has been that it was an attack not against the Tangut, but against Tibet, occasioning not only the submission of the Tibetans to the authority of Chinggis-khan, but also his conversion to Tibetan Buddhism. From a fearsome warrior, he is supposed to have become an active propagator of the Buddhist faith. This interpretation has persisted even though all the available evidence clearly points to the conclusion that Chinggis-khan never came close to Tibet, let alone became a Buddhist proselytizer and engaged in a Buddhist holy war. It originated in later-date pious Mongol and Tibetan historiography, the first to be translated into a Western language, which created the alleged conversion and submission for purely ideological reasons. When the Mongols converted to Tibetan Buddhism in the sixteenth century, this legend assured the cultural dominance of Tibet and its monks over the Mongols. It also provided the Mongol rulers of that time with a historical legitimation for their relations with Lhasa. The historical reality of Tibetan-Mongol relations during the period of the world empire is that Tibet was one of the last countries to be attacked by the Mongols. Horses, after all, are not very practical in mountainous terrain. The Tibetans, well aware of what had happened elsewhere in the world, immediately recognized Mongol suzerainty, thus avoiding having their country overrun by the undiscriminating Mongol forces, then under the command of Chinggis-khan's son and successor, Ogodei (1229–1241).[19]

The Conquest of North China

In 1167 the Jürchen had established themselves as the nominal suzerains over the emerging Mongol tribes. They must have known about the developments on the steppe, although it is no longer possible to determine exactly what information was available to them. Furthermore, an alliance had existed since 1117 between the Jürchen and the Tangut, and it is highly unlikely that the Jürchen court had not been informed by the Tangut court about the Mongol attacks. Moreover, in 1209 Chinggis-khan stopped sending the annual Mongol tribute to the Jürchen court. These actions could have, and should have, been interpreted by the Jürchen court as overt hostility. Contrary to expectations, the Jürchen did not originate any punitive actions whatsoever; instead, they concentrated on their own internal problems and began military preparations for a retaliatory war against the Southern Sung on account of the actions of its revanchist party. For two years after the submission of the Tanguts, Chinggis-khan gathered detailed information about the state of military readiness of the Jürchen empire, as well as about its political situation. His investigation was helped substantially by the defection of disgruntled Chinese and Ch'i-tan officials of the Jürchen dynasty. These officials, the first of whom appears to have defected in 1208, urged Chinggis-khan to attack the Jürchen; one of them, a Ch'i-tan named Yeh-lü Nieh-erh, actually offered him a complete plan of conquest.[20]

The Mongols launched their attack on the Jürchen in the spring of 1211. With this attack began a war of conquest that was to last until 1234, almost a decade after the death of Chinggis-khan. How far he had planned to penetrate into Jürchen territory is not known, but he appears to have proceeded with caution. Throughout 1211 and 1212, the Mongols concentrated their forces against the Jürchen northern defenses, located mainly in present-day Chahar province. They easily gained control over the three principal strongholds, Fu-chou, Hsüan-te, and Te-hsing (respectively, present-day Chang-pei, Hsüan-hua, and Cho-lu). The Jalair Muqali, one of Chinggis-khan's commanders (later to be his commander-in-chief for the North China campaign) was able to conquer two important strategic passes, those of Hsüan-erh-tsui and Chü-yung-kuan. Control over these passes opened the road to the Jürchen capital, Chung-tu, roughly present-day Peking. In 1213 the Mongols launched a massive three-pronged attack against the Jürchen central defenses, and early in 1214 they laid siege to Chung-tu.[12] While Chinggis-khan took control of the siege, his commanders Jochi-qasar and Muqali captured the territory to the north, east, and west of the Liao River, thus protecting the Mongol rear. It is doubtful whether, at this point, Chinggis-khan intended to invade the city. It was a large city, well defended and well supplied, and the Mongols clearly did not have the desire, or the manpower, for a prolonged siege. A Jürchen-Mongol truce was negotiated, and the Jürchen agreed to pay the Mongols a substantial tribute. Thereupon Chinggis-khan withdrew from the walls of the city and began his return to the steppe. Barely had the Mongol troops left when the Jürchen moved their capital to the city of Pien, the former K'ai-feng of the Sung. The Mongols interpreted this as a hostile action. Immediately Chinggis-khan dispatched forces to attack Chung-tu, and in May 1214 the Jürchen capital fell into Mongol hands. The fall of Chung-tu marked the end of the first phase of the Mongol conquest of North China.[22]

The Jürchen move to a more southern capital did not lessen their problems. As a matter of fact, they became more complicated, for the move brought the Jürchen uncomfortably close to the hostile Sung dynasty. While attempting to halt the Mongol advances in the north, they embarked on a war with the Southern Sung. In essence, this was a defensive maneuver:[23] far-fetched as it may appear in hindsight, an alliance between the Mongols and the Sung was within the realm of possibilities.

During the first phase of the Mongol campaign, substantial numbers of Chinese and Ch'i-tan units of the Jürchen army defected to the Mongols, and many of them were, in modern terms, combat engineering units; thus, the art of siege warfare no longer presented the Mongols with any serious problems. It is estimated that more than half of the army under Muqali's command when the second phase of the campaign began were former

Jürchen units. The number of strictly Mongol troops is estimated at twenty-three thousand.[24]

The reasons for Chinggis-khan's return to the steppe after the "peace" treaty with the Jürchen and the subsequent fall of Chung-tu are not clear. He must have felt, however, that his presence on the North China battlefield was not necessary to the successful conclusion of the campaign's second phase, essentially one of consolidation. Command over these operations was entrusted to Muqali, and by the end of the year 1216, the Mongols controlled virtually all of the northeastern provinces of present-day China. In the fall of 1217, Muqali was back in Mongolia, at Chinggis-khan's camp on the Saghari-kegher. During this visit, whose purpose was obviously to discuss the strategy for the remainder of the North China campaign, the Mongol emperor bestowed great honors upon his commander. He declared that Muqali's orders with regard to North China had to be obeyed as if he himself had issued them.[25] Furthermore, the Mongol emperor granted Muqali several important Chinese-style titles, such as *Kuo-wang* ("Prince of State"), *Ti-shih* ("Grand Imperial Preceptor"), *Tu-hsing-sheng* ("General Regional Commander"), as well as *Ping-ma Tu-yüan-shuai* ("Commander-in-Chief of the Infantry and Cavalry").[26] After the ceremonies that accompanied the awarding of these honors, Muqali returned to North China, apparently with orders to consolidate the Mongol hold over their conquests and, in time, to begin a southward expansion into the remainder of the territory under Jürchen control.[27]

Muqali's mopping-up campaign lasted until 1218. During this period more Chinese and Ch'i-tan officials joined the Mongols. At the same time, the Tangut were actively supporting the Mongols against their erstwhile allies, the Jürchen. In 1218 Muqali began his southward movement, but he did not attempt to penetrate deeply into Jürchen-held territory until 1220. Only a few raids, primarily for reconnaissance, were staged, undoubtedly because part of Muqali's forces, especially the Mongol units, must have been called back to participate in the Mongol punitive campaign against Qwarezm, which Chinggis-khan had begun in 1218. These raids, however, had shown a weakened Jürchen state that offered little resistance.

The southward campaign began in earnest in the spring of 1221. From then on the Mongols began to suffer repeated and serious setbacks. Muqali had apparently vastly underestimated the resources still available to the Jürchen, as well as their morale.[28] Had it not been for the military skills of such commanders as Mongke-buqa, Shih T'ien-ni, and others, the Mongols might actually have been driven out of the territory they already occupied. Indeed, by the beginning of 1222 the Jürchen were on the offensive. Throughout 1222 Muqali's forces continued to suffer serious setbacks, and the Jürchen chances of recovering their lost territory appeared good. Mongol advances had been brought almost to a halt. It is not known whether Muqali informed Chinggis-khan of this state of affairs in North China.

At this time, almost four years after Chinggis-khan had left Mongolia, resentment in the Tangut state against highhanded Mongol rule began to reach serious proportions. The Tangut, who had submitted only under duress, decided to rejoin the Jürchen in their fight against the Mongols. This defection presented a serious threat to Mongol supply and communication lines. Muqali must have been informed of the Tangut defection sometime in 1222. He immediately took steps to protect these lines and prepared to attack the Tangut. The first attack occurred in November 1222. Throughout the spring of 1223, Muqali continued to raid Tangut territory while maintaining a defensive posture against the Jürchen. In attempting to secure his supply lines, Muqali was forced to let the Jürchen regroup and consolidate. His campaigns against the Tangut were far from successful. In April 1223, Muqali died of an illness while campaigning in Tangut territory.[29]

Bol, Muqali's twenty-six-year-old son, assumed his father's functions and continued the campaign. He concentrated his efforts on the Tangut front, while his deputy, Daisan, conducted the war in Jürchen territory. In the late fall of 1224, after defeating a Tangut army and sacking the important city of Yin-chou (Mi-shih, Shensi), Bol returned to Mongolia to pay his respects to Chinggis-khan, who had returned from a successful campaign in the Middle East. While Bol was away from the Jürchen scene, several of the officials who had defected to the Mongols now rebelled against them. Chinggis-khan must have learned about the Tangut defection towards the end of 1222, and of Muqali's death during the summer of 1223. In the discussions held in Mongolia in the winter of 1224, it was decided to proceed with a final attack against both the Tangut and the Jürchen. The destruction was to be thorough and methodical: first the Tangut, then the Jürchen. The entire Mongol army was to be under Chingiss-khan's direct command. The Mongol emperor was able to carry out the first part of the plan, but he died after the successful conclusion of the Tangut destruction. The destruction of the Jürchen empire followed several years later and was accomplished by the second Mongol emperor, his son Ogodei.

The Jürchen empire was the first totally sedentary state conquered *and* occupied by the Mongols. This was a first not only for the Mongols, but for any of the nomadic empires of Central Asia. The occupation, to be profitable, required some form of administration, another nomadic first. In their conquest of North China, the Mongols had been aided by defectors from the Jürchen, and when in need of an administrative structure to exploit the conquered territories, it was to these defectors that the Mongols turned.[30] Between 1216 and 1227, the year of Chinggis-khan's death, some forty officials, thirty-one of whom were Chinese, went over to the Mongols. These officials were put in charge of important administrative and sometimes even military affairs. Of all the civil authorities who held office during this period, only one is known to have been a Mongol. In the towns and villages that had been conquered by the Mongols, local officials were retained as long as they obeyed Mongol commands and requests. Although it seems certain that the Mongols would have conquered North China without the help of these defectors, holding on to it and exploiting it would have been difficult without their administrative advice. Although the Mongols had relied on Uighur secretaries for their administration until the early years of the conquest, China provided the real model on which the Mongol empire was to be structured. After all, China was, and had been for centuries, the cultural beacon for the nomads of Central Asia, including the Uighurs.

The Middle East and Beyond

After the fall of the Jürchen capital, Chinggis-khan returned to the steppe, where he must have arrived late in 1215 or early in 1216. Information about the next few years in his career is almost nonexistent. Probably he was simply enjoying the fruits of his conquests and, like his nomadic predecessors, planning to expand his raids into other territories.

At some point—the time is undetermined, but it was clearly after his enthronement—a mission arrived at Chinggis-khan's court from the empire of Qwarezm, in the Middle East. As the Persian sources make abundantly clear, this mission was nothing more than an attempt to begin trade with the newly created empire; it appears to have been a strictly commercial affair. In the minds of the Mongols, however, trade and diplomacy were almost synonymous, a notion fostered by the historical traditions of the steppe. After a few initial difficulties, brought about by mutual distrust, the trading mission was received and treated as a diplomatic mission. At its conclusion, Chinggis-khan assembled a group of Mongol nobles to accompany the three Muslim traders back to Qwarezm. The message, as given by Juvaini, which his envoys were to deliver to the Sultan of Qwarezm made the Mongols' desire for friendly trade relations quite clear.

> Merchants from your country have come among us, and we have sent them back in the manner that you shall hear. And we have likewise dispatched to your country in their company a group of merchants in order that they may acquire the wondrous wares of those regions; and that henceforth the abscess of evil thoughts may be lanced by the improvement of relations and agreement between us, and the pus of sedition and rebellion be removed.[31]

There is no indication that Chinggis-khan had hostile intentions towards Qwarezm or any of the regions beyond it. The exact composition of the Mongol mission is not known, but the mission was a substantial one and almost all of its members were representatives of the ruling families. When they arrived in Otrar, the governor of the town, Inalchuq, detained and imprisoned them. What happened at Otrar is not quite clear, but it is certain that Inalchuq had no real idea of whom, or what, the mission represented and that he was interested solely in obtaining, free of charge, the merchandise they were carrying. He informed the sultan of Qwarezm that he had arrested these traders. The latter thereupon ordered the execution of the prisoners and the confiscation of the merchandise. All but one member of the Mongol mission were executed and, if the Persian sources can be believed, in a particularly cruel fashion. Although no precise date can be given for these events, they appear to have occurred prior to 1218. That was the year the Mongol emperor set out in retaliation for Qwarezm and for what was to be one of the more sensational conquests in world history.

As soon as Chinggis-khan was informed about the fate of his mission to Qwarezm, he began preparations for a full-scale attack against the arrogant sultan. Traditional historiography on the Mongols presents the western campaign as a well-planned conquest of the entire Middle East. A closer examination of the sequence of events suggests that although the campaign was well planned, no full conquest was envisaged, but only a massive punitive raid on Qwarezm alone. The Mongol army crossed Transoxiana without any major difficulties, settling some old scores with nomadic tribes along the way. In the summer of 1219, the Mongol emperor and his army crossed the Irtysh River and in the later summer of that year attacked the town of Otrar. From there the invading force, encountering little resistance, proceeded through the Qizil-qun Desert via the town of Nur, which was essentially left untouched, towards Bukhara, one of the major trade emporiums in the Middle East. The siege of Bukhara, which took place in February 1220, lasted but three days. Stubborn resistance was maintained only in the city's citadel, which, as a consequence, was razed to the ground with the defenders inside. From Bukhara the Mongols proceeded toward the other principal trade emporium of Qwarezm, the city of Samarqand. They arrived there late in the spring of 1220 and ransacked the city. According to the Muslim chroniclers, hardly an unbiased source, by the time the Mongols ended their massacre, there were not enough people left to populate a single neighborhood within the city. This undoubtedly is an exaggeration, but it is an indication of the extent of the Mongol emperor's revenge on Qwarezm.

Although the forces at the disposal of Muhammad, the sultan of Qwarezm, were numerically superior to Chinggis-khan's, they were ill organized, badly trained, and even more badly commanded. After a few engagements with the Mongol advance units, many of the sultan's units chose to surrender to the Mongols rather than to offer what appeared to them a futile resistance.

After the sack of Samarqand, Chinggis-khan dispatched several detachments to conquer other towns within the Qwarezm empire, a relatively easy task, and his commanders Jebe and Subudei to cross the Amu-darya and begin a relentless pursuit of the sultan, avoiding cities that he did not occupy in person. The chase took them to the castle of Farrazin, near the modern Arak on the road between Hamadan and Isfahan in Iran, and from there to Armenia. Each time Jebe and Subudei were about to close in on the sultan, he managed to escape: one has the impression that the Mongols allowed him to. Under the constant harassment of Jebe and Subudei's troops, Muhammad was unable to organize any resistance, or even a semblance of it. He began to be deserted by his allies and his own forces, and finally, in late December 1220 or early January 1221, he died, in absolute misery, on a small island in the present-day bay of Astarabad, on the Caspian Sea.[32]

While Jebe and Subudei pursued the sultan, Chinggis-khan spent the summer resting in the grazing lands in the vicinity of Samarkand and, as he had done in North China, organizing the conquered territories by using local officials. In the fall of 1220, Chinggis-khan moved against the city of Tirmidh on the northern bank of the Oxus, roughly the present-day border between Uzbekistan and Afghanistan. After a ferocious siege, in which the Mongols used Islamic siege weaponry, the city was captured, and Chinggis-khan decided to spend the winter in the area, which had excellent grazing grounds. Even though Jebe and Subudei were successful in preventing Qwarezmian resistance, as a precautionary measure Chinggis-khan dispatched a force under the command of Boghurchi against the capital of Qwarezm, the city of Gurganj. Among this force were Chinggis-khan's sons, Chaghatai and Ogodei. The city, under the command of the sultan's mother, was captured, and she was sent into captivity in Mongolia.

To the Mongols, the conquest of Transoxiana and of the Qwarezm empire must have been much easier than they expected. Undoubtedly, the Muslim traders from whom they had initially obtained intelligence had exaggerated the sultan's strength. Probably because of the ease of the conquest, it was decided, during the winter of 1220/1221, to proceed further into the area and secure the conquered territories.

On the states of the Middle East, however, the Mongol conquest of Qwarezm had a devastating psychological impact. None of the Muslim armies, many of which were of Turkic origin, had been able to offer any serious resistance to the invading nomads. Furthermore, unlike previous attackers from the steppe, the forces of Chinggis-khan had no difficulty in dealing with city walls and moats. The nomads used strategies and tactics that they had never used before, and none of the sedentary states was able to counteract them. With the defeat of Sultan Muhammad, organized resistance had temporarily disappeared. Soon afterwards, however, his son Jalal al-Din, who had fled from Qwarezm to the neighboring states, began to organize them to resist the Mongol advance and reconquer his father's lost empire. To quell this potential resistance and counterattack, the Mongols went on the offensive. In the process, they invaded and conquered almost the entire Middle East.

Chinggis-khan probably learned of Jalal al-Din's intentions while he was in winter quarters. In the spring of 1221, the main Mongol army crossed the Oxus and destroyed the town of Balkh so thoroughly that the city of the same name in modern Afghanistan is not located on or near the ruins of the old city; in fact, the location of the old city is not precisely known. After the destruction of Balkh, the Mongol army was divided into two wings, one under Chinggis-khan, the other under his son Tolui, and the Mongols proceeded with a two-pronged attack on Persia. Tolui's task was to conquer Khurassan, and he accomplished it so thoroughly that the region never fully recovered from the Mongol onslaught. The forces under Chinggis-khan's command appeared under the gates of the city of Merv on 25 February 1221. The city offered serious resistance. When it was finally overcome by the Mongols, some seven hundred thousand of its inhabitants were put to the sword to demonstrate the futility of resistance. Shortly after the conquest of Merv, the news reached Chinggis-khan that in the city of Nishapur, which had submitted to him in November 1220, a rebellion had broken out and one of his favorite commanders had been treacherously killed there. To prevent other uprisings of this kind, especially in the cities to his rear, Chinggis-khan decided to make an example of this city as well. He issued an order "that the town be laid to waste, that the site could be ploughed upon and that in the exaction of vengeance not even cats and dogs should be left alive."[33] Almost no one survived the slaughter carried out by what was a very small force. After the total destruction of Nishapur, the city of Herat underwent almost the same fate.

The history of the conquest of the Middle East—the countries beyond Qwarezm—is essentially the history of the war between Chinggis-khan and Jalal al-Din. The latter's initial efforts to organize the Muslim armies into a force capable of resisting the Mongol invasion were not very successful. Mistrust about his ambitions and dissension among the Muslims made the organization of serious resistance difficult, if not impossible. Many Muslim rulers continued to view the Mongol onslaught as a mere nomadic invasion.

Jalal al-Din escaped from Nishapur just before the Mongol massacre there and moved to Ghazna. During the winter of 1221 and the spring of 1222, he managed to organize an eclectic force of some sixty thousand men, and he moved his army to Parvan, intending to make it the headquarters of his anti-Mongol campaign. Near Parvan the Mongol army suffered the sole serious defeat of its entire western campaign, and a Mongol advance unit was completely wiped out. The victory, however, clearly revealed the weakness of Jalal al-Din's coalition. Quarrels over the distribution of loot broke out immediately after the battle, and whatever unity Jalal al-Din had been able to achieve was soon dissipated, leaving him with only a small force, not too well trained at that, to oppose the seasoned Mongol army. Realizing that the Mongol army would come to his pursuit soon after the news about the Parvan defeat reached Chinggis-khan Jalal al-Din prepared to escape to India.

The two wings of the Mongol army regrouped at Taliqan, where Chinggis-khan resumed command over the entire force. It was at Taliqan that the news of the Parvan disaster reached him. The Mongols began their pursuit of Jalal al-Din, but upon reaching Ghazna, they learned that he had proceeded towards the Indus River. It was near the present-day Kalabagh on the Indus that the forces under Chinggis-khan caught up with the only Islamic leader who was capable at that time of organizing an anti-Mongol resistance. The battle at Kalabagh was a ferocious one. Although the strength of the Mongol forces was vastly superior to his own, Jalal al-Din put up a valiant resistance that drew the respect of even Chinggis-khan. The Muslim forces, as expected, were defeated, and with but a handful of followers, Jalal al-Din managed to reach the other bank of the Indus.[34]

The victory at Kalabagh marked the virtual end of the western campaign, which had left a path of destruction throughout the Middle East. Jalal al-Din's defeat, however, did not end his attempts to oust the Mongols from his domains. A few years later, during the reign of Ogodei, he returned and was able to organize the Muslim states. It was in vain, however, for the Mongols returned and stayed for slightly more than a century.

After the victory over Jalal al-Din, Chinggis-khan apparently remained in the Indus valley area for a while. It must have been at about this time that he received word of the Tangut defection, for a decision was taken to return to Mongolia not via Tibet, as originally planned, but via the well-known routes from Samarkand. Tradition has it that the reason for the decision not to return via Tibet was that the mountain passes were snowbound and some of his units had seen a unicorn (most likely a rhinoceros), an event that was interpreted as an evil omen.[35] The reality probably was that the route through Tibet was unknown and that the situation in North China did not permit a venture into unknown territory. Chinggis-khan was back in Mongolia by the winter of 1224, and immediately began preparations for attacks on the Tangut and the Jürchen.

Chinggis-khan's campaign against Qwarezm witnessed not only Mongol penetration into Persia, but also the chance invasion of Russia. Having relentlessly pursued the ruler of Qwarezm, Jebe and Subudei learned that their chase had come to an end because of Muhammad's death. For reasons totally unknown, the two commanders turned northwards toward the Caucasus instead of continuing towards the rich city of Baghdad. Thus began what must be, by any criteria, one of the most sensational raids in history. Crossing the Caucasus, Jebe and Subudei penetrated the Qipcaq steppe where, in May 1223, they defeated an alliance of Qipcaq and Russian forces. Their raid brought the Mongols as far north as Novgorod, as far west as the Dnieper, at no time encountering serious resistance. Loaded with loot, the forces of Jebe and Subudei returned to Chinggis-khan's camp near Samarqand, where the entire Mongol army spent the winter of 1223.[36]

It was during the same winter that Chinggis-khan received the famous Taoist monk Ch'ang-ch'un (1148–1227). This visit has given us one of the most interesting travel accounts of that time, namely the *Hsi-yu chi* ("Account of a Journey to the West") written by one of Ch'ang-ch'un's disciples, Li Chih-chang (1193–1256).[37] Ch'ang-ch'un was the leader of the Ch'üan-chen, a syncretist sect which, in theory at least, attempted to combine the teachings of Taoism, Confucianism, and Buddhism. He had been invited to Chinggis-khan's court by Yeh-lü Ch'u-ts'ai (1189–1243), a Sinicized Ch'i-tan who, after serving the Jürchen, had joined Chinggis-khan in 1218 as court secretary and astronomer-astrologer. After he joined the Mongol emperor's court, it appears that Yeh-lü Ch'u-ts'ai attempted to give it a veneer of what he considered culture. He clearly hoped that the allegedly syncretist teachings of the Ch'üan-chen sect would have a favorable influence upon his ruler. As it turned out, however, Ch'ang-ch'un was not the great scholar Yeh-lü Ch'u-ts'ai had expected but an advocate of esoteric and magical doctrines. Chinggis-khan received the Taoist monk warmly and accorded him several audiences. Ch'ang-ch'un attempted to exploit this cordiality to promote the interests of the Taoists and neutralize the Buddhists in North China. Apparently he was able to obtain a decree, later rumored to be false, giving the Taoists tax-exempt status as well as power over religious affairs in China. Feeling betrayed by Ch'ang-ch'un, Yeh-lü Ch'u-ts'ai, a Buddhist himself, felt compelled to justify his actions for posterity and he wrote the *Hsi-yu lu* ("Record of a Journey to the West").[38] His, however, was not a travelogue but a polemical work that severely criticizes and condemns Ch'ang-ch'un, as well as the actions based on the alleged decree from Chinggis-khan. We will return to this problem when dealing with the state of religion in the Mongol empire.

The Second Tangut War

As we saw earlier, Chinggis-khan was back in Mongolia by the winter of 1224 and held a council to decide the final campaign against the Tangut and the Jürchen. According to the *Secret History*, once he returned to Mongolia Chinggis-khan reminded the Tangut of what he considered Li An-ch'üan's betrayal. There is, however, some confusion in the Mongol records as to who the Tangut ruler was. The Tangut-Mongol alliance was breached by Li Tsun-hsü, the successor to Li An-ch'üan. Moreover, by the time Chinggis-khan returned to Mongolia, Li Tsun-hsü had abdicated and had been succeeded by his son Li Te-wang. Li Te-wang was thus not completely distorting the truth when he claimed that he had neither betrayed nor insulted the Mongol emperor.

The Tangut court, however, no longer enjoyed the unity that had existed earlier. While Li Te-wang attempted to convince Chinggis-khan of his innocence and thus prevent a Mongol attack, the Tangut general Asha-gambu, the real power in Hsi Hsia, rashly issued a challenge for battle in the Alashan mountains. Although the Mongols did not easily overcome the Tangut army, Asha-gambu had definitely overestimated the strength of his own forces, especially when confronted with the seasoned and well-disciplined Mongol army. While the war was in progress, from 1225 to 1227, Li Te-wang died and was succeeded by his son, Li Hsien, the last of the Tangut rulers.

Convinced that further resistance to the Mongols was useless, Li Hsien sued for peace in 1227 in an attempt to save some parts of his empire from Mongol destruction. Chinggis-khan accepted and, in turn, exacted a heavy tribute from the Tangut. Furthermore, he granted Li Hsien the honorific title of *sidurghu* ("loyal"). In reality, however, Chinggis-khan had no intention of allowing the Tangut empire to survive, even as a semi-independent entity within the Mongol empire. On instructions from his father, Tolui had Li Hsien executed. This occurred almost immediately after

Li Hsien had received his honorific title and at a time when he must have felt that he had saved his state from a fate worse than life under the Mongols. He was mistaken, however, for at the time of his execution, a large number of Tangut intellectuals and ordinary people were also put to the sword. The remnants of the Tangut population, like so many others before and after them, were absorbed into the Mongol empire. The Mongol destruction of the Tangut state was so thorough that even today, most of the literature of that once flourishing nation cannot be read and its history for all intents and purposes remains to be written.

The Death of
Chinggis-khan

The second and final campaign against the Tangut was not only the end of Tangut civilization but also of Chinggis-khan's career. In the course of the war, which appears to have been the most violent and most ferociously fought one in the short history of the Mongol empire, the Mongol emperor either was wounded or contracted a fever and died as a consequence. There is still some controversy in the scholarly world about the exact date and place of Chinggis-khan's death, as well as about his burial place. Without going into the details of this controversy, it can be said that he died between 18 and 29 August 1227, most likely in Tangut territory, and was transported to Mongolia, where he was buried and where his death was announced. The burial place is unknown, but taking into consideration Chinggis-khan's background, a logical place would have been the Burqan-qaldun area. Unless, by a stroke of almost unimaginable archeological luck, the actual tomb is discovered, its precise location will remain unknown.[39] It was a Mongol tradition to hide the burial place of their ruler. The ground was trampled, and trees were planted on it until the place could no longer be distinguished from the surrounding countryside; moreover, those actually involved in the burial were executed, so that within a relatively short time, the precise location of the burial place was forgotten. It seems that during Mongke's reign, about thirty years after Chinggis-khan's death, the Mongols no longer knew precisely where their first emperor was buried.

The Consolidation
of the Empire

The Reign of Ogodei,
1229–1241

Well before his death, Chinggis-khan had designated his third son, Ogodei, as his successor. Apparently, he had hesitated for a long time between Ogodei and Tolui, his youngest son, after the death of his oldest son, Jochi, while the second son, Chaghatai, was never considered. In the end, he followed the Mongol tradition that made the youngest son the keeper of the ancestral homelands. Thus Tolui was charged with this task, and Ogodei was designated to become emperor. At the time he named Ogodei as his successor, Chinggis-khan defined the tasks of his three sons.

> And whoever wishes to have good knowledge of the yosun and the biligs, let him go to Chaghatai. And whoever has an inclination for generosity and liberality and seeks wealth and riches, let him approach Ogodei. And whoever wishes for valor, and fame, and the defeat of armies, and the capture of kingdoms, and world conquest, let him attend upon Tolui.[40]

Although Ogodei's election as Great Khan was to be but a formality, two years passed between Chinggis-khan's death and Ogodei's enthronement. The title and function of Great Khan was not yet hereditary; it had to be conferred and confirmed by an assembly, or *quriltai,* of all the Mongol nobles. As many Mongol princes were still campaigning in different places throughout the world, gathering the *quriltai* took some time. During the actual deliberations, there appears to have been some hesitation about Ogodei's qualifications. He was known to be hedonistic and to drink wine and alcohol in excessive amounts, vices for which he had been reproached several times by his father. Chaghatai's intervention in favor of his younger brother removed all doubts, and thus, in August 1229, the Mongols had a new emperor. The *quriltai* that confirmed Ogodei was to be the last deliberative *quriltai* insofar as the election of a new emperor was concerned.

The reign of Ogodei is one of the most important in the history of the Mongol empire. It lasted nearly twelve years. During this period, the empire began the slow transition from a military state into a centralized bureaucratic one. Ogodei realized the change was inevitable and necessary for the survival of the empire, and thus he reluctantly agreed to it.

At the time of Chinggis-khan's death, many countries had felt the power of the Mongols, but only one, Hsi Hsia or the Tangut empire, had been fully conquered. The conquest of North China was by no means concluded, and that of Southern China had not even been begun. The Middle East was slowly but surely recovering from the Mongol onslaught and had found in Jalal al-Din, returned from India, a leader capable of providing resistance against the new nomadic empire. In Russia, the fear of a Mongol return was slowly fading, and the European kingdoms and the papacy did not know what had happened: reports from the Crusader Kingdoms spoke merely of a certain King David, obviously a Christian, who, somewhere in the East, had been inflicting serious defeats on the infidels. At this time, too, the Mongols were rich and could have lived comfortably until the need arose for replenishment of resources through another raid. The pleasure-loving, wine-drinking Ogodei, however, was more of a statesman than his contemporaries anticipated, and soon after his enthronement, the wisdom of Chinggis-khan's selection was obvious.

Immediately after his accession, Ogodei began preparations to continue and consolidate the conquests begun by his father. This involved three

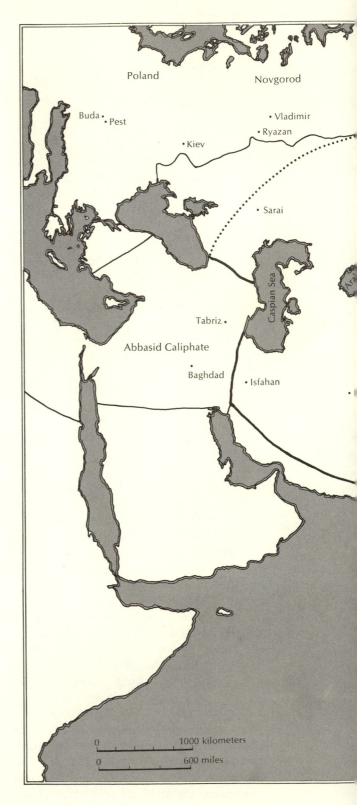

Map 2
*The Mongol Empire
circa 1230 A.D*

············

Limit of the empire under Chinggis

Poland
Novgorod
Buda • • Pest
• Vladimir
• Ryazan
• Kiev
• Sarai
Caspian Sea
Tabriz •
Abbasid Caliphate
• Baghdad
• Isfahan

0 ————— 1000 kilometers
0 ————— 600 miles

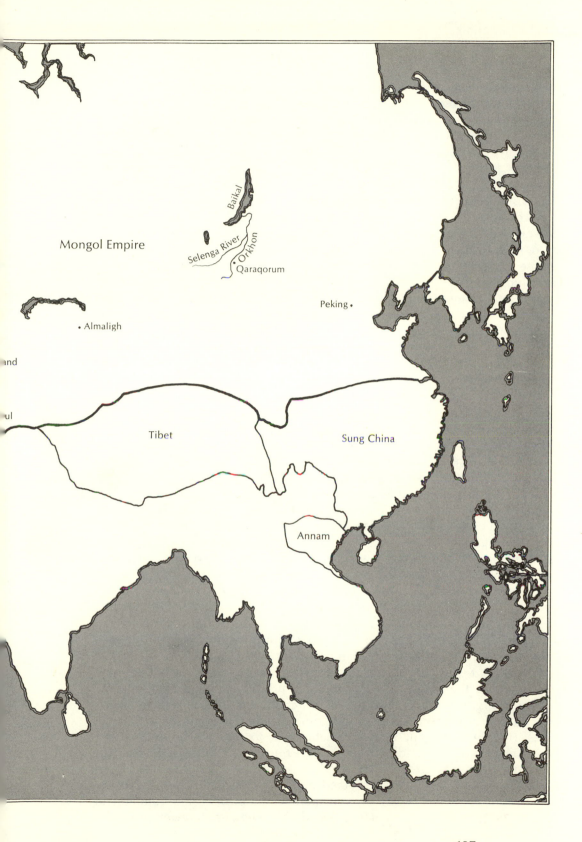

Mongol Empire

Baikal

Selenga River

Orkhon

•Qaraqorum

Peking•

•Almaligh

and

ul

Tibet

Sung China

Annam

major battle plans: first, the liquidation of the Jürchen and the consolidation of control over North China and Korea; second, the elimination of the threat posed by Jalal al-Din in Persia, consolidation of the Mongol hold there, and possibly expansion into the territories of the 'Abbasids; and finally, the conquest of the rich territories of Russia and Eastern Europe. The new Mongol emperor planned not only to continue, and to some degree expand, the conquests of his predecessor, but also to establish Mongol administration in the territories conquered.

According to Ogodei's plans, local administrations were kept in place and given a large degree of freedom, as long as the Mongol court received its required tribute. They were, in theory, under the direct supervision of the central Mongol administration in Qaraqorum, the capital city created by Chinggis-khan around 1220. The central administration was clearly based on a Chinese model, whereas the local administrations were continuations of existing institutions. In creating a central administration for the conquered territories, Ogodei created what must have been the first truly supranational bureaucracy. Its personnel included not only Mongols, Uighurs, and the like, but also Chinese, Jürchen, Ch'i-tan, Persians, and even Europeans.

The architect of the administration instituted by Ogodei was the Sinicized Ch'i-tan Yeh-lü Ch'u-ts'ai. As was indicated above, he had joined the court of Chinggis-khan in 1218 but did not achieve real prominence until Ogodei's reign, when he became the Mongol emperor's principal advisor on administration. Most likely he had already provided Chinggis-khan with advice on these matters, but for that no documentary evidence exists. His first officially documented action took place in the year of Ogodei's enthronement, when he introduced a series of fiscal reforms whose purpose was to bring some order to the confused and rather *ad hoc* system of the Mongols, and to bring fiscal administration into line with a Chinese model. A direct consequence of these reforms was the creation of a network of civil officials. Yeh-lü Ch'u-ts'ai, however, had more in mind than the fiscal health of the empire when he proposed his reforms. Armed with the "decree" given to them by Chinggis-khan, the Taoists, supported by some Mongols in North China, had attained political control. Yeh-lü Ch'u-ts'ai attempted to curb Taoist excesses through his fiscal reforms, since revoking Chinggis-khan's decree would have been difficult, if not impossible.

Yeh-lü Ch'u-ts'ai, after the warm reception of his reforms by Ogodei, was appointed to the office of prime minister (*Chung shu-ling*).[41] During his tenure in this post he proposed the introduction of a Chinese-style examination system for the recruitment of civil officials and the granting of monastic titles. The purpose of the first examination was to provide the state with a reservoir of competent administrators. The purpose of the examination for monastic titles was twofold. As religious institutions and their members were tax-exempt, many people joined monastic communities to avoid the steep Mongol taxes. The abuses were particularly evident and common in China. The proposed examination tested the religious knowledge of the monks. Those who failed it were to be returned to lay status and obliged to pay taxes. The second purpose was another attack on the Taoists, the worst offenders in the granting of monastic titles. A strict enforcement of the examination would have dealt a devastating blow to them, for, most frequently, they sold these titles. Many Mongols, however, felt that the system was too Chinese—that is, it relied too much on conquered people—and removed Mongols from positions of authority, and so it was rejected. In 1236 Yeh-lü Ch'u-ts'ai proposed new, streamlined fiscal reforms. From these proposals it is clear that he had in mind the welfare of the state, not that of the individual Mongol princes. These proposals, like his previous, pro-Chinese ones, alienated too many people and cost him his influential position. With his fall, Chinese influence at the Mongol court declined seriously, at least until the beginning of Qubilai's reign.

In spite of the administrative structure developed by Ogodei, the Mongol empire remained a military one. The conquered territories were treated as such and essentially were under military occupation. During the early years of the empire, the difference between civil and military authority was a small one.[42] Nevertheless, a characteristic of the Mongol empire that had appeared during Chinggis-khan's reign became much more evident in the years following his death. The empire of the Mongols combined nomadic and sedentary features, the most important sedentary feature being the creation of a geographically fixed capital for the Mongols themselves, the city of Qaraqorum. For the first time in his history, the nomad ceased to rule from horseback. At the time of Ogodei's accession, Qaraqorum was still essentially a tent city. During his reign the construction of permanent buildings, especially store and treasure houses and religious buildings of all kinds, was begun. Soon the city became the effective center of the Mongol empire and, to a certain degree, of the world empire. It was to Qaraqorum that the envoys of the popes and the European and other kings travelled. The accounts left by these travellers indicate that Qaraqorum's wealth was striking.

No statistics are available as to the amount of loot acquired by the Mongols. If, however, a survey is made of the economic conditions in the conquered territories before and after the Mongol conquests, it becomes clear that the wealth arriving in Qaraqorum must have been staggering, even if large amounts of it were skimmed off during transport. To this loot and the collected taxes must be added the tribute sent to the Mongol emperor by the submitted states. The city contained artisans of all kinds in large numbers; continuing a practice started by the Ch'i-tan, each time the Mongols captured a city, its artisans were rounded up and sent to the court to put their skills to use for the Mongol emperor. The Mongol state was rich, and it cannot be said that Ogodei was a miser. He generously distributed the wealth to both deserving and undeserving subjects, not by the handful, but by the cartload, to the great dismay of his bureaucrats. Many stories, most of them probably apocryphal, have come down to us showing that Ogodei thought of himself not as a barbarian, but as one of the most generous rulers in history.[43] His reign was only the beginning of the great splendor of the Mongol empire, which reached its zenith during the reigns of Mongke and Qubilai.

The reforms that took place under Ogodei were essential to the survival of the empire created by his father. Nevertheless, without renewed campaigns to finish and consolidate those begun by Chinggis-khan, the Mongol conquests would have assumed the ephemeral nature of previous nomadic invasions. Thus, like his father's reign, Ogodei's was characterized by war throughout the then-known world. Unlike his father, however, Ogodei actively participated in only one of the campaigns he ordered begun, the completion of the North China conquest, undertaken not only because the Mongols wanted the steady food supplies the area provided, but also because it had been the last plan of Chinggis-khan. Already in 1229, Ogodei had clearly expressed his intentions with regard to the Jürchen. At his enthronement an envoy of the Jürchen court was present,[44] who desired, in the Chinese tradition, to present funeral gifts because of Chinggis-khan's death. Although undoubtedly aware of the ceremonial nature of these gifts, Ogodei abruptly dismissed the envoy and told him that the Jürchen bore the responsibility for the fact that Chinggis-khan spent his life campaigning. Ogodei argued that if the Jürchen had submitted in 1211, during Chinggis-khan's lifetime, he might have died enjoying the fruits of his conquests rather than on the battlefield.[45]

To the Jürchen it appeared that Mongol interests lay in the west, and thus it was rational to assume that the Jürchen state would be able to maintain at least a semblance of independence. Since 1224, moreover, Jürchen armies had been able to reconquer substantial portions of what is today Honan province. In particular, they regained control over two strategically important locations: the Wei River valley and the heavily fortified strategic town of Tung-kuan. That the Jürchen expected to arrive at some kind of agreement with the Mongols is evidenced by the presence of their envoy, Wan-yen Nü-shen, at Ogodei's *quriltai*. What the Jürchen court's reaction was to his abrupt dismissal is not known; it does appear, however, that it did not expect war. This proved erroneous. Skirmishes between Jürchen and Mongol troops occurred throughout 1230. In March 1231, two Mongol armies, commanded by Ogodei and Tolui, penetrated the Jürchen domain, recaptured the Wei valley, and began their march through Honan.[46] The campaign had the desired surprise effect. Indeed, contrary to custom and expectations, the Mongols had not assaulted Tung-kuan, but bypassed it in a large circular movement; all Jürchen troops in the town were cut off from the rest of the empire, a devastating blow to Jürchen strategy. In order to accomplish this maneuver, part of the Mongol troops had to pass through Sung territory, for which the Sung readily accorded permission—indeed, the Sung court saw in the events in the north a repetition of those that had led to the destruction of the Ch'i-tan empire. Aiding the Mongols could help them recover North China, or at least substantial portions of it. Most of the year 1232 was spent in fierce fighting. Despite almost insurmountable odds, the Jürchen had no intention of surrendering and put up a strenuous resistance. An unexpected respite was granted them in the winter of 1232 when Ogodei temporarily halted the campaign on account of Tolui's death.[47] In May 1233, after prolonged resistance, the Jürchen capital fell into Mongol hands. Intervention by Yeh-lü Ch'u-ts'ai saved the city from total destruction, the fate of so many others that had resisted the Mongols. The Jürchen emperor managed to escape. In February 1234, in desperate straits, he abdicated and committed suicide. Thus came to an end the Jürchen dynasty.[48] Northern China was firmly in the hands of the Mongols and would remain so for more than a century.

Ogodei's second priority was the Middle East. When Chinggis-khan left it, the area was not under firm Mongol control. The unstated purpose of the campaign—punishment for the murder of the Mongol envoys—had been fulfilled by Jalal al-Din's defeat at Kalabagh. However, the Qwarezm empire had survived, although in disarray, and when Jalal al-Din returned to the Middle East after a few years in India, he was able, at least partially, to restore it. Its center was now in Western Persia. It is clear that Jalal al-Din had seen Chinggis-khan's campaign for what it was, a punitive raid, and he did not expect the Mongols to return. They occupied parts of Khurassan, but their hold there appeared rather precarious.

For his return to power, Jalal al-Din used a combination of military campaigns and diplomatic alliances. Nevertheless, his power base proved fragile. Although his military tactics were often brilliant, Jalal al-Din was by no means an astute politician. Often entering into alliances, he just as often broke them, and he did not hesitate to attack his allies when such an action was beneficial to him. In the process, of course, he antagonized many of them and, more importantly, antagonized many potential allies. Jalal al-Din's careless policies and disregard for his allies resulted in the formation of a powerful military alliance against him, in which the Saljuq sultan Kai-Qabud and the Mamluk Malik al-Ashraf had the most important roles. In August 1230 a major confrontation between the two sides took place in which Jalal al-Din was defeated and from which he never recovered. He was still trying to regroup his forces when, suddenly, he was faced with a Mongol army of thirty thousand who had come to avenge Jalal al-Din's massacre of four hundred Mongols at Isfahan the preceding year.

After his return from India, Jalal al-Din had had many skirmishes with the Mongols. In August 1228 he suffered a minor defeat during one of these battles, which took place near Isfahan. Then, using a Mongol ruse, he was able to draw three thousand Mongols into a trap. The Mongols suffered heavy losses, and four hundred of them were taken prisoner. Jalal al-Din took revenge upon these prisoners for all the humiliations the Mongols had inflicted upon his father and himself. He organized a victory celebration in Isfahan, one of whose attractions consisted in dragging the feared Mongols through the streets of the city and then publicly executing them, to the great joy of the local populace.

When news of the massacre reached Ogodei, he dispatched the commander Chormaghan and thirty thousand soldiers with the order to eliminate Jalal al-Din once and for all. Caught completely off guard by the arrival of the Mongol troops, the sultan fled northwards, since the road to India had been closed by the Mongols. While travelling through the Hakkar mountains, he was assassinated in his sleep by a band of Kurdish robbers. This left the Mongols with only one serious opponent between them and the Mediterranean coast: Jalal al-Din's brother, Ghiyath al-Din. He was assassinated by Baraq Hajib, the first of the Qutlugh Shahs of Kirman. Baraq had Ghiyath al-Din's head sent to Ogodei. Qwarezm no longer existed.[49]

The elimination of Jalal al-Din had proved unexpectedly easy. To the great relief of the Mediterranean coastal states, Chormaghan did not turn towards Baghdad and Damascus, but went north instead. The Mongols penetrated Azerbaidjan and from there proceeded towards Georgia, forcing its queen, Russudan, to flee. After the destruction of the queen's capital, the Mongols invaded and occupied Greater Armenia, sowing destruction in their path. Only the king of Little Armenia submitted before they invaded his domain and thus saved his country from the Mongol onslaught. Thus, indirectly, Jalal al-Din's escape to the north had expanded the Mongol empire.

Because of his unscheduled conquest of Armenia and Georgia, Chormaghan was unable to execute personally the second order he had received from Ogodei: to bring political and administrative stability to Khurassan. He assigned this task to the non-Mongol Chin-temur. The Mongols reoccupied Khurassan in its entirety and systematically and ruthlessly established a military government. One of the tasks confronting Chin-temur was the elimination of pockets of anti-Mongol resistance. He was relatively successful; the only major exception was the Ismailis, a Muslim sect considered heretics by other Muslims and sometimes better known under the name "Order of the Assassins." In their mountain strongholds, they held out against the Mongols for another thirty years; one of the forts allegedly resisted an eighteen-year-long siege. Nevertheless, the situation in Khurassan remained confusing, and Chin-temur's steady campaigning did not prevent anti-Mongol uprisings. Thereupon, Ogodei dispatched Dayir with the task of putting down the principal rebel, a Turk named Qaracha, who had taken refuge in the citadel of Sistan. After a siege of nearly two years, Qaracha finally surrendered.[50]

It was around this time—1232–1233—that the first open quarrel between Mongol commanders occurred; there were to be many later on. Both Dayir and Chin-temur claimed governorship over Khurassan with Ogodei's blessings, and they were close to fighting it out when Ogodei decided in favor of Chin-temur. Later, Dayir was placed in charge of an invasion of India and died, in 1241, before the city of Lahore. The dispute was a minor one. It was, however, indicative of the centrifugal tendencies present in the empire, tendencies that became much more evident after Ogodei relaxed his hold over the government of the empire in favor of the wine cup.

Towards the end of 1233, for all practical purposes the military objectives that existed at the time of Ogodei's enthronement had been achieved. It was then that Ogodei decided to hold a *quriltai* on the banks of the Orkhon to celebrate his victories and discuss the future course of the empire. The *quriltai* took place in June 1234. A series of administrative and legal decisions were taken, and important appointments were made.[51] It was also decided to continue the military conquests, whose targets were now Korea, Russia, and the Southern Sung. The Korean campaign had the lowest priority of the three. The Mongols already had penetrated the Korean peninsula in 1231, but were confronted with many anti-Mongol rebellions. The renewed invasions that took place in 1236 placed Korea solidly within the Mongol orbit. The Korean court itself succeeded in escaping to a small island, where it kept a semblance of independence until 1241, ignoring and being ignored by the Mongols. After 1241 Korea was an integral part of the Mongol empire, and during the reign of Qubilai, it became the staging area for the Mongol missions to Japan.

When the Southern Sung decided to give the Mongols assistance against the Jürchen, its intention was to reclaim lost Chinese territory. The Sung court was inclined to view the Mongols as it had viewed the Central Asians of the past, and it did not entertain the notion that the Mongols might be unwilling to give up Jürchen territory. That, however, is precisely what happened. After the Mongols had conquered the Jürchen, they returned northwards, virtually abandoning the southern part of the Jürchen empire. This incited the Sung to make preparations to retake the important cities of K'ai-feng, Lo-yang, and Kuei-te. A Sung force of fifty thousand men planned to march first towards K'ai-feng, then towards Lo-yang, and afterwards secure the region by occupying Tung-kuan. The Mongols quickly brought these plans to a grinding halt. In the spring of 1235, three Mongol armies attacked the Southern Sung; one penetrated Szechuan, the other Hsiang-yang, and the third attacked Hupei and Anhui. In this first planned campaign against the Southern Sung, the Mongols encountered a skillful opponent in the Sung commander Meng Kung,[52] the only really competent commander the Sung had in its war with the Mongols. By 1239 Meng Kung had halted the Mongol advance and reoccupied Hsiang-yang. Afterwards, and for several years after Ogodei's death, the Mongol campaign was conducted rather haphazardly. Most of the action, in the form of raids, took place in Szechuan. Ogodei, however, did not seem to be much interested in the conquest of the Southern Sung, and throughout the remainder of his reign, he took no action to strengthen the Mongol forces against it. The whole campaign remained a minor one.

The major military action of Ogodei's reign was the consolidation of Mongol control over the Qipcaq steppe and the imposition of Mongol authority over Russia, Hungary, and other parts of Europe. It is clear that Ogodei and the Mongols viewed the Western campaign as much more important than the one against China. A great number of troops were assigned to it, as well as many ranking Mongol nobles, among them the future emperors Guyuk and Mongke. The leadership of the campaign was given to the very experienced general Batu, a grandson of Chinggis-khan, who had received from his grandfather the Qipcaq steppe as his appanage.

The Mongol army struck in full force against the Volga Bulghars during the fall of 1237, occupying the city of Bulghar. In pursuit of the Volga Bulghars, the Mongol forces penetrated Russia proper. By December 1237 the city of Veronez, and with it Ryazan, was in Mongol hands. After the fall of the city, the Mongols relentlessly continued their attacks on Russia, in spite of what is described as a very harsh winter. In quick succession, they captured a large number of secondary cities, among them Moscow. On 1 February 1238, they took the principal city, Vladimir. From there, the Mongol army swung westwards in the direction of Poland and the Baltic states and advanced with lightning speed, leaving a path of destruction behind it. The city of Great Novgorod was saved from the Mongol onslaught only by virtue of the fact that the fierce resistance of the town of Torzok (which was destroyed) delayed the Mongols until the onset of the great thaw. The countryside turned to deep mud, and the Mongols' great thoroughfare, the frozen rivers, became useless. The westward movement was temporarily halted, and the remainder of the year was spent in consolidating Mongol authority throughout conquered Russia.[53]

The Mongol attack had come as a surprise to the Russians. Batu and his forces did not encounter any serious resistance, because the Russians had mistakenly viewed the Jebe-Subudei raid as but one of the many nomadic raids they had suffered. To the Russians, the steppe forces presented no real threat, in spite of the victories of Jebe and Subudei; more often than not, the Russians had been able to repel nomadic attacks.

Batu had to deal with one of the consequences of the Jebe-Subudei raid: the resistance of the Cumans. They had come under Mongol control—at least so the Mongols thought—at the time of the raid. Then they had sought refuge with the Russians and had been involved in the murder of Mongol envoys to that nation. This was a matter the Mongols never took lightly. Troops were thus dispatched southwards, and in December 1238 the town of Sugdaq, once ransacked by Subudei, was again thoroughly looted. Many Cumans found asylum in Hungary after this battle. In pursuit of the Cumans, the Mongols began to invade the principality of Kiev and conquered the city in December 1240. Its ruler, Michail Chernigov, fled to Hungary and was given asylum at the court of Bela Kun. With the fall of Kiev, the Mongols controlled practically the whole of Russia.

Hungary, which had granted asylum to the enemies of the Mongols and refused to release these refugees to them, was the next victim of the Mongol onslaught. To prevent the formation of a coalition between Hungary, Poland, and Bohemia, the Mongol armies were divided into three wings, each of which was to penetrate Hungary from a different direction. One wing, under the command of Qaidu, marched through Silesia; the one under Qodan entered Wallachia through the Eastern Carpathians. The main force, led by Batu, went directly through the Carpathians towards the Hungarian capital. The Hungarians, caught by surprise, were able to field only a small army, and the heavy armor of the European knights proved a fatal handicap against the lightly equipped, highly mobile Mongol cavalry. On 11 April 1241, the Hungarians suffered a decisive, humiliating defeat, and Hungary became part of the Mongol empire.[54]

Meanwhile, the Mongols were equally successful in Poland, where city after city fell into their hands. For a better defense against the Mongols, the Polish and the German orders of knights united under the authority of Duke Henry I of Silesia. By the European standards of that time, this represented a spectacular and powerful army, one, it was undoubtedly thought, that would scare the Mongols and certainly defeat them. The Mongols remained undaunted. The knights and the Mongols faced each other near Leignitz on 9 April 1241. At the end of the day, the knights were utterly defeated, leaving numerous dead and wounded on the battlefield. European cavalry tactics, the straight line charge, and the shining armor of the knight, like the moats and walls of the cities, had ceased to be a defense against the mobile and well-disciplined Mongol army.

The European courts feared that the next victim of the Mongol onslaught would be Germany and that nothing would be able to stop the "barbarians." Preparations for a Holy Crusade against the Mongols were begun but never completed. Ironically, this probably contributed to saving the rest of Europe from a Mongol attack, since nothing could have guaranteed such an invasion more than an attack on the Mongols themselves. Suddenly, however, the Mongol advance came to a halt, and the Mongols actually withdrew from some of the conquered territories without having suffered a single defeat. Although an attack on Germany undoubtedly had been planned, it never took place.

The reasons for this sudden halt in the conquest and the subsequent withdrawal are not clear. It is known that there was a conflict of authority between Batu and Guyuk, Ogodei's son. The latter probably felt that as the son of the emperor he should have more authority than the son of one of Chinggis-khan's sons whose legitimacy was sometimes in question. In the spring of 1240, Guyuk reported to Ogodei that the conquest of the West had been completed, an opinion with which Batu certainly was not in agreement. Whatever the cause of the conflict between Batu and Guyuk, Ogodei recalled both Guyuk and Mongke and their troops in December 1240.[55] News of the recall must have arrived on the European front in the spring of 1241. The removal of these units left Batu's units spread too thinly and his supply lines overextended, so that he must have thought it wise to withdraw and consolidate before engaging in a new campaign. Early in 1242 Batu learned of Ogodei's death in December 1241, and preparations for the renewal of the campaigns were stopped. Batu returned to Qaraqorum to attend the *quriltai* for Ogodei's successor. Thus, only by chance did the rest of Europe escape the fate of Russia. After Batu's return eastward, Mongol interests shifted back to Asia. Europe was not to be threatened again, but Russia remained under Mongol control until the sixteenth century.

Ogodei had remained in Qaraqorum since the 1234 *quriltai*. There, he had begun to indulge in the more pleasurable aspects of his role and to neglect governing and policy making. His interests lay in the embellishment of Qaraqorum, the hunt, and the festivities that accompanied it. His drinking had become so excessive that his older brother, Chaghatai, ordered him to restrict it to a specific number of cups per day. Ogodei did not disobey his brother's order; he merely changed the size of the cup, and the hapless official whom Chaghatai had appointed to prevent Ogodei from drinking was unable to do so. Ogodei's death was the result of his excessive wine consumption at one of his celebrations.[56]

The Reign of Guyuk, 1246–1248

Ogodei's death plunged the Mongol empire into a deep state of confusion. Guyuk had not yet returned from the West and, in any case, he had not been named as his father's successor. During his lifetime, Ogodei had designated his third son, Kochu. When the latter died, he chose Kochu's third son, Shiremün; but Shiremün was still an infant when Ogodei died. This made Kodon, Ogodei's second son, a candidate for the succession, especially since it was rumored that Chinggis-khan had designated him as a successor to his father, but Kodon apparently did not exercise this option. Many Mongols, however, disapproved of the nomination of Shiremün, for obvious reasons.

The most vocal opposition to Shiremün was the faction led by Ogodei's wife, Toragana. An energetic and strong-willed woman, she wanted her son Guyuk, Ogodei's first son, to succeed his father. Support for Guyuk, however, was not unanimous; other members of the House of Chinggis-khan wanted to be emperor. Among them was Otchigin, who was one of Chinggis-khan's brothers and quite old at the time. He assembled his forces and was marching to the capital when he was dissuaded by his own son and by the news that Guyuk had returned from his campaign in the West. From 1242 until 1246, Toragana assumed the regency of the empire and sent out emissaries to round up support for Guyuk at the forthcoming *quriltai*. Nearly four years after his father's death, Guyuk was confirmed as emperor during a *quriltai* held at Koke-naghur in the late summer of 1246. However, in promoting her son rather than a compromise candidate, Toragana had done irreparable harm to the unity of the empire, even though at that time it was not evident. The regency had completely alienated Batu, and the favoritism shown to the descendants of Ogodei did not sit well with the descendants of Chinggis-khan's other sons. Civil war was narrowly avoided through the confirmation of Guyuk.

The details of what happened at the *quriltai* of 1246 are not known, even though the festivities are better known than those of any other *quriltai* because the first papal envoy to the Mongol court, John of Plano Carpini, had arrived at the imperial encampment about one month before it took place; returning to Europe after his reception by Guyuk, he gave the Europeans their first eyewitness account of the feared Mongols, or Tartars, as they were then known. It is known that almost all Mongol nobles were present, with the notable exception of Batu, and that Guyuk obtained from them an agreement that henceforth the position of Great Khan was to be restricted to the descendants of Ogodei. This promise was to have ominous consequences for the empire after Guyuk's death. During his short reign, however, Guyuk's main problems were Batu and the maladministration that had begun during Ogodei's reign and had grown worse during the Toragana regency.

Batu's absence from the *quriltai* by no means reduced the legitimacy of Guyuk's appointment. It increased, however, the tension between the two men which had probably originated in events of the Western campaign about which the sources are silent. When Batu learned of Ogodei's death, he disengaged himself from the European front and returned to the steppe. Upon his arrival in the Qipcaq steppe, he must have learned about Toragana's regency and her lobbying efforts in favor of her son. Batu decided to set up his own court on the Qipcaq steppe, to consolidate his control over that area and Russia, and to await further developments. In fact, he set himself up as an independent ruler, and with regard to certain foreign missions travelling to Qaraqorum, he acted as the Great Khan of the empire.

Since Batu was the oldest living descendant of Chinggis-khan, and as long as no new Great Kahn was appointed, his actions were entirely within the Mongol tradition. However, after Guyuk had become the Great Khan and summoned the Russian prince Alexander Nevskii to Qaraqorum, Batu received Nevskii in audience, dismissed him, and sent him back to Russia. This was a clear violation of the tradition and an open defiance of Guyuk's authority.[57] Thereupon, Guyuk decided to go to war with Batu. Already he had attempted to curb Batu's power by sending a force to Arran, nominally under Batu's control, to govern in his, Guyuk's, name. This attempt had failed, and in the process Batu had executed Guyuk's envoy. Early in 1248 Guyuk began to move his troops westwards. Officially, he was going to his own appanage of Emil, in present-day Sinkiang, for his health. His intention, however, was to make a surprise move against the well-trained forces of Batu. He was informed of Guyuk's movements and intention by Sorqoqtani Beki, the widow of Ogodei's younger brother, Tolui.[58] Thereupon Batu began an eastward movement, and a major clash between the rivals seemed inevitable. Approaching the gates of Samarqand in March 1248, Guyuk died suddenly, most likely of the same cause as his father. With his death the threat of civil war had been removed, and Batu became the kingmaker.

The antagonism between Batu and Guyuk was but the most acute expression of a general problem besetting the empire at that time: maladministration by the central government, which led to a degree of regional autonomy that threatened the empire's cohesion. These tendencies were already apparent during the last years of Ogodei's reign, when he relaxed the reigns of government for the stem of the wine cup. Under Toragana's regency, centrally controlled administration for all practical purposes had ceased. Regional commanders assumed full autonomy, issued their own decrees, collected their own taxes, and failed to transmit to Qaraqorum the central government's share. When Guyuk became the third emperor, this situation was seriously threatening the unity and the financial base of the empire. Intent on keeping the empire united, Guyuk attempted to curb the growing autonomy of the different branches of the Mongol imperial house and to assure, in the process, the sole dominance of the House of Ogodei. He systematically replaced commanders and administrators, not necessarily with more competent people, but with people who were personally loyal to him. He did not hesitate to intervene in the affairs of the other imperial houses: for example, the House of Chaghatai. Chaghatai had been succeeded by his grandson Qara-Hulegu, the son of his second son, Moghetuken. The decision to appoint Qara-Hulegu had been made by Chaghatai himself, undoubtedly because of the heavy drinking and general incompetence of his fifth son, Yesu-Mongke. Yesu-Mongke was still alive at the time of the succession and had been denied any participation in it. Guyuk removed Qara-Hulegu and appointed Yesu-Mongke instead, making sure that the latter knew that he owed his position to Guyuk and no one else.[59]

Through the appointment of officials, Guyuk apparently hoped to restore central control over the empire. In doing so, he did not hesitate to eliminate officials appointed by his mother. For example, Toragana had appointed 'Abd al-Rahman governor of North China, or *Qitai*, as the Mongols called it. In this position he committed numerous excesses and failed to report adequately to the court. His administration was resented to the point that a rebellion in North China seemed likely. Guyuk ordered 'Abd al-Rahman executed and appointed a new governor.[60] Furthermore, immediately after his enthronement, Guyuk nullified all decrees, edicts, and regulations, such as tax exemptions, issued by local Mongol officials or their representatives. He reaffirmed all the laws and decrees issued by his father; documents that did not have his father's seal were declared invalid. Guyuk's reign, however, was too short to have any lasting effects. His sudden death at Samarqand found the empire in as great a state of confusion—if not a worse one—as at the time of Ogodei's death.

Upon Guyuk's death, and following the practice that had begun with Toragana, his widow, Oghul Qaimish, assumed the regency until such time as a *quriltai* could be convened. Once again, political intrigues were the order of the day. In conformity with the promise extracted by Guyuk during his *quriltai*, Oghul Qaimish desired that her own son or a nephew of Guyuk should assume the throne. But the death of Guyuk had left Batu the major force within the empire and the sole arbiter of family disputes. Batu's intense dislike for Guyuk and his followers was well known. Guyuk's promotion of certain branches of the House of Ogodei, moreover, had created bitter resentment among many princes. Batu thus decided that the throne should go to a member of the House of Tolui, and he selected Mongke because of the distinction he had won during the European campaign. The unilateral appointment of Mongke did not diminish the resentment of the ruling families, and many refused to accept Batu's decision. It took several years of both friendly and unfriendly persuasion before it was accepted. In July 1251 a *quriltai* was held from which many members of the House of Ogodei were absent, and it confirmed Mongke's position as Great Khan.

In essence, Batu's actions and Mongke's accession to the throne represented a coup d'état. Mongke, however, had Chinggis-khan's qualities and none of Ogodei's or Guyuk's vices. He appears to have been a temperate man, a rarity among Mongols of that time. The princes who opposed Mongke, most of them of the Houses of Ogodei and Chaghatai, were weak and disorganized. The new Mongol emperor, backed by Batu's armies, took advantage of this situation by physically eliminating many of the younger princes of these Houses on the pretext that they were planning a coup. Those who were not executed were banished to the distant frontiers of the empire. Some serious rivals and potential contenders were, however, not eliminated, for reasons that are unclear and may have been related to military balances within the empire. One of these contenders was Qaidu, a grandson of Ogodei.

Mongke was forty-three when he acceded to the throne, and his reign was a brilliant one. The empire was ailing when he took over, and for several years he was hampered by his alliance with Batu, who for all practical purposes ruled independently over the Western domains of the empire until his death in 1255. Mongke's personality and the excellence of his rule kept the empire together. If Chinggis-khan was the founder of the Mongol world empire, Mongke was to be its first real emperor.

7

The Mongol
World Empire

By the time Mongke assumed the throne of Chinggis-khan, nearly half a century had passed since the Mongols began their conquest of China. From a small group of nomads, the Mongols had become for all practical purposes the rulers of the then-known world. By the middle of the thirteenth century, they controlled the largest continuous empire in history. Embassies from all over the world, including the European kingdoms and the papacy, undertook the long, but now safe, voyage to the Mongol court in Qaraqorum. Even states that did not send envoys, like the Mamluks of Egypt, were compelled to consider the Mongol empire as a major factor in their foreign policy decisions. Even so, at the time of Mongke's *quriltai,* the empire had not yet reached its maximum size. Mongke ordered the complete conquests of Persia and Southern China, which were fully completed by the last quarter of the thirteenth century.

Having conquered a world empire, the Mongols were confronted with the problems inherent in ruling such an empire. No steppe empire before them had ever attempted to rule both the nomadic and the sedentary worlds. A Chinese maxim, probably dating from Han times, stated: "Though the empire can be conquered from horseback, it cannot be ruled from horseback."[1] Of all the steppe people, the Mongols were the first to draw the consequences of this saying, which the Chinese had used for centuries to prove the supremacy of their system. To govern, the nomad dismounted: a symbolic act with important and long-lasting consequences for both the nomadic and the sedentary worlds.

The Reign of Mongke, 1251–1258

Mongke, who had been selected by Batu for his military and administrative qualities, found the empire created by his grandfather in sad shape. In the ten years that preceded Mongke's enthronement, the empire had suffered from a lack of governance. Ogodei might well have coined the phrase "après nous le déluge,"[2] for his behavior during the last couple of years of his reign fitted its meaning. Guyuk made ineffectual attempts at governing, but was preoccupied with the problems created by Batu's challenge; moreover, his reign of less than two years was too short to allow for much change. The regencies of Toragana and Oghul Qaimish did not involve governing, only political maneuvering with regard to the succession. During that period, Mongol discipline became lax, and regional autonomy increased greatly. In the conquered territories, many Mongol princes led lives of extravagant luxury, in the process accumulating huge debts. They had seized authority and privileges never granted by the Great Khan, although they acted in his name. Abuses were rife. Had these trends not been checked, the Mongol empire would have gone the way of the previous steppe empires. Its only claim to fame would have been that it had conducted conquests on a scale never undertaken before and that it had reduced wealthy sedentary states to poverty.

Hampered by the semi-independence of Batu, to whom he owed his throne, Mongke nevertheless immediately undertook a series of drastic measures. In one of his first decrees, he abolished all rights and privileges not specifically granted by the central government, that is, by the Great Khan himself. These rights included the granting of tax exemptions and the withholding of tax collected for personal use. The decree abolishing these privileges further specified that the only valid tax exemptions were those granted by Chinggis-khan. Consequently, a great number of people rejoined the ranks of the taxpayers. Quick action by Mongke, assisted by Batu's troops, eliminated complaints and open discontent. Mongke also ordered that all debts contracted by Mongol princes, whether in the name of the central government or privately, be paid forthwith and to the last cent. This action was intended to quell the discontent, and possible rebellion, of people living within the conquered areas, on whom the Mongols had to rely for both supplies and intelligence. Thus, Mongke immediately made it clear that his rule would be a sober and well-disciplined one, and that he intended to rule over an empire in good financial condition.

The creation of an efficient administration for such a large empire had never before been attempted by any society, nomadic or sedentary. It was clear to Mongke and his entourage that it would be impossible to continue governing in the casual manner of his two predecessors. The Chinese administrative model was ready-made, but it provided for the restraining influence of the bureaucracy on the emperor's authority, an aspect that Mongke, and many other Mongols, did not welcome. Instead, Mongke created a governmental system that combined the centralized bureaucratic features of the Chinese system with characteristics of feudalism in an almost European form. Mongol princes, instead of being granted people as their appanage, were assigned to specific territorial domains, irrespective of the people within those domains.[3] Their task was to administer the domains and to account for their administration to the central government in Qaraqorum. Moreover, Mongke clearly and unmistakably established the supremacy of the Great Khan in Qaraqorum over any prince, regardless of his lineage, and over any clan or family alliance. In Qaraqorum, the Great Khan presided over a strong bureaucratic structure, modeled on the Chinese central administration but, in its key positions, staffed by non-Chinese, whose task was to administer the empire efficiently and to collect the revenue generated by the vast domain under Mongol control. Because he maintained the capital on the steppe, it appears that Mongke conceived of the Mongol empire as one in which the sedentary and nomadic modes of life could peacefully coexist, although this was never specifically stated and the concept had never been tried before. Under Mongke's stern and authoritarian leadership, the Mongols resumed the work begun by Chinggis-khan and their domain became an empire in the true sense of the word.

The administrative reorganization wrought by Mongke still presented problems in that the emperor himself had to make all decisions for all sections of the empire. Consequently, for the first time in a steppe empire, Mongke introduced the viceroyalty. He appointed five viceroys, who were responsible for the administration of their domains and personally accountable for that administration to the Great Khan. Henceforth, the Great Khan acted as the supreme overlord. Of the five appointees, three were Mongke's brothers. Mongke himself was the first son of Tolui and Sorqoqtani Beki, and he appointed only his full brothers. His younger brother, Ariq-buqa, the sixth son of Tolui, was appointed governor of the Mongol heartland, an office which involved the administration of the capital, Qaraqorum. Hulegu, Tolui's fifth son, was appointed viceroy over the Middle Eastern territories and instructed to finish the conquest there and eliminate the resistance of the Ismailis, which had been going on since the days of Chinggis-khan. Qubilai, Tolui's fourth son, was appointed viceroy over the richest part of the empire, China. Mongke intervened in the House of Chaghatai, where he appointed Qara-Hulegu to replace Yesu-Mongke. The latter, caught in the power play between the House of Tolui and the House of Ogodei, was executed after a summary trial. It was also decreed that, henceforth, the rule over the Chaghatai Khanate was to remain within the lineage represented by Qara-Hulegu. As to the Golden Horde, the Mongols on the Qipcaq steppe, it was clear that Mongke could not intervene as long as Batu was alive. In any case, the Golden Horde did not appear to threaten Mongke's personal authority or that of the Great Khanate. When Batu died in 1255, Mongke could have intervened but did not, even though Batu's two sons, Sartaq and Ulaghchi, had ephemeral reigns. They were succeeded by Batu's younger brother, Berke, the second son of Jochi, Chinggis-khan's oldest son, to whom the founder of the Mongol empire had given the Qipcaq steppe as an appanage. By confirming Berke's authority, Mongke avoided a conflict similar to the one between Batu and Guyuk.

As was indicated earlier, during the first years of his reign, Mongke's authority was challenged primarily by the members of the House of Ogodei, who had been left out of the redistribution of power that accompanied his accession. On the initiative of Shiremün and Naqa, two of Ogodei's grandsons, a coup was plotted. News of the plot reached one of Mongke's falconers, Kesege of the Qangli tribe. When Kesege informed Mongke of the imminence of the attack by the conspirators, his accusations fell on deaf ears: it was apparently inconceivable to him that the decisions made at a *quriltai* could be challenged in this manner. After prolonged pleading by Kesege, Mongke finally ordered an investigation led by high-ranking princes, among them his brother Moge. The plot was discovered, and its principals were executed after a public trial.[4] Later, Mongke was forced to consider the possible threat posed by Guyuk's widow, Oghul Qaimish, and her son Qaja. The latter had planned not to recognize Mongke's authority and to stage an uprising against him. However, he had a change of heart, allegedly at the urging of his wife, and submitted to Mongke, who granted him an appanage to the north of Qaraqorum. Oghul Qaimish, however, refused, on the basis of the promises made by the Mongol princes during the *quriltai* of Guyuk, to recognize Mongke as the legitimate great khan. She was seized and summarily executed.

Mongke resumed the conquests begun by his predecessors and temporarily interrupted during Guyuk's reign. Two primary targets remained: Persia and the domains of the 'Abbasid caliphs, and the Southern Sung. The campaign in the Middle East was assigned to Hulegu. After extensive preparations, he left Qaraqorum for Persia and crossed the Amu-darya in January 1253. Eight years later, his mission was accomplished, and Persia became the domain of the Il-khans. The campaign against the Southern Sung was under Mongke's personal supervision. An initial penetration into Szechuan and the Ta-li kingdom took place under Qubilai. There the Mongols encountered stiff resistance, but under constant Mongol pressure it began to weaken. After a *quriltai,* held early in 1258, it was decided to strike a final blow against Szechuan, and from there against the center of the Southern Sung. In May of that year, a massive three-pronged attack took place, and it appeared at last that the days of the Southern Sung were numbered. Then, on 11 August 1258, Mongke died of a disease contracted during the campaign, and the conquest of China was again halted, while the Mongols fought over the succession. However, war with China continued sporadically for nearly two decades. Its outcome was never in doubt.

During the reign of Mongke, the city of Qaraqorum became the true political and economic center of the world. The roads leading to it were filled with people on their way to pay their respects to the Mongol emperor and engage in trade at the Mongol capital. Among the travellers were Western Europeans, one of whom was Wilhelm van Ruysbroeck, the first missionary to the Mongols. The relations between the Mongols and Europe will be discussed elsewhere in this chapter. Qaraqorum, however, had not only become the political and economic capital of the Mongols, but also their cultural and religious center. Travel accounts give extensive descriptions of the artistic activities within Qaraqorum and the open display of works of art. The artisans working at the Mongol court were not only involuntary exiles from the conquered territories, but also people who had travelled on their own initiative to the Mongol capital to offer their services. Among these, for example, was a goldsmith from Paris, a certain Guillaume Boucher.[5] Regrettably, none of these artisans have left us accounts of their lives at the Mongol capital, nor have any of their artistic creations survived.

China:
The Yüan Dynasty

The death of Mongke, coming not long after the death of Batu, reopened the quarrels between the House of Ogodei, represented by Qaidu, and the House of Tolui, represented by Qubilai. As soon as Mongke's death was known, Ariq-buqa convened a *quriltai* and was duly elected Great Khan. He based his claim to the succession on the fact that he was the guardian of the Mongol homeland, and his claim was further supported by Mongke's widow, by the Houses of Chaghatai and Ogodei, and, in particular, by the ambitious prince Qaidu. When Ariq-buqa held his *quriltai*, Qubilai was campaigning in China, and, for strategic reasons, was not able to act immediately. Hulegu was campaigning in the Middle East, and, in any case, he learned of Mongke's death only in 1260, two years afterward.

Qubilai spent the winter of 1259 in China. In the spring of 1260, in the city of K'ai-p'ing, he held his own *quriltai*. Like Ariq-buqa's, it was a rump meeting, as only the princes in Qubilai's camp attended. On 5 May 1260, Qubilai was proclaimed Great Khan. He was to remain in China, and for the next four decades to dominate the Mongol empire from his base in the sedentary world.

At the time of his accession to the position of Great Khan, Qubilai was forty-five years old. He was to be the most active of all Mongol emperors, and one of the most active emperors China had ever known, until his death on 18 February 1294 at the age of eighty. If the period of his reign is well documented, the period that preceded it remains a total mystery. The sources, without exception, are strangely silent about his youth and his adult career prior to the accession of Mongke. He is mentioned for the first time in 1252, when Mongke assigned him the post of viceroy for China and the responsibility for its conquest. From the Persian sources it appears that Qubilai was not in good health.[6] His sudden accession to eminence without any evidence that he had earned his laurels campaigning or in some other manner is without precedent in Mongol history, and, in fact, in the history of all the steppe empires. The absolute silence of all sources for Mongol history, whether of primary or secondary importance, suggests either that a deletion was ordered or that it was a strictly forbidden subject. Qubilai's early career, unquestionably, is one of the greatest mysteries in Mongol history. On the other hand, it is also without question that he was the most capable of the Mongol emperors.

Once he assumed the functions of Great Khan, Qubilai acted quickly, but prudently, to assert his authority. He sent envoys to Hulegu and Berke to inform them of his accession, and a similar mission was sent to Ariq-buqa himself. An armed conflict was inevitable, for Ariq-buqa had no intention of surrendering his position. However, Qubilai needed peace in China in order to do battle with Ariq-buqa. Thus, on the advice of Hao Ching, one of his numerous Chinese counsellors, Qubilai entered into peace negotiations with the Sung. These were concluded successfully, and afterwards, again on Hao Ching's advice, Qubilai made sure that there would be no interference with his communication routes in China itself. For the next several years, until the settlement of the succession, Qubilai maintained a more or less peaceful attitude towards the Sung.[7] While thus assuring his rearguard, Qubilai apparently received word from Hulegu and Berke that they supported him in his claim to the throne.[8] Thereupon Qubilai began his war against Ariq-Buqa, his younger brother.

The first engagement of the war occurred in the former Tangut territory. Qubilai emerged as the victor, and his forces continued into the steppe. There were two more engagements. In the last, Ariq-buqa's main force was defeated and routed. Instead of pursuing the defeated army, Qubilai returned to China and began an economic blockade of the steppe, whose effects were soon felt in Qaraqorum as foodstuffs became more and more scarce. To obtain the necessary supplies, Ariq-buqa had to exact them from his own allies, in particular from the Chaghatai Khanate, the only area with agricultural zones that had followed him. Alughu, the Khanate's ruler, was Ariq-buqa's appointee, but the exactions soon turned Alughu against him. Armed conflict broke out between the two, and although Ariq-buqa scored a victory, it was a pyrrhic one: Alughu escaped and was able to regroup his forces, and, moreover, he switched his allegiance to Qubilai. Ariq-buqa thus found himself without support on the steppe, and with dwindling resources. In 1264, three years after the first engagement between the two brothers, Ariq-buqa surrendered to Qubilai. He relinquished his claim to

146

the throne and recognized Qubilai as the Great Khan. Two years later, while under house arrest in Peking, he died of an illness. Qubilai's authority as Great Khan could no longer be challenged.

Of all Mongol emperors, Qubilai was unquestionably the most impressed with Chinese civilization. In the earliest documents about his career, he is shown surrounded by Chinese advisors. Well before he became emperor, he was working with them to create an administrative structure that would be beneficial to the Mongols without exhausting the resources of China.[9] One of his first decisions as Great Khan was to transfer the Mongol capital from Qaraqorum to Peking: from the nomadic to the sedentary zone. This was an important break with the traditions of the steppe empires, and with what was conceived of as Mongol tradition. Qubilai, however, was convinced that without actual control exerted from within the sedentary zone, a steppe empire, no matter how powerful, would not survive long. The success of the strategy used against Ariq-buqa reinforced his conviction. The shift from Qaraqorum to Peking, however, added an extra dimension to the problems created by the size of the empire. The distances from the capital to the other parts of the empire were increased substantially, increasing the time needed for communication.[10]

Qubilai's accession to the throne of Chinggis-khan had been contested by Mongols on the central steppe, but after Ariq-buqa's surrender, they reluctantly recognized him as the Great Khan. However, when it became clear that the capital's transfer was a permanent one, they again rejected Qubilai's authority. The leader of the rebellion was none other than Qaidu, Ogodei's grandson. Sometime in 1268 or 1269, Qaidu and his allies held a *quriltai* on the banks of the Talas. The decision was taken to reject Qubilai's authority and to recreate the empire as it had existed under Chinggis-khan and Ogodei. This decision, resulting in a thirty-year-long civil war, was to have serious consequences for the Mongol empire as a whole. Nevertheless, it never endangered Qubilai's authority, and he was able to confine the conflict to the steppe.

Qubilai's strategy was in essence the same as the one he had used against Ariq-buqa, except that it was conducted on a much grander scale: the economic strangulation of the steppe. This did not preclude armed conflict—on several occassions, Qubilai sent armed forces into the steppe—but, until quite late in the war, it did not appear that he seriously intended to defeat Qaidu militarily. Only twice was there combat in earnest. The first time was in 1285, when Qaidu attempted to take advantage of a rebellion by the Tibetan 'Bri-gun-pa sect to penetrate Southern China; the second was when Prince Nayan rebelled against Qubilai in 1287.[11] Both times Qaidu's forces were thoroughly defeated. Finally, in 1292, Qubilai appointed Bayan of the Barin tribe, the victor over the Southern Sung, as commander-in-chief of the forces in charge of eliminating Qaidu.[12] Bayan's strategy followed Qubilai's: no direct combat until the enemy was completely exhausted. Thus began a running battle with Qaidu that ended with his death in 1301, almost seven years after Qubilai's death. The war did not come to a formal end until two years later, when the remainder of Qaidu's forces surrendered to the new Great Khan, Qubilai's successor, Temur (1294–1307).

The wars with Ariq-buqa and Qaidu were important to Qubilai, but he treated them as a family matter; the consequences of these wars were not realized until long after his death. It appears that neither of these conflicts ranked high among Qubilai's concerns. Ever since he had been appointed by Mongke as governor of the Chinese domains, his primary goal had been to gain control over the Southern Sung and organize an efficient adminis-tration throughout the whole of China. The Southern Sung officials realized that the peace they had gained in 1260 was only a respite: once the prob-lems of the succession were settled, the Mongols would return. At about that time, however, the Sung court was going through upheavals of its own. An infant emperor assumed the throne, and the reigns of government passed into the hands of the prime minister, Chia Ssu-tao. Although he is depicted as an evil minister and a traitor by traditional Chinese historians, Chia Ssu-tao made a desperate attempt to use the interval given to the Sung by the Mongol fraternal wars to put the Sung government and mili-tary on a sound and solid basis. He failed. The drastic measures he took alienated him from the elite, whose financial resources were needed, so that he only further weakened the Southern Sung by creating more dissen-sion.[13] Hostilities resumed in 1268, and on 2 October 1274, three Mongol armies under the command of Bayan of the Barin began the final assault against Sung defenses.

The massive attacks on the Southern Sung posed serious strategic prob-lems for the Mongols in that the area they controlled had strong natural defenses in its rivers, lakes, and marshes; it was a terrain not well suited to the cavalry warfare the Mongols normally conducted. Furthermore, Sung resistance proved much more stubborn than had been expected. In many a city under siege, loyal Sung officials were able to rally the local popula-tion to resist the Mongols at all costs; often this required the execution of those who desired to surrender. The Mongols were able to overcome the natural defenses as well as the resistance, and slowly but surely they marched towards the Sung capital. One of the most decisive battles was fought on 19 March 1275, near the Ting-chia prefecture. The Mongols defeated a large Sung army, allegedly one million men, under the command of Chia Ssu-tao. The Sung forces were routed, but, more importantly, the Mongols proved that they were able to defeat the Sung's last defense, the river navy. In the naval battle that took place, in which Bayan of the Barin personally led the Mongol troops, the Sung lost some two thousand vessels.[14] This defeat sealed the fate of the Southern Sung. As the Mongols were approach-ing the Sung capital, the court attempted to use a tactic that had worked fairly well with the Border Empires, namely, recognizing Qubilai as their superior: they would address him as "uncle," whereas he could address them as "nephew," and they offered an annual payment in silk and silver. This time, however, the "barbarians" were not interested, for complete control over China was within reach. On 21 February 1276, the Sung surrendered, and the infant emperor was sent as a hostage to Qubilai's court.

The surrender of the Sung capital and court did not mean, however, that the Mongols had conquered the entire South; stubborn resistance continued in China's extreme southern provinces. The Southern Chinese selected another throne pretender, the nine-year-old Ti-ping, a member of the Sung imperial family. The Mongol forces, however, continued their march through the south, and although elite forces were no longer involved, Sung resistance crumbled. Port city after port city fell into Mongol hands. By the end of 1278, there was little Chinese territory that was not under Mongol control. Sung resistance formally ended on 3 April 1279, when the resistance forces escaped from the mainland with the throne pretender, only to have their ships intercepted by a Mongol flotilla. In the ensuing skirmish to the south of Canton, the pretender drowned. Thus, in the minds of the traditional Confucian historians, did the Sung come to an end. For Qubilai and the Mongols, however, the Sung had ceased to exist long before that. It was in 1271 that Qubilai adopted the dynastic title "Yüan," a name derived from the *Book of Changes*.[15]

Although Qubilai had forces engaged in the South and, to a limited degree, on the steppe, he was intent on expanding his sovereignty over other areas as well. It appears that he wanted to be recognized as emperor by all the states which, at one time or another, had recognized the T'ang emperor and which had not been conquered by the Mongols. Such a recognition became mandatory from the moment he proclaimed the Yüan dynasty[16] as the legitimate successor of previous Chinese dynasties. One of the more important states that refused to recognize Qubilai was Japan. After the failure of several missions to Japan via Korea, now a docile vassal of the Mongol court, Qubilai decided to use force. The sequence of his actions makes it doubtful that he actually intended to occupy Japan, for recognition appears to have been the most important element in his decision. Two armed missions were sent to Japan, both times using Korea as a staging ground. The first mission left in 1274, and though it landed near Tsushima, it was driven back by Japanese forces. After a few more diplomatic missions, the Mongols decided to use a regular force. After extensive preparations, which dragged on because of the difficulties in constructing ships to transport forty-five thousand Mongols and their horses, as well as the sudden death of the mission's commander, the force finally set out for Japan in 1281. The Mongol fleet, divided into two sections, anchored off the coast of Kyushu. While battle was raging, a typhoon struck and the greater part of the Mongol fleet was destroyed, forcing the Mongols to withdraw and abandon many casualties. To the Japanese, this typhoon became known as the *kamikaze*, the "divine wind." Although Qubilai planned another campaign, the plans were dropped in 1284, when military expeditions in Southeast Asia also failed to achieve the desired results.

Mongol penetration into Southeast Asia was probably based on the same premise as the attempts to establish relations with Japan. The first country to come under partial Mongol occupation was Burma, where, in 1277, Mongol forces occupied the Bhamo pass and thus won control over the Irrawady Valley. Their control, however, was not permanent; the Mongol forces made sporadic thrusts into Burmese territory in order to keep its allegiance and tribute, and in 1287 they looted the Burmese capital. The main Mongol effort, however, was against the Annamese and Champa kingdoms, in present-day Vietnam, as well as against the Khmer empire in Cambodia. Territory was difficult to win, and, once won, even more difficult to control. The Annamese especially put up a fierce resistance, and their techniques of guerilla warfare, practiced in semitropical jungles, were unfamiliar to the Mongols. The campaign was under the command of Qubilai's eleventh son, Toghon, who was killed in an engagement near Tai-kiêt in 1285, an event that probably contributed to Qubilai's decision to cease campaigning in Southeast Asia.[17]

Mongol forces also made attempts to gain control over Sumatra and Java. The reasons for these campaigns are not obvious. Possibly they were inspired by a desire to protect sea communications between China and the Middle East, especially since the Qaidu war had made crossing the steppe hazardous. The straits around these islands were pirate-infested, however, and Mongol attempts at conquest were completely unsuccessful. They gained a toehold and were able to loot the Javanese capital, but then they were forced to withdraw. The reverses the Mongols suffered in these campaigns should not be interpreted as showing a decline in Mongol strength, for the Mongol units involved were small and the auxiliary troops (frequently surrendered Sung forces) were inefficient. Moreover, the climate in these regions did not suit men from the Central Asian steppe, or, for that matter, Chinese from north of the Yangtze.

From the preceding paragraphs, the impression could be gained that Qubilai was a typical steppe ruler, primarily concerned with conquest. Although he engaged in these campaigns, most of them were of low priority. Unlike many Mongols, and in sharp contrast to his predecessors, Qubilai was not a military man but an organizer, a person interested in the efficient administration of the empire. The only time Qubilai appears to have actively assumed a military command was between the years 1251 and 1260. Even then, he does not seem to have done much of the actual campaigning himself, but merely to have acted as the coordinator of the attacks; most of the fighting was left to his commander Uryangkadai.

Qubilai drew the ultimate conclusions from what had already become evident in Mongke's time: the empire could not be ruled from horseback. From the moment he appeared on the political scene, Qubilai was surrounded by Chinese and Tangut Confucian advisors. That Qubilai would look to China and the Confucian state doctrine when it came to organizing his empire was natural. For centuries, China had been the cultural beacon of Asia, and Mongol contact with the Middle East and Europe did not give the Mongols a favorable impression of their state structures to counter it. China, in fact, possessed the only system of statecraft that could readily be adapted to the needs of a world empire. Up to the reign of Qubilai, the glory and splendor of the Mongol empire were based on spoils, and spoils could be replenished only by continued conquests and continued exploitation. Both options had become difficult by the time of Qubilai's accession. Most of the richest areas in the then-known world had been conquered. (Europe apparently did not much impress the Mongols.) Further exploitation of conquered populations could only have led to rebellions, which, in view of the relatively small number of Mongols,[18] could have meant the destruction of the empire. Therefore, on the advice of his Confucian counsellors, Qubilai deliberately set out to transform the structure of the empire so that it could continue to enjoy the fruits of conquest without unduly and prematurely exhausting the conquered territories. In this process, many Mongols began to assume sedentary lifestyles.

Confucianism is commonly thought to represent a static, unadaptable system of thought. Such an interpretation, which is based on an extrapolation from the state of Confucianism in the Ch'ing dynasty, is completely unwarranted for the period under consideration. In the decades that preceded the Mongols' formal establishment of an administrative system in China, Confucianism was a dynamic system of thought, undergoing the drastic changes commonly described as Neo-Confucianism, which led to a more pragmatic approach to state affairs during the difficult years of the Sung dynasty. Under the Mongols, however, Neo-Confucianism became a state doctrine, which eventually led to its ossification. The details of the development of Confucianism into Neo-Confucianism and hence into a state doctrine cannot be discussed in the present volume,[19] but all the advisors with whom Qubilai surrounded himself participated in the debates involved in the process. Even though few of them have left philosophical writings, their surviving memorials, letters, petitions, and the like clearly prove them active participants.

When Qubilai became governor of China, and later Great Khan and emperor of China, the political, administrative, and economic situation there was one of utter chaos. The Mongol conquest had sown destruction and disorganization everywhere, and the lackadaisical administration of Qubilai's predecessors had aggravated an already bad situation. To the Confucian scholar-officials who had joined the Mongols, the only way to restore a semblance of order was the reintroduction of a civil administration dominated by scholar-officials, albeit Mongols, rather than by military men in Mongol service. This was a pragmatic approach, for it reintroduced Confucian values into North China, values the local population knew and could easily understand, and at the same time, it kept Mongols the ruling and socially dominant elite.

Among the many Chinese scholars who surrounded Qubilai, one in particular—Liu Ping-chung (1216–1274)—seems to have been most influential in providing him with plans for the administration of the empire.[20] Liu Ping-chung joined the Mongol court in Qaraqorum around 1240, as part of a group of Buddhist monks active there. About 1250 he submitted to the

Mongol court a lengthy memorial in which he gave first historical reasons for the organization of an effective administration and thereafter a detailed ten-point plan for its implementation. Four points stand out in his memorial: first, the establishment of an orderly, hierarchical bureaucracy based on merit; second, a reduction in the level of taxation; third, the formulation of a uniform code of law; and fourth, the establishment of a school system along traditional Chinese lines. At that time Qubilai was not in a position to implement programs like the one proposed, but he must have felt that one day he would be, for he solicited similar proposals from other Chinese scholars. Some of Liu Ping-chung's proposals were tested when Qubilai was governor of China. The success of the implemented reforms further convinced Qubilai of the validity of Confucian statecraft.[21]

The administrative reforms were accomplished within a decade of Qubilai's assumption of the title of Great Khan. By and large he followed a Jürchen-T'ang model, since most of his Chinese counsellors had been officials for the Jürchen Chin dynasty. Nevertheless, a major innovation was introduced that guaranteed the absolute power of the emperor. The government was divided into three major offices, the emperor being the acting head of each. The first and most important office, the Central Secretariat (*Chung-shu sheng*), had been introduced by Yeh-lü Ch'u-ts'ai during Ogodei's reign. Whereas under Ogodei and his successors the office was merely a secretariat, its positions filled primarily by Chinese, under Qubilai it became the principal government institution, the office that coordinated all the others. Its president was the heir-designate, and all its key positions were occupied by non-Chinese personnel. The second major office was the Bureau of State Affairs (*Shu-mi yüan*), which reported directly to the emperor and whose major responsibility was military affairs, broadly interpreted, in China, Mongolia, and Central Asia. This office was also dominated by non-Chinese and had within its authority two offices that were of crucial importance in keeping the peace within the empire: the Surveillance Bureaus (*Lien-fang-ssu*) and the Pacification Bureaus (*Hsüan-wei-ssu*). The third major office was the Censorate (*Yü-tai shih*). In the past, its essential task had been to see to it that the emperor and the central administration functioned according to Confucian principles. It also fulfilled this function under Qubilai, but received two extra assignments: the open surveillance of the provincial administrations and the secret surveillance of all lower government echelons.

Qubilai's concerns, however, were not limited to the organization of the central administration. The purpose of the organizational proposals was to restore China's war-devastated economy and provide revenue for the Mongol court. China had always been an agricultural country, and this was the only aspect of economic life that found grace in the eyes of the Confucians, although they did not attempt to promote or regulate it by government policy; trade to them was but a necessary, though lucrative, nuisance. The Mongol approach to the economy differed radically. For the first time in Chinese history, an office was created within the central government with the specific task of promoting agriculture: the Great Office of Agricultural Affairs (*Ta-ssu-nung-ssu*). To prove the importance of agriculture, Qubilai had printed and widely distributed under its auspices a work entitled "Collection of Items on Agriculture and Sericulture" (*Nung-sang chi-yao*).[22] Under Qubilai there was a deliberate development of agriculture in areas that, before the Mongol empire, had been only marginally productive. The main attempt at agricultural colonization was concentrated in the Kansu corridor and the Tarim basin.[23] While thus actively promoting agriculture, the Mongols also promoted trade of all kinds: interregional specialization, intraregional, and foreign. Their unabashed purpose was to generate revenue. The account left by Marco Polo of China's cities during Qubilai's reign suggests that the policies he had initiated were successful. China appeared to have recovered from the devastation of nearly half a century of intermittent warfare.

For a "barbarian" dynasty, Qubilai and the Mongols attached great importance to the promotion of intellectual activities. Qubilai followed, deliberately, a policy of promoting the establishment of schools and Confucian education. In a country that traditionally attached the utmost importance to education, such a policy was welcomed and favored. Rather than force loyal Sung officials to join the government or be unemployed, Qubilai encouraged them to join or create learned academies, surmising, quite correctly, that the likelihood of their promoting resistance or rebellion would be seriously reduced once they were on government stipends. Within this context, Qubilai reactivated the Chinese Han-lin Academy and created a special Mongol Han-lin Academy,[24] and even an academy reserved exclusively for painters. The latter provided the world with some of its most beautiful Chinese paintings.

In China, with its Confucian orthodoxy, all forms of religion, and especially those that advocated a supreme deity, were looked upon with suspicion; the Mongols, on the other hand, were extremely tolerant. Under Qubilai, Mongol tolerance for all religions prevailed and led to the creation of a series of offices, unique in Chinese history, that dealt specifically with religious affairs. The most important was the Office of Buddhist Affairs (*Hsüan-cheng yüan*), often erroneously translated as the "Office of Buddhist and Tibetan Affairs" because one of Qubilai's favorite monks, the Tibetan 'Phags-pa Lama, was also its first chief. The authority of this office, however, covered *all* Buddhists within the empire.

The importance of the relationship between Qubilai and the 'Phags-pa Lama—and hence that of Mongol-Tibetan relations—has frequently been overstated. It was but a minor aspect of Qubilai's reign, but it illustrates how Qubilai, through the careful manipulation of a cleric, was able to control a territory as vast as Tibet (some four hundred seventy thousand square miles) with a minimum of military forces.[25] The 'Phags-pa Lama's principal claim to fame lay in having invented a peculiar script, briefly adopted as the Yüan dynasty's official script,[26] and in having been an excellent philosopher.

While actively occupied with the numerous aspects of the administration of his domain, Qubilai also consciously strove to make the Yüan a legitimate Chinese dynasty. The adoption of the title *Yüan* and the final collapse of the Southern Sung were the initial prerequisites for the "Mandate of Heaven." Legitimacy, however, required also the acceptance of certain Chinese ceremonies and customs. In 1269 Liu Ping-chung proposed the reintroduction of traditional Chinese rites and music. After a study of the Jürchen practices in that area and their adaptation to Mongol requirements, new rites and music were promulgated in 1271.[27] Another equally important element was the adoption of a calendar. Initially the Mongols followed the Jürchen calendar. This was replaced by a calendar devised by Yeh-lü Ch'u-ts'ai, which in turn was replaced by a calendar compiled by the Persian astronomer Jamal al-Din. None of these calendars gave full satisfaction. After a prolonged study, a new calendar, entitled *Shou shih li* ("Calendar delivering the seasons"), was adopted as the official Yüan calendar in 1281. Finally, the construction of a new capital, Yen-ching, was begun in 1267. This imperial city, which later became known as the Forbidden City, was completed in 1292, two years before Qubilai's death.

Qubilai's reign as emperor of China and Great Khan of the Mongol empire was an exceptional one. He was, in the words of an eminent Sinologist, an anomaly in the tradition of steppe rulers.[28] Although the Mongols were in China as an occupation force and intended to remain there as such, Qubilai's reign saw a dramatic improvement in the living conditions of the average Chinese, especially when the war-torn and maladministered decades that preceded him are taken into consideration. When Qubilai died in 1294, China was once again a flourishing and powerful nation. Some of the destructive consequences of the conquest were still visible, but on the whole, Mongol reign proved beneficial to both the conqueror and the conquered.

That Qubilai was a "Son of Heaven" is undisputed. There has been argument, however, as to whether or not he actually was a Great Khan in the same sense as his predecessors. It is customary to divide the Mongol empire after the death of Mongke into four separate entities that had in common only the fact that they had been founded by Mongols. I use the traditional division in this study, but do not adhere to the theory that the world empire ended with the reign of Mongke. Although much more research needs to be done before a final study can be written on this topic, sufficient material has now been published to permit us to determine that Qubilai *was* a Great Khan in the tradition of Mongke and his predecessors.

Qubilai was clearly recognized as Great Khan by Alughu, the ruler of the Chaghatai Khanate during the war with Ariq-buqa. However, the best evidence for viewing Qubilai as a traditional Great Khan comes from the history of the Mongols in Persia, the Il-khans. The term *Il-khan* itself, adopted by Hulegu, is an indication of submission, for it signifies "viceroy." As was indicated earlier, Hulegu recognized Qubilai as Great Khan in 1260, and when Abaqa succeeded his father in 1265, he continued to reign in Hulegu's name until he received confirmation of his appointment as Il-khan from Qubilai.[29] The same delay occurred when Abaqa was succeeded by his son Arghun in 1284. At that time, too, Qubilai appointed a personal representative to the Il-khanid court, one Bolod Cingsang, who was active in Persia at least through the reign of Ghazan (1295–1304).[30] Qubilai's position with regard to the Golden Horde is less clear, undoubtedly because of the present state of research in the field. Berke's attitude towards Qubilai was ambiguous, but there is no evidence of open hostility or rejection.[31] Two of his successors, Mongke Temur and Tode Temur, were confirmed by Qubilai in 1267 and 1283 respectively. Tode Temur actually requested that a *quriltai* be held.[32]

The transfer of the Mongol capital from the arid steppe to the more fertile sedentary area of China does not argue against Qubilai's status as Great Khan. On the contrary, it provided a more solid economic and financial base for the seat of the empire. As was shown in the wars with Ariq-buqa and Qaidu, it made the seat of the empire immune to challenges from the central steppe itself, or at least to the immediate consequences of such challenges.[33]

Upon Qubilai's death, the function of Great Khan passed to his grandson Temur, who reigned until 1307. To a very large degree, he continued his grandfather's policies. The most outstanding event of his reign was the end of the Qaidu war, and the reconciliation among the divisions of the empire after the final surrender, in 1303, of Qaidu's last allies. Temur, whose health had never been good, died on 10 February 1307, without heirs. The last phases of the war against Qaidu were commanded by Qaishan, his nephew. Qaishan, who was still in the steppe when the news of Temur's death reached him, took immediate action to assure that the throne would be his. At the capital, a group tried to promote another candidate, Qaishan's younger brother, Ayurbarwada. With Temur's death, therefore, factionalism entered the Mongol court in Peking. After prolonged threats, backed by military pressure, Qaishan assumed the throne on 21 May 1307. Once again, experience on the steppe had been a deciding element in the succession; however, judging from these events, the idea had circulated at the court that steppe experience was not necessarily a prerequisite.

When Qaishan died in January 1311, he was succeeded by his younger brother, Buyantu, even though he had two sons. This succession had not been a smooth one, and Buyantu had agreed that his successor would be from the line of Qaishan. From that moment on, however, serious political infighting began to dominate the court, for Buyantu wanted to make sure that his own son, Shidebala, inherited the throne. Qaishan's sons were sent to different parts of the empire, far from the capital. In 1317 Shidebala was named heir apparent, and succeeded his father upon his death in 1320. This succession, however, was not to the liking of several factions at the court, especially the group that supported Qaishan's son Qoshila. Another faction supported the other son, Tughtemur. Qoshila's faction was associated with experience on the steppe;

Tugh-temur's was considered the "Chinese" faction, for it deliberately adopted Confucian attitudes towards government in an attempt at legitimation. Both subsequently became emperors, but the rivalries between these factions culminated in what became known as the Restoration of 1328, a coup d'état in which the "Chinese" faction emerged as the victor.[34]

From that year on, with the exception of a brief period between 1335 and 1340, the principal characteristic of Yüan administration was an increasingly thorough Confucianization, a trend that transformed the Mongol empire in China into a Mongol Chinese dynasty, reminiscent of the Jürchen Chin dynasty. Tugh-temur's accession brought with it dramatic changes in the Yüan bureaucracy: from a predominantly supranational institution, it again became a predominantly Chinese one. Although the new bureaucracy was still dominated by Mongols and Central Asians, they differed in many respects from their predecessors; first, the steppe was essentially alien to them, and second, they deliberately fostered a Confucian approach to the government of the empire. The Confucian elite, however, was by no means a monolithic structure. Many factions existed and vigorously opposed each other, and in the process they created a dangerous political vacuum and paralyzed the central government. Forty years after the so-called Restoration, the Mongol empire in China collapsed. The emperor, Toghon Temur, confronted with increasing economic and military difficulties, left Peking and returned to the steppe in September 1368. He planned to return to China, and still claimed to be its legitimate emperor, but he died on the steppe. The events that led to the collapse of the Yüan, as well as its underlying causes, will be examined in Chapter 9.

Persia: The Il-khans

Although Chinggis-khan and Ogodei had conquered the greater part of the Middle East, Mongol authority was not felt with equal strength throughout the area. Mongol control was firmly established solely in the domains of the former Qwarezmian empire. Throughout the rest of the Middle East, Mongol authority was exerted in the form of sporadic raids to collect tribute and remind local rulers of their allegiance to the Mongols; it was a rather inefficient system of rule over conquered territories, but one typical of steppe empires. With the appointment of a civil administration, Ogodei began a serious attempt to bring the area's administration into line with the rest of the empire. But his lackadaisical attitude towards government, particularly during the last years of his reign, was also reflected in the Middle East, where political strife between the Mongol civil and military authorities was the order of the day. It was Guyuk who appointed the first viceroy to the area, Arghun Aqa, under whose vigorous leadership peace and stability began to take hold. When Mongke made his purge of Guyuk's appointees, Arghun Aqa was one of the few who were confirmed in their functions. In fact, Arghun Aqa, who had proceeded towards Qaraqorum to attend Mongke's *quriltai* but arrived there too late, was sent back to the Middle East with increased authority.[35]

When Mongke sent Arghun Aqa to the Middle East, it was clear that his function was that of acting viceroy until such time as Hulegu and his armed forces arrived in the area. Upon his departure, Mongke gave him a series of decrees dealing with the financial administration of the Middle East. In fact, these decrees provided the legal support for what Arghun Aqa had attempted to do until that time on his own authority. First, all privileges acquired or extended by Mongol princes without approval from Qaraqorum were revoked. Second, Arghun Aqa was ordered to carry out a census of the population and to establish a fixed tax on the basis of that census. This action provided urgently needed tax relief for the local population, for the Mongol conquests had resulted in a dramatic drop in the population of the Middle East; before Arghun Aqa's reform, however, taxation was based on census records dating from before the conquest. A new maximum tax was set at seven dinars for a rich man, and one dinar for a poor man. He also issued regulations reducing the demands Mongol officials could make on the local population with regard to lodging and travel. Officials on government business could use only the horses of the government's postal relay stations. A maximum of fourteen horses was allowed, and it was strictly forbidden to seize horses or other pack animals from the local population. Merchants, who had been illegally making use of the free facilities of the postal relay stations, henceforth had to provide for their transportation from their own resources. Arghun Aqa was able to defuse the hostility which could have threatened Mongol control over the area. He continued his administration until the arrival of Hulegu near Samarqand in the fall of 1255, when he turned the government of Persia over to Mongke's brother and the first official Il-khan, or Viceroy. He continued to function in the Il-khanid administration until his death in 1275.[36]

Hulegu's general orders were to complete the conquests begun by Chinggis-khan and to consolidate the subdivisions of the Middle East into a single administrative unit. To do this required three military campaigns and one administrative task. The first item on Hulegu's agenda was the elimination of the Ismaili sect, a powerful sect viewed by other Muslims as heretics. Their elimination would give the "heathen" Mongols stronger support in Islamic lands. Although the Ismailis did not occupy a specific territory, they nevertheless formed a political and spiritual state, centered in different mountain strongholds, heavily fortified, built in strategic locations, and able to withstand prolonged siege warfare. The second—an almost routine task for Mongol forces—was to repress rebellious movements in Kurdistan and Lur. The third task was, in fact, an extension of the conquest in that it involved obtaining the submission of the center of Islamic intellectual and spiritual dominance, the 'Abbasid caliph in Baghdad. As long as the caliph had not recognized Mongol suzerainty, the Islamic population in the conquered lands had an allegiance to a higher authority than the Mongols. Fourth and finally, Hulegu was to arrange fiscal and economic administration so that the Mongols would derive maximum profit from the conquered areas.

It was not until two years after his appointment that Hulegu left the Mongol homeland; it can only be assumed that during this time he was preparing for the campaign. In any case, he did not appear to be in a great hurry to accomplish his task, for it took him and his army nearly two more years to arrive in the vicinity of Samarqand. From Samarqand he continued towards Kish, where, in the fall of 1255, Arghun Aqa joined him and where he established his temporary headquarters. Thereupon Hulegu sent messengers throughout Persia to inform all local rulers, Mongol and non-Mongol alike, of his presence as the viceroy appointed by the Great Khan. At the same time, they were ordered to provide him with assistance in the campaign against the Ismailis; any refusal to do so would be punished in the customary manner: by destruction. Once this was accomplished, Hulegu established a temporary capital in Tus.

The war between the Mongols and the Ismailis was one of nerves, each side attempting to avoid open battle. Hulegu sent several embassies to the Ismaili Grand Master, Khur-shah Rukn al-Din b. Muhammad III, ordering him to surrender to Mongol authority and to begin dismantling the mountain castles. His responses were not outright rejections, but evasive maneuvers aimed at gaining time. By promising Rukn al-Din safe passage, Hulegu attempted to lure him into a false sense of security and thus to obtain his surrender without a major battle; but Rukn al-Din was waiting for winter, when snow would make an attack impossible. The winter of 1255, however, was exceptionally mild. Confronted with Rukn al-Din's consistent refusal, Hulegu ordered a siege of the nearly impregnable castle of Maimun-Diz, Rukn al-Din's residence. The castle was subjected to heavy bombardment. Nearly a year later, on or about 19 November 1256, Rukn al-Din surrendered, having been promised clemency. Immediately the dismantling of the castle was begun; its famous library and all its astronomical instruments were saved from destruction on orders of the "barbarian" Hulegu. Rukn al-Din's surrender made it relatively easy for Hulegu to obtain the surrender of the other Ismaili castles, many of which could have withstood several years' siege. As the leader of the sect, Rukn al-Din was sent to Mongke's court, but was assassinated on the road to Qaraqorum. Rukn al-Din's departure from Hulegu's camp was the signal for the massacre of all the Ismailis, women and children included. This marked virtually the end of the Ismaili sect.

Hulegu spent the remainder of that winter on the grazing lands near Qazvin. In the spring of 1257, at a deliberately slow pace, his forces began their move towards the capital of the 'Abbasid caliph and of Islamic orthodoxy, the splendid city of Baghdad. In Hamadan Hulegu's army set up camp and was joined by other Mongol forces stationed throughout the Middle East. For some time thereafter, Mongol forces travelled back and forth between Hamadan and Tabriz. The sources offer no reason either for this crisscrossing of Central Persia or for the slow advance of the Mongol forces, but in this rebellion-prone area, Hulegu most likely wanted to impress upon the local officials and population that any resistance against Mongol rule would be in vain. Furthermore, as he appears to have done during his slow trip from Qaraqorum, he must have occupied himself with consolidating the Mongol administration and centralizing it in the hands of the Il-khan.

In the late summer of 1257, Hulegu's attention again focused on Baghdad and several missions travelled back and forth between that city and Tabriz. Hulegu's ambassador carried a message ordering the caliph, al-Musta'zim, to formally submit to the Mongols, either by coming to Hulegu in person or by sending his highest officials. It is extremely doubtful that, at that time, the caliph would not have known who the Mongols were and what military might and determination they possessed. In any case, his reply to Hulegu was one of utter contempt. The reaction to such an answer came as expected. In the fall of 1257, the Mongols formally decided to attack Baghdad and began their march through Iraqi territory, in the process expanding the Mongol empire. On or about 16 January 1258, the Mongol army crossed the Tigris and immediately thereafter routed the caliph's armies. By 22 January the Mongol troops were in the suburbs of Baghdad. The attack on the city itself began on 29 January and, after a serious resistance, it fell into Mongol hands on 13 February. To obtain the city's surrender, Hulegu had promised safe passage to those citizens who left it voluntarily. As they left, however, they were slaughtered one by one. Hulegu allowed his forces to loot Baghdad, the richest city in the Middle East, from 13 February to 20 February. The caliph, al-Musta'zim, was put to death in the Mongol fashion, that is, without shedding a drop of his blood on the soil. The center of the Islamic world was now in the hands of the Mongols and the Il-khan, a non-Muslim, was the undisputed master of the Middle East. The only exceptions were the Mamluk possessions in Syria, in particular the wealthy city of Damascus.[37]

After the destruction of Baghdad and the 'Abbasid caliphate, Hulegu returned to Tabriz, the city his son Abaqa had made his principal residence. There plans were made to invade Syria and to seize Damascus. The Mongol army set out for Syria in the early winter of 1259. On 18 January 1260, the inhabitants of Aleppo, to the north of Damascus, suddenly found themselves besieged by the Mongol army. The siege lasted a week, and when it ended, Aleppo was subjected to the same systematic plunder and slaughter as Baghdad. News of the destruction of Aleppo spread like wildfire. City after city surrendered to the Mongols, and on 1 March 1260, without having had to give combat, the Mongols entered Damascus. From Damascus, the Mongols pushed further into Palestine, and by the summer of that year had penetrated as far as Gaza. Hulegu clearly intended to penetrate Egypt, the heart of the Mamluk empire. Suddenly, in a manner reminiscent of Batu's European campaign, the Mongol advance ground to a halt. Apparently it was near Gaza that the news reached Hulegu that his brother Mongke had died. He left behind a rearguard of some five thousand men under the command of one of his best generals, Kit-buqa, and immediately returned to Tabriz. Towards the end of the summer of 1260, he learned that Qubilai had become the Great Khan. Thereupon Hulegu abandoned plans to return to the steppe, at least for the time being.

Before returning to Tabriz, Hulegu had sent ambassadors to the Mamluk ruler in Egypt with the standard Mongol message: either submit into allegiance or face the consequences of a massive invasion. The Mamluks, however, were not a typical Islamic state, but a well-organized, professional military one, founded by Türks, descendants of the steppe; in the Islamic world, the Mamluks were the only serious military force. Hulegu's envoys were summarily executed, and the Mamluk armies were readied to drive the arrogant Mongol out of Syria. Kit-buqa's small rearguard force was no match for the large Mamluk army. Vastly outnumbered, the small Mongol army put up a ferocious resistance, but on 3 September, in a battle at 'Ain Jalat, they were completely defeated.[38] Kit-buqa was captured and executed. As a consequence of this defeat, the remainder of the Mongol forces in Syria left for Persia. Word of Kit-buqa's defeat and the disastrous end of the Syrian campaign reached Hulegu at about the same time as the news of Qubilai's enthronement.

The victory scored by the Mamluks was, in fact, a minor one. A Mongol counterattack was not forthcoming, even though they had killed Mongol ambassadors and a Mongol commander. What the outcome would have been, at that time, of a full-scale battle between the Mamluk army and the main Mongol army cannot be determined; chances are, however, that the Mongols would have won. The primary reason no Mongol counterattack took place was that the conflict between Qubilai and Ariq-buqa had repercussions within the Il-khanid domain, forcing Hulegu to concentrate his forces against the Golden Horde. Berke, then the Horde's ruler, felt that Hulegu was encroaching upon Arran and Adherbaidjan, areas he considered his territories. When Chinggis-khan gave the Qipcaq steppe as an appanage to his son Jochi, it apparently included these two territories. The Il-khan, on the other hand, had received administrative authority over them from Mongke. With Mongke's restraining influence gone, the Golden Horde was determined to regain control. Moreover, since the fall of Baghdad, mistrust had begun to grow between the two khans.[39] War broke out in the fall of 1262, and on 13 January 1263, Berke's forces defeated Hulegu's. The Golden Horde had won the battle, but not the war: several years later, Hulegu's successor was to drive the Horde out. The main consequence of the battle was that it assured the Mamluk state that no attack would be forthcoming from the Mongols in Persia. Furthermore, as Berke had converted to Islam, the Mamluks sent a mission to the Horde to establish diplomatic relations and come to an agreement regarding their common enemy, the Il-khan.[40]

Hulegu died on 8 February 1265 in his winter headquarters on the Jaghatu. His son Abaqa was appointed as his successor. For a brief period following Hulegu's death, it appeared that civil war over the succession was imminent. Abaqa's brother, Yashmut, intended to challenge the succession but withdrew when he found that he did not have strong support among the other princes. Abaqa assumed the Il-khanate on 19 June 1265; as was indicated above, until he received confirmation from the Great Khan, he acted in Hulegu's name. He kept his capital at Tabriz and a second residence on the Jaghatu. There, on 20 November 1270, Abaqa was officially enthroned as Il-khan after word arrived of the confirmation of his title.[41]

Almost immediately after his accession to the throne in 1265, the war between the Golden Horde and the Il-khanid empire flared up. This time, however, the tide of battle went in favor of the Il-khan. Berke's troops were defeated, and while escaping towards Tiflis, Berke died. Abaqa, not wanting to prolong the hostilities, released important prisoners he had taken during combat, among them Mongke-Temur, Berke's successor. Abaqa then went to spend the winter of 1266/67 in the Mazandaran area. Peace had been established in Persia; it was, however, of short duration. In 1269 the Qaidu-Qubilai war spilled over into the Il-khanid domains in the form of an invasion by Qaidu's principal ally, Baraq, the ruler of the Chaghatai Khanate. On Qaidu's instructions, Baraq set out to conquer the Badghis meadows in Khurassan. Although Abaqa was willing to make peace with Baraq on terms favorable to the latter, Baraq rejected his overtures, and Abaqa was forced into a full-fledged war. On 22 July 1270, in what became known as the Battle of Herat, Baraq's forces were defeated, and he himself barely managed to escape, only to be executed soon after, apparently on Qaidu's orders. From the time of the Battle of Herat, the eastern border of the Il-khanid domain remained relatively peaceful until the rise of Timur-i-leng, Tamerlane, at the end of the fourteenth century.

Foremost in the plans of Abaqa, even before Baraq's defeat, was the renewal of the Syrian conquest and retaliation against the Mamluks, and his resolve was strengthened by the fact that the Mamluks had been raiding the Il-khanid border. He appointed his brother Mongke-temur, who was quite inexperienced in warfare, commander of the campaign. The army was ordered to advance in September 1281, and in the vicinity of Hims, the Mamluk and Mongol armies gave battle. Abaqa's mistake in choosing his commander was immediately evident. Inexperienced and ill advised, Mongke-temur was unable to respond to the enemy's maneuvers, and on 29 October 1281, the Mongol army suffered a disastrous defeat. When he was informed of this defeat, Abaqa ordered the responsible officials punished, stated that he would lead the campaign personally the next year, and went hunting. After a trial of officials in Baghdad, Abaqa went to Hamadan, where he died on 1 April 1282.

Abaqa's was to be the first, but not the last, contested succession in the history of the Il-khanid empire. The conflict was between Teguder, a son of Hulegu, and Arghun, Abaqa's son. In the negotiations that followed Abaqa's death, Teguder was chosen as the successor on 6 May 1282 and enthroned on 23 June 1283. Arghun reluctantly accepted the outcome of what can be considered a *quriltai*. However, quite soon after the official enthronement ceremonies, open antagonism flared up.[42] In the spring of 1284, Teguder decided to move militarily against Arghun, who was deliberately ignoring and provoking the official Il-khan. The civil war lasted through the spring and early summer of that year and ended with Teguder's defeat. He was taken prisoner and executed on 10 August 1284, whereupon Arghun was unanimously elected as his successor. Teguder's reign was of little consequence in the history of the Il-khans, for it was Arghun who acted as the policy maker during it. The only noteworthy event, other than the war itself, was the fact that Teguder became the first Il-khan to embrace Islam; hence, the Persian sources refer to him by his Islamic name, Ahmad.[43]

Like Teguder, Arghun had two enthronement ceremonies, the first when Teguder was executed, the second on 7 April 1286, when his envoys returned from Qubilai's court with the official decree appointing him Il-khan.[44] Arghun's objection to Teguder's appointment had been that Abaqa had designated him (Arghun) as his successor, and the shortness of the interval between Arghun's unofficial and official enthronements tends to support this allegation.

Although, in a sense, Arghun had gained the throne through a military coup, his reign was devoid of major military undertakings. There were a few minor conflicts with the Golden Horde, again over the possession of Arran and Adherbaidjan, but they were only raids and in no way threatened the empire. In February 1288 an armed clash took place with a raiding party of some thirty thousand men sent by Qaidu. Il-khanid forces were able to push them back, but not until they had looted Balkh and Merv.

The most serious threat to Il-khanid rule came from within: the rebellion of the governor of Khurassan, Nauruz, the son of Arghun Aqa. Neither the causes nor the evolution of the rebellion are known. There was some speculation that Ghazan, Arghun's son, was behind the rebellion, for Nauruz was the second-in-command of Ghazan's armies. This theory has it that Nauruz was testing the waters for Ghazan's attempt to remove his ailing father from the throne. Serious confusion arose when, after some initial successes, Nauruz turned against Ghazan himself, for a while threatening the empire's survival. Towards the end of 1289, however, the joint forces of Arghun and Ghazan were able to contain the rebellion. It was, however, not repressed until the reign of Ghazan and then in a manner that tended to confirm earlier suspicions about the affair: Nauruz surrendered to Ghazan and was not punished.

One of the leading personalities of Arghun's reign was a Jewish physician, Sa'ud al-Daula, who obtained Arghun's confidence in 1289 and soon was the major official at the court. His principal task was the financial administration of the empire and, as was customary, he used his position to improve the standing of his family, appointing one of his brothers governor of Baghdad, a very lucrative position. Sa'ud al-Daula was one of only three officials who had access to Arghun. These two elements combined to make him the focus of discontent at the Il-khanid court, especially after Arghun's withdrawal from active government increased Sa'ud al-Daula's power.

Arghun was in search of the elixir of longevity, the lodestone of Asian alchemists, and on the advice of either a Tibetan or a Kashmiri Tantric monk he drank, for eight months, a potion composed primarily of mercury and sulphur. He became ill, his behavior became erratic, and plots were spun to remove him and all those directly associated with him, especially those viewed as having been, at least in part, responsible for his illness. Arghun died on 10 March 1291. In May the latent resentment against government officials broke out, and Sa'ud al-Daula was arrested and executed. His execution marked the beginning of the looting of the houses of all those even remotely associated with him.[45]

With this event began a chaotic period in Il-khanid history that lasted until 1295. Not only was the empire torn apart by the lingering Nauruz rebellion and the civil disorders that followed Arghun's death, but there were three contenders for the Il-khanid throne: Arghun's brother Geikhatu, who resided in Rum; Ghazan, then campaigning in Khurassan; and Baidu, Arghun's cousin, who was in Baghdad. A *quriltai* was held to choose a successor, but in reality, political intrigues were the means of selection. Ghazan was confronted with a *fait accompli,* for he was informed of the *quriltai* after it took place, and Baidu did not have strong military backing. Thus, on 23 July 1291, Geikhatu became the Il-khan. There is no indication that he sought confirmation from Qubilai.

Geikhatu's accession to the throne inaugurated one of the darkest periods in Mongol history. The Mongols certainly were not a prudish people, but all contemporaries describe Geikhatu as a profoundly immoral person. In the words of the Syriac historian Bar Hebraeus:

> He had no thought for anything except the things that were necessary for Kings and which they were bound to have and how he could get possession of the sons and daughters of the nobles and have intercourse with them. . . . And very many chaste women among the wives of the nobles fled from him, and others removed their sons and daughters and sent them away to remote districts. But they were unable to save themselves from his hands or to escape from the shameful acts which he committed with them.[46]

Stories about Geikhatu's vices may be exaggerated; however, it is indisputable that during his reign of less than four years the Il-khanid empire came close to collapse.

Although Persia had never fully recovered from the economic devastation of the Mongol conquest, at least by the time of Arghun's reign conditions had begun to stabilize. Under Geikhatu they took a turn for the worse. All blame cannot be placed on him, for a natural disaster struck the Mongol herds and decimated them, thus contributing to the depletion of the treasury. But Geikhatu and his sycophants precipitated a major economic catastrophe by introducing Chinese-style paper currency as a means of replenishing the treasury. Although Bolod Cingsang, Qubilai's representative at the Il-khanid court, advised against this measure, having explained how the Chinese system worked, his words of caution were ignored. The order to issue paper money was given in August 1294. Almost immediately economic activity throughout the empire ground to a halt, and the markets of Tabriz suddenly were empty. Less than two months later, the edict had to be revoked.[47]

By themselves, Geikhatu's immorality and his economic mismanagement would have led to an uprising. He had, however, set the stage for a challenge to his reign when, on a whim, he imprisoned Baidu in June 1294. Freed shortly thereafter, Baidu returned to his domains and began plotting rebellion. The uprising broke out early in 1295 and progressed with lightning speed. On 24 March 1295, Geikhatu was arrested and strangled, apparently without Baidu's approval. Immediately Baidu assumed the position of Il-khan. Groups loyal to Ghazan, who had not given up his claims to the throne, informed him of Geikhatu's death. The support that Baidu enjoyed at the time of his uprising crumbled as soon as it was known that Ghazan claimed the throne. Sometime in September, his own officials arrested him and brought him to Tabriz. There are indications that Baidu was willing to relinquish the throne in Ghazan's favor; the latter, however, refused to meet with him and had him executed on 4 October 1295. He had held the Il-khanid throne for a mere six months.

A major problem confronting the Il-khans was the fact that the population, as well as many officials, was Muslim, whereas they were not; thus, in keeping with tradition, there was little personal allegiance to the alien rulers. Ghazan, who had been a Buddhist, was convinced by Nauruz, with whom he had been reconciled, that as Il-khan he should adopt Islam as his personal religion, as well as his state one. Although Ghazan never appeared to be a serious and devout Muslim, except for the first two years of his reign, he did see a substantial political benefit from the conversion. He adopted Islam in a public ceremony on 19 June 1295, and was followed in his conversion by his Mongol officials. Thereupon the campaign against Baidu was interrupted on account of the holy month of Ramadan. The political impact of these largely symbolic gestures was enormous. When Ramadan ended and the campaign against Baidu resumed, Muslims who had been supporting Baidu switched their allegiance to Ghazan, eliminating the need for battle; the campaign against Baidu was in reality not a military campaign at all, but a triumphal march. Ghazan's conversion kept Persia indisputably within the cultural realm of Islam.

Ghazan was the most brilliant of the Il-khans. The state over which he ruled, however, was no longer a Mongol empire; it was an Islamic state that happened to be ruled by Mongols. As soon as Ghazan arrived in Tabriz on the day of Baidu's execution, he ordered the immediate implementation of his first decree: the destruction of all churches, synagogues, and Buddhist temples in Tabriz, Baghdad, and throughout the empire. Even the Buddhist temples built by his father were not to be spared. To this persecution Ghazan brought the zeal of the new convert, at least for a while.[48] Although he and his officials had converted to Islam, many external symbols of Mongol dominance, or steppe dominance, remained. In November 1297, the Il-khan Ghazan decided to eliminate them. In a formal and public ceremony held in Tabriz, he and his officials exchanged their broad-brimmed Mongol hats for traditional Persian headgear. This symbolic act meant that the steppe, and its traditions, had ceased to be important in the conduct of state affairs. The Il-khans now identified themselves with the people of their empire, rather than with their ancestors in Inner Asia.

It seems to have been a perennial dream of the Il-khans, and Ghazan was no exception, to occupy Syria and defeat the Mamluks. Ghazan, however, had slightly more success in this endeavor than his predecessors. In December 1299 his armies attacked Syria and laid siege to Aleppo and Hims. On 8 January 1300, the Mongols occupied Damascus. It was during this campaign that the only major battle between the Mongols and Mamluks took place. In the battle at the Wadi al-Hazander, to the west of Hama, the Mamluk army was thoroughly defeated and routed. Instead of pursuing the remainder of the Mamluk army, however, Ghazan merely appointed governors for Damascus and Syria and returned to Persia.[49] It appears that he did not want to continue the war against the Mamluks unless the Christian West participated in the campaign. On 12 April 1302, Ghazan sent a letter to that effect to Pope Boniface VIII. His overtures were received with suspicion in the West, however, for he was a Muslim. As in the past, no alliance came about. On 11 May 1304, at the age of thirty-three, Ghazan died of an illness.

At the time of his death, Ghazan had been actively engaged in reviving the economy of the Il-khanid empire, and the first results of these reforms were beginning to appear. The state of the Il-khanid treasury improved as the overall economic situation did. Ghazan's brother, Khar-banda, who had assisted in the implementation of the reforms, was quickly informed of Ghazan's death and forthwith assumed the title of Il-khan. Immediately he took ruthless action to eliminate possible rivals for the Il-khanid throne, including his cousin Ala-Fireng, who was executed with several other imperial princes. Khar-banda's prompt actions probably prevented a repetition of the bloody conflicts that had followed the death of his father, Arghun. The official enthronement ceremonies took place on 19 July 1304. Khar-banda changed his personal name to Khuda-banda and adopted the reign title *Oljeitu*, "the Fortunate, the Auspicious," a title under which he became known to history.[50]

Although Oljeitu's accession to the throne was not completely legitimate, it was a most splendid continuation of his brother's reign. Firmly intent on continuing his brother's successful economic policies, he sought a reconciliation with the Golden Horde; this not only served economic goals but was part of a trend throughout the Mongol world after the final collapse of Qaidu's attempt to restore a pure steppe empire. The Golden Horde, apparently for similar reasons, was desirous of a reconciliation, for in December 1304, envoys from the Horde's ruler, Toqto (1291–1312), arrived at Oljeitu's court. Oljeitu viewed these events as signalling the restoration of the Mongol empire as it had existed during the

reign of Mongke, his great-great-grandfather. This is evident from his letter to Philippe le Bel in April 1305. After referring to dissension among
the Mongols, he stated that these quarrels had ceased and that, as before,
the empire was united from the Chinese to the Caspian seas.[51]

Like his brother, Oljeitu hoped to conquer the Mamluks and to enlist
the aid of Europe in this venture; that was the purpose of the letter to
Philippe le Bel. Oljeitu as a ruler was a Muslim, but it appears that he was
brought up a Christian; throughout his reign he remained rather sympathetic to Christians in general. As in the past, however, Europe did not react
positively to Mongol overtures, even though both the European kings and
the papacy realized that such an alliance could mean the reconquest of the
Holy Land. Oljeitu decided to attempt the conquest alone. In the winter of
1312, his troops crossed the Euphrates and laid siege to the fortified town
of Rahbal al-Shams. Confronted with strong resistance, and suffering heavy
casualties, the Il-khan did not persist long and, at the end of January 1313,
returned to Persia. The Mongols earnestly desired an alliance with the
West, and if the West had been less reluctant to deal with a Mongol
Muslim ruler, there is no doubt that the survival of the Mamluk state would
have been seriously jeopardized. As it happened, the West waited too long:
after the siege of Rahbad al-Shams, the Il-khans abandoned their dream of
conquering the Mamluk empire. When, after 1313, the West began to consider the Mongol overtures seriously, the opportunity for an alliance had
passed.

Oljeitu's reign was essentially a peaceful one. In the midst of the Mongol
empire, however, a small state had escaped forced submission to the Mongols; the state of Gilan, a territory to the south of the Caspian Sea, had
remained unconquered because of its inaccessibility, its unhealthy and
humid climate, and its dense, marsh-like forests. Oljeitu dispatched his
principal commander, Qutlugh-shah, to subdue the area. The initial phases
of the campaign went in favor of the Mongols, but the Gilakis were soon
able to draw the Mongols into combat on terrain of their own choosing.
The Mongol cavalry, unable to maneuver in the marshy terrain, suffered a
disastrous defeat, and Qutlugh-shah was among the many victims.[52] His
death was a serious blow to the political stability of the Il-khanid empire,
for he was succeeded in his post as vizier by the less than scrupulous emir,
Choban.

The problems that confronted Oljeitu, however, were not so much of a
military as of a political nature: namely, interfactional rivalries at the court.
These had been a constant feature of life at the Il-khanid court and usually
were most evident at the time of succession. During Oljeitu's reign a major
conflict broke out between his two most important viziers, Rashid al-Din,
the well-known historian and vizier for Central and Southern Persia and
Khurassan, and 'Ali-shah, vizier for Northwestern Persia, Mesopotamia, and
Asia Minor. Each wanted to eliminate the other and become vizier for the
entire empire. Although the conflict between the two men was bitter, Oljeitu
managed to keep it under control. His successor, however, proved unable

to do so, and this inability was an important factor in the collapse of the Il-khanid dynasty.

Oljeitu died at the age of thirty-six on 7 December 1316, and as for so many Mongol rulers and princes, the cause of his death was intemperance. He was succeeded by his son Abu Sa'id, then twelve years old. Rashid al-Din, 'Ali-shah, and the ubiquitous Choban remained in the service of the new Il-khan; in view of his age, it was inevitable that one of the three would attempt to seize full control by eliminating the others. Throughout the first years of Abu Sa'id's reign, Choban remained on the sidelines, as the conflict between Rashid al-Din and 'Ali-shah increased in intensity. 'Ali-shah emerged as the victor, and Rashid al-Din, the empire's historian, was executed on 17 July 1318.

The first years of the new reign witnessed not only court conflicts, but also a series of internal uprisings, to which the Golden Horde gave generous assistance. The Il-khanid state, although beset with problems, was by no means a weakened state, and it reacted vigorously. In a fierce battle near Mianeh in June 1319, the uprising was crushed. In this battle, the young Il-khan participated personally, and the Il-khanid victory was largely due to his actions. Consequently he earned the title *Bahadur Khan,* "the heroic ruler." During the same battle Choban also distinguished himself and earned the young ruler's full confidence. A close personal relationship was created when Choban was given Abu Sa'id's sister in marriage.

Early in 1324, the vizier 'Ali-shah died, the only Il-khanid vizier to die of natural causes, and his death opened the way for Choban to become ruler of the empire in all but name. With power concentrated in Choban's hands, court intrigues came to dominate Il-khanid politics. Choban, taking advantage of the Il-khan's trust, promoted the interests of his family and his allies, not those of the state, and began to intrigue against his benefactor. Then, as if the intrigues at the court and the rebellions within the empire did not create enough difficulty for the Il-khanid state, Abu Sa'id suddenly fell in love with the princess Baghdad Khatun, who had been promised to one of Choban's sons. Abu Sa'id's inflexibility, together with his decision to take rule into his own hands, aggravated the political crisis, especially after he ordered Choban's execution. Many officials appointed by Choban turned against the Il-khan. The latter, who had forcibly married Baghdad Khatun, was poisoned by her on 30 November 1335. With Abu Sa'id's death, the empire created by Hulegu disintegrated.

Russia:
The Golden Horde

Two of the subdivisions of the Mongol world empire remained essentially within the steppe: the Golden Horde and the Chaghatai Khanate. The Golden Horde was the larger, and unlike the Yüan and the Il-khans, it exerted control over a sedentary area—Russia—without actually being located within its boundaries. When Chinggis-khan distributed the spoils of empire among his sons, he awarded Jochi, his eldest son, the territories along the Irtysh River and the Altai mountain range and ordered that he should control the Qipcaq steppe and the territories beyond it. When Jochi died, during Chinggis-khan's lifetime, his appanage was given to his second son, Batu. During the European campaign ordered by Ogodei, Batu was able to enlarge the territory under his control to include the Qipcaq steppe, the Bulghar territory, and the Russian principalities. The last recognized Mongol overlordship, an overlordship that lasted, in one form or another, until well into the sixteenth century.

The domain of the first real ruler of the Golden Horde, Batu (1237–1255), was immense; a good sense of its size can be gained from the travel account given by the missionary Wilhelm Van Ruysbroeck. Unlike the cities within the Chaghatai Khanate, the Horde's cities played an important role in its political and economic life. One of its principal cities was the trading emporium of Bolghar on the Kama, where the rulers of the Golden Horde located their mint. Later, at the mouth of the river, they built a capital city, Sarai.[53]

Almost from its inception, the Horde found an accommodation between its own nomadic traditions and those of the conquered sedentary areas. Although it remained on the steppe, it felt a need for fixed geographical locations to administer its domain efficiently. In time, this use of cities led to a sedentarization of the Horde and transformed it into a nomadic-sedentary state. The development of the Horde was minimally affected by developments within the other domains of the empire. Under Batu's leadership, the Horde was the first subdivision of the Mongol empire to assume a semiautonomous course—this at a time when the Great Khan still ruled from Qaraqorum. The Horde never lost this autonomy.

Batu's reign was essentially one of consolidation and expansion. He was not only a brilliant military commander, but an excellent administrator as well. It is likely that he realized that settling within the conquered sedentary areas would create needless problems for his administration; it was more practical to rule through the representatives of these areas. Through skillful manipulation of the rivalries among the Russian princes and use of the Orthodox Church, Batu established himself and his successors as the uncontested overlords of the Russian principalities, achieving this with a minimal amount of Mongol manpower. He appointed or dismissed at will the Russian Great Princes and required them to come regularly to pay homage to him. Batu also organized the Horde on a solid financial basis, in contrast to some of the other parts of the empire. Among his own people, he was immensely popular as a ruler, as evidenced by the numerous epic stories about him that exist on the Qipcaq steppe. Batu began the consolidation and organization of the Horde's domains after the death of Guyuk and the enthronement of Mongke. When he died, in 1255, his reforms were not completed. His first two successors, Sartaq and Ulaghchi, did not reign long enough to have any impact. Batu's work was continued when his brother Berke became khan of the Golden Horde in 1257.[54]

It is not known by what process Berke was chosen as his brother's successor; in any case, he had at least Mongke's implicit approval. An early convert to Islam, he was a worthy successor to his brother, and finished the work begun by him. The Horde's control over the Russian principalities and certain areas beyond them was consolidated. In 1259 Mongol forces penetrated Poland and laid siege for three months to the city of Cracow, in the meantime thoroughly looting the countryside and making forays into the Baltic areas. This raid confirmed the superiority of Mongol forces over the European knights. To a large degree this facilitated Berke's control over the Russian principalities closer to the Qipcaq steppe, especially after the death of the Mongols' staunchest supporter among the Russian princes, Alexander Nevskii.[55]

Whereas during the first few years of his rule, Berke's attention was concentrated on the areas to the north of the Qipcaq steppe, during the years that followed Mongke's death, his attention focused on the areas to the south, in particular Arran and Adherbaidjan. After his victory over Hulegu, Berke began negotiations with the Mamluk and Byzantine empires in an apparent attempt to establish an anti–Il-khanid alliance. Success was not achieved with the Byzantine empire. For political and strategic reasons, the Byzantine ruler, Michael VIII Palaialogus, favored an alliance with the Il-khans, who ruled over Rum and large portions of Asia Minor. In the summer of 1263, Berke launched an invasion of Thracia to press the basileus into an alliance with the Horde. For a while the Horde's forces threatened Constantinople, but then they withdrew. Another attempt was made in the summer of 1265. Instead of bringing the Byzantine empire within the Horde's sphere of influence, Berke succeeded only in driving the basileus to establish closer ties with the Il-khans.[56]

Sometime in July 1263, an alliance was created with the Mamluks. Although in his correspondence with the Mamluk rulers, Berke indicated that his actions against the Il-khans were inspired by their treatment of Islam, particularly the execution of the 'Abbasid caliph, it appears that this was a mere political expedient. Prior to the creation of the treaty, Mamluk envoys had arrived in Sarai. From them, and probably from other sources as well, Berke must have learned that the Mamluk ruler was eager to find allies against the Il-khans; even though they had defeated the forces of Hulegu at 'Ain Jalat, the Mamluks realized that the Mongols were a serious threat. From Berke's viewpoint, this eagerness could be exploited for two purposes: trade and territorial acquisition. What influence Berke's independent actions had on Qaidu is unknown, but probably his unchallenged authority and his ambitions had an impact on the outcome of the Talas *quriltai*. Berke's plans came to nought when he again attacked the Il-khanid empire, this time to be thoroughly defeated by the forces under Abaqa's command. Retreating through Georgia, Berke died in Tiflis early in 1267.

Batu's grandson, Mongke Temur (1267–1280), succeeded Berke and re-versed the politics of the Golden Horde. Whereas Berke's policies were aimed at independence from the Great Khan, Mongke Temur placed the Horde again under the authority of Qubilai.[57] Although he reverted to a proimperial policy with regard to the other subdivisions of the empire, Mongke Temur maintained independent relations with the Mamluk and Byzantine empires. To the Mamluks, Mongke Temur's reconciliation with the Il-khan boded ill, but the Horde did not take any hostile action against them. Finding his policies confusing, the Mamluks sent envoys to the Il-khan, sometime in 1271 or 1272, to determine the exact nature of the relations between the two Mongol rulers.[58]

Mongke Temur was succeeded by his brother Tode Temur (1280–1287), a devout Muslim but an inept politician. The *de facto* ruler of the Horde was Noqai, who had been chief of the armed forces under Berke and Mongke Temur and was a member of a distant branch of the House of Jochi.[59] Noqai was a military man in the true sense of the word and had established his own power base between the Don and the Dnieper. Through a series of campaigns into Russia and Poland, Noqai had become the intermediary between the Russian principalities and their tribute and the khan of the Golden Horde.

With Tode Temur's death began one of the strangest civil wars in Mongol history. Noqai never assumed the throne or the title of khan, but contented himself with appointing new rulers and controlling them. First he appointed Tole-buqa (1287–1291), then Toqto (1291–1312). Both rulers proved less malleable than expected and attempted to rid themselves of Noqai, whose forces, however, proved too strong for them. Tole-buqa was assassinated on Noqai's orders, and Toqto's forces were defeated in a fierce battle on the Dnieper in 1297. Noqai, however, made a serious strategic mistake after the battle: he failed to pursue the defeated forces of Toqto and totally destroy them during their retreat to Sarai. Overconfidence and old age are the only readily available explanations for such a mistake on the part of the Horde's most experienced commander. For the next two years, Toqto regrouped and prepared for another battle, which took place, again on the Dnieper, in 1299. This time Noqai was thoroughly defeated, and Toqto emerged as the Horde's sole ruler. On several occasions Noqai's descendants rebelled, but they never seriously threatened the Horde's political unity.[60]

When Toqto died, his succession was fiercely contested. The victor in the political infighting was Oz-beg (1313–1341), the son of Toqto's brother.[61] Under Oz-beg the Golden Horde reached a new height in its political and economic history. Relations with the Il-khan remained strained but peaceful, although the dispute over the possession of Arran and Adherbaidjan had not been resolved. The peaceful situation permitted Oz-beg to devote more attention to the Horde's Eastern European and Russian domains, where resentment of Mongol overlordship was on the rise, accelerated by the apparent weakness of Oz-beg's predecessors. Oz-beg was able to bring the problem under control, but the increasing restlessness of the population of the Russian principalities required a reorientation of the Horde's interest from the Caucasus to Russia. While consolidating his hold over the Russian domains, Oz-beg maintained friendly relations with Egypt, which, however, was itself undergoing serious internal problems. When, in 1324, war broke out between the Golden Horde and the Il-khan, the help promised by the Mamluks never arrived, and relations with the Mamluks were broken off. Ten years later, after Abu Sa'id's sudden death, Oz-beg again attacked the Il-khanid empire, only to be defeated by Abu Sa'id's successor, Arpa Ke'un.

Oz-beg's main problems were concentrated in Europe. Prior to his reign, many areas in Eastern Europe had ceased to pay tribute to the Mongols. Oz-beg began a series of punitive raids to make it clear that the Mongols had no intention of relinquishing control. Hungary was raided three times between 1331 and 1337; the city of Lublin was subjected to a regular siege in 1340; raids were staged in East Galicia and Prussia during the same year; in 1339 the city of Smolensk, which had stopped paying tribute in 1313, was thoroughly sacked by a Mongol-Russian force. But Lithuania, its power on the increase, maintained the anti-Mongol resistance. Oz-beg began a campaign against it; on his way towards Lithuania, however, he died. He was succeeded by his son Tini-beg (1341–1342), who at that time was campaigning in the former territories of Qwarezm. He returned to Sarai, only to be assassinated by his own brother Jani-beg (1342–1357), who then assumed the throne of the Golden Horde.

With Jani-beg, the Golden Horde had passed the apogee of its power and had begun an almost irresistible decline; the only important success the Horde achieved during his reign was the conquest of Adherbaidjan, after nearly a century of attempts. The most serious challenge to the Horde's authority came from Lithuania, which, after Oz-beg's death, rejected Mongol overlordship. The Horde, torn apart by political infighting, was not in a position to challenge this rejection, and consequently the Russian principalities began to follow suit. They were emboldened when the Horde fell into political chaos after Jani-beg's death, and one of the first manifestations of their independence was the cessation of the annual tribute payments. Unquestionably the power of the Russian principalities had grown considerably by the middle of the fourteenth century, but one must conclude that they were confronting a weakened and leaderless state.

Around 1380 it appeared that the end of the Golden Horde was imminent, and that it would break up into a group of petty states. Then Toqtamish, the leader of a minor Mongol group, the White Horde, staged a coup and seized control over the Golden Horde. Toqtamish provided the Horde with the leadership it needed for survival as a unified and politically powerful state. The Russian princes, however, paid no attention to this development, and after they had defeated Toqtamish on the Kulikovo in 1380, they became overconfident. When Toqtamish issued an ultimatum that they submit to the Mongols and resume the payment of tribute, they ignored it. Immediately,

Toqtamish invaded Russia, sowing destruction in his path. On 31 August 1382, his forces occupied Moscow, looted it, and burned it to the ground. Russia was to remain under Mongol dominance for more than a century thereafter. With Toqtamish, the Golden Horde began a new period in its history.

The Steppe:
The Chaghatai Khanate

The only truly Central Asian and nomadic subdivision of the Mongol empire was the appanage of Chinggis-khan's second son, Chaghatai. Named after its ruler, the Chaghatai Khanate covered Turkestan and Transoxiana, although it never possessed precise borders.[62] It included such magnificent cities as Samarqand and Bukhara, but the Khanate's orientation was towards neither urbanization nor sedentarization. In fact, except for a few brief years, the Khanate ignored its cities, so much so that its seventh ruler, Baraq (1266–1271), thought nothing of having these cities sacked each time cash for the armed forces was needed. Unlike the Golden Horde, the Khanate never had a formal capital, although it did have a central rallying point, the town of Almaligh on the Ili River.[63] It was the only subdivision of the empire where the bulk of the conquered area was inhabited by Turkic people leading a nomadic or seminomadic existence. Outside of the Mongol heartland, the Khanate was the only region with which the Mongols had common traditions. In time, this led to the complete "Turkicization" of the Mongols and the creation of what can be called a new language: Chaghatai Turkish.

True to its nomadic traditions, the Chaghatai Khanate did not leave many documents, and its history is thus the least well known of all the subdivisions of the Mongol empire. Most of the information has to be culled from other sources, in particular from the sources for the history of the Il-khanid domain. In a sense this silence represents the position of the Khanate within the Mongol empire, especially after the death of Chaghatai in 1242. It played a secondary role, politically as well as economically, within the empire. The Khanate existed for slightly over a century, but autonomy from the Great Khans was achieved only during the reign of its tenth ruler, Du'a (1282–1307).

Modern historians have devoted little attention to the Khanate. René Grousset, who wrote the first scholarly history of the steppe, made a rather unfair assessment of the career of Chaghatai, its founder. Comparing him with Qubilai and the rulers of the Il-khanid empire, he described him as representing the backward type of Mongol, the Mongol who ignored or rejected the refinements of sedentary life.[64] Rashid al-Din, the empire's historian and not an unbiased observer, paints quite a different portrait: according to him, Chaghatai did not possess the same zest or dynamism as his brothers; he was successful because of steady work, not strokes of genius. After his father's death, however, he became the elder statesman of the empire and an active supporter of his brother Ogodei.[65] Although Chaghatai clearly had influence over his brother, once the latter was the Great Khan, he assumed the attitude of a subordinate.

The Khanate had nineteen rulers, but only four had reigns of any importance. Alughu (1260–1266), the Khanate's fifth ruler, caused the collapse of Ariq-buqa's claim to the position of Great Khan. For most of his reign, Alughu attempted, with a fair degree of success, to establish the Khanate as a semiautonomous entity; as long as he supported Qubilai, there was little intervention in the Khanate's affairs.

The reign of Baraq (1266–1271), the Khanate's seventh ruler, coincided with Qaidu's dominance over the Central Asian steppe. The two met in battle, and Baraq was defeated and recognized Qaidu as his sovereign. In a sense, the Chaghatai Khanate ceased to exist during this period, becoming a mere subdivision of Qaidu's domain. On the latter's orders Baraq invaded Khurassan, with the disastrous consequences described above. Two rulers succeeded him, each holding the position of Khan for less than a year. Thereafter, the Khanate entered into a decade of civil war, whose eventual victor was Baraq's second son, Du'a, an ally of Qaidu. He acceded to the throne in 1282 and became the Khanate's tenth and most brilliant ruler.

War, in one form or another, had been the most constant feature of the Khanate since the reign of Alughu. Du'a's primary concern was to restore peace in the Khanate itself and bring some order to its economic and financial affairs; under Du'a, the Khanate also knew war, but this time outside its own boundaries. He actively participated in Qaidu's last campaign against the Great Khan Temur. This war, which took place in 1301, marked the end of Qaidu's restoration effort; Qaidu was killed, and Du'a himself was wounded.[66] Du'a recognized Qaidu's son Chapar as his suzerain but at the same time began peace negotiations with the Great Khan's court. As soon as these were completed, sometime in 1303, Du'a went his own way. For the first time in its history, the Khanate was autonomous, as were the other subdivisions of the empire at that time.

For the remainder of his reign, Du'a attempted to restructure the Khanate along the lines of the reforms promulgated by Ghazan in Persia. After a reign of nearly twenty-five years, the longest in the Khanate's history, Du'a died in 1307, without completing all the reforms he had proposed. His efforts were continued, however, by his successors and especially by Kebek (1318–1326), the Khanate's fourteenth ruler. Kebek was the only one of the Khanate's rulers who preferred sedentary, urban life to the nomadic existence of his predecessors. During his reign, the cities of Samarqand and Bukhara underwent a revival, setting the stage for the splendor of the empire of Timur-i-leng near the end of the fourteenth century. Kebek himself built his palace to the south of Samarqand, and the palace in time became a city in its own right. His reign was peaceful, and, limited though it may have been, it was the apogee of the Khanate's power.

Kebek was succeeded by his three brothers, Elchigidei, Du'a-temur, and Tarmashirin, in that order. Tarmashirin, reigning from 1326 to 1334, was the Khanate's last ruler. Under him the Khanate revived the warlike traditions of the steppe empire, and conducted constant raids in the borderlands. His two principal targets were, in order of importance, the sultanate of Delhi in India and the Il-khanid domain. He was the first ruler of the Khanate to embrace Islam, attempting to make it the state religion as well.[67] After he was severely defeated at the gates of Delhi, his military and religious policies precipitated a civil war, which in turn led to the division of the Khanate, in 1334, into two new states.

The Mongols and the West

Frequent reference has been made to attempts by the Mongols to enter into an alliance with the Christian West, that is, the Western European kingdoms and the papacy. The following paragraphs give a brief outline of the earliest relations between the Mongols and Europe. A detailed description and analysis of these relations and their influence on interstate relations within Europe itself cannot be given in the present volume: in Mongol history, these relations and contacts are of minor and secondary importance. Although Europe came close to being invaded by the forces of Batu, and later by the Golden Horde, there is no evidence that the Mongols ever seriously considered such an invasion.[68]

Sometime around 1220, rumors circulated among the Crusader states that somewhere in the East a new king had arisen: a Christian king who was inflicting defeats on the infidels and who had been sent by God to eliminate the teachings and the followers of Islam. Although there was no evidence of his existence, these rumors were accepted as true by the Crusader states, an acceptance facilitated by earlier legends of a lost Christian community in Asia. According to Jacques de Vitry, this new leader's name was King David, and in a sermon at Damietta he described him as "A God-sent envoy to destroy the execrable law and the pestilential teachings of the treacherous Mohammad."[69] A careful comparison of these stories about King David with sources for Mongol history clearly indicates that the rumors concerned the destruction of the Qwarezmian empire by Chinggis-khan. Europe and the papacy were convinced that Chinggis-khan, alias King David, would help them reconquer the Holy Land. This conviction was so profound that in 1221 Pope Honorius III mentioned it in a papal bull to the bishops of France and England.

From the Crusader states, the papacy received optimistic and encouraging reports. Their optimism was suddenly clouded when a letter arrived from Russudan, Queen of Georgia, informing the papacy and the European kingdoms of the destruction wrought upon her kingdom by the Mongols. After 1223 more disquieting news was received, including the information that the Mongols made no distinction between Christians and Muslims. Other discordant notes were forthcoming from the Cistercian abbeys in Hungary, the two primary informants being Jacob of Pecoraria, the abbott of Trois-fontaines, and Robert, the archbishop of Esztergom, who had been involved in missionary work among the Turkic Cumans.[70] The papacy, however, credited the more optimistic views from the Crusader states. This was all the easier as the first Mongol alert, the raid of Jebe and Subudei, ended without an incursion into Europe.

Less than twenty years later, however, this image of the Mongols was rudely shattered when under Batu's command they laid to waste Russia, thoroughly defeated the forces of Hungary, and destroyed several orders of knights. Suddenly it was realized that the Mongols presented a serious threat to Europe, and thus to the security of Christianity. Confronted with the imminent possibility of an invasion of Germany, a council held in Merseburg in April 1241 called for a Holy Crusade against the Mongols, which was to be under the orders of Conrad IV, the son of Frederic II; internal European politics, however, prevented its departure. Shortly thereafter, Batu returned to the steppe on account of Ogodei's death, thus removing the immediate threat to Europe. However, by June 1243, when Sinbaldo de Fieschi became Pope Innocent IV, the West was more than ready to consider seriously the Mongol menace.

When the Council of Lyons convened in 1245, it was evident that one of the most pressing matters on the mind of Innocent IV was the danger created by the Mongols in Eastern Europe. No policies, religious or political, could be formulated, because the information available on the Mongols was contradictory. The need for more accurate information had been felt prior to the Council of Lyons, and a list was drawn up of nine questions to which answers were urgently needed.[71] It was decided to send diplomatic missions to the Mongol leaders and to investigate them. Contrary to what has sometimes been suggested, missionary work was not on the pope's mind.[72]

The best-known and most successful mission was that led by John of Plano Carpini. He left for Mongolia via Russia in April 1245, and arrived at Batu's court a year later. After presenting the pope's letter to Batu, he was ordered to proceed to Qaraqorum, where the mission arrived in July 1246. As the *quriltai* for Guyuk's confirmation had not yet taken place, the mission stayed in the vicinity of the Mongol ruler's camp. They were received by Guyuk in August and presented him with the pope's letter. Extremely dissatisfied with its tone, Guyuk dismissed the envoys.[73] They took with them his reply, which ordered the pope and the European kings to submit to Mongol authority or face Mongol wrath. In November 1247 John of Plano Carpini was back in Lyons, where he wrote his report to the pope, the famous *Historia Mongolorum*.[74] It was the first objective, detailed, and sobering eyewitness account of the life, customs, and military organization of the Mongols. It painted a bleak picture of the prospects for a defense against a renewed Mongol attack.[75]

At the same time as John of Plano Carpini's journey, two other missions left to seek contact with the Mongols, one headed by Ascelin, the other by André de Longjumeau. Neither mission reached Qaraqorum, and neither left a detailed account of its travels. Ascelin travelled through the Mediterranean and from there through Georgia and Armenia. When he arrived at the camp of Baiju, the son of Chaghatai, he refused to go farther; he considered his mission accomplished when he handed Baiju the pope's letter. As Ascelin refused to submit to Mongol protocol, it is somewhat surprising that his mission returned at all.[76] The mission of André de Longjumeau, which was in fact sent by Louis IX, did not travel in the direction of the Mongol capital but through Islamic territory, and, from there, to the Mongols in Persia. This mission was probably the first attempt to create an alliance between the West and the Mongols, an alliance that never materialized.[77]

These initial contacts between the West and the Mongols were followed by the intriguing mission of Wilhelm van Ruysbroeck. A Franciscan, he observed to the letter the task of his order and went to the Mongols to preach the Gospel. It was a completely private undertaking; he had a few letters of introduction from the king of France, but these contained no political allusions, but merely a request that the missionary be permitted to settle among the Mongols. In May 1253 he left from Constantinople, and in the same year arrived in the camp of Batu's son, Sartaq. There Ruysbroeck was able to establish contact with the Nestorians, but by this time, he had lost all desire, or courage, to preach. The Mongols insisted on equality among all religions, and religious intolerance was severely punished. Luckily for posterity, Ruysbroeck did not have the makings of a martyr. From Sartaq's camp, he was sent to Mongke's court in Qaraqorum, where he arrived sometime in June 1254. He stayed in Qaraqorum about three months and was allowed to practice his religion freely; he did not dare, however, to proclaim the supremacy of Christianity and the pope. He left Qaraqorum in August and was back in Europe by the middle of 1255.

Wilhelm van Ruysbroeck left an account of his travels. If Plano Carpini's is the account of an experienced diplomatic observer, Ruysbroeck's is a much more personal one and shows a profound sympathy for the Mongols. It cannot entirely be trusted, however, especially when he discusses religious affairs.[78] Although Ruysbroeck had hoped to obtain privileges for the Christian Church, he apparently never dared to raise the subject, in sharp contrast to King He'tum I of Little Armenia, present in Qaraqorum at about the same time, who was able to obtain from Mongke decrees protecting the Church in Armenia.[79]

With Ruysbroeck's return to Europe, the first phase of European-Mongol relations came to a close. Its main achievements were firsthand accounts of the Mongols and the situation in some of the conquered countries. Europe's interest in the Mongols, however, strongly diminished once the immediate danger of a Mongol invasion had vanished. When the Golden Horde subsequently plundered Eastern Europe, the Western European courts considered it a distant, localized problem.[80] Later, both the Mongols and the Europeans desired an alliance against the Mamluks, but European distrust of the Mongols prevented its realization. Yet the Church retained an interest in the Mongols, albeit a purely missionary one; towards the end of the Yüan, it even created a diocese of Peking.

1.
Fragment of the stele dedicated to Kül-tegin
in Turkic Runic inscriptions *(Inscriptions de
l'Orkhon: Recueillies par l'expédition
finnoise de 1890,* Société Finno-Ourgrienne.
Helsingfors, 1892. Table 27.)

2.
Sung Dynasty. Paintings of falconers, probably Ch'i-tan (*Chung-kuo li-tai ming-hua chi.* Peking, 1965. Volume 2, plate 80.)

3.
Yüan Dynasty. A foreign mission (*Chung-kuo li-tai ming-hua chi*. Peking, 1965. Volume 3, plate 88.)

4.
Qubilai Khan as Emperor of China (*Chung-kuo li-tai to hu hsiang*. Shanghai, 1934[?].)

5. *(Opposite)*
Qubilai hunting outside the Summer Palace
(*Chung-kuo li-tai ming-hua chi*. Peking, 1965.
Volume 3, plate 14.)

6.
Fragment of a Japanese woodblock of 1293
illustrating Mongol defeat (Moko shurai
ekotaba, 1916 facsimile of a scroll made in
1293.)

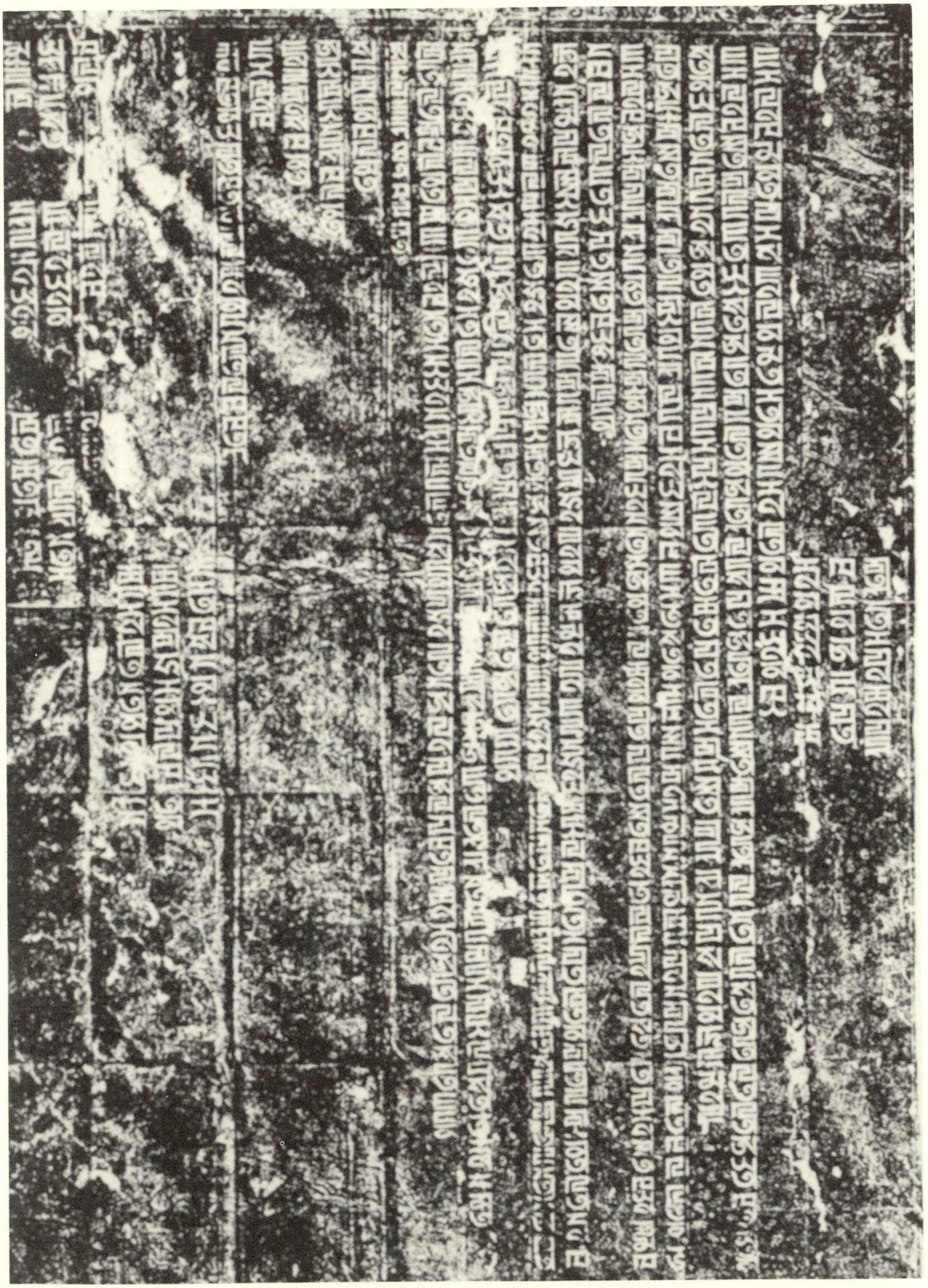

7. *(Opposite)*
Edict of Buyantu Khan, 1314, in the ephe-
meral 'Phags-pa script (N. Poppe, *The
Mongolian Monuments in Hp'ags-pa Script.*
Wiesbden, 1957. Plate 3, facing p. 56.)

8.
Firdawsi, Shah-nama, illustrating the develop-
ment of Persian miniatures under Mongol
influence (A. U. Pope and Ph. Ackerman,
*A Survey of Persian Art: From Prehistoric
Times to the Present.* Oxford, 1938-39.
Volume 9, plate 838.)

9.
Sultaniyeh, the mausoleum of the Il-khan
Oljeitu (A. U. Pope and Ph. Ackerman, *A
Survey of Persian Art: From Prehistoric
Times to the Present*. Oxford, 1938-39
Volume 8, plate 381.)

8

The Structure of
the Mongol Empire

The best-known aspect of Mongol history is the political history of the early empire and, to a lesser degree, of its subdivisions. An empire's history, however, does not consist solely of politics and conquests, an image all too frequently conveyed when it comes to steppe empires in general and the Mongol empire in particular. To survive past its formative period, an empire needs structures of some kind in almost all aspects of its internal functioning; this is all the more true for a nomadic people who conquer and rule sedentary areas without abandoning their nomadic realm. The structure of the Mongol empire has rarely been touched upon: a few monographs, primarily dealing with the Yüan dynasty, are available, but no overall view has been attempted.

To understand fully the structure of the Mongol empire, it is necessary to be acquainted with the structures of the sedentary states in which the Mongols established it. With regard to the empire's formative years, the absence of material complicates the matter. Although some research has been conducted, it will be some time before the structure of each subdivision is fully understood and before a more than superficial comparison between subdivisions can be successfully accomplished. Therefore, the present chapter does not pretend to provide a full and detailed overview of the empire's structure.

The Sociopolitical Structure

Until quite some time after the beginning of their conquests, the Mongols were nomads and were not inclined to abandon their nomadic customs. This fact is important in understanding the transition from a steppe tribal confederation to a bureaucratically structured empire. It also played a role in the social stratification that occurred among the Mongols after the creation of their empire under Chinggis-khan's leadership. This stratification found its clearest expression in the formation of princely houses headed by the founder's sons, in essence the formation of a Chingizid dynasty.

Prior to the rise of Chinggis-khan, the sociopolitical structure of the Mongols appears to have been quite simple. Essentially, it was a typical tribal structure with few aristocratic and feudal features and a definite trend towards military activity as a means of political expression. There were different categories of families or clans, with one of them dominating the others within a tribal arrangement. This domination was based not so much on ancestry as on military prowess and the ability to lead the tribal organization in its migrations across the steppe, a hostile environment. The structure was simple and adapted to the needs of relatively small groups. Whenever a larger tribal confederation developed, usually under military pressure, the basic structure remained unaltered but there was a substantial increase in military-aristocratic influence. When several larger confederations coalesced to form a steppe empire, a monocratic military system was adopted in which social stratification was based exclusively on an individual's military capabilities.[1] Only after Chinggis-khan's death did ancestry become a determinant factor in stratification.

During the formative years of the empire, Mongol society appears to have been divided into three strata. Initially these were contained within the clan itself, but with the expansion of the Mongol confederation they were taken over into the interclan structure. The top stratum was that of the chieftains or khans. Within their hands was concentrated all military, political, and administrative authority over the clan. The members of the different clans formed the middle stratum of Mongol society and provided the khan with his officers, both civil and military. At the lowest social level were the serfs and the slaves, the former acting primarily as vassals of more powerful groups, and the latter fulfilling primarily domestic functions.[2] The position of these groups was a consequence of downward interstratic mobility, most frequently as a result of military conflicts.

When the Mongol confederation expanded, the various clans allied themselves on a tribal basis known as the *irgan*. The *irgan* was a relatively unstable formation; although it most frequently followed bloodlines, tribal affiliation was just as frequently determined by purely economic and military considerations. By the time of Chinggis-khan's youth, the *irgan* had increased in importance to the point that the function of khan was held by the leader of the *irgan* and no longer by the leader of the clan. When Chinggis-khan became the supreme emperor of the Mongols, the title of *khan* was restricted to the emperor himself. With the accession of his son Ogodei, however, the emperor assumed the title of *qaghan,* roughly meaning the "khan of khans" while the title *khan* reverted to nobles of lower rank.[3]

The clans that made up an *irgan* were known collectively as the *oboq.* Its composition was unstable; members of a clan could separate from it and form a new clan with groups that had separated from other clans. Although initially clans were based on lineages within a single family, this practice appear to have disappeared by Chinggis-khan's time. Nevertheless, within each newly formed clan, an allegiance to a common ancestry, known as a "bone," continued to be the major criterion for clan membership. In one sense, the bone constituted a blood lineage, but in time it lost its precise meaning, so that several clans could claim to belong to the same bone without being directly related to each other. Nevertheless, membership in the same bone prevented marriage between people from the clans thus related. The need to marry outside of one's own bone was a major factor in the instability of the clan itself.

When the empire was established, the instability of the clan seems to have already disappeared, and it had become the basic social and political unit. With the establishment of the empire and its subsequent expansion, stratification among the clans themselves began. Before the 1206 *quriltai,* the prominence of a clan was determined by the number of its followers and its military abilities. Afterward, the role it had played in the formation of the empire, and later in the conquest, became the criterion by which a clan's importance was determined. The years immediately preceding and following the *quriltai* witnessed the formation of a conquest aristocracy among the clans and a hierarchizing among the members of the clan itself.

The elite positions were occupied by the clans that had participated with Chinggis-khan in the formation of the empire; the leaders of these clans then became the empire's elite. From that time, too, ancestry began to have a more important role than military prowess in social stratification within the clan. While interstratic upward mobility remained high during Chinggis-khan's reign, it decreased substantially during the reigns of his immediate successors. For all practical purposes it ended during Mongke's reign; from that time on, stratification was primarily based on clan affiliation and ancestry. The two most important clans were the Qonggirad and the Borjigid.[4] The importance of ancestry was already manifest during the reign of Ogodei, as evidenced by the conflict between Guyuk and Batu.

At the lowest social stratum, the distinction between serfs and slaves was apparently based on whether or not they belonged to the same bone as the military victor. Warfare between unrelated clans was a common occurrence, but so was warfare between related clans, that is, those claiming a common bone or *yosun*. If it belonged to the same *yosun,* the defeated clan became a vassal of the victor; if it was outside the *yosun,* it was reduced to slave status. What degree of upward interstratic mobility existed for the members of these two classes is not precisely known, but it seems likely that the needs of an expanding empire enabled a substantial number of them to improve their social position.

When the empire was established and the conquests began, the social position of all Mongols, regardless of their preconquest status, was improved, for they became the dominant stratum of the new society created by Chinggis-khan. The conquest permitted drastic upward mobility. Although individuals are known to have improved their own positions substantially, the evidence suggests that for most Mongols the upward mobility was determined by the addition of conquered and submitted people at the bottom of the sociopolitical ladder. Tribes and nations that submitted voluntarily to the Mongols became vassals, whereas those who were conquered were reduced to slave status. It must be pointed out, however, that conquered Mongol tribes, such as the Merkid, nevertheless occupied a higher sociopolitical position than non-Mongol tribes that had submitted voluntarily, for example, the Tangut and the Uighurs.

The Mongol empire is most commonly defined as feudalistic, both politically and socially. Some historians continue to accept this definition for the entire history of the Mongol empire. Strictly speaking, *feudalism* describes relations between man and man during the European Middle Ages, but it has recently been extended to include the domination of one clan by another, an extension that distorts the original meaning.[5] It is evident that with a few minor modifications, the basic definition is an acceptable one. The main difference between the feudalism of Europe and that of the Mongols was that the latter did not involve the allocation of land to those admitted into vassalage. The basis of the Mongol economy was the horse, and appanages were expressed in terms of animals and people, usually people who had either submitted or been conquered.[6]

The Mongols' elementary feudalism changed substantially during the reign of Chinggis-khan. This change was an integral part of the changes Mongol society was undergoing as a consequence of the establishment of an empire and its expansion. Whereas feudal relations had been minimal before the empire's formation, they became a dominant factor after the 1206 *quriltai* and the formation of an aristocratic conquest elite, as conquered and submitted people were assigned to Mongol princes on a permanent basis. After the initial phases of the conquest were over, Chinggis-khan introduced the notion of territoriality into the Mongol political structure: not only did he assign people to Mongol princes, but he also allotted each of his sons an appanage expressed in specific territorial terms. The sons in turn apparently assumed the responsibility for further division of the territory to other Mongol princes, while retaining the overlordship for themselves. This territoriality became the basis of the geographic subdivisions of the empire, and later, a primary source of conflict between the different Chingizid houses.[7]

The tendency towards a territorial and aristocratic division based on ancestry continued during the reigns of Chinggis-khan's successors, clearly contributing to the quarrels between the princely houses as each of them sought to dominate the others. During Mongke's reign, the imperial feudal structure of the Mongols attained its final form and continued unmodified at least until the reign of Qubilai's first successor, Temur (1294–1307). The Great Khan, whether in Qaraqorum or Peking, was the absolute emperor to whom the viceroys of the various subdivisions owed their allegiance and to whom they were accountable for their administration. They in turn appointed a second series of lords within their domains. All Mongols, regardless of rank, assumed a privileged position within these domains, a privilege based on the facts of conquest.

It appears that the structure assumed during the reign of Mongke was continued in each of the subdivisions of the empire and, in one way or another, maintained until the fall of the empire itself. With the exception of the Yüan, very little information is available on the subdivisions. The Chaghatai Khanate, the subdivision that adhered most closely to steppe traditions, appears to have been the least affected by social and political modifications. Although it remained monocratic until its collapse, the form of feudalism within it appears close to traditional nomadic feudalism as it existed before Mongke's accession to the throne. On the other hand, the Golden Horde, because it occupied both nomadic and sedentary areas, appears to have developed a system in which traditional steppe feudalism coexisted with the newly developed territorial feudalism. This situation, however, was conducive neither to the formation of stable borders nor to permanent stability within the Golden Horde itself, thus permitting centrifugal tendencies to come to the fore.[8]

Within the Il-khanid and Yüan domains aristocratic and territorial feudal forms assumed their fullest expression. In both cases, these structures persisted until the collapse of the dynasty and aggravated centrifugal tendencies within the empire, especially towards the end of each dynasty. The system permitted Mongol lords to possess military forces distinct from those available to their overlords, the Il-khan and the Yüan emperors. The situation in the Il-khanid domain has not yet been subjected to a serious critical examination, but a cursory survey of readily available material confirms this perception of its political and social structures.[9] The Yüan has been the subject of studies that clearly support the above description of the evolution of its sociopolitical structure.[10] The main difference between these two subdivisions is that in China, the feudal lords were supplanted by the bureaucracy, a situation that never developed in Persia.

The backbone of Mongol social and political structure, however, remained the army. From time immemorial the principal means of upward social mobility on the steppe had been through military action, and to this tradition the Mongols were no exception. Military campaigns enabled Chinggis-khan to become the supreme emperor of the Mongols, and military expeditions were the basis for the empire's expansion and consolidation. Why most steppe societies were primarily military has not yet been thoroughly investigated, but the history of the Uighurs demonstrates that it was not an inevitable consequence of life on the steppe. From what is known about Mongol forces during the formative years, the Mongol army was of a neferic type. In time, however, under the pressure of an increasing feudalism and a decline in central control, the military adopted a tallenic structure, and, towards the end of the empire, a ritterian one.[11]

Many myths have been propagated, and are often still accepted, about the Mongol army, especially about its size and tactics. The basic structure of the Mongol army was a unit of ten men, the *arban,* which was further organized into groups of one hundred and one thousand. The latter combined into the Mongol army's basic operating unit, the group of ten thousand men known as the *tümen.* All of the *tümen*'s subdivisions, with the exception of the *arban,* were commanded by members of the Mongol conquest aristocracy. Within each unit all commanders had close personal relations, partly as a consequence of the Mongol social structure. In turn, most of the commanders of a *tümen* had close ties with Chinggis-khan, either through their participation in the Baljuna Covenant, or as members of his immediate family.

While the personal ties within the army provided for a high degree of cohesion, strict legal prescriptions for the Mongol soldier provided for an equally high level of subordination. Contemporary accounts are replete with descriptions of the Mongol soldier's discipline and obedience to his commanders.[12] Mongol law, the so-called *yasa,* was particularly severe regarding the soldiers' behavior in battle. Retreat without permission was punished by death. The same punishment was meted out to any soldier who did not assist another in combat. On the other hand, the law also provided for an equitable distribution of loot, resolving a source of frequent internecine warfare on the steppe. The law also attempted to ensure the cohesion and subordination of the troops by forbidding any man, prince or commoner, to leave the unit to which he was assigned for another one; this was an offense punishable by death, regardless of status.[13]

Within the regular army structure, Chinggis-khan had created a special unit: the *keshik,* or imperial bodyguard. The *keshik,* apparently founded around 1203, was composed of three types of soldiers: the bodyguards or *keshiktu,* the nightguard or *kebteghul,* and the dayguard or *turqughut.* The *keshik* was an independent *tümen* under the emperor's personal command; initially, it was composed solely of members of the Mongol aristocracy. In battle, it surrounded the emperor and intervened only to finish off an enemy or give assistance to units in difficulty.

The *keshik* was continued within the Yüan military structure, and throughout the reigns of Qubilai and Temur the size, and the tradition established during Chinggis-khan's reign were maintained. After 1312 this changed. The size of the *keshik* increased, and non-Mongols, even Chinese, were allowed to become members.[14] Although the rulers of the other sub-divisions of the empire had bodyguards, the Chingizid *keshik* continued only within the Yüan.

At the beginning of the empire's expansion, the army was relatively small, especially in comparison with the armies of China and the Muslim states. Though it was numerically inferior, the Mongol army's superiority lay in the ability of its commanders and in their tactics. The formative years of the empire appear to have been a period exceptionally rich in military com-manders. A survey of the campaigns shows that all Mongol commanders were as capable of leading successful campaigns as Chinggis-khan himself; they frequently had to act independently and at great distances from the Mongol emperor. Perhaps Chinggis-khan's most remarkable action was selecting these highly competent commanders and motivating them to act as a single body.

The command structure and tactics of the Mongol army gave them a technological advantage over their opponents in the sedentary states. Their operational structure made the Mongol forces unbeatable and enabled them to maintain their advantage for nearly a century. The Mongol army represented the apogee of nomadic warfare. The Mongol troops adopted the tactics created by the Ch'i-tan, which consisted of highly disciplined cavalry maneuvers used together with ruses to trap the enemy. By the time of Chinggis-khan's rise to power, however, the sedentary states, and China in particular, had begun to develop defenses against the new style of cavalry warfare. The military genius of Chinggis-khan was to continue the traditional forms of nomadic warfare while incorporating into them the defensive strategies of sedentary warfare. This meant that for the first time in the history of the steppe, the nomad engaged in siege warfare, making the sedentary state's traditional defense against the horseman—the moat and the city wall—useless. Furthermore, it appears that Chinggis-khan made the most of intelligence information before launching an attack; thus, the nomad no longer struck haphazardly, but at the enemy's weakest point.

The scope of their conquests made the expansion of the Mongol armies a necessity. The Mongols incorporated the armies of conquered tribes and nations, but always as separate units. The first to join the Mongols in this fashion, other than the Turkic tribes of the central steppe, were the forces of the Uighurs and the Tangut. Information about the western steppe is scanty, but there is no reason to presume that the situation was substantially different from that on the East Asian front; in fact, acceptance of Muslim units was probably easier than acceptance of Chinese units, as many of them were made up of people of Turkic origins. The incorporation of conquered troops into the Mongol army had several important conse-quences, other than the increase in the army's size. The bulk of the in-corporated troops were from the sedentary states, providing the Mongols with units well trained in sedentary warfare and thus improving their strategic and tactical advantages. Furthermore, these forces provided the Mongols with useful intelligence.[15]

When the empire was firmly established, during Mongke's reign, the

Mongols did not modify the military nature of their sociopolitical structure; although sedentary administrative techniques were adopted, they always remained secondary to the military organization. Until close to the collapse of the empire, the Mongols remained a conquest dynasty, and the conquered areas remained essentially under military occupation. As far as can be determined, the military structure of the Golden Horde and the Chaghatai Khanate remained the same as that of Mongke's time. The only serious modification was the progressive replacement of the Mongols by the dominant Turkic population, a consequence of the demographic balances of these subdivisions. Within the Il-khanid domain, too, the military structure does not appear to have been modified substantially; the major change was the incorporation of large numbers of infantry units.

It was in China that the military aspect of Mongol society underwent substantial changes in both function and structure. These modifications began shortly after 1260, when Qubilai made his capital within conquered domains. The subsequent conquest of the Southern Sung only accelerated the transformation begun several years earlier. The driving force behind the structural change was the large number of Chinese troops that had to be either disbanded or incorporated. Although Qubilai and his advisors undoubtedly considered disbandment, such a policy presented too many political and military risks. Thus, the Chinese armies were incorporated into the Mongol armies, and a threefold division was created. At the top were the Mongol and the so-called *tammachi* troops, units made up of people assimilated to the Mongols (for example, the Türks). These troops formed the elite of the Mongol army in China and supplied the guard units at the capital and in the principal provincial centers. At the second level were the North Chinese troops, including Jürchen troops, and at the third and lowest level were the newly incorporated troops, that is, the armies of the Southern Sung. These troops were stationed primarily in the provinces—but never in their province of origin—although they were also used on the borders. Qubilai made substantial use of them in his pacification of the Kansu corridor. The Chinese troops also provided the bulk of the personnel for the military colonies, which were agriculturally self-sufficient units. Although Mongol units were also assigned to military colonies, they were not required to cultivate the land.[16]

Although necessity forced the Yüan to alter the Mongol military structure substantially, the Mongols nevertheless remained the military elite and the dominant social stratum. Although this is frequently glossed over by Chinese historians, the Mongols in China *did* maintain their customs and traditions, as well as the conquest elite structure that had arisen after Chinggis-khan's accession to power.[17] Perception of the Yüan dynasty's social structure is obscured by the apparent dominance of Chinese institutions. A closer examination of the evidence reveals that within China two societies—Chinese and Mongol—coexisted, each with its own sociopolitical structure. The Mongols formed the superstructure, a conquest elite that deliberately kept itself at a distance from the Chinese. The scholar-official class, the elite of Chinese society, provided the administration of the country for the benefit of the Mongol conquest elite, at least until about two decades before the Yüan collapse.[18]

From this brief description of the sociopolitical structure of the Mongol empire, it is evident that Mongol society was based on and oriented toward military activity. It was unquestionably a militocracy, and thus it continued and brought to its culmination the steppe tradition.[19] The militocracy maintained itself in all subdivisions of the empire. Only in Yüan China did the Mongols have to make a deliberate effort to maintain it, for there they were subjected to the pressures created by a centuries-old tradition of bureaucratic and civilian rule. It is quite possible that the Mongols were able to maintain themselves on the eastern steppe long after the collapse of the empire precisely because of Yüan efforts to maintain their original social and political structure, although more comparative investigation of this possibility is needed.

However, a different interpretation of Mongol sociopolitical structure during the imperial period exists, according to which administration and religion formed the basis of the sociopolitical structure. This theory considers military activity only within the very restrictive context of the administrative and the religious spheres: the military was needed for a peaceful operation of the administration, which worked for the benefit of religion. This theory is known as the "Two Orders" and originated in Tibetan Buddhism. It penetrated Mongol historical thought after the Mongols' conversion to Tibetan Buddhism in the sixteenth century and became the standard interpretational framework for the Chingizid empire by the late eighteenth or early nineteenth century. On the basis of historical literature in Mongol and Tibetan, Western scholarship has sometimes accepted this theory, at least as far as the Yüan is concerned. A recent study places the origins of this theory in the reign of Qubilai and implies that Qubilai himself inspired it.[20] This study analyzes and translates the primary source in Mongol for the Two Orders theory, the so-called *White History* (*Caghan teüke*), and ignores all the Chinese evidence that would contradict it. When that evidence is taken into consideration, the only conclusion that can be drawn regarding the sociopolitical structure of the Yüan is that it was a militocracy which, towards the end of the dynasty, began to give evidence of an increasing bureaucratization.[21]

The Administrative Structure

At the time when Chinggis-khan created the Mongol empire, administrative functions were kept strictly to a minimum. Military and civil functions were held by the same persons, usually officers of the Mongol army. According to the *Yüan shih,* only two major functions existed during the formative years, that of commander of a myriarchy and that of *tuan-kuan-chih,* or judge, the Mongol *jarghuci*. The latter function referred specifically to an official, military or not, who was in charge of all criminal and civil affairs.[22] These officials were assisted in their functions by secretaries, *bichegchi*, mostly of Uighur origins.

This very rudimentary administrative structure was sufficient for a nomadic society, and for the Mongols as long as they were not in control of large sections of non-Mongol territory. Once the initial conquests were over, it must have become apparent to the Mongols and to Chinggis-khan that this system was inadequate.[23] Administrative reforms were necessary for efficient exploitation of the conquered areas. The process by which a decision was reached in this matter is not known, but two requirements must have been clear to the Mongols: the need for a geographically fixed gathering point, and an official to take charge in each conquered area. The first need led to the creation of the Mongol capital, Qaraqorum. Founded by Chinggis-khan around 1220, the city was built up and walled by Ogodei after 1235.[24] The second led to the creation of the office of *darughaci*, roughly translated as "governor," an office that for the duration of the Mongol empire was always occupied by a Mongol.[25]

When the Mongol emperor began his campaign against the Jürchen Chin dynasty, his forces were assisted by a number of foreigners, primarily Uighurs, Ch'i-tan, and Chinese, who formed a rudimentary chancellery-secretariat in charge of strictly administrative tasks, such as requisitions, communications, and the like. If needed, these officials could be pressed into military service. The formation of this chancellery-type office probably took place after the Tangut and Uighur submission, for the Mongols did not personally administer these territories. With the success of the Jürchen campaign, the Mongols found themselves in control of a vast territory inhabited almost exclusively by sedentary people. Stories have it that Chinggis-khan had intended to eliminate this sedentary population and to turn the whole of North China into one vast grazing area; whether the stories are apocryphal or not, this undertaking would not have been quite feasible, and, in any case, it was realized that more profit could be derived if the area was administered by someone for the Mongols. In order to accomplish this, however, the Mongols needed a type of official that they could not supply themselves: for one thing, there were not enough Mongols, and, for another, the Mongols had neither an administrative nor a bureaucratic tradition. During the conquest, many officials of the Jürchen had defected to the Mongols, and it was among these defectors that the conquerors found a ready supply of trained administrators.[26] By using these defectors, who often were reappointed to the area they had administered before defecting, the Mongols assured themselves of an official presence in the conquered areas. Furthermore, this practice guaranteed them the revenues and the supplies they wanted and at the same time provided a buffer against rebellions.

When the first phase of the North China campaign ended, after the fall of the Jürchen capital, the territory that had come under Mongol control was in disarray. The Mongols needed the logistical support the area could give, but a quick restoration of the administrative infrastructure was required before they could obtain it. As the Mongols did not possess an adequate structure of their own, they essentially adopted the one that existed in North China. The conquered territory was divided into a number of large areas called *hsing-sheng*. The task of the officials appointed to administer these areas was one of coordination between military and civilian activities. The Mongol mobilization of local troops and the need for a fast and efficient communications network contributed substantially to the revival of the battered Jürchen administration and, to a more limited degree, to the revival of the area's economy because of the exploitative nature of Mongol occupation. How many administrative regions were operative in North China during Chinggis-khan's reign is not known, but during Ogodei's reign there were ten.[27] The administrative center for North China was the former Jürchen capital of Chung-tu.

At the beginning of the North China conquest, most of the administrative tasks were in the hands of the Ch'i-tan and the Chinese. Quickly, however, the latter outnumbered the former. There is no indication that ethnic Jürchen joined the Mongols in substantial numbers. Thus, though the existing institutions had been taken over without visible modification, there were subtle but important changes. Before the Mongol conquest, a prerequisite for an administrative position was membership in the Confucian scholar-official class. The Mongols dropped this requirement: what counted for them was competence, not success at an esoteric examination. The Mongols appointed both scholar-officials and professionals to administrative positions. Thus, the conqueror permitted an upward social mobility for classes otherwise deprived of this opportunity.

Another subtle change was brought about by the large number of Ch'i-tan in the Mongol administration of North China, which resulted in a return to older forms of government, in particular forms inspired by the Chinese T'ang dynasty as described in the T'ang codex *Chen-kuan cheng-yao*. The most visible return of certain Ch'i-tan practices was the reintroduction of the *paizas*: gold, silver, and silver and gold tiger-shaped tablets that indicated specific ranks within the administrative structure. Furthermore, an increasing number of people from outside East Asia, in particular Persians, were appointed to office in North China. Thus began the multiracial, supranational administration that was so characteristic of the Mongol empire, an administration that permitted a Marco Polo to hold an important office in China without knowing Chinese.

The increasing reliance of the Mongols on Chinese and on Sinicized Ch'i-tan for the day-to-day administration of the country—especially of the conquered territories—resulted in cultural inroads by Chinese-style officialdom into traditional Mongol practices. This found its clearest expression in the increasing complexity of the administrative structure and in bureaucratic restraints on the conqueror. This transformation was facilitated by the fact that these defectors were incorporated into Mongol society under the concept of the *nokor,* a free association between groups, one being in a service relationship.[28] This was not an uncommon practice during the reign of Chinggis-khan; in fact, it had contributed to his rise to power.

Even though large numbers of Chinese and Ch'i-tan joined the Mongols in a privileged position, this did not mean that the Mongols accepted Chin administrative practices wholesale. In fact, they did so rather haphazardly, according to immediate needs rather than long-term plans. The *ad hoc* procedures and the lack of consistency must have been a difficult problem for the Chin defectors, who wanted to serve the Mongols, but, at the same time, to maintain what they felt were important aspects of Chinese civilization. This desire was, more often than not, incompatible with the actions of the Mongols. Probably this desire played a role in Yeh-lü Ch'u-ts'ai's attempts to convince Chinggis-khan of the superiority of Chinese practices and his subsequent invitation of the Taoist monk Ch'ang-ch'un to the court. As was shown earlier, this attempt did not have the expected results.

For most of Chinggis-khan's reign, the administrative structure of the empire did not develop beyond the adoption of some elementary Chinese-inspired changes. When Ogodei succeeded him to the Mongol throne, the size of the empire had increased considerably. While the empire's expansion occurred at lightning speed, the elaboration of the administrative structure needed to govern it efficiently lagged far behind. During the conquest, little attention was paid to administration, but immediately thereafter, the Mongols were confronted with an administrative problem which could not be solved by recourse to precedent, Chinese or other. Indeed, the administrative structure of the western territories was drastically different from that of the eastern territories. The compromise developed, apparently on the initiative of Yeh-lü Ch'u-ts'ai, was that each area would maintain its existing administrative structure, while in the Mongol capital, a centralized bureaucracy based on a Chinese model was to be established. Of all the administrative models at the Mongol emperor's disposal, the Chinese was the only one readily adaptable to the growing size of the Mongol empire.

As was indicated earlier, Yeh-lü Ch'u-ts'ai's primary function at Chinggis-khan's court, which he joined in 1218, appears to have been that of astrologer and secretary. Though there is no evidence of his holding other offices, he was probably also involved in creating an administration for his employer. That would explain his sudden success as an administrator when, shortly after Ogodei's accession to the throne, he was able to introduce fiscal reforms. In 1230 he became the first president of the Central Chancellery, an institution which remained in existence throughout the Yüan dynasty and which, until the time of Qaidu's surrender, handled relations between the subdivisions of the empire.[29] His policies, however, antagonized many Mongols, and soon he lost his influential position to a Persian, 'Abd al-Rahman, who was appointed minister for North China and continued the policy of ruthless exploitation that had existed before Yeh-lü Ch'u-ts'ai's reforms.

The reigns of Ogodei and Guyuk were characterized by maladministration:

for all practical purposes, the empire was not administered at all. Their reigns were strictly within the steppe tradition. The Mongols lived off their loot and the tribute they exacted, without regard for the possible consequences—depletion of resources, economic collapse, and so on. Of the two, Ogodei was less inclined to forethought. He was an extravagant spender, and although his advisors cautioned, they were completely powerless to stop or restrain him. One of the most important consequences of the absence of administrative direction and control was that many Mongol princes ceased to forward the central government's share of revenue to Qaraqorum. The brevity of Guyuk's reign was probably a factor in the empire's survival. The extravagance of the Mongol court could not have continued.

When Mongke acceded to the throne, the administration of the empire had been totally disrupted. Drastic and ruthless measures were needed to restore the empire's financial base, and Mongke did not hesitate to take them. After eliminating potential contenders from the House of Ogodei, he abolished all the privileges that local chieftains had granted themselves and simultaneously returned to the dual administrative structure begun in the reign of Chinggis-khan. His most important reform, however, was the division of the empire into a territorially based feudalism consisting of four regions which maintained their traditional administrative structures but which were controlled by a Chinese-style bureaucracy in Qaraqorum. Nevertheless, he affirmed Mongol preference for a non-Chinese, indeed a non-native, officialdom within this central bureaucracy, for it would have the interests of the empire as a whole in mind and would be less biased in favor of its own territories. Thus, the supranational bureaucracy was formally institutionalized during Mongke's reign.[30]

One of the prerequisites for efficient administration was the standardization of fiscal matters and practices throughout the empire; thus, Mongke revived Yeh-lü Ch'u-ts'ai's ideas. The very able Muslim official, Mahmud Yalavach, who had already participated in the Ogodei reforms but had lost favor during Toragana's regency, was appointed to direct the fiscal reforms. These were reminiscent of the 1229 and 1236 reforms in that their primary aim was to rationalize the hodgepodge of practices that existed. Standardization was necessary to provide Qaraqorum with a steady supply of revenue, since it was remote from the revenue-producing regions of the empire.

Most of the details of Mongke's administrative reforms are not known. At the time of his death, the empire was well on its way to having a formally centralized bureaucracy, and it appears unquestionable that, had it not been for Mongke's premature death, the Mongol empire might have assumed a substantially different administrative structure from the one that came into existence under Qubilai. Mongke's reforms were the last attempt to place the entire empire under one centralized bureaucratic administration in Qaraqorum. With Qubilai's accession to the throne, each of the empire's subdivisions was to adopt an administrative structure modeled on the one that already existed in the area it occupied. To what degree central administration of the empire as a whole continued to exist during Qubilai's reign cannot be determined for lack of information. Nevertheless, in certain economic matters, particularly taxation, the subdivisions maintained nearly identical policies for a long time, suggesting that there was some form of centralized decision making.

When Qubilai became governor of China, he assumed control over a country that had a long tradition of bureaucratic administration. Chinese society has been described by Etienne Balaźs as a permanent bureaucratic society, and, indeed, understanding Chinese society is difficult unless one is familiar with its political and institutional history.[31] China, an agrarian society, was dominated by a class of scholar-officials, which, although extremely small in numbers compared to the total population, was almost omnipotent and without which no ruler could be expected to govern this vast and varied territory. Chinese society is best described with a maxim attributed to Mencius: "Some labor with their minds and some labor with their brawn. Those who labor with their minds, govern others; those who labor with their strength, are governed by others. Those who are governed by others, support them. Those who govern others, are supported by them."[32] The scholar-official class was also self-perpetuating; the essential and virtually sole criterion for admission to it was education, and it held a monopoly over the educational system. Although the scholar-official fulfilled many functions—such as, for example, teacher or judge—its real *raison d'être* was the administration of the empire.

When or how Qubilai became familiar with Confucian political thought is one of the many unknowns in his early career. Contemporary documents give the impression that he was thoroughly familiar with the Confucian ethic.[33] From the start of his career, and before he became emperor, Qubilai was surrounded by an important group of Chinese advisors, all of whom have left proposals addressed to him for a Confucian-style government for the empire. In 1260, as soon as he had proclaimed himself Great Khan, Qubilai adopted these proposals and began their implementation. Thus, he provided his domains with an adequate administrative structure that not only gave him and his court the necessary tools of government, but guaranteed permanent benefits from the conquered Chinese territories.[34] The system adopted by the Mongol emperor was a combination of the T'ang and the Jürchen administrative systems.

Although Qubilai adopted the Chinese bureaucratic system, he did not slavishly follow existing practices. On the recommendation of his Chinese advisors, in particular Liu Ping-chung (1216–1274), Shih T'ien-tzu (1202–1275), and Hsü Heng (1209–1281),[35] certain important modifications were adopted within the central structure itself. The Mongols intended to remain in China as conquerors and as such needed more control over the bureaucracy than previous emperors had enjoyed. It was necessary to reshape the bureaucratic superstructure so that the emperor had direct and absolute control over the bureaucracy and political sabotage on the part of this bureaucracy, which remained predominantly ethnically Chinese, could be reduced to an absolute minimum.

At the top of the bureaucratic structure, under the direct authority of the emperor, was the Central Secretariat (*Chung-shu sheng*), which was in charge of all state affairs. From it depended the traditional Chinese Six Ministries (*Liu pu*), the Provincial Administration (*Hsing-sheng*), and the Pacification Office (*Hsüan-fu sheng*). In previous dynasties, the Six Ministries were policy-making bodies from which all other offices depended. During the Yüan, however, they were merely technical bureaus for the implementation of the policies formulated by the Central Secretariat. Nominally under the Central Secretariat, but actually under the emperor's direct control, were two other offices of crucial importance for the maintenance of Mongol superiority: the Bureau of Military Affairs (*Shu-mi yüan*) and the Censorate (*Yü-shih t'ai*). In previous dynasties, the *Shu-mi yüan*'s primary function was handling general affairs of state. During the Yüan this function was removed and transferred to the Central Secretariat, while the *Shu-mi yüan* retained strictly military functions. Nevertheless, throughout the Yüan dynasty, it is often difficult to maintain a clear distinction between these offices. The normal task of the Censorate had been one of supervising the bureaucrats in the central administration and the provinces. Moreover, through remonstrances, it was supposed to keep the emperor within the Confucian structure, a task not always observed literally.[36] During the Yüan it became an additional instrument for the emperor, and hence the Mongol elite, to exert strict control over the Chinese population and Chinese officialdom.[37]

Qubilai also created several other offices which had no precedents in Chinese administrative history. As will be discussed below, since the formative years of the empire, the Mongols had used religious institutions as a means of control over the local population; it is therefore not surprising that the special and unique offices created by Qubilai dealt with the religions found in China. Up to four offices were created, all theoretically belonging to the Board of Rites (*Li pu*), one of the traditional Six Ministries, but in fact under the direct rule of the Central Secretariat.

The most important of these offices was the *Hsüan-cheng yüan*, the Office of Buddhist Affairs.[38] This office was created, albeit under a different name, in 1260, and its first nominal head was the Tibetan 'Phags-pa Lama, who also received the honorific title, carried later by other holders of the post, of *Kuo-shih,* or Imperial Teacher.[39] Probably because its first head was Tibetan, the office has often been described as concerned primarily with Tibet, and this interpretation, to a certain degree, enhances the status of Tibetan-Mongol relations during the Yüan. Nothing in the available evidence warrants such a conclusion. Tibetan affairs were only part of the office's responsibilities, and its primary activity was political control over the Buddhist community within China proper.[40] The offices of the Christian, Taoist, and Islamic cults were grouped under the aegis of the *Chi-hsien yüan,* a Sung title normally referring to the imperial library. It appears to have had a decidedly less important role than the *Hsüan-cheng yüan,* for not only is little information available about it, but it appears to have been a sinecure for retired officials.⁴¹

Exerting strict control over China and its population, however, was not Qubilai's sole concern. Equally important was the restoration of China's economy and especially of its mainstay, agriculture. It is ironic that agriculture, the foundation of the Confucian state, was to receive administrative recognition during the reign of a conquest dynasty whose orientation before its occupation of China was antagonistic to agriculture. Qubilai showed his interest in agricultural revival in China from the moment he assumed the throne. He ordered the Pacification Office to actively promote agriculture. In 1270 an Office of Agricultural Affairs was created, the *Ssu-nung-ssu,* which eventually became the Great Office of Agriculture, *Ta-ssu-nung.* Its basic administrative unit was the *she,* which has been defined by Matsumoto Yoshimi as "an organization for the advancement of agriculture designed to restore and further agricultural production which had been hurt by warfare and turmoil."⁴²

By and large, the reorganization of the administrative structure and the creation of new offices were completed within a decade of Qubilai's accession to the throne. What emerged was in essence a typical Chinese structure with one major and important modification: an institutional transformation that gave the emperor much more power than any previous emperor had enjoyed. The emperor now had direct, unhampered control over a vast bureaucratic system. None of the emperors who succeeded Qubilai, Chinese or other, ever changed this situation. The Chinese emperor now was a full fledged autocrat.

To staff this vast bureaucracy, Qubilai used the regular Chinese recruitment channels, with the exception of the examination system. Edicts were issued for the recommendation of "worthy" individuals, and serious material inducements were offered to attract the scholar-official class. The Chinese thus recruited, however, never held the key positions within the administration; these were in the hands of the non-Chinese conquest elite. Among the Chinese themselves a discriminatory factor existed in that, until the final decades of the dynasty, it was nearly impossible for a Southern Chinese to hold any post of importance.

In the past, the examination system was the normal road to officialdom, assuring the government a steady supply of officials qualified in Confucian thought. Qubilai's pragmatic orientation and his desire to keep the Chinese from dominating the administration were probably behind his decision not to use the examination system. This created certain problems, since there was no other system to provide the government with a reservoir of potential officials. In 1315, therefore, the examination was reintroduced. It differed, however, from the system of the Sung dynasty in emphasizing the Four Books with their Chu Hsi commentary and in paying no attention to rigid metrical composition. At the same time, a quota system was created to assure the Mongols and other Central Asians a numerical advantage over the Chinese.[43] The examination was again abolished as part of the anti-Confucian program of Bayan of the Merkid. This, however, also worked to the disadvantage of many Mongols and thus attracted resentment against Bayan, who soon lost power. After his demise, the examination system became, once again, the standard entrance to the bureaucracy.

The establishment of a formal administrative structure of the Chinese type was not only a practical matter, but also formed part of Qubilai's policy to legitimate Mongol rule in terms of Chinese political concepts. Legitimation, however, required more than the adoption of a Chinese administration. It also required the establishment of proper rites and music, integral parts of the Chinese political and administrative structure. Former Jürchen officials were charged with the development of appropriate forms, which were officially promulgated in 1271. Equally important was the maintenance of the academies, and in particular of the Han-lin Academy, the Imperial University. Qubilai actively promoted education and went so far as to create a special Mongol Han-lin Academy, about which very little is known.

The last step in legitimation was the adoption of an appropriate Chinese reign title. This was accomplished in 1272, when Qubilai adopted the title *Ta-Yüan,* derived from *I-ching,* the "Book of Changes," and thus symbolic. Roughly translated, it means the "great origin," or the "great first." The adoption of these formal symbols of Chinese statehood, however, did not mean that the Mongols in China had abandoned all their own customs and symbols. Although the matter has not been subjected to much study, it appears that the Mongols maintained a dual administrative and political structure, similar to the one that had existed under the Ch'i-tan and the Jürchen. This is most clearly shown in the Yüan military structure, but the Mongols also maintained their own rites, quite distinct from the Confucian ones they had formally adopted. The separation between Mongol and Chinese can be found in nearly all aspects of the structure of the Yüan, even in cultural affairs.[44]

The Yüan dynasty, however, was and remained a conquest dynasty. Reforms were carried out with only two goals in mind: the control of the population and the derivation of maximum benefit from the country's economic resources without exhausting them. Throughout the reign of Qubilai and his first two successors there was not the slightest need for the Mongol rulers to make their interests coincide with those of the population at large; that they did so only facilitated their task. Even the reforms of Toghto (d. 1356), which could be superficially interpreted as having the welfare of the people in mind, were in reality aimed at restoring and preserving Mongol control. His failure resulted in the collapse of the central authority.[45] It is therefore not surprising that the military remained the Mongol rulers' principal administrative branch, and that next to the Central Secretariat, the Bureau of Military Affairs had the most important role. From the information available, the guard units stationed in the capital totalled about two hundred twenty-five thousand men. The Mongol provincial troops were quartered in garrison towns and acted as occupation forces. A total of ten thousand men per province (a unit consisted of a thousand men) was the theoretical distribution of the troops. If all the soldiers in these units were not necessarily Mongols, all commanders were Mongols or Central Asians. By 1308 the military in the provinces numbered some seven hundred twenty thousand men, substantially more than the number of officials in the bureaucracy. In 1315 the latter numbered around twenty-two thousand five hundred.[46]

Our knowledge of the administrative structure of the Il-khans and the Golden Horde, not to mention the Chaghatai Khanate, is much more limited than our knowledge of the Yüan. There are many reasons for this, but the principal one is simply that less information has survived because the Islamic world did not have as strong a historiographical tradition as the Sinitic world. The problems resulting from this situation are compounded by scholarly neglect of the western part of the Mongol empire. Thus, much has to be inferred, cautiously, from the situation as it was immediately before and after the Mongol empire.

When the Mongols invaded the Middle East, they were not confronted, as had been the case in China, with a homogeneous population. The original Persian and Arab populations had intermingled with people of Turkic origins. Many of the ruling houses—for example the Saljuqs and the Mamluks—were also of Turkic origin. As was shown earlier, even descendants of the Ch'i-tan had settled in the area. The ruling houses and the entire population, however, were Islamic, and this was most important. Many of the Turkic tribes that conquered areas in the Middle East and created their own empires, moreover, belonged to the Islamic faith at the time of the conquest, or shortly thereafter.

Although a sharp dichotomy existed between the ruling classes and the people, that is, between the Turkic and the non-Turkic populations, all social classes were united by a common respect for the religious law of the *shari'at*.[47] The sultan was described as the "Shadow of God" on earth. The common man was expected to pay his taxes and pray for the ruler, who, in turn, provided him with protection and justice. He was the supreme worldly judge, and it was recommended that he devote at least two days a week to dispensing justice.[48]

The power of the sultan was, in theory, absolute and totally arbitrary. More frequently than not, it was obtained and maintained by force and required for its survival the concentration of the administration of the state in the sultan's hands. Bureaucracies existed solely to carry out the desires of the ruler; they never acquired the semi-independent status that the Chinese bureaucracy had maintained both before and during Mongol rule.

The primary function of the administrative structure in the Middle Eastern territories was the collection of taxes. The bureaucracy had three levels: the central, provincial, and district administrations. By and large, the latter two were reflections of the structure of the central bureaucracy. The central administration was headed by the vizier (*wasir*), in essence, the head of the State Chancellery (*dīwān i-īnshā*), which exerted control over five major offices, three of which dealt specifically with the state's finances. These were the Superior Financial Administration (*dīwan-i istīfā-i mamālik*), the Superior Accounting Administration (*dīwan-i ishrāf-i mamālik*), and the Superior Financial Inspection Administration (*dīwan-i nazar-i mamālik*). The other two major offices were the Military Administration and the Postal Administration. At the provincial level, the structure differed only in that there were a governor and a provincial vizier and the only administrative offices were the financial ones. At the district level, one found the same structure, with the addition of the Tax Collector (*'āmil*) and the Irrigation Officer (*mi'mār, āmīr-āb*).[49]

Although the Middle Eastern states, in particular the Saljuq and the Qwarezm states, had powerful bureaucratic structures, they were organized on a feudal basis according to the so-called *iqtā'* system. Its principal notion was the distribution of land, part of whose revenue was to be transmitted to the sultan. The concept of the *iqtā'* and its forms underwent substantial modifications and led to various definitions. The system that the Mongols inherited was primarily that of the Saljuqs, under which the *iqtā'* had largely become a military system, and the holder of the *iqtā'* merely a guarantor for the tax income.[50] When the military became the principal tax collector—a practice that easily led to abuses, especially in a society without institutional restraints on authority—this situation gave rise to political unstability. If the sultan was a powerful man, the system contributed to the general wealth of the state. If, on the other hand, he was weak, the tax system contributed to a disintegration of the political system and to serious economic disruption. These tendencies were aggravated by the fact that the *iqtā'* had become hereditary, thus removing the sultan's control over *iqtā'*-land distribution.

The administrative system with which the Mongols were most familiar, even before their conquests, was the Chinese one. Like other steppe people before them, the Mongols were oriented towards the Middle Kingdom and, as was shown in the previous chapters, they conquered the Middle East more by chance than by plan. The Chinese administrative structure, however, did not particularly appeal to the Mongols, primarily because it placed too many restraints on the ruler—hence, Qubilai's major reforms. When the Mongols began their systematic conquest of the Middle Eastern countries, they encountered an aristocratic, feudal system that was quite congenial to them. Consequently, they adopted the existing system without major changes.[51]

Throughout the reign of the first six Il-khans, whatever administrative system there was was aimed at one thing: the maximum exploitation of the conquered territories without regard to the consequences. After the disastrous monetary experiments of Geikhatu, however, it was clear that administrative and economic reforms were necessary if the Mongols were to continue to exploit the area. As soon as Ghazan assumed the throne, he began a series of drastic reforms. He sought to recreate a strong central authority within the framework of the traditional Persian centralized feudal government. Although Ghazan died before he was able to accomplish all the reforms necessary to create a stable and economically secure government, his reforms put Persia on the road to recovery.

Ghazan's reforms were successful because he realized, more than any of his predecessors had, the importance of Islamic law. For a ruler to be effective over a long period of time, irrespective of his own personality, it was necessary for him to respect the *shari'at*; through this he obtained the allegiance of the people. In a sense, the Il-khan had to legitimate his rule. Ghazan accomplished this through his public and formal adoption of Islam as both his personal and his state's religion. The Mongols in Persia, like those in China, had to adopt the symbols of legitimacy in order to continue reaping the benefits of conquest. In Persia, too, the Mongols refrained from eliminating the local elite and incorporated them into the political and administrative structure. In contrast to the Yüan emperor, the Il-khan appears to have had little direct control over these coopted elites.

Unlike the Yüan and the Il-khans, the Golden Horde controlled territory that comprised both nomadic and sedentary areas. Their administrative structure reflected this duality; however, they never actually occupied the sedentary areas, and consequently there was a special branch for these areas, primarily Russia, within the administrative structure for the nomadic areas.

Like the Il-khan or the Islamic sultan, the ruler of the Golden Horde was an absolute ruler whose decisions were not to be questioned. The problem of legitimation never confronted the Golden Horde, primarily because of the Horde's early conversion to Islam and because not only the local elite, but also the general population was of Turkic origins. These factors facilitated contact between the two groups and, eventually, led to the complete Turkicization of the Golden Horde. Nevertheless, to be legitimate, the ruler of the Golden Horde had to be a member of the House of Jochi. This rule, although unwritten, was strictly enforced, and even as powerful a challenger as Noqai did not dare violate it.

Although a nomadic state, the Golden Horde was no longer a steppe empire in the traditional sense. Its primary economic orientation was towards the sedentary states, and trade, not looting and tribute, was the basis of its relationship with them. It controlled several subordinate states and had established extensive diplomatic and economic relations with the Byzantine and the Mamluk empires. Commercial relations had also been established with Venice and Genoa.[52] To deal adequately with diplomatic and trade affairs, the collection of local taxes, and the receipt of tribute, an administrative structure was required. Having created the city of Sarai, its capital,[53] on the lower reaches of the Kama, the Horde, probably under the influence of its predominantly Turkic population, adopted a system similar to that of the Saljuqs, and thus quite close to that of the Il-khans.

At the head of the administrative structure was the ruler of the Golden Horde. He was assisted by a regent, usually the crown prince, who assumed his functions when the ruler was away from the capital for a prolonged time. The Horde was alone in having this arrangement, which dated back to the time of Batu, when seasonal hunting expeditions often kept him away from the principal encampment. Directly below the ruler was the prime minister, the vizier, whose functions appear to have been similar to those of his Il-khanid counterpart. The ministries that made up the central administration were the same as those in the Il-khanid empire; the Horde, however, had a special chancellery for foreign relations, including relations with the submitted states. At the provincial and district levels, the administrative units were strictly of a financial and a police nature. The provinces were administered simultaneously by a governor and an emir; the distinction between these two offices is rather blurred, for they possessed basically the same authority. The primary function of the Horde's administration, if not the exclusive one, was financial.

In the submitted territories, like Russia, the Golden Horde did not create an administrative structure but ruled through existing institutions. Throughout most of the thirteenth century, Mongol presence was clearly felt, for the Mongols collected the tribute themselves. Early in the fourteenth century, this practice changed. Local princes and even the Orthodox Church were appointed to collect the tribute, so that the Mongols never became deeply involved in local politics, but nevertheless maintained a degree of control. These appointments were made by special decree, the *jarlyg*. To the Mongols, however, it did not matter who actually exerted the power conferred by the decree; in time, it was granted to whatever noble gave the Mongols the largest financial gift, and eventually the decrees were resold among the local princes themselves. Whenever the submitted states began to waver in their allegiance, the Mongols staged a punitive raid, after which they appointed new tribute collectors. In the end, however, the Golden Horde's policies contributed to the rise of the Muscovite state.[54]

Of all the empire's subdivisions, only the Chaghatai Khanate remained a steppe domain, even though within its borders were the territories of previous sedentary states and important cities such as Bukhara and Samarqand. Its steppe orientation was reflected in the administrative structure of the Khanate; in accordance with the steppe tradition, administration was kept to an absolute minimum. It was only when its last ruler, Tarmashirin, converted to Islam that changes came about in the Khanate's administration. The major cities within it served only as rallying points, and the ruler's capital remained a mobile tent camp pitched near one city or another. In the areas where there had been an administrative structure prior to the Mongol conquest, it was allowed to continue. No attempt was made to unify the different structures or to eliminate them in favor of the nomadic world order.[55] Whatever administrative structure existed at the ruler's court was probably limited to financial matters, and even this does not appear to have been important or much developed. The Khanate's rulers did not hesitate to sack their own cities when in need of funds: witness Baraq's sack of Samarqand.

To assure effective control over the administrative and the political structures of a conquest empire, an efficient and fast communications network was essential. This existed in all subdivisions of the Mongol empire in the postal relay system, the 'yam. The system provided, by means of an intricate relay network, for quick communication from one end of the empire to another. Such a system had already existed in Chinggis-khan's time, and probably was the continuation of a pre-existing communications network. Networks of this type, with major differences between them, existed not only on the steppe, but also in the conquered sedentary states. The Mongols reformed and streamlined the existing networks to obtain efficient, fast, and nearly uniform networks throughout their empire. Special administrations were created within each of the empire's subdivisions for these networks, which were known as 'yam, the postal relay system. The relay stations provided accommodations as well as fresh mounts to the couriers. Special legislation was established governing the obligations of both the relay station managers and the couriers.[56]

The Economic Structure

Before their conquests and the establishment of their empire, the Mongols had a typical pastoral economy. To the steppe, with its limited resources, trade was of vital importance; its staple product, the horse, had to be bartered for agricultural products and other goods. Contrary to a common misconception, the Central Asian nomad was an excellent trader, and because of the importance of trade, he frequently equated it with diplomacy.[57] Although the nomads' primary orientation, political and otherwise, was always towards China, there was a major conceptual difference between them with regard to economic matters. Agrarian China was basically self-sufficient and had only a limited need for the steppe's products. Furthermore, the Confucian ethic viewed trade as a necessary evil, to be practiced as little as possible and kept always under strict control. Usually, then, China was reluctant to engage in trade with Central Asia, and frequently this reluctance was a cause of war. In contrast, trade relations between Central Asia and the Islamic states were excellent, and Islamic traders were often the most important middlemen in Central Asia's trade.

As was indicated earlier, the exact causes of the Mongols' conquest of the world are unknown. Political ambition, the historical traditions of the steppe, and economic considerations were probably equally important. The economic situation on the steppe on the eve of the Mongol conquests is among the least-known features of this period's history. It is safe, however, to assume that the steppe's economy was thriving: serious difficulties in animal husbandry would have deprived the Mongols of their principal means of conquest, an adequate supply of horses.

Soon after the Mongols began their conquests, it became clear that economic considerations were part of the Mongol ruler's plans. Rather than merely loot the conquered areas, the Mongols established political control over them and began to exert full control over their financial and economic resources. It appears that, for the first time, the nomadic horseman wanted to assure himself a steady supply of foodstuffs, luxury products, and tax revenues, in a sense, to gain control over the means of production. The Mongol conquest of the Islamic world revealed a similar pattern, although not during Chinggis-khan's lifetime: the sole purpose of his western campaign was to punish the Qwarezmian empire. When, however, Ogodei resumed the campaign, he clearly intended to gain full political and economic control over the Islamic states.

The Mongols' primary interest in the conquered territories was the profit they could derive from them. Hence, they were interested primarily in revenues and did not pay close attention to how these revenues were actually raised. This attitude prevailed through the reign of Mongke; during that period, the economic structure of the Mongol empire and its tax-collecting structure were synonymous. The Mongols first seized control over the custom houses, thus obtaining control over the traditional tolls on commerce and manufacturing. These tolls, known in Mongol as the *tamgha,* began almost as soon as the Mongols had secured a particular region, and for a while it was the principal form of revenue. Once control was firmly established and the conquerors had gained a knowledge of the local situation, the traditional levies of the sedentary states were continued, with payment to the new rulers or their representatives, and to these traditional tax burdens, the Mongols added new ones. Traditional nomadic taxation forms were extended to the sedentary states; the tribute (*alban*) and the levy (*qubchiri*) were the principal ones. The tribute was a standardized form of payment, whereas the levy was an extraordinary exaction to fill specific needs. All taxes were paid in cash, in kind, or through special forms of service.[58]

The system that existed, if it can be called a system, led to confusion. On several occasions, attempts were made to streamline it, in particular by Yeh-lü Ch'u-ts'ai and Mahmud Yalavach, but the reforms initiated by these two men brought only temporary order to the hodgepodge Mongol taxation system. At the time of Mongke's death, the system was basically unchanged, except that Qaraqorum exerted more control over the collection agents. Following Mongke's death, the subdivisions assumed a more independent role than before. Consequently, no further attempts were made to unify the taxation system, although everywhere both *alban* and *qubchiri* were maintained, frequently under a drastically different nomenclature. The *de facto* financial independence of the empire's subdivisions led to important policy modifications. In the two subdivisions created in the sedentary areas, the Yüan and the Il-khans, an economic rather than a fiscal policy was developed. In the Golden Horde and in the Chaghatai Khanate, the traditional nomadic fiscal practices continued more or less unchanged.

Qubilai was unquestionably the most enlightened of the Mongol rulers. Even before he assumed the Mongol throne, he must have realized that the existing disorderly state of exploitation ran counter to the Mongols' long-term interests. When he assumed the throne and began his administrative reforms in China, he introduced measures to revive the seriously disrupted Chinese economy. As was shown earlier, one of his most important reforms, both administratively and economically, was the revitalization and restructuring of agriculture. The success of these reforms, ironically, was the basis for China's economic resurgence. Another major reform initiated by Qubilai was the creation of a standardized paper currency system throughout his domain.

Paper currency as such was not a Yüan innovation; it had been created during the T'ang dynasty. However, the Yüan was the first to apply it on a systematic and uniform basis and also to give it, at least until near the end of the dynasty, a solid backing in silver and other precious materials. By Chinggis-khan's time the Mongols were already familiar with printed paper money through their contacts with the Jürchen Chin dynasty. The Jürchen, in turn, had derived their knowledge of the system from the Sung dynasty, even though the use of paper currency changed between the periods of the Northern and the Southern Sung.[59] During these two dynasties, however, metal currencies remained the primary form of payment.

Before Qubilai's accession to the throne, the Mongol conquerors issued a paper currency three times, but these first issuances were intended mainly as stopgaps for the treasury. No attempt was made to put the paper currency on a sound financial basis, nor was there any attempt to unify the different systems.[60] In 1260—almost immediately after his coronation—Qubilai began to bring some order to the situation. An edict was issued creating a new paper currency known as the "exchange notes" (*chiao-ch'ao*). These notes came in different denominations and were convertible into either silver or copper. In the past, exchange rates had fluctuated drastically, and counterfeiting had been rife. Therefore, simultaneously with the edict creating a new currency, edicts governing the exchange rates were issued, along with new laws against counterfeiters. A solid backing in precious metal was created at the central treasury, and the number of places where currency could be issued was severely restricted to permit the central government to exert more control.

Throughout Qubilai's reign this system functioned well and was carefully administered. Under his successors, however, a tendency to use the printing press to fill financial deficits became evident, thus aggravating the rampant inflation that began to disrupt the country's economy after 1350. On several occasions, the central government resorted to drastic measures to regain control over the financial crisis, including official devaluation of the currency, but to no avail. The worsening political conditions after 1329 contributed substantially to the worsening economic situation. Furthermore, laxness in enforcing the currency laws resulted in an increase in counterfeit notes, as well as unauthorized currency emissions. Nevertheless, the paper currency system created by the Yüan was an efficient one and was adopted by the two succeeding dynasties with but minor modifications.[61]

The revival of agriculture and the creation of an efficient currency system were only part of Qubilai's efforts to revitalize the Chinese economy. It was equally important to stimulate internal and external trade, but this required the restoration of the country's road and waterway infrastructure. Most of Qubilai's first two decades of rule were spent on this project, and one of his more impressive achievements was the restoration of the Grand Canal linking the North and the South, neglected since the fall of the Northern Sung. The restoration of the communications infrastructure served two purposes, and while economic restoration was the primary one, the fact that it would permit Mongol forces to move quickly from one area to another was not lost on Qubilai. Mongol interest in trade caused the Confucian censure to fall into neglect. Many people, especially those of the scholar-official class, who prior to the Mongols engaged only cautiously in this activity, were now able to do it quite openly. As Marco Polo's account shows, Qubilai's efforts at revitalizing China's economy were quite successful. This period was one of the few in which foreign trade was an important factor in the Chinese economy. China's ports were bustling with activity, and imports from all over the world flowed into China.[62]

Qubilai's economic reforms were not aimed at improving the lot of the common people, but at assuring the conquerors a steady source of revenue; that the reforms also benefited the population at large was serendipitous, for it reduced the chance of rebellion. So far as Qubilai's aims are concerned, the economic infrastructure of Yüan China served primarily for the collection of individual and business taxes. This was a common purpose throughout the Mongol empire. The Yüan taxation system can be divided into three major categories, individual, monopoly, and commercial taxes. The principal difference between the Yüan and the other subdivisions of the empire was that the Yüan revitalized tax-producing institutions.

The individual taxes levied fell into three categories: the land tax, the head tax, and the household tax. In general these taxes were payable, respectively, in grain, in cash, and in corvée labor. The organization of the tax collection system along Chinese lines resulted in a twofold division of the population: those who received preferential treatment, and those who paid the full load of the tax burden. The first group consisted of the conquerors themselves and the people assimilated to them, and the clergy, with Buddhists the largest group. The other group was divided into four classes, although the specific differences between these classes are not yet clear. The bulk of the population in this group must have belonged to the first category, those subject to full taxation. The three other classes were tax exempt in varying degrees.

The monopoly taxes and commercial taxes were levied on all businesses. Since the Han dynasty, the central government of China had established a monopoly over the production and sale of certain commodities; the principal one was salt. Since its introduction, the salt monopoly had constituted one of the primary sources of revenue for the central government. The Mongols followed this practice, and for them, too, the salt monopoly was the primary source of commercial tax revenue.[63] Other state monopolies were those on tea, liquor and vinegar production, and mining of precious metals. These monopolies were less efficient in producing revenue, for they were much harder to control. The commercial tax was levied on all forms of production, all sales, and all means of transportation, including the use of roads and bridges.

The Chinese economy continued to be healthy during the reigns of Qubilai's first two successors. As the Mongol court became more and more involved in palace politics, the court's control over the activities of the other members of the ruling classes, especially in the provinces, declined. As the extravagant luxury of the court increased, so did taxation and corvée labor. About thirty years after Qubilai's death, taxation had returned to the exorbitant level of the pre-Qubilai reforms. Court extravagance and maladministration coincided with the increased Confucianization of the court and the upper levels of the administrative system. These elements combined to contribute to the economic crisis, which was further exacerbated by inflation and constant currency devaluation.

The scholar-official class and the Mongol nobility, relying primarily on salaries for their income, were seriously affected by the economic decline, and consequently they began to look for other sources of revenue. The most convenient sources were the peasants in the territories under their jurisdiction. The exactions of the officials, combined with the already heavy taxation and monetary instability, aggravated the plight of the peasant. Another indirect result of the Confucianization and the economic uncertainty was that the upper classes and the monasteries again began to acquire vast tracts of land. Most of this land, whether acquired legally or illegally, became tax exempt; the resulting extra tax burden fell on the peasants, who had less land to farm, and thus less revenue, while taxes continued to climb. The crushing burdens to which they were subjected by Chinese and Mongols alike led to rebellions that helped to topple Mongol control in China.

Persia's economy before the Mongol conquests, in contrast to China's, was based on agriculture, pastoral nomadism, and crafts.[64] The Mongol invasion, as described by contemporary sources, was a major catastrophe. The Middle East witnessed a sudden and drastic drop in its population: the contemporary accounts reckon that five million people were killed in the cities of Nishapur, Merv, Herat, and Baghdad alone. Quite possibly these numbers are inflated, but both anti-Mongol and pro-Mongol sources give high figures and an impression of utter devastation. The devastation was so enormous that Persia did not fully recover until long after the disappearance of the Mongols themselves. Marco Polo (in the late thirteenth century) and Ibn Battuta (in the 1330s) were struck by the same desolate scene that had been witnessed nearly a century earlier by the Taoist monk Ch'ang-ch'un. There is a stark and appalling contrast between their reports and those of pre-Mongol travellers. In Tus, for example, a mere fifty houses were occupied, and the once-flourishing city of Nishapur was at one time completely deserted. Many cities and villages were never rebuilt.[65] That killing on such a massive scale caused economic dislocation goes without saying, but the drop in population was only one of the factors in Persia's economic decline. Two other causes were equally important: first, an increase in nomadism at the expense of agriculture, and, second, the fiscal policy of the Mongols.

Persia included semiarid and arid areas where the principal form of economic activity was pastoral nomadism; this is true of some of these areas even today. Under the Ummayyads and the Saljuqs, however, pastoral nomadism did not play a very important role, and agriculture was the mainstay of the economy. The Mongols, with their inbred dislike for the peasantry, favored nomadism. The population decline made it easy to convert excellent agricultural land into excellent pasture land, sharply reducing the amount of arable land available. Although the agricultural output fell off, it continued to be the basis for the Persian economy. The feudal exploitation of the peasantry, combined with the Mongol disinterest in agriculture, led to a centuries-long stagnation: the agricultural tools used at the beginning of the present century were not much different from those used at the time of the Il-khans. Even though agriculture was one of the prime sources of revenue, the Il-khans, in sharp contrast to the Yüan, never expressed any interest in it.

If the declines in population and agricultural production adversely affected the Persian economy, it was delivered a near death blow by Mongol taxation. The Mongols never took the drop in population into consideration, but left the existing taxes at pre-conquest levels. They were, however, unable to collect taxes at those levels and so added new taxes of their own; furthermore, they modified the tax collection system to obtain more cash. The basic tax, usually paid in kind, was on the land, and the new Mongol collection system placed an extremely heavy burden on the peasantry, since it required cash payments and forced the peasants to sell their entire crop to obtain the necessary cash. Subsequently, they had to purchase their own food, often at inflated prices, for purchases were also subject to taxation. The peasant became permanently indebted.

The new taxes introduced by the Mongols were, with the exception of the *tamgha,* variants of nomadic taxation forms. The *tamgha* was levied on all forms of trade and appears to have been about 10 percent of the value of each transaction. The *'avarid* tax was normally used only to cover extraordinary expenses, but it was levied frequently and was not fixed or predictable. The *tarh* tax involved the compulsory sale of products to the ruling classes at prices well below market value. These taxes were accompanied by physical forms of taxation, such as corvée labor, billeting of troops, carriage duty, and an obligation to provide animals, without reimbursement, to the postal service. In sum, it was an extremely heavy tax burden. Nevertheless, the total amount collected during the Il-khanid period never approached the amount collected before the Mongol conquests:[66] the Il-khans collected about 20 percent of what their predecessors had amassed. When it is remembered that the Mongols exploited their domains to the utmost, the difference is a clear illustration of the dramatic consequences of the Mongol conquest.

The first two Il-khans, Hulagu and Abaqa, were excellent rulers, but only from the Mongol point of view. Their policies never took into consideration the seriousness of the economic situation, nor did they even consider that the constant application of their policies could result in economic collapse. Once, at the time of Geikhatu's attempt to introduce a Chinese-style paper currency, the entire economy of the Il-khanid empire ground to a halt. Of all the Il-khans, only Ghazan was concerned with the long-term consequences of his economic policies. Like his predecessors, he was not particularly interested in the well-being of his subjects, but merely with a steady supply of revenue for the Mongol elite. Consequently, he followed Qubilai's example and introduced measures to revive the Persian economy.[67] Most of Ghazan's reforms dealt with taxation, the principal cause of the Il-khanid economic problems. A new, more equitable method of collecting the land tax was established. Payments were partly in kind, partly in cash. All taxes, including the land tax, were set at predetermined rates and, instead of being collected haphazardly according to the court's needs, they were collected twice a year, in spring and fall. Many taxes, like the *tamgha,* were halved, and most of the extraordinary levies were abolished. Physical forms of taxation were drastically reduced, and care was taken not to impose them during periods crucial to agriculture and not to overburden any one category of people. Ghazan also attempted to restore a viable currency system, a dire necessity after Geikhatu's experiments. He ordered the adoption of fixed exchange rates for silver and a uniform system of weights and measurements throughout the empire. Nor did Ghazan neglect the agricultural sector. His most important order was the restoration of the crucial irrigation system, which his predecessors had allowed to deteriorate because canals interfered with the freedom of movement desired by the nomadic horsemen.[68]

As a result of these reforms, the Persian economy began a slow upturn. Although Ghazan reduced the overall tax burden, revenues of the central *divan* (the treasury) increased. Prior to the reforms, the *divan* collected some seventeen million dinars; after the reforms, twenty-one million dinars. The beneficial consequences of Ghazan's reforms continued to be felt during Oljeitu's reign, when the administration of the *divan* was in the hands of the very talented Rashid al-Din. When political intrigues eliminated him, the Il-khanid state quickly returned to a situation similar to that of the pre-Ghazan days. With Rashid al-Din's death, the Mongol aristocracy regained the power it had lost because of Ghazan's reforms. The political intrigues and the civil wars during and after the reign of Abu Sa'id brought to nought all attempts to recreate a vital economic structure in Persia, and under the Il-khanid successor states, the situation did not improve. In fact, it got worse, as a consequence of the rise to power of Timur-i-leng, better known as Tamerlane. It was not until well into the reign of the Safavids, some three hundred years later, that the dire consequences of the Mongol invasion began to disappear.

Unlike their kinsmen in China and Persia, the Mongols of the Golden Horde never left the steppe. The Golden Horde avoided many of the problems of the Mongols in China and in Persia by not settling in the agricultural sections of their domains; the separation of agriculture and pastoral nomadism was facilitated by the geographical features of the Horde's domain. Moreover, the destruction in this part of the world, although great, did not come close to that dealt in China and Persia, and the economy was proportionately less affected. Although the land was fertile, the Horde's basic economic activity was pastoral nomadism, with a minimum of agriculture. It was not until the fifteenth century that agriculture began to dominate.[69]

As the Golden Horde resided in the Qipcaq steppe, not in the submitted sedentary areas, their fiscal system differed slightly from that of the Yüan and the Il-khans in that the nomadic population, whether Turkic or Mongol, was also subject to taxes. These taxes were based on the size of the herd, but were much lighter than those exacted from the conquered people. The taxes levied on the latter were basically the same as those of the Il-khanid domain prior to Ghazan's reforms. Taxes were levied regardless of economic conditions, and the Golden Horde was as harsh in exacting them as the other subdivisions of the empire were. According to al-'Umari (1301–1349), the Horde's taxes were so high that when a natural disaster struck, people were forced to sell their children into slavery to raise the exacted amounts.[70]

Taxes and tributes were important sources of revenue for the Golden Horde, but trade played an equally important role, a natural consequence of both the Horde's strategic location and the Mongols' generally favorable attitude towards trade and traders. Located between Northern Europe and the Black Sea and on the trade routes between the Mediterranean, Persia, and China, the Horde found itself in an excellent position to become the principal intermediary in trade. Trade had always been important to the Crimea. With the Mongol occupation of the Qipcaq steppe and adjacent areas, the once unruly and dangerous hinterland had become peaceful. As long as unity prevailed within the Horde, it was safe and convenient to travel through the steppe. This safety was a major factor in the development of a bustling trade activity, which principally benefited the Horde. Trade was subject to taxation, but taxation was never onerous enough to hamper or destroy trade patterns. Trade was disrupted only when dissension broke out within the Horde.[71]

Once again, as was the case with the sociopolitical structure of the subdivisions of the Mongol empire, it can be noted that there were more similarities than differences. The essence of the economic structure was exploitation. In each of the subdivisions of the empire,[72] the Mongols created a similar taxation system and superimposed it on the existing tax structures, restructuring the latter only to the extent that the revenues were channeled directly into the Mongol treasuries. It is only in the details of the application of these policies, and in the names given to the different taxes, that there were major differences. With the notable exceptions of Qubilai and Ghazan, none of the Mongol rulers ever engaged in long-term economic planning. Even the reforms of these two rulers are seen, upon close scrutiny, to be aimed more at short-term profit than the long-term viability of the economy of the territories under their control.

Religion
under the Mongols

The religion of the Mongols, which did not basically change during the imperial period, was a shamanistic form of animism. The Mongols did not have a structured religion, but an amalgam of superstitious beliefs fitted into a rather loose framework of causal relations. Its features reflected life on the steppe. The principal deity, *Tengri,* was a rationalization of the forces of nature as embodied in the sky. Uncertainty about nature and its manifestations can be said to be the principal element of this belief.[73]

The Mongols were undoubtedly familiar with the organized religions of the sedentary states. From the beginning of the conquest, Chinggis-khan and the Mongols adopted a policy of absolute tolerance towards these religions. The common explanation for this attitude has been that the Mongols wanted to play it safe when it came to their own hereafter, supposedly because of the uncertainty of the Mongols' own religion and the impossibility of determining which of the many deities in the conquered territories was a real one. The Mongols, like most people of that period, were superstitious; this probably does partially explain their tolerance. It is a fairly simplistic explanation, however. When the career of the Mongol emperors is examined, it is clear that the tolerance was dictated to a very large degree by purely political considerations. To Chinggis-khan, the organized churches in the conquered territories seemed a useful tool for establishing Mongol authority because of their influence over the population at large. Therefore, he issued a series of edicts exempting religious institutions from all taxes, including corvée labor. Moreover, he ordered that the Mongols respect all religions and, in particular, treat them all equally. With regard to his personal beliefs, Chinggis-khan apparently never abandoned the traditional shamanistic and animistic beliefs of his ancestors.

Ogodei, like his father, remained true to the traditional religion of the Mongols, and he obeyed his father's orders to treat all religions equally. When Guyuk succeeded him, this state of affairs changed somewhat, even though Guyuk personally followed Chinggis-khan's decree. During his reign, both Nestorianism and Buddhism began to have a more important role at the court in Qaraqorum. The importance of Nestorianism was a consequence of the fact that Guyuk's mother belonged to that faith and exerted a great deal of influence over her son. The form of Buddhism at both Guyuk's and Ogodei's courts was the austere Chinese Buddhism of the Ch'an sect, better known under its Japanese name, *Zen*. Ch'an's attraction for the Mongols is by no means clear, but it may have been a consequence of Chinggis-khan's order that religious groups devote their time to praying for the Mongols' rulers.[74]

The reign of Mongke was no different from that of his predecessors. From some historians the impression can be gained that Mongke favored Confucianism, but Mongke's interest was limited to those aspects of Confucianism that dealt with statecraft. His principal advisor on Confucian matters was not even a Chinese, but a former Tangut official, Kao Chih-yao.[75] Mongke does not appear to have had a serious interest in religion as such; his preoccupations were the organization of the empire and the conquest of the Southern Sung. There are some indications that he was inclined, as far as his personal beliefs were concerned, towards Buddhism, but what variety of Buddhism is not known, and on the basis of the present evidence, his personal beliefs can best be described as pantheistic with some preference for Buddhism. In 1256 he is reported to have compared the great religions within the Mongol empire to a hand, the fingers representing Confucianism, Taoism, Christianity, and Islam, and the palm of the hand, Buddhism.[76] This statement cannot be taken at face value, for it is reported by an interested party: the Buddhists. Nevertheless, Mongke's reign is important from the religious-political viewpoint in that it witnessed the beginning of a serious dispute between the Buddhists and the Taoists, which had serious consequences for the state of religion in China.[77]

The conflict dated back at least to the reigns of Chinggis-khan and Ogodei and reflected centuries-old antagonisms. It was essentially of a political nature. During Mongke's reign, the nature of the conflict remained political, but both sides used philosophical arguments in their attempts to discredit each other. The critical date for the conflict is 1251, the year when Mongke appointed the Ch'an Buddhist Hai-yün as the leader of the Buddhist community and Li Chih-chang, a disciple of Ch'ang-ch'un, as the leader of the Taoist community. Previously, the conflict had taken place in China; following these appointments, and the resultant jockeying for political influence, the conflict erupted in Qaraqorum, where it would have been impolitic to engage in the physical violence that had characterized the dispute in North China. What brought the conflict into the open was the publication by Li Chih-chang, shortly after his appointment by Mongke, of a work entitled *Lao-tzu pa-shih-i hua-t'u* ("Eighty-one Illustrations on Lao-tzu"), an illustration to a Taoist work entitled *Hua hu ching* ("The Conversion of the Western Barbarians"). The gist of this work was that Lao-tzu, the legendary founder of Taoism, had gone to the Western Lands (that is, India) and that the Buddha was one of his disciples. Hence, Taoism preceded Buddhism, which was but a variant of Lao-tzu's teachings, and therefore Taoism should occupy the most exalted political position.

The philosophical arguments used by both sides, although intricate, are basically irrelevant to the dispute. Its importance lay in the fact that it cleared the way for Buddhism, including Tibetan Buddhism, to play an important role at Qubilai's court. As a result of the accusations and counteraccusations, Mongke decided that the issue had to be settled in a public debate. This occurred in the summer of 1255, and the Taoists were defeated. They did not admit defeat, however, and shortly after the first debate, the controversy arose again. In 1258 it was necessary to hold a second public debate, and this one was presided over by Qubilai. On the Buddhist side, there was the skillful debater the 'Phags-pa Lama, who, like all Tibetan monks, was an expert not only in debating, but also in Indian Buddhism. For fairness, Qubilai appointed a group of Confucians as referees in the debate, an appointment that favored the Buddhists, as most Confucians looked down upon Taoism. The Taoists were soundly defeated, and it was ordered that all the disputed books be burned. Having suffered a serious political setback, the Taoists nevertheless attempted a comeback, only to be severely persecuted by Qubilai in 1281. They never recovered from this persecution, in spite of an increase in popularity towards the end of the Yüan dynasty.

After these debates the 'Phags-pa Lama was appointed by Qubilai as the head of Buddhist affairs within the empire. As was shown in the previous chapter, Qubilai's favoritism towards Tibetan Buddhism was more apparent than real, and his motivations were purely political. Qubilai bestowed favors not only on Tibetan Buddhism, but also on Chinese Buddhism. The political importance of Buddhism is reflected in the creation of a special administration for Buddhist affairs, the *Hsüan-cheng yüan*. Although the role of Chinese Buddhism during the Yüan dynasty has never been examined seriously, one can say confidently that the favors bestowed upon it by the dynasty were politically motivated. Indeed, secret societies, many of which had a Buddhist foundation, presented a serious risk of rebellion,[78] and the Buddhist clergy appear to have had a strong hold over the local population, and even over a substantial number of officials. The Yüan spent large amounts on gifts and religious ceremonies and exempted almost all Buddhist institutions from taxation. Therefore, it is not surprising that in such a favorable atmosphere, Buddhist institutions assumed an important nonreligious role, becoming wealthy landlords and engaging on a large scale in such worldly activities as trade and banking: a far cry from the prayers requested by Chinggis-khan.

The growing monastic population soon became a major problem for the Yüan dynasty. Soldiers fled the army and peasants abandoned their fields to avoid taxes by joining Buddhist and Taoist monasteries, in such numbers that they soon began to threaten the military stability of the empire and were a drain on the treasury's resources. The court consequently adopted a policy aimed at restricting the size of the monastic population, as well as the amount of tax-free land the religious institutions were allowed to possess. Qubilai issued a decree to that effect in 1264, but with little success, as the law was not enforced. A serious attempt was made early in 1295. The decree stated that the religious institutions in Tibet, North China, Yünnan, and the Uighur territories were allowed to keep tax-free land if it had been acquired before the first month of that year (19 January–17 February 1295). All land acquired after that date, as well as land owned by religious institutions elsewhere, was subject to regular taxation.[79] But none of these laws was ever strictly enforced, and the religious institutions, especially those in China proper, became centers for antidynastic agitation.

The Yüan rulers basically followed the tradition of tolerance established at the time of Chinggis-khan. Whatever religious beliefs they possessed did not significantly affect court policies. This attitude on the part of the Yüan elite was facilitated by the dominance of the very worldly traditions of Confucianism, a politico-philosophical system that, at that time, cannot be described as a religion. During the Yüan dynasty two persecutions took place, one of the Taoists and one of the Muslims, the latter shortly after the 1328 coup.[80] These persecutions, however, were not carried out for religious reasons, but for purely economic and political ones. In that sense, the Yüan fitted into the Chinese tradition begun with the Buddhist persecutions of the T'ang dynasty in 841. During the Yüan, as under nearly all other Chinese dynasties, religion played no important political or social role because of the dominance of the Confucian ethic.

The case of the Mongols in the Middle East was substantially different. There they were confronted with a single, homogeneous, structured religion: Islam. At the time of the conquest, the Middle East had been dominated by Islam and divided into two major sects, the Sunni and the Shi'i. In Persia, the bulk of the population belonged to the Sunni sect. Mongol occupation of Persia deeply affected the religious structure of the area. It was the first time the Islamic world had been ruled by a non-Islamic group, one which, moreover, had no particular sympathy for Muslims. The elimination of the Ismailies and the death of the 'Abbasid caliph were severe blows to the faith, as well as to the Sunni sect. Most of the Muslim advisors to the Il-khans belonged to the Shi'i sect, and consequently the latter began to dominate the religious scene in Persia.[81] Under the Mongols, Persia slowly became a Shi'i state and has remained so until the present day.

The revival of non-Islamic tradition in Persia was a direct consequence of the great religious tolerance imposed by the early Mongol rulers. Nestorianism, which appears to have been widespread among Mongol women, resulted in a sympathy towards Christians in general; this attitude was probably a factor in the persistent Mongol attempts to establish a political alliance with the Christian West against the Mamluks. The Jewish community also assumed a more important role. Two Jews who held high political posts were the well-known Rashid al-Din and Sa'ud al-Daula, personal physician and minister to the Il-khan Arghun.[82] The most intriguing aspect of religious life under the Il-khans, however, is the role of Buddhism, about which not much is known, not even which form of Buddhism was predominant, and because of the lack of sources, not much will ever be known. It appears that Buddhist monks either accompanied the Mongols on their conquests or arrived in Persia shortly after Hulegu's campaigns. They appear to have replaced the Mongol shamans: hence the supposition that they were Tantric Buddhists. Of all the Il-khans, Arghun practiced Buddhism most conscientiously. It was during his reign that Buddhist temples were built in Persia. The principal characteristic of religious life under the Il-khans was that religion was a personal matter, not a state affair, similar to the situation under the Yüan.

The first of Sha'ban in the year 649 of the Hegira (16 June 1295 A.D.) is perhaps the most important date in the history of the Il-khans. It was the day on which Ghazan publicly converted to Islam, a conversion which, as was shown earlier, was based on political expediency rather than religious conviction. As soon as he acceded to the throne, shortly after his conversion, he ordered the persecution of the Buddhists throughout Persia and the destruction of all Buddhist temples. The *Jami'ut al-tawarikh* provides us with an interesting insight into Ghazan's beliefs.

> When the Lord of Islam, Ghazan, became a Muslim he commanded that all the idols should be broken and all the pagodas destroyed, together with all other temples, the presence of which in Muslim countries is prohibited by the shari'at and that all the communities of Idolaters [that is, Buddhists] be converted to Islam. . . . But some persevered in their hypocrisy while others returned to their wicked beliefs. And Ghazan said: "My father was an Idolater and died an Idolater and built for himself a temple which he made *vaqf* for that community [of Buddhists]. That temple I have destroyed; go ye there and live on alms."[83]

While Ghazan applied Islamic law rigorously during the first years of his reign, once his position on the throne was secure he relaxed his severity. The Islamic adherence of Ghazan and his successors seems to have been a function of political considerations and the religious orientation of their advisors. Oljeitu was raised as a Christian and then became a Buddhist. After his conversion to Islam, he belonged successively to the Hanafi, the Shafi, and finally the Shi'i sects. Abu Sa'id, Oljeitu's successor, was raised as a Shi'i Muslim, but upon coming of age he adhered to the Sunni sect. With his reign, however, there was no longer a question about the religious orientation of the Il-khanid state. It was no longer a purely Mongol state, but an Islamic state that happened to be ruled by Mongols. The Mongols, like the Türks who had preceded them in the Middle East, had come full circle. In contrast to the Mongols in China, the Mongols in Persia adopted the religion of their subjects and soon thereafter were absorbed into the Islamic world.[84]

The Mongols of the Golden Horde maintained their ancestral traditions until the accession of Berke. The latter converted to Islam, and from that moment on it became the principal religion in the Horde. There is some controversy about when Berke converted; some sources state that it was before he became the Horde's ruler, others, afterwards. Conversion in the Golden Horde was strictly a personal matter, and there appears to have been no political significance attached to it. Only the elite of the Horde converted to Islam, however; among the commoners shamanism continued to predominate. When Oz-beg acceded to the throne in 1313, he formally adopted Islam as his own and his state's religion, but did not require that other members of the Horde follow suit. Nevertheless, even though he was not a fanatical Muslim, he expelled the shaman priests and thus, indirectly, promoted Islamic dominance. By the end of his reign, the Horde, too, was an Islamic state. Unlike the Il-khans, who followed the Shi'i sect, the Golden Horde followed the Hanafi.[85]

As the Golden Horde also controlled Russia, it had to deal with the Orthodox Church. Christians were present at the Horde's court, but those Mongols who were Christians did not create a political problem for the Horde's ruler. During the first period of the Horde's history, it followed Chinggis-khan's tolerance edict. At no time was the practice of the Orthodox faith hindered, even though the Mongols plundered quite a number of churches and monasteries; in fact, relations between the Orthodox Church and the Horde were excellent. After 1267 the Horde granted the Church special *jarlygs* which enabled it to act in the Horde's name. A problem arose when Franciscan missionaries sent by the Roman Catholic church began activities in the Black Sea area in 1258. During Oz-beg's reign a political conflict broke out between the Horde and the Franciscans, and neither side wanted to recognize the moral superiority of the other. Although the papacy tried to activate the missions, while downplaying some of its inherent political claims, the missionary efforts cannot be said to have been successful. After 1375 only Islam and the Orthodox Church had any political role within the Horde. Two religions of the Yüan and Il-khanid domains, Buddhism and Judaism, appear not to have existed in the Golden Horde.

The Khanate of Chaghatai held within its borders two major religions, Islam and Buddhism, each occupying a specific geographical area; Islam was predominant in Transoxiana; Buddhism dominated the Turkestan area. Unlike the Golden Horde, the Khanate's rulers did not adopt Islam, but many commoners did, probably as a consequence of their contacts with Muslim Türks. The first ruler of the Chaghatai Khanate to adopt Islam was also its last, Tarmarshirin. When he converted, he ordered all members of the Khanate to convert also, an order that was not well received by the Buddhists.[86] Religion suddenly assumed a political role. His conversion order led to a schism between Transoxiana and Turkestan, and, with his disastrous military campaigns, to the Khanate's collapse.

Cultural Life under the Mongols

The differences between the subdivisions of the Mongol empire were most pronounced in the area of culture. As a nomadic people, the Mongols did not have a highly developed cultural life. Literature was limited to oral tradition; the arts were essentially decorative, as everything had to be mobile. The exact sciences were limited to their practical aspects, to what was needed for animal husbandry and survival on the hostile steppe. To the people of the conquered areas, especially China and Persia, the Mongols seemed crude barbarians. The Mongols, on the other hand, were interested in the cultural trappings of the societies they conquered. Their practical orientation led them away from literature, philosophy, and the like, but towards the promotion of the visual and decorative arts.

Cultural life in the conquered territories, whether scientific or artistic, was at its highest in China. If the Sung dynasty cannot be rated highly in military affairs, there is common agreement that culturally it was one of the most brilliant periods in Chinese history. Literature, philosophy, and poetry flourished; its paintings and porcelains are among the most treasured possessions of modern museums. Even in the exact sciences, China dominated the rest of the world.[87] In the Chinese intellectual and cultural tradition, letters were supreme, and therefore it is important to assess the Mongol attitude towards literary endeavors.

Although Qubilai himself seems to have had a rather poor knowledge of Chinese, his interests in the literary aspects of Chinese culture manifested themselves in several ways. He promoted the Han-lin Academy and the schools in the province, and even if his basic motivation was political, his efforts kept Chinese traditions alive. He also realized that if his successors were to continue to dominate China, they needed more than a rudimentary acquaintance with Chinese culture in general and Chinese literature in particular. It is known that he provided his first heir apparent, Jingim, with both a Mongol and a Chinese education. The latter's success in absorbing Chinese culture seems to have been quite limited; he was foremost a man from the steppe and remained one. Nevertheless, it created an important precedent. At least two of the Mongol emperors, Buyantu and Qutuqtu, were thoroughly familiar with Chinese and Chinese culture.[88]

Of the two, Qutuqtu was probably the more erudite. During his reign, cultural activities again flourished at the court. He himself was a skilled calligrapher, and he had a serious interest in both literature and painting. He created a new government institution, the *K'uei-chang-ko,* an academy devoted to artistic activities and to which the foremost painters of the Yüan dynasty belonged. During the same period, many Mongols and Central Asians had fully adopted Chinese culture and had begun to produce literary works in Chinese.[89] It cannot, however, be said that the Yüan produced literary works of any importance, at least from a Chinese point of view.

Compared to other Chinese dynasties, the literature of the Yüan, whether written by Chinese or not, is not very interesting, but there was one major innovation. If the Mongols were not particularly interested in literature as such, they were very much interested in drama. Thus, under Mongol influence, the Chinese literary scene began to produce pieces for the theater. Most of China's great plays, as well as its theatrical traditions, trace their origins to the Yüan dynasty. The theater required the use of the vernacular, and soon it became a popular literary form, its popularity fueled by the

Mongols' lack of interest in scholarly purity. Chinese was no longer written in the classical literary style, and this relaxation of literary standards resulted in China's first two popular novels: the famous *All Men Are Brothers,* also known as the *"Water Margin,"* and the *Romance of the Three Kingdoms*.[90] This tradition of popular fiction was continued, except for a brief period after the Yüan, in the two succeeding dynasties.

The general cultural atmosphere under Yüan rule was one of relaxation of official controls and benign neglect on the part of the Yüan emperors. The Mongols were tolerant of the scholars' activities, and, unlike many other dynasties, never undertook a literary persecution. This attitude resulted in freer forms of expression and less government censorship. As a consequence, much more information—both positive and negative—about life under the Mongols is available. However, because of their less formal style, Chinese scholars of the Ming and Ch'ing dynasties considered the Yüan works too poorly written to be worth preserving, and many works were thus lost.

The Mongol impact on Chinese culture was most strongly felt in the area of the visual arts, primarily because of government sponsorship. They promoted and financed paintings, and some of the most brilliant Chinese paintings date from this period. Mongol practicality led to a decline in the artistic value, but an increase in the quality, of lacquer ware and jewelry. Under the Mongols, the exact sciences, especially mathematics and astronomy, were allowed to fully develop, and they flourished. During the succeeding Confucian Ming dynasty, however, these sciences sank into oblivion. Only modern scholarship has recently begun to rediscover the highly advanced state of the sciences in Yüan China.

In Persia, too, the Mongols were confronted with a flourishing culture, although one of quite a different nature because of its Islamic orientation. The Mongol conquest had serious consequences for Persia's cultural life, simply because a great number of intellectuals and artisans lost their lives. As Yüan rule in China witnessed the increasing use of the vernacular, so too Il-khanid Persia promoted the use of Persian over Literary Arabic. But, as in China, the Mongols themselves did not produce any works of importance; even less is known about the Il-khans' familiarity with Persian literature than about the Yüan rulers and Chinese literature.

Under Mongol rule, historiography reached its apogee, and the principal works produced under the Il-khans are among the greatest ever written under an Islamic regime. The two most famous historians are 'Ala al-Din'Ata-Malik Juvaini and Rashid al-Din Fadl Allah. Juvaini wrote, around 1260, the well-known history of Chinggis-khan and the early Mongol rulers, the *Ta'rikh-i Jahan-Guzha*. Rashid al-Din, one of the world's greatest historians, wrote or directed the writing of the *Jami'ut al-tawarikh,* the "Compendium of Histories," the world's first really universal history. The sophistication of these and other histories was not equalled until the famous Ibn Khaldun. Historiography was by far the most brilliant literary activity at the court of the Il-khans, but poetry and prose were enthusiastically practiced.

Other art forms also flourished in Persia. Under Oljeitu architecture was revived. One of the most famous buildings, still seen today, is Oljeitu's mausoleum in Sultaniyeh. But, as in China, Mongol influence and sponsorship found its best expression in painting. During the Il-khans, a new form of painting emerged, the Persian miniature. The epic art of illustrating books on Persia's past is a purely Il-khanid creation. Its best examples can be found in the resplendent illustrations of the *Shah-nama*.[91]

Not only the arts, but also the exact sciences were promoted by the Il-khans. It has been noted that the famous philosopher-astronomer Nasir al-Din Tusi was one of Hulegu's advisors. Almost all the Il-khans were interested in astronomy, and under their direction large observatories were built, some of which are still extant. The most famous of these is at Maragheh. The information available on the instruments at Maragheh, as well as the studies conducted there, shows that astronomy was much further advanced in Persia than in Europe, where it was not until the sixteenth century that Tycho Brahe "invented" instruments similar to those constructed at Maragheh by Ma'ayyid al-Din al-'Urdi and made the observations that later permitted the theoretical advances of Kepler. Under the Il-khans, astronomy was so advanced that Persian astronomers were active even at the Yüan court.

There is some evidence that both the Golden Horde and the Chaghatai Khanate cultivated the arts and sciences, but our information is fragmentary. What is clear, however, is that even though the Mongols themselves did not produce any cultural works, they actively promoted cultural life in the conquered areas. The Mongol occupation channelled cultural life into areas that had not been attempted before because they went against traditional, orthodox standards. The dynamism released by Mongol sponsorship did not completely disappear after the collapse of the Mongol empire.

9

The Collapse of
the Mongol Empire

Until quite recently, the emphasis in Mongol historical studies has been on the early decades of the empire, its formation and heyday. Western historians have only recently begun to devote attention to the causes of the collapse of the Yüan,[1] and even now, very little attention is given to the overall causes of the collapse of the world's largest empire.

Historians have traditionally approached Mongol history from the Chinese, the Middle Eastern, or the Russian viewpoint. This is understandable when one considers that the historical sources do not deal with the empire as a whole. Most of the material dealing with the Mongols is written in Chinese, yet almost nothing can be learned from it about the empire's condition outside the Chinese cultural sphere. The Chinese sources are, for all practical purposes, silent about developments in Persia and Russia; likewise, the records of the Il-khans and the Golden Horde barely mention the Yüan. Then, too, information on the Mongols is recorded in a great number of languages, well beyond the reach of an individual historian.[2] The traditional

225

approach has led to the easy acceptance of a stereotyped division of the Chingizid empire. Mongol history has been divided neatly, but simplistically, into five major parts. Only the first covers the empire as a whole, beginning with the rise of Chinggis-khan and ending with the death of Mongke. The other four, all beginning with the death of Mongke, are based on a geographical division of the empire: the Yüan dynasty located in China, the Il-khans in Persia, the Golden Horde in Russia and the Qipcaq steppe, and the Chaghatai Khanate on the southern central steppe.[3] Thus the traditional historical periodization of the Mongol empire has been an awkward combination of a temporal one, the first period, with a geographical one, the other four. An inevitable consequence of this periodization has been the treatment of the empire's subdivisions as having little or no connection with each other, as if they were five empires distinct from each other but founded by people of the same ethnic group.

It is evident that the traditional division of the Chingizid empire is not a true historical periodization and that its application tends to obscure the nature of events that affected all the subdvisions in more or less the same way. Conceptually, the Mongol empire was much more unified than an examination, within the traditional framework, of the linguistically isolated sources would indicate. As has been shown in the previous chapters, attitudes and developments within each of these supposedly independent subdivisions were remarkably similar; their differences appear more pronounced because each adopted the external trappings of legitimate statehood associated with the areas under its control.

To understand the overall causes of the decline of the Mongol empire, a true historical periodization must be attempted, and to achieve this, it is necessary to analyze conditions within each of the traditional five subdivisions, focusing on those elements that affected all of the subdivisions. It will then be possible to determine when those changes occurred that eventually caused the collapse of the empire in its entirety. A periodization thus obtained will provide a clearer perspective on Chingizid imperial rule.

Disruptive Forces in the Nomadic Tradition

The influence on the Mongols of the historical traditions of the steppe has been largely overlooked. The Mongols were and remained true heirs to the steppe traditions, and their historical presence cannot be written off as "the wrath of God." Attention to the histories of the Türks and Uighurs and the other steppe empires sheds quite a new light on the Mongol collapse.

Very little information is available on the political situation on the steppe during the last decades of the twelfth century. What there is, however, clearly points to an area in constant turmoil and undergoing violent and abrupt changes. There was no unified force or single group that dominated. Some groups, like the Tatars, enjoyed at one point or another a position of supremacy on the steppe. Like many groups before them, however, their position depended on the ever-changing alliances that had characterized steppe politics for centuries.[4] The reunification of the steppe under the leadership of a single group headed by a single ruler, or khan, did not occur until the first decade of the thirteenth century.

A large number of clans and tribes were active on the steppe during the late twelfth and early thirteenth centuries. The numerous attempts at unification and the desire to recreate a powerful Central Asian empire led to fierce battles between the contending clans for supremacy. More often than not these resulted in the debilitation of the attacked group: witness the fate of Chinggis-khan's own clan after the murder of his father, Yesugei, by the Tatars. The final unification process, under Chinggis-khan himself, was also a bloody affair. Many clans were forcibly conquered, while others submitted voluntarily to the rising new ruler to avoid attack by the ever-growing coalition.

The Mongols followed the traditional pattern in the creation of their empire. Former steppe empires had usually been made up of relatively homogeneous groups, while the new steppe empire led by the Mongols had incorporated other tribal groups not of Mongol origin, which nevertheless became an integral part of the new empire. These non-Mongol groups, which recognized the authority of Chinggis-khan well before the formal establishment of the Mongol empire, were primarily of Turkic extraction.[5] However, the confederation that thus came about was held together primarily, as in the past, by the charismatic personality of its leader, Temujin, and by his ability to use to his own advantage the community of economic interests of the steppe people. Past nomadic empires came into existence because of a charismatic leader and collapsed because of tensions and conflicts directly related to this kind of leadership. Modern historians have too often ignored this fact.

Chinggis-khan was by no means the only ambitious leader on the steppe. Two major conflicts early in his career, well before his authority was firmly established, illustrate the warring factionalism that characterized steppe politics. The first was between Chinggis-khan and his sworn brother, Jamuqa. The excuse for the conflict was a difference of opinion on the distribution of the properties and spoils of war. A closer examination of the conflict, however, clearly indicates that its real cause was the fact that both Jamuqa and Chinggis-khan aspired to become the sole leader of the budding confederation. Chinggis-khan emerged as the victor of a ferocious fractricidal war. The war's real importance, however, lies in the fact that it is indicative of the serious personality clashes that existed within a nomadic confederation. The idea advanced by Vladimirtsov[6] in his study of the career of the first Mongol emperor—that the conflict between these two men was one of the aristocratic tradition, represented by Chinggis-khan, versus the lower classes of society, represented by Jamuqa—does not make much sense. It rests on painfully twisted evidence, and furthermore goes against all the historical traditions of steppe empires.

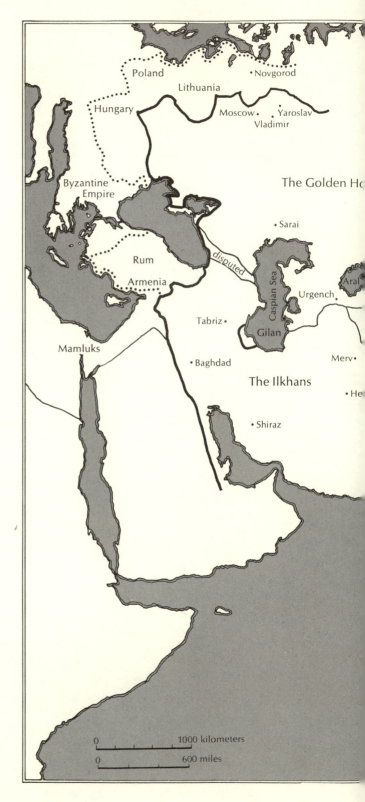

Map 3
*The Mongol Empire
circa 1280 A.D.*

——————

Limit of actual Mongol dominance

············

Limit of nominal Mongol control

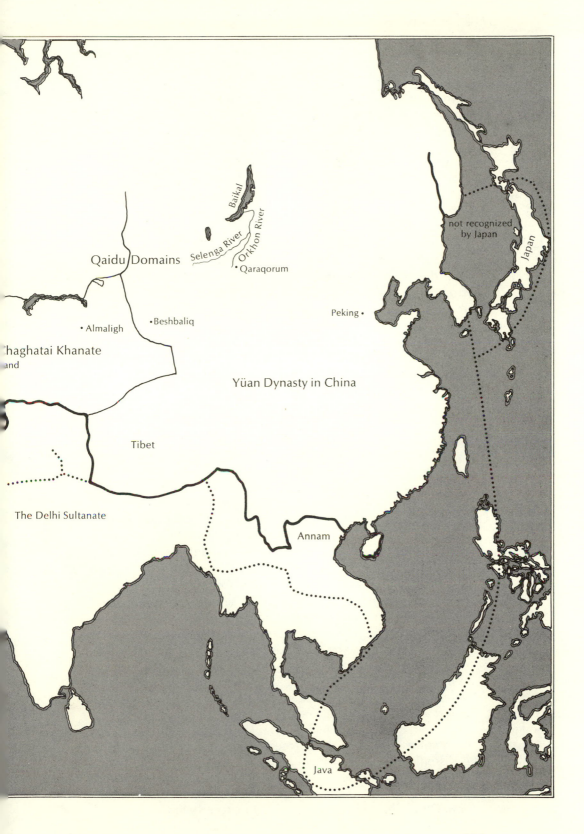

Qaidu Domains

Baikal

Selenga River

Orkhon River

• Qaraqorum

not recognized
by Japan

Japan

• Almaligh

• Beshbaliq

Peking •

haghatai Khanate
and

Yüan Dynasty in China

Tibet

The Delhi Sultanate

Annam

Java

The second conflict—with his erstwhile ally and overlord, Toghril-khan or Wang-khan—occurred shortly after the Mongol ruler had been elected emperor and assumed, during the 1206 *quriltai*, the title *Chinggis-khan*. This conflict, very much in the steppe tradition, shows the nomadic emperor's need to eliminate all who could lay claim to an authority over the steppe that antedated his own coronation. The war between Chinggis-khan and Toghril-khan resulted in the total elimination of all challengers and potential challengers to Chinggis-khan's newly established authority. Subsequently, and throughout his entire career, his authority was never challenged from within the confederation.

Chinggis-khan thus possessed all the characteristics of a nomadic emperor. He proved himself to be not only a brilliant general but also an excellent and charismatic leader of men, without question the most brilliant leader ever to come from the steppe. Almost immediately after establishing his authority, he promulgated a series of measures aimed at eliminating one of the major sources of discontent in the previous nomadic empires, the distribution of the spoils of conquest. He issued strict but equitable orders. Loot was distributed on what was perceived as a fair basis, and everyone, from the common soldier to the leading prince, benefited from the emperor's rule. This and several other measures detailed earlier in the present volume seem to account for the fact, as contemporary accounts testify, that the Mongol armies were seldom confronted with a disciplinary problem.

Although Chinggis-khan took steps to prevent his empire from undergoing the same fate as the previous nomadic empires, he made several decisions that sowed the seeds of the discord that became a characteristic of the Mongol empire several decades after its founder's death. The first decision, to allow military commanders almost complete independence in the conduct of war, was unavoidable given the scope of the Mongol conquests. Commanders received a general strategic directive, but adapted their tactics to local circumstances. This decision permitted successful and far-flung campaigns from China all the way to Russia.[7] Its inherent danger, best described by the term *regionalism*,[8] became evident soon after Chinggis-khan's death. Independent military action led to the creation of semi-independent fiefdoms, thus placing a strain on the empire's unity. When Mongke, Chinggis-khan's grandson, assumed the throne, he was forced to devote many of his resources and a great deal of his time to the elimination of these fiefdoms.

In the long run, an even more fateful decision was Chinggis-khan's division of the empire among his sons. Because Chinggis-khan's decisions had the force of inalterable laws, this one created a situation where potential conflicts of interest could easily degenerate into fratricidal warfare. In Chinggis-khan's time, no quarrels broke out, or at least none that threatened the unity of the empire. Even Ogodei's accession to the throne did not provoke serious dissension among Mongol princes. Chinggis-khan had personally appointed his third son as his successor, and this was accepted without question by everyone in the empire, including Chaghatai, Chinggis-khan's second son. Ogodei's reign, however, was to exacerbate the problem of regionalism created by Chinggis-khan's first decision. His legendary lackadaisical attitude towards the empire's administration encouraged the formation of independent fiefdoms and aggravated the difficulty of controlling the regional overlords.[9] Mongke attempted to eliminate the factionalism brought on by his grandfather's actions, but because of his premature death, his reforms were not fully carried out, and within two years the empire was in the throes of a civil war that lasted more than a quarter of a century.

The conquests launched by Chinggis-khan had created a large empire for the Mongols. Even though he had conquered territory in the West, his campaigns there had been essentially massive raiding parties, and at the time of his death, it seemed that the Mongols might lose control over the area. Ogodei's reign is important because he started a series of campaigns to consolidate the work begun by his father, including one against Russia. This campaign, which led to the conquest not only of Russia but also of a major portion of Eastern Europe, also saw the beginning of an important quarrel between two Mongol princes, one the commander of a powerful and seasoned army, the other soon to be the new emperor. The European campaign was under the general command of Batu, and among his subordinates were Guyuk, the son of Ogodei, and Mongke, the son of Tolui. Only scant information is available on the relations between Batu and Guyuk during this campaign, but what there is points towards hostility between them. At one point or another during the campaign a clash must have occurred, for Guyuk returned, or possibly was sent, to Qaraqorum well before the European campaign ground to a halt as a result of Ogodei's death. This enmity was to have major consequences for the empire as a whole.[10]

The first indication of trouble came almost immediately after Ogodei's death. During the relatively short regency of Toragana, Guyuk's mother, a *quriltai* was convened with the purpose of confirming Guyuk's appointment to the throne. Batu refused to participate, an unprecedented action on the part of a Mongol prince, and began extensive preparations to march against the new emperor. Although dissuaded by other princes from executing his plans, Batu never recognized Guyuk's authority and openly showed disdain for him; among the numerous incidents was Batu's refusal to permit Alexander Nevskii to proceed towards the court in Qaraqorum.[11]

Even to those only remotely involved in the empire's government, it soon became clear that an armed conflict between Guyuk and Batu was unavoidable. When Guyuk suddenly moved westwards, under the pretext of looking for new pasture land and returning to his own appanage, it appeared that the expected armed conflict was imminent, especially since Guyuk's movement had also set in motion, in an eastward direction, the troops of Batu. But fate, in the form of the Mongols' notoriously excessive consumption of alcohol, saved the Chingizid empire from a potentially disastrous fratricidal war. On his way to the battle field, when he was approaching Samarqand, Guyuk died of an overdose of alcohol. War was avoided, but problems were not. Batu took immediate steps to make sure that the new emperor would be sympathetic towards him and that he would not be a member of the House of Ogodei. His choice was Mongke, Tolui's oldest son, who was not only a good general and administrator, but also a sober man. Since the princes of the Houses of Ogodei and Chaghatai refused to participate in a *quriltai* that denied them a choice, two *quriltai*s had to be held before Mongke was duly appointed emperor. Shortly after this recognition, which took place in July 1251, rumors circulated that certain members of the House of Ogodei were planning a coup. Whether these rumors were true or false, Mongke used them as an excuse to ruthlessly crush the rather disorganized House of Ogodei well before it could threaten his throne.[12]

The empire inherited by Mongke was unsound and by no means resembled the empire at the beginning of Ogodei's reign. Ogodei had shown no serious interest in the administration of the empire; he was interested only in its revenue. Regionalism and its accompanying abuses spread; the areas worst hit were China and the Middle East, the two richest parts of the Chingizid domain. When Ogodei died, the empire was torn apart by intense political rivalries and serious maladministration. Toragana's regency and Guyuk's short reign of less than two years only aggravated an already bad situation. To Guyuk's credit was the fact that he attempted to stem the ever-growing regionalism by replacing incumbent officeholders with people loyal to him. His choices, however, were not the best. His appointment of Yesu-Mongke to rule the Chaghatai Khanate was a disaster, as alcoholism totally debilitated the new ruler. There is some indication, however, that had it not been for the consequences of his own alcoholism, Guyuk might have been able to bring his attempted reforms to a successful conclusion.

With the reign of Mongke, it became clear that to survive, the empire had to find a middle way between the traditions of the steppe and those of the sedentary empires. Mongke established a centralized administration, inspired by the Chinese model; even more importantly, he almost eliminated the House of Ogodei and made his brothers viceroys over the empire. Although he weakened the House of Ogodei, he did not eliminate everyone who could possibly threaten him: the principal survivor of his purge was Qaidu. Why Qaidu was spared is not clear; perhaps it was because, at that time, his forces were such that they could easily be kept under control by the combined forces of Mongke and Batu, and because he did not seem to have had a close relationship with Guyuk. Mongke's magnanimity was to lead to disaster for the empire.

For all of Mongke's excellent qualities as a ruler and an administrator, the way in which he had obtained the throne was a handicap. He was able to intervene, and he did so vigorously, in the affairs of the empire as a whole, with the exception of Batu's domain. Even after the latter died in 1255, Mongke decided not to intervene in the affairs of the Golden Horde. There were many reasons for this but two stand out; first, he did not want to antagonize the group to which he owed the throne, and second, he was deeply involved in the restructuring of the empire's administration and the conquest of the Southern Sung, and he deemed it advisable to leave the Horde alone. The Horde was not hostile to his rule, and the empire did not need another fratricidal confrontation.

Unlike his two immediate predecessors, but like his grandfather, Mongke died, in 1258, from wounds received while on campaign. His death was unexpected, and no orderly succession had been arranged. There is some evidence that it was his intention that Qubilai, the viceroy of China, the empire's richest possession, was to be his successor, especially since Qubilai's talents seemed to lie in administration rather than in the conduct of war.[13] It was Ariq-buqa, however, who quickly convened his own *quriltai* and had himself appointed emperor. As the youngest brother of Mongke and governor of the Mongol homelands, he felt that the succession was rightfully his. Although it is true that, according to Mongol law, the youngest son was always in charge of the homestead, Ariq-buqa's *quriltai* was of dubious legality, as the other two viceroys, Qubilai and Hulegu, as well as Berke, the ruler of the Golden Horde, had not participated in it. At the time of the *quriltai,* Qubilai was campaigning in China, and when he learned of it, in 1260, he convened his own *quriltai* of equally dubious legality. He was, of course, duly elected emperor, and this led to war. The war between the two emperors, fought mainly on the steppe, lasted about four years. Qubilai emerged as the uncontested victor, but, nevertheless, soon thereafter his rule was challenged by Qaidu.

Civil war was not limited to the eastern part of the empire. Mongke's appointment of Hulegu as governor over the Middle East had created resentment in the Golden Horde, primarily because Hulegu had been given authority over two areas, Arran and Adherbaidjan, which had been given by Chinggis-khan himself to the House of Jochi, and hence to Batu. Once the restraining influence of Mongke was gone, war between Hulegu and Berke over these territories broke out. Traditionally it has been claimed that the cause of the war was the resentment of Berke, a Muslim, over Hulegu's killing of the 'Abbasid caliph. When one looks at the conflict somewhat more skeptically, especially in light of Berke's own attitudes, it becomes clear that it was a territorial dispute. The mysterious deaths of three members of the House of Jochi at Hulegu's court were used as a pretext, and swords were crossed.[14] The first phase of the war went against Hulegu, and in the winter of 1263, he was defeated on the Terk River. The war continued nevertheless, and neither Hulegu nor his opponent, Berke, lived to see the end. Abaqa, Hulegu's successor, routed Berke's troops in July 1265, and the latter died while fleeing towards Tiflis, Georgia. Thus ended the first of many wars between the Il-khans and the Golden Horde over Arran and Adherbaidjan.

This shifting pattern of alliances and warring factions is typical of steppe politics. However, the debilitating effect of these wars pales in comparison with the effects of the war begun by Qaidu, leader of the House of Ogodei, which lasted over thirty years and was the single most important factor in the collapse of the Chingizid empire. It is indeed quite remarkable that neither this war nor its principal figure has received any serious scholarly attention.[15]

Although Qaidu's military effort is traditionally described as a rebellion because of its aims, it would be more appropriate to call it a war of restoration. Indeed, Qaidu wanted not only to restore the House of Ogodei to its former glory, but also to recreate a nomadic empire with its dynamic center located in the steppe.

The War of Restoration

Qaidu, a grandson of Ogodei, controlled primarily the Ili and Tarbagatai area. At the time of the dispute between Ariq-buqa and Qubilai over the legitimate succession, he recognized the former as emperor. For the remainder of his life, he steadfastly refused to recognize Qubilai's authority, even after the latter had become, through Ariq-buqa's surrender, the legitimate successor to Mongke. This refusal was based on two factors. First, he claimed correctly that not all Mongol princes had been invited to or were able to attend the *quriltai* that appointed Qubilai emperor. Second, and probably more importantly, he strenuously objected to the fact that Qubilai had held the *quriltai* in a conquered sedentary area rather than in the Mongols' homeland, as required by tradition. Qaidu also protested against the transfer of the capital from the steppe to the sedentary area, from Qaraqorum to Peking; such a transfer was an unheard-of breach of tradition. Exploiting this theme, Qaidu came to represent the defenders of steppe traditions, those Mongols who had remained on the steppe and who, because of political intrigues, did not benefit from the empire's wealth. Sometime after Ariq-buqa's surrender to Qubilai in 1264, Qaidu apparently decided to challenge militarily the House of Tolui, which dominated the empire, and thus attempt the restoration of the House of Ogodei.

Sometime in either 1268 or 1269, on the banks of the Talas, Qaidu and his allies held a *quriltai* to discuss the state of the empire.[16] Our sources, quite understandably, do not reveal much about the matters discussed during the *quriltai,* but it appears that three decisions were made. First, Qaidu was to be the leader of the new federation. Second, an attempt was to be made to restore the Chingizid empire to its nomadic traditions. Third, and most importantly, the new coalition refused to recognize the sedentary areas under Mongol control as belonging to the Mongol world. For them, the Yüan and especially the Il-khans had ceased to be real Mongols. Soon after the Talas *quriltai,* raids reminiscent of those that took place during Chinggis-khan's life resumed, ending what could be called the Pax Mongolica on the steppe.

Qaidu's initial efforts were aimed primarily at the Chaghatai Khanate and at some of the Chinese border areas only nominally under Qubilai's control.

Strategically, it was important for Qaidu to obtain the allegiance of Baraq, and his efforts were successful: the fact that the Chaghatai Khanate was a nomadic state probably made the planned restoration rather attractive. Soon after Baraq's defection, Qaidu's strategy became evident. He directed his own forces against the domain of Qubilai, while Baraq, on Qaidu's orders, began a campaign against the Il-khans that was designed to acquire Khurassan, and in particular the Badghis meadows. There were three reasons for Qaidu's decision to fight the war on two fronts. In the tradition of the nomadic emperors, he did not want the ambitious Baraq to be too close to his own throne. Second, the resources of the steppe were limited and could not support two armies for long. Third, the Il-khans recognized Qubilai as the Great Khan. By massing two armies on the Chinese border, Qaidu would have left himself open to an attack from the Middle East.

It appears that Qubilai did not pay much attention to Qaidu's activities, at least not initially. However, in 1271, because of the continuing growth of Qaidu's movement, he was forced to take preventive measures. At first, he sent a few military columns against Qaidu, but they were unsuccessful and returned. Then, in a display worthy of a modern public relations man, Qubilai sent an army under the command of his own son, Nomuqan,[17] thereby proclaiming that this was an important campaign. This imperial army was to proceed towards the Chaghatai Khanate and from there attack Qaidu. At the time this army was sent, Qaidu was about to realize an alliance with the Golden Horde, a grand alliance of all the nomads against Qubilai. Although the alliance never materialized, it had consequences for Nomuqan's army, whose leadership had been divided from the start. Probably as a result of rumors about the grand alliance, Nomuqan's officers rebelled against him, joined Qaidu, and handed over Qubilai's son as a prisoner.[18]

It seems, though, that Qubilai had anticipated the defection of his son's army. Soon after its departure and throughout 1284, he sent several other military units against Qaidu. Although the campaigns ended inconclusively, they were but diversions; Qubilai's real strategy was to block Qaidu's access to foodstuffs and other products of the sedentary area. In Qubilai's mind, the time when a traditional steppe empire could dominate the surrounding sedentary areas without actually occupying them was over. An army based on the traditions of the steppe, which also had at its disposal the economic resources of the sedentary areas, would, in the long run, always prevail over the traditional armies of the nomadic horsemen. Thus Qubilai systematically developed a strategy based on the agricultural colonization of the Kansu corridor and the oasis states. The defense troops stationed there were *Chinese*: Chinese troops were less likely to join Qaidu, and farmers would not throw in their lot with the nomads.[19] By 1285 it was evident that Qubilai's plan was beginning to work.

This plan, however, was based on the relative ease of communication between China and the oasis states. Since the year 990 and the creation of the Tangut state, these routes had run through Northern Tibet,[20] mostly through the territory of one of Tibet's major sects, the 'Bri-gun-pa. In 1285 an incident occurred that seriously threatened Qubilai's plans. Resenting Mongol overlordship, as well as Mongol preferential treatment of their principal rivals, the Sa-skya-pa sect, the 'Bri-gun-pas rebelled and threatened to cut off the communication routes. The danger was aggravated by the fact that they were supported by an unidentified group of Mongols, probably allies of Qaidu.[21] Qubilai's reaction was quick and ruthless: his troops crushed the rebels and destroyed their monasteries. This proved to be a major setback for Qaidu. Although after this date he staged regular raids on Qubilai's domain, he no longer presented a major threat to the security of China, which had by that time recovered from the devastations of the conquest.

The dwindling fortunes of Qaidu received unexpected support in 1287, when Prince Nayan rebelled against Qubilai and threw in his lot with the Central Asian confederation.[22] As his economic strategies had been successful, Qubilai decided to put an end to Qaidu's ambitions once and for all, by military means. As the commander-in-chief of this operation, Qubilai appointed Bayan of the Barin, who had played such an important role in the conquest of the Southern Sung.[23] Bayan quickly crushed the rebellion, even before Nayan had had time to join with Qaidu's forces. Then he began a running battle with the latter's forces, draining them of whatever strength they had left. Qaidu's attempt at restoration ended seven years after Qubilai's death. In 1301 his army was defeated, and he himself died while fleeing the battlefield.[24] In 1303, some thirty-five years after it had begun, the Central Asian confederation came to an end. Qaidu's surviving allies throughout the empire made peace with the House of Tolui.

Although Qubilai, and through him the Yüan dynasty, had been Qaidu's principal opponent, other divisions of the Chingizid empire were also affected by the attempted restoration. When Baraq allied himself with Qaidu, he was instructed to attack the Il-khanid empire. Baraq launched his attack early in 1270, and by May of that year he had conquered practically the whole of Khurassan, and the city of Nishapur had once again been laid waste. The Il-khan, confronted with other problems, did not particularly want to engage his forces in a fratricidal war, especially not over Khurassan. Thus, towards the end of May, Abaqa proposed to Baraq a very generous peace, offering him the areas he wanted, including the Badghis meadows. Baraq, who apparently aspired to become Il-khan himself and interpreted Abaqa's offer as a sign of weakness, refused to accept the offer. This was a major mistake. Abaqa was forced to launch his well-trained and seasoned army in an all-out attack on Baraq. The latter's forces were utterly defeated in what became known as the Battle of Herat, and Baraq himself lost his life, assassinated on Qaidu's orders after his return to the steppe.[25] This defeat was a serious setback for the Qaidu confederation, for it meant the end of their southward expansion and closed off their access to a fertile region.

Though Baraq's invasion had threatened the security of the Il-khanid domain, the major consequence of the Qaidu-Baraq alliance and the attempted restoration was the war between the Il-khans and the Golden Horde, which kept the Il-khans from concentrating their military efforts against the Mamluks in Egypt, saving the latter from the fate of the other Middle Eastern states. The relations between the Golden Horde and the Il-khans alternated between tenuous friendship and half-hearted warfare. The Golden Horde itself did not suffer any serious consequences from Qaidu's restoration war. Nomadic themselves and occupying the western steppe, they did not look favorably upon the rise of a new nomadic force on the central steppe that could challenge their control over the western areas. Thus the Horde, although often strongly tempted, refrained from giving any serious assistance to Qaidu, and this, of course, definitely weakened his chances of success.

Qaidu's attempt to restore the empire under the House of Ogodei seriously drained the economic resources and military strength of the Chingizid empire. His attempt, however, was not only consistent with the traditions of the steppe, but was a natural consequence of the personality clashes that had existed within the Chingizid empire ever since its creation. Qaidu became the ultimate representative of these clashes and also of those Mongols who, after Chinggis-khan's death, had been cut off from the benefits of the empire. The destructive forces at work within the empire, best expressed by Qaidu's restoration attempt, were noted even by non-Mongol contemporaries. Su T'ien-chüeh, a scholar at Qubilai's court, wrote, "The reason why these princes rebel is on account of their fathers."[26]

The recovered Mongol unity, referred to in Oljeitu's letter to the papacy,[27] did not survive long. The disintegrative forces triggered by the Qaidu wars could no longer be stopped; each division of the empire had taken a course that favored disunity rather than unity. Local conditions within each subdivision would precipitate the final collapse within half a century of Qaidu's death.

The Fall of the Yüan

With the exception of the Qaidu wars on the border, the reigns of Qubilai and his first successor were essentially untroubled; no event occurred that could be said to imperil the dynasty's survival. In fact, a devastated China had been restored to the greatness it had known under the T'ang dynasty. Economically, politically, and culturally, China was once again a flourishing nation, probably the most advanced in the then-known world. The major difference was that China was now governed by a people from the steppe who, in a breach of their own tradition, had set up their capital within China itself. This move had been dictated by the need to occupy a more advantageous economic position, but, in the long run, it alienated the rulers from the steppe and its traditions. By adopting the symbols of Chinese power, the Mongols were inevitably drawn into the turmoil of Chinese court politics and its multiple factions.

In addition, the continual feuding among Qubilai's successors, like the feuding among the successors of Chinggis-khan, Ogodei, and Mongke before them, weakened the power of the Mongol emperors. In 1307 Qaishan, a great-grandson of Qubilai, assumed the throne but lost it a mere four years later to his brother Buyantu. Court intrigues kept the imperial succession away from Qaishan's descendants, and the resulting discontent among Qaishan's followers led to a coup in 1328. The years 1328 and 1329 were a political watershed for the Yüan, for it was then that the tensions between Qubilai's descendants and the various court factions, both Chinese and Mongol, broke out into the open.

The coup of 1328, led by the Qipcaq El-Temur and the Merkid Bayan, neither of whom belonged to the imperial house, laid the foundation for the ensuing Confucianization[28] of the Yüan dynasty. Although the leaders of the coup did not act consciously within a Confucian framework, their actions fitted the Confucian political world view; indeed, the coup was interpreted as a "restoration" of the legitimate imperial line. This apparent legitimation meant that its leaders, probably to their great surprise, received substantial support from the Confucian bureaucracy. The coup reduced the absolute power of the Mongol emperor on two counts. He now owed the throne directly to two leaders from outside the Chingizid houses, and the coup had given the bureaucracy, dominated by the Chinese, an opportunity to involve itself in Mongol politics. Compromise, personal ties, and loyalties henceforth dominated the country's administration.

Prior to the "1328 restoration," the Yüan administration was truly the first supranational government. In order of importance, high positions were held by Mongols, Central Asians of all kinds, including Europeans and Persians, and Northern Chinese. An indirect consequence of the coup was the ever-decreasing role of the non-Chinese element in the bureaucracy. Remarkably, the person most responsible for the increasing role of the Confucian elite was the Merkid Bayan, who can by no means be described as a Confucian or even a Confucian sympathizer. In fact, after he claimed that Qubilai's reign had been an anti-Confucian one, he adopted a series of measures aimed at eliminating the Confucian influence on the empire's government. The stimulus for the reforms was Bayan's perception of the Confucian bureaucracy as a monolithic structure, which he felt had to be broken up. His failure to realize that it was far from monolithic prevented him from exploiting its inner weaknesses and contradictions to the advantage of the ruling Mongols. He succeeded only in alienating the Chinese and Mongol elites, which began to perceive him as an upstart from a clan that had been conquered by Chinggis-khan. In the reaction against him and his policies, cliques comprising all ethnic groups were formed to neutralize or eliminate him.[29]

The political infighting at the court and within the bureaucracy had important repercussions throughout the provinces. In China, tendencies towards regional autonomy were commonplace at the first sign of weakness by the central authorities, and the Mongol's natural tendency towards autonomous action has been pointed out several times in the previous chapters. It is not surprising, therefore, that while Bayan and the central bureaucracy wrangled, the provinces decided to go their own ways. Conflicts, tensions, disputes, and misunderstandings came to a head in 1340 and resulted in the disgraceful ouster of Bayan, his subsequent banishment to the south, and his death. The steppe and its traditions, however, did not emerge as the victors in this conflict. It was the Chinese Confucian elite, supported by some Mongols, who reaped the benefits created unwittingly by Bayan. They were now the dominant group within the country's administration.

It could normally be assumed that because the traditional Chinese governing corps had resumed its age-old role, the country's problems might begin to be solved. In reality what happened was exactly the opposite. Soon after Bayan's fall, it became clear that the Confucian elite was divided into two major parties, each of which was subdivided into multiple factions with sharply defined areas of disagreement. The two major groups can be called the reform and the conservative parties. The Reformers, consisting primarily of Neo-Confucians,[30] were the better organized. Their approach to problems was characterized by pragmatism and an intolerance towards other opinions. The Conservatives were essentially Confucians of the old school, not well organized and, in theory, more concerned with the well-being of the people at large than with that of the state.

It was not long before political and ideological conflicts broke out between the two parties. Instead of concerning themselves with the country's problems, the bureaucracy was torn apart by parties, and factions within those parties, striving for dominance. Eventually, these rivalries effectively paralyzed the government,[31] causing the provincial authorities to take steps to protect their own interests, which did not necessarily coincide with those of the empire as a whole. The latent regionalism of the 1340s became an active drive towards some form of regional autonomy during the 1350s. The political options available to the court and the emperor became increasingly limited, and they eventually reached the point, around 1350, where they no longer had the means, or the desire, to initiate actions against the disastrous developments within the country. The court lost effective control over the whole area south of the Yellow River, and to the north it had to rely, tenuously, on the local Mongol warlords to ensure its control. In this precarious situation, the court managed to alienate the most powerful of the warlords but succeeded, in a final shudder of authority, in eliminating him.[32] In doing so, however, it also eliminated all vestiges of the court's control over the north.

The reign of the last Mongol emperor in China is seriously obscured by the requirement of traditional Chinese historiography that the reign of a last emperor was necessarily one of decadence and neglect.[33] This stereotype was a requirement for the new and succeeding dynasty to justify its own assumption of power, especially since the same tradition demanded that the new dynasty write the history of the preceding one. The official history of the Yüan does not vary from the traditional model. The Yüan annals, however, were compiled with undue haste and very carelessly,[34] and consequently with less stereotyping than was the case for some other dynasties. Moreover, many unofficial accounts by contemporaries have survived, and it is possible to obtain a fairly accurate picture of the last years of the Mongols in China. This picture is substantially different from that found in many textbooks on China, most of which follow the standard Confucian interpretation.[35]

The fall of the Yüan gave birth to numerous legends. According to the Chinese version of the principal one, anti-Mongol sentiment culminated in a general conspiracy to overthrow the hated rulers. An agreement was reached between the conspirators, and the uprising was to occur on the fifteenth day of the eighth month, which was an important holiday, an occasion to give mooncakes to friends and relatives. In the year 1368, with little advance warning, the Chinese people were informed of the date of the uprising through slips of paper hidden in the mooncakes. At the appointed time, the oppressed people rose en masse and overnight threw out the hated alien rulers. The Chinese version is rather prosaic and certainly not as colorful and imaginative as the Mongol one. According to the latter, the fault lay with the Tibetan lamas and the greed of an emperor. One lama was assigned per every ten households, and among his many privileges and obligations were the *ius primae noctis* and the task of cutting off the thumbs of each newborn male: while the first antagonized the population, the second made sure that no Chinese would ever be able to use a bow. But the emperor was so corrupt and greedy that he was bribed to suspend the thumb law for three months. During this very short period, all of China's future leaders were born, and kept their thumbs. Once of age, they became the great conspirators, and here the Mongol story rejoins the Chinese.[36]

These legends are just that—legends. The fall of the Yüan is more prosaic and more complex. Close scrutiny of the facts indicates that the Yüan's collapse did not quite resemble those of the previous dynasties in China. Although the dynasty had become politically impotent, to a large degree its military strength remained intact but useless, as the main armies were concentrated in the capital. The traditional assumption that the barbarian conquerors of China eventually were Sinicized and that at that time the "Chinese" element once again began to dominate is a convenient rationalization on the part of the Chinese themselves. Sinicization was a phenomenon of the Ming dynasty, not the Yüan, or certainly not on a large scale.[37] During the Yüan, the Mongols adopted the external trappings of a Chinese dynasty, but they remained Mongols. Even though some Mongols became Chinese literati,[38] most Mongols never knew the language.

The most commonly accepted explanation for the fall of the Yüan is that the Mongols were incompetent in the financial administration of a large empire. The proponents of this theory argue that the Mongols did not understand the paper money system created by the Sung, and used the printing press to cover their financial needs, thus creating uncontrollable inflation. Although this is a politically and historically simplistic explanation for the inflation that existed during the final decades of the Yüan, it still finds credence in certain circles. What the advocates of this theory generally ignore is the fact that the financial administration was largely in the hands of the Chinese elite, the same elite that had created the system. It is, as a matter of fact, rather surprising that the theory is still accepted two decades after Herbert Franke demonstrated that the amount of money in circulation was not the cause of the inflation and that inflation was not one of the causes of the dynasty's collapse.[39] It cannot be denied that there were abuses in the issuance of paper currency, but their impact on the dynasty's declining fortunes was minimal.

The principal reason for the Northern Chinese inflation was a dramatic increase in the cost of food supplies. The North, dependent on the South for its food, found that the regular supply route had been cut off on account of the increase of rebellions and banditry in the central area and piracy along the coast. To this essentially political problem must be added the fact that the Yellow River area, the North's principal supplier, had undergone a series of natural disasters. These had seriously affected the crops and thus contributed to the scarcity of food supplies in the North. Natural shortages combined with artificially created shortages (hoarding, for example) were the primary force behind the ever-worsening inflation.

The court was acutely aware of these economic problems. It proposed corrective measures, but these were never implemented. The existence of two diametrically opposed factions within the bureaucracy, both of which were largely beyond the court's control, was the main reason behind this inertia. With no serious corrective measures forthcoming, or even expected, from the central administration, dissatisfaction increasingly found its expression in violence, not only on the part of the Chinese population, but also among the Mongols themselves. To compound the court's problems, many Chinese and Mongol officials outside the capital were also disaffected. Since their salaries did not keep up with inflation, they resorted to a series of measures to increase their income.[40] The direct victim of their abuses was the Chinese population itself. Indirectly, because they diminished much-needed revenues and added more uprisings to the already large number taking place, they aggravated the court's problems. The court was perceived as indifferent, which further antagonized a large section of the population. The most serious effect of this perception was on the loyalty of the Mongol troops stationed in the provinces. Many a Mongol soldier was reduced to a mere subsistence level, quite a change from the beginning of the dynasty. In their plight, Mongol soldiers and officers alike began to identify with the Chinese population among which they lived and which they were supposed to control.

The events of the last years of the Yüan are interpreted by traditional

Chinese historians as the portents that always announced the end of a dynasty. Unquestionably, the historians of the Ming dynasty saw numerous signs during the reign of the last Mongol Yüan emperor, Toghon Temur (1333–1368). Ming interpretations, however, should be taken with more than a few grains of salt, for they justify the way in which they had obtained the "Mandate of Heaven." Of all of Qubilai's successors, Toghon Temur had the longest reign, a fact that certainly did not fit the traditional model. Moreover, many of the so-called portents were defined by the Ming historians only in hindsight, for if the Ming had not assumed power, these events would never have been called portents. Ming historians exaggerated minor events and simply invented those that were necessary to fit the traditional patterns.[41] However, it cannot be denied that by 1360, China was in disarray and that without drastic action, the days of the Mongol dynasty were numbered.

If there is a constant in Chinese history, it is the presence of rebellions and uprisings. The history of the Yüan was no exception to this general rule. Most of the rebellions had been concentrated in Southern China, their traditional place of occurrence, and kept under control rather easily by both Mongol and Chinese troops. By the middle of the fourteenth century, as a result of the court's paralysis, they began to threaten the stability of the empire. The nature of these rebellions has been obscured by the Ming historians for the same reasons that they invented the necessary portents: Chinese historians would like us to believe that anti-Mongol sentiment was behind them. Close scrutiny, however, reveals that these rebellions were not against the Mongols per se but against the *dynasty*; it did not matter whether the emperor was Chinese, Mongol, or something else. The southern rebellions initially were a reaction against the court's apparent lack of interest in the economic and social problems of the country. When even this did not force Peking to act, the nature of the rebellions changed. By the 1360s, the court had essentially given up trying to control anything outside the capital. The absence of military intervention south of the Yellow River allowed the antidynastic rebellions to develop into a pure and simple Chinese civil war for control over the South. Mongol units stationed in the South participated actively in this civil war and joined one of the several groups vying for control.

By the middle of the 1360s, the southern rebellions began to spill over into the North. The multiple rebellious movements coalesced into six major groups. The Mongols, in a reversal of a traditional Chinese policy, tried to play one group of rebels against another, without much success. The rebellions increased in scope, size, and ambition. Control over the South was no longer sufficient; now the goal was control over the whole empire. Eventually, the group under the leadership of Chu Yüan-chang (1328–1398)[42] emerged as the victor and began a march towards the empire's capital. In 1368 Chu Yüan-chang's forces occupied Peking without a fight; the Mongols had abandoned it and returned to the steppe. Chu Yüan-chang then proclaimed the Ming dynasty. He became known as Ming T'ai-tsu, and his reign as the Hung-wu reign. Toghon Temur and the Yüan court, however, had not given up their claim to legitimate rule over China. Their withdrawal to the steppe was a strategic one, not the rout of a defeated group. It appears that their plan was to regroup on the steppe, obtain assistance from the Golden Horde, and begin the reconquest of China. This plan, however, failed to materialize. The expected assistance from the Golden Horde did not appear, for at that time the Horde itself was in a state of upheaval. In 1371 the Ming armies were able to capture the town of Ying-chang, the last major city in Mongol hands, and thus brought to an end formal Mongol rule over China. On the steppe, however, the Mongols set up the Northern Yüan dynasty, and they continued to be a serious threat to the Chinese border areas until well into the fifteenth century.

Chu Yüan-chang's victory over his rivals was not the result of any major victory by Chinese forces over Mongol ones. It appears that in the face of ever-increasing difficulties, the Mongol court slowly withdrew to the North and to the steppe, and then simply abandoned China. Not all Mongols, however, returned to the steppe. Many found the return route to the steppe cut off by rebel forces, and an equally important number of Mongols, born and raised in China, had no particular desire to return to the steppe they had never known, which, in comparison with China, must have struck them as beyond the last outpost of civilization. Thus many Mongols remained in China and became loyal subjects of the Chinese emperor.

It would be a great mistake to claim that there was one single major event or cause leading to the ultimate collapse of the dynasty. The Qaidu wars, Confucianization, the economy, or the rebellions by themselves did not end Mongol rule in China. It was the combination of these elements with the contradiction inherent in the presence of a nomadic empire in a sedentary state that led to the collapse. Numerous times it has been said—and it is still being said—that by the middle of the fourteenth century, the military strength of the Yüan had been exhausted. The historical evidence, however, points to a somewhat different conclusion. Although the military strength of the Yüan was no longer as great as it was in the early decades of the dynasty, towards its end, the major problem was the army's inability to act on account of political dissension among the leadership at the court. The Mongols were not expelled—they left. In a sense, the Yüan resembled the master chessplayer who, having dominated the game, becomes overconfident, makes a wrong move, and has to end the game in a draw. Although the Mongols wanted one, they were not able to gain a rematch, for reasons that are enumerated in the next chapter.

The Mongol emperor's acceptance of the political tenets of Confucianism first limited his options and eventually eliminated military and political options that, from a strictly Mongol viewpoint, would have been viable. Consequently, the Yüan, though aware of the deteriorating conditions within the empire, was unable to take those measures that would have assured its survival, or at least prolonged its existence. The end of the Yüan was not the result of the Chinese people's reaction against the alien "oppressor," but the inevitable consequence of a political and military situation for which the Mongols themselves were responsible.

The Disintegration of the Il-khanid Empire

The chronology of the events leading up to the demise of Mongol rule over Persia is quite clear. The key date is 30 November 1335, the date on which the last regularly appointed Il-khan, Abu Sa'id, was poisoned by his jealous and vengeful wife, Baghdad Khatun. There is some truth to the story that Abu Sa'id was a victim of his wife's emotions, for he had acquired her from her first husband, against his and her will, by using his powers as Il-khan. Baghdad Khatun, however, was not the only person dissatisfied with Abu Sa'id's behavior, and at the court few people regretted his premature passing. Although his death did Baghdad Khatun no good—she was executed—it gave the court factions an opportunity to promote their candidates for the Il-khanid throne.

Not unlike Toghon Temur, the last ruler of the Yüan, Abu Sa'id was highly intelligent, and a good general and administrator; he even had serious literary inclinations. He became Il-khan when he was still a child and the regency was assumed by the emir, Choban. Upon reaching his majority, he took the necessary steps to assure his independence by physically eliminating Choban and his allies, and to assure a strong and vital central government, rigidly under his own control. Unquestionably, these actions led to dissatisfaction within the court cliques. Thus when Abu Sa'id died "unexpectedly" and without offspring, the politics of the court factions swung into full gear, each faction promoting its own candidate; the candidate, of course, was one who would not oppose the interests and the activities of the faction that pushed him. The political agitation was facilitated by the fact that the death of Abu Sa'id meant the virtual end of the House of Hulegu. The Il-khanid empire, which never achieved a reputation for political stability, erupted into political and military turmoil. The serious problems confronting an already weakened empire were compounded by threatened invasions by the Mamluks and the Golden Horde, the latter still interested in the territories of Arran and Adherbaidjan.

The first successor to Abu Sa'id, Arpa Ke'un, was a descendant of Ariq-buqa. He was a strong and energetic ruler who employed drastic and ruthless means to prevent a repetition of Abu Sa'id's fate and consolidate his own position. He ordered the execution of Baghdad Khatun and of all the Chingizid princes, including infants, who could possibly or even remotely challenge his authority. He married Abu Sa'id's sister, the widow of Choban, in an attempt to secure the allegiance of the surviving Chobanites.[43] He proved his military capabilities by repulsing an attack by the Golden Horde, then under the rule of Oz-beg. Arpa Ke'un's reign, however, did not last long. Apparently he was not a Muslim and was thus unable to obtain the allegiance of the majority of the officials and the population. Moreover, he seemed to have misjudged the political realities within the Il-khanid empire. The Oirat governor of Baghdad, 'Ali-Padshah, had proclaimed as Il-khan a descendant of Baidu and thus a distant member of the House of Hulegu. The two Il-khans went to war. Arpa Ke'un's forces were defeated in April 1336 on the banks of the Jaghatu, and he himself was captured while fleeing towards the capital of Sultaniyeh. He was executed in May of the same year, and with his death the last of strong Il-khan rulers disappeared. Civil war became the day-to-day politics of the empire, which was ruled simultaneously by a slew of puppet Il-khans.

The situation after Arpa Ke'un's death can best be described in a single word: chaos. Shaikh Hasan-i-Buzurg, the first husband of Baghdad Khatun, proclaimed as Il-khan a certain Muhammad, a descendant of Mongke Temur. 'Ali-Padshah persisted with his own Il-khan, Musa. The governors of Khurassan, hostile towards both 'Ali-Padshah and Hasan-i-Buzurg, appointed as their Il-khan a certain Togha-temur, a distant descendant of Chinggis-khan's brother Jochi-qasar. Three Il-khans were obviously two too many. War broke out, and when the dust cleared, there were no more Il-khans. The empire had disintegrated into a series of successor states.

The distintegration of Hulegu's empire occurred during 1336 and 1337. Hasan-i-Buzurg attacked the Musa forces and defeated them in July 1336. Musa managed to escape, but his patron, 'Ali Padshah, was killed. In the meantime, Togha-temur and his supporters attacked Adherbaidjan and Persia. Hasan-i-Buzurg made a quick strategic withdrawal and left them practically the whole of present-day Iraq. To simplify matters, Hasan-i-Buzurg and Togha-temur agreed to join forces against Musa. The latter was defeated and executed in July 1337. His death resulted in the partition of of the empire: Togha-temur ruled over Khurassan and Mazandaran; Hasan-i-Buzurg over the rest. The myth of a unified empire, however, was maintained.

The arrangement certainly did nothing to clarify the existing confusion. Shortly thereafter, the Chobanites reacted. The new challenger was Shaikh Hasan-i-Kuchuk, a grandson of Choban and the son of Temur-tash, the former viceroy of Rum. With the aid of a slave, who impersonated Temur-tash, Hasan-i-Kuchuk was able to rally to his cause many of Choban's former supporters, as well as Oirats. The new coalition attacked Hasan-i-Buzurg in July 1338 and forced him to flee. Muhammad, the official Il-khan, was captured and executed. As the usefulness of the false Temur-tash was nearing its end, he tried to take advantage of his masquerade to seize power for himself. He was, however, unsuccessful in his attempt to assassinate his employer.

The years following the first clash between the two Hasans are among the most confusing in the history of the Il-khanid empire. Both continued to appoint new contenders for the Il-khanid throne, contenders so unimportant that in many cases their names are all that is known about them. In June 1340 the Jaghatu was, once again, the scene of a pitched battle between the Hasans and again Hasan-i-Buzurg suffered a setback. He withdrew to Baghdad and ended the pretense of maintaining the Il-khanid empire. He deposed the puppet Il-khan and proclaimed his own dynasty, that of the Jalayirs (1336–1432). Togha-temur, the last contender for the Il-khanid throne, as well as the last of the Chingizids in the Middle East, died in battle in 1353. After that, Hulegu's empire was divided into successor states. The Sarbardars had replaced Togha-temur and ruled over Khurassan and Mazandaran; the Jalayirs ruled over Baghdad and Tabriz; the Muzaffarids and the Karts ruled, respectively, over Fars and Herat. The political vacuum lasted until the end of the century when a new conqueror, of Turkic origin but claiming to represent the Chingizid tradition, reunited the territories of the defunct Il-khanid empire, at least for a while. The conqueror was Timur-i-leng, better known as Tamerlane.[44]

The causes of the chaos at the end of the Il-khans are somewhat more difficult to determine than the causes of the Yüan collapse, simply because the historian has much less material at his disposal. Nevertheless, a careful examination of the sources, combined with the knowledge of the political and economic situation in the Middle East prior to the Mongol conquest, allows us to understand the principal causes of the Il-khanid debacle.

It must be kept in mind that, unlike China, the Middle East did not have a homogeneous population. Moreover, since the Saljuq period, its society had been divided into two major groups, a local population of primarily Semitic and Persian origins, and a ruling class composed essentially of Türks, a group with close linguistic affinities to the Mongols. The sole bond between these ethnically and linguistically different groups was a common belief in Islam. Thus, by the time of the Mongol conquest, the Middle East was used to "alien" rule; even Egypt was ruled by a group of Turkic origins, the Mamluks. There was, however, an essential difference between the Turkic and the Mongol conquests. Most of the Turkic conquerors of the Middle East were already Muslims when they began their conquests. The Mongols, on the other hand, were heathen, and were regarded as a plague sent by 'Allah. It was not until the reign of Ghazan that large-scale conversion occurred and the Il-khans began to identify themselves somewhat more with the Middle East than with the Central Asian steppe.

Many Turkic people had joined the forces of Chinggis-khan well before the beginning of the Middle Eastern expedition. The close affinity between Türks and Mongols, the presence of Türks within the Mongol army, and the fact that the Mongols were quite evidently the strongest force of their time made it easy for the Turkic rulers of the Middle East to submit to Mongol authority. It also facilitated Mongol acceptance of this submission; often the Mongols permitted these Turkic rulers to continue their rule as before, at least as long as they satisfied all the Mongol requests. The existence of a leadership of Turkic—thus of steppe—origins led Hulegu to adopt an administrative structure quite different from the one adopted by his brother Qubilai.

To a very large degree, the Middle East still, at the beginning of the thirteenth century, had a feudal aristocratic system.[45] Unlike China, which had certain built-in safeguards against regional autonomy, the administration of the Middle Eastern states was based solely on the authority that a ruler could command. Whereas in China the bureaucracy more often than not had a restraining influence on the ruler, in the Middle East almost its sole *raison d'être* was the collection of taxes for the ruler. In China, Qubilai modified the existing institutions so that an emperor could exercise absolute control, and through his manipulation of antagonistic parties he was able, unlike his predecessors, to prevent bureaucratic sabotage of his policies. In Persia, Hulegu merely took over the existing system and gave it a Mongol veneer; he took no steps to avoid or reduce regional and political factionalism. Consequently, as has been shown earlier, the political situation within the Il-khan's domain was always extremely volatile. Violence and premature death were a constant of Il-khanid political life; only one of the Il-khanid viziers died of natural causes. The volatility of politics had existed before Hulegu formally established the Il-khanid empire; in China, a similar situation developed only during the last two decades of Mongol rule.

Thus, with hindsight, it becomes quite clear that one of the major reasons for the instability that characterized the Il-khanid empire was the Mongols' failure to modify and seize firm control over the existing political structures. Misled by the large Turkic presence in the area, the Mongols failed to grasp either the reality of this situation or the consequences of their acceptance of it for the long-term survival of their rule. In defense of Hulegu's actions it must be said, however, that the volatile political situation did not strike the Mongols as abnormal; they themselves came from an area not known for its political stability, and the political situation in the Middle East resembled the one they were accustomed to. This mistaken perception was at the basis of the Il-khans' continuing problems with sedition and rebellion.

Anti-Mongol activity was always rationalized on at least two grounds: first, the Mongols were heathen, not Muslims, and thus allegiance to them was only relative; second, submission to the Mongols had always occurred under duress: there was a real threat of annihilation if one dared to resist them. Neither point can be denied, and the Mongols themselves would probably have agreed with the second one. To cite but one example: one of Hulegu's faithful allies after his surrender had been Badr al-Din Lu'lu' of Mosul, who died in 1261. His son Salih established close relations with the Mamluks, which Hulegu viewed as a betrayal and also as a serious threat to his borders. The Mongols laid siege to Mosul, and after one year of desperate resistance, the city finally surrendered. Its entire population was massacred, and Salih and his infant son were executed. Thus ended the dynasty founded by 'Imad al-Din Zangi, the great champion of Islam against the Crusaders.[46]

The example of Salih's "rebellion" points to a problem peculiar to the Il-khans: they, unlike the Yüan, were confronted with multiple border defenses and forced to conduct war on several fronts, in addition to the military requirements within the empire itself. Unlike the Yüan, whose military campaigns were of its own making, the Il-khans had many a war thrust upon them. Most of the wars with the Golden Horde were not serious, but nevertheless they required the diversion of military resources, from other places where they were sorely needed. The Il-khans' major enemy was the Mamluks in Egypt. From the time of Hulegu until well into the reign of Oljeitu, the Il-khans attempted to conquer the Mamluk domain, or at least its Syrian and Palestinian components. Although the Mongols were able to penetrate the Mamluk domain as far as present-day Gaza, and although they were able to occupy Damascus, most of the time their attacks took the form of massive raids; no occupation ever lasted long.

The Il-khanid dispersal of their military resources contributed to their failure to conquer the Mamluk territory permanently, but it was not the only factor. The Mamluks, of all the sedentary people of that time, were the only ones thoroughly familiar with the tactics of the steppe warrior. They were Türks and, moreover, a professional military organization. Thus, they were the only serious opponents the Mongols ever faced in the West.

Adding together the wars with the Mamluks, the Il-khanid feuding with the Golden Horde and the Chaghatai Khanate, the Qaidu restoration attempt, and their own internal rebellions, one can see that the military problems faced by the Il-khans were staggering. Eventually they had less and less control over these problems, which were thus an important factor in the empire's disintegration. Yet if military problems were the only ones with which the Il-khans had to deal, they probably would have found a solution. The Middle East, however, had literally been laid waste by the Mongol conquest, and consequently many serious economic and social problems existed. According to I. P. Petrushevsky, the socioeconomic history of Persia at the time of the Il-khans falls into three distinct phases.[47] The first phase, from the 1220s to the 1290s, was characterized by a colossal economic decline, a drastic increase in taxes and feudal rents, and insurrectionary movements. The second phase, from the 1290s to the 1330s, witnessed the expansion of large-scale and unconditional land-ownership at the expense of both the state and the peasantry; the attempted revival of the preconquest economy met with only limited success. The third phase, from the 1330s to the 1380s, saw the empire sink into a state of anarchy, whose consequences have been described above.

Ghazan was the first Il-khan who seriously attempted to halt the disintegrative forces at work within the empire. To do this, he had to restore the economic life of the cities, which, prior to the Mongols, had been large and rich trade emporiums, and regular agriculture in the countryside. To accomplish these aims, Ghazan needed the allegiance of the autochthonous population, peasant and noble alike. In a society held together by a common belief in Islam, this meant that the Mongols had to adopt Islam as their own faith. As was noted earlier, Ghazan obtained the much-needed allegiance by formally and ceremoniously adopting Islam and rejecting the external symbols of the steppe in favor of those of Persia.

From Ghazan's actions after his "conversion" to Islam, it is clear that he did not have in mind the welfare of the people in his reforms; that was a useful side effect. His primary aim was to assure the court of stable and increased revenues. Such measures were a dire necessity after the economic catastrophe of Geikhatu's experiment with Chinese-style paper money. Ghazan's measures brought some vitality back to the Il-khanid economy, and, because of them, revenues collected reached their peak for the Mongol period. Nevertheless, even though the improvement was spectacular, revenues remained far below the levels of the preconquest era. Ghazan was unable to complete his reforms, especially the political ones needed to ensure economic stability, for an unidentified disease felled him in the prime of life. His two successors, Oljeitu and Abu Sa'id, clearly intended to continue the work he started but lacked the personal popularity and the military backing Ghazan had enjoyed when he became Il-khan; Abu Sa'id was still a child when he acceded to the throne. Their weakness permitted the reactionary forces, who were most threatened by the reforms, to act against them, and in the process they plunged the empire into anarchy.

In China it was possible to witness a slow but unmistakable transition from conquest dynasty to a native-oriented dynasty, but a similar development is not evident for the Il-khans. Though under Ghazan, the Il-khans assumed the external trappings of local Islamic rulers, once the throne had been firmly established, Mongol rather than Islamic traditions were followed more often than not. Throughout their reign, the Il-khans remained the rulers of a conquest dynasty, never identifying themselves with their subjects. This attitude was, ironically, nourished by the existence of Turkic conquest dynasties and their survival, in one form or another, after the Mongol conquest. Further research is required on this topic, a difficult proposition because of the scarcity of material. Nevertheless, it appears that this outlook was the major cause of the difficulties confronting the Il-khans. The Türks, once their conquest was over, had identified themselves with the region and survived. The Mongols did not and disappeared.

The Partition of the Steppe

As was shown in the previous chapter, the political histories of the Golden Horde and the Chaghatai Khanate, the empire's steppe subdivisions, were substantially different from those of the Yüan and the Il-khans. China and Persia were oriented towards agriculture; the Golden Horde and the Chaghatai Khanate, towards nomadism. Moreover, the bulk of the population that had come under their control was of Turkic origin. The affinities between the Mongols and the Türks led to a blurring of the differences between them and, in both cases, to the domination of the Mongol element by the Turkic. It is therefore not surprising that the nomadic subdivisions of the empire underwent a decline that was quite different from that of the rest of the empire.

Of the two Central Asian subdivisions, the Chaghatai Khanate was the less structured from both the political and administrative viewpoints. It was a loose coalition of Türks, Uighurs, Qaraqitais, Persians, and others under the leadership of a tiny Mongol minority. With no fixed geographical capital, the city of Almaligh served as the Khanate's central rallying point, and it was the city to which the envoys of the Great Khans were sent. Like the nomadic founders of the Mongol empire, the Chaghatai rulers, with but one exception, were so contemptuous of city and sedentary life that they plundered and looted their own cities more than once.

The Chaghatai Khanate was the stepchild of the Chingizid empire. It did not enjoy the same wealth, political influence, or economic resources as the other subdivisions, including the Golden Horde. It was not allowed semiautonomy, for not only did the Great Khans intervene constantly in its affairs, but the other subdivisions did not hesitate to do likewise. Turmoil and instability are the words that characterize the history of the Khanate. Frequent changes in leadership, not uncommon in a nomadic kingdom, were one of the major causes of the Khanate's political instability. Between 1227, when it was created, and 1338, when it was partitioned, the Khanate had nineteen rulers, only two of whom had relatively long reigns: Chaghatai himself, from 1227 to 1242, and Du'a, from 1282 to 1307. Seven of the other rulers stayed on the throne for a year or less. The turnover in leadership, as well as the outside intervention in its political affairs, began when Guyuk appointed a personal friend, Yesu-Mongke, as replacement for the successor chosen by Chaghatai himself. Yesu-Mongke, a perpetual drunk and political innocent, became caught up in Qaraqorum power politics and was replaced and executed on Mongke's order.

During the reign of Alughu (1260–1265), the Khanate attempted for the first time to establish some form of independence from the Great Khans. Initially, Alughu had allied himself with Ariq-buqa, but when the latter began to make exacting demands on the Khanate, Alughu switched his allegiance to Qubilai. His actions resulted in Ariq-buqa's defeat and a brief period of autonomy for the Khanate. Within a couple of years, the Khanate was drawn into the Qaidu restoration attempt, and Qaidu became its *de facto* suzerain. It was not until the reign of Du'a in 1282, which coincided with the declining fortunes of Qaidu, that the Khanate was able to reassume an autonomous existence. By the 1330s it had freed itself completely from outside interference, and, in fact, roles were now reversed as the Khanate intervened in the affairs of its neighbors through its constant raids.

These characteristics of the Khanate were completely within the tradition of steppe nomadism and steppe warfare. Throughout its existence, the Khanate knew only one anomalous rule, that of Kebek (1318–1326), who was interested in the amenities of city life, especially life in Samarqand, to the south of which he built his own palace. During the reign of Tarmashirin, also known as Sultan 'Ala al-Din, the Khanate engaged in massive raids against its neighbors. One of these raids was to lead to the partition of the Khanate, essentially along religious lines. In 1327 Tarmashirin led an attack against the Delhi sultanate and was soundly defeated. As his second name indicates, Tarmashirin was a Muslim, and his conversion to Islam had antagonized the largely Buddhist population of the Ili area. When Tarmashirin proved to be a less than brilliant general, the popular discontent erupted into violence. In the civil war that followed the Delhi disaster, the Khanate split into two states, and the Nestorian faith, which had played such an important role in the empire, was almost completely destroyed in the process.

The two new states were known as Transoxiana and Mogholistan. The rulers of Transoxiana were primarily puppets of their emirs or prime ministers, even though they were direct descendants of Chaghatai. The emirs, rather than working to keep the state together, were constantly at odds with each other and thus seriously weakened the richest part of the erstwhile Khanate. On the other hand, in Mogholistan a new force arose under the leadership of Tughluq Temur (1347–1363), who was rumored to be a descendant of the Chaghatai ruler Esen-buqa (1310–1318). Tughluq Temur was a strong personal ruler, the image of the traditional nomadic ruler. The various forces in the Ili area coalesced around him, and as soon as he was firmly established in his reign, he claimed Transoxiana as rightfully his. In 1360 he invaded and occupied it. From that time until the much larger unification under Timur-i-leng, the Khanate was once again united. The state created by Tughluq Temur, however, was not a restoration of the Khanate, but a completely new state.

Terms such as *decline* or *fall* are not really applicable to the Chaghatai Khanate. Its political evolution, the absorption of the nomadic Mongol minority by the nomadic Turkic majority, and its vestigial administrative structure point towards the typical evolution of a nomadic kingdom, formed and held together by the community of interests of its constituents. Once these common interests ceased to exist or lost their importance, the normal course of events was the rise of a new coalition, which, eventually, would be strong enough to create a new kingdom. Thus, unlike the Yüan and the Il-khans, the Chaghatai Khanate witnessed a progressive transition from a unified but heterogeneous state to two smaller but homogeneous ones.

It appears that the average life of the subdivisions of the Chingizid empire was approximately one century. The sole exception to this was the Golden Horde, which did not come to a formal end until well into the sixteenth century. The Horde's longevity does not mean that it was able to maintain its power throughout its existence; quite the contrary: the Horde had its ups and downs, and several times came close to total disintegration. Its problems were basically the same as the Il-khans'; like all the subdivisions, it had its share of political infighting, rebellions, economic problems, and external wars. What seems to have ensured its survival after the other Mongol subdivisions had become past history was its structure and, more specifically, the structure's adaptability to changing circumstances. Nevertheless, on several occasions pure luck seems to have been the most important factor.

Like the Chaghatai Khanate, the Golden Horde occupied a territory primarily inhabited by Türks, but unlike the former, it developed a geographically fixed capital. From about the middle of the fourteenth century, the Horde ruled its domain and conducted an active diplomatic intercourse with the Mamluks and the Byzantines from the city of Sarai.[48] Moreover, almost from its inception, the Horde was able to accommodate both the agricultural and the nomadic populations within its domain. The coexistence of these essentially inimical groups was facilitated by geography, as the zones were fairly clearly delineated. Although its taxation system was as exploitative as those applied elsewhere in the empire, the Horde did not interfere with trade or cities, and thus found itself on a sounder financial and economic basis than either the Il-khans or the Chaghatai Khanate.

Another important difference, perhaps the most important one, between the rest of the empire and the Horde was its relationship to the conquered territories. The Chaghatai Khanate settled in the nomadic zone and did not really control any group; the Yüan and the Il-khans settled in the sedentary areas. The Golden Horde settled in the nomadic zone and incorporated the nomadic population into its state structure; and from the nomadic zone it controlled the conquered sedentary areas, primarily Russia. The Horde preferred to follow the steppe tradition of acting as distant overlords rather than directly. It contented itself with collecting taxes and tribute, which were gathered for it by the subjected population, appointing princes, and acting as arbiters in disputes. This policy meant that the Horde rarely became embroiled in local politics and it never identified its interests with those of its Russian subjects.[49]

Around the middle of the fourteenth century, however, it seemed that the Golden Horde was about to undergo the same fate as the rest of the empire. Its ruler, Jani-beg, died in 1357, and almost immediately a twenty-year-long civil war erupted. This was remarkably similar to the events following the Il-khan Abu Sa'id's death. Various factions contended for the throne, and no single powerful leader emerged. It was not until 1377, when Toqtamish, a leader of the White Horde,[50] forcibly took the throne, that unity once again appeared within the Horde. Toqtamish's accession meant that rule over the Horde had passed out of the hands of Batu's descendants.

During the two decades preceding Toqtamish's assumption of power, civil war was not the only problem confronting the Horde. The Russian principalities, well aware of the Mongols' weakness, moved to reject the Mongol yoke. They ceased their annual tribute payments and prepared for war. On 8 September 1380, a major clash occurred near Kulikovo, and the Russians were able to defeat the much-feared Mongol armies. Emboldened by this victory, they rejected Toqtamish's ultimatum to resume forthwith the payment of tribute. Toqtamish could not allow the situation to continue without endangering his own power. He invaded Russia and severely punished the Russians. On 13 August 1382, his forces completely destroyed Moscow. The victory re-established Mongol authority over Russia for almost another two centuries, and the Horde was once again a major power in the area.[51]

Things, however, were not the same as before, and Toqtamish's reign turned out to be a period of transition. A new power—the empire created by Timur-i-leng—had established itself in what was once the Chaghatai Khanate and had begun to expand at the expense of the surrounding states. By the time of the Horde's reassertion of power over Russia, several areas of the Middle East and the southern Central Asian steppe had come under Timur's control. His avowed aim was the reconstruction of the Chingizid empire, and it appears that this was his main reason for not attacking the Golden Horde and the Qipcaq steppe. But Toqtamish began to intrude on what Timur considered his domain and consequently war over the possession of a large portion of the Qipcaq steppe broke out in 1395. Toqtamish and his armies suffered a disastrous defeat. The defeat did not mean the end of the Horde, but it marked the beginning of a radical change in its nature, even though it continued under that name. After Toqtamish's debacle, the Horde's rulers were mere figureheads, and real power passed into the hands of the emirs, the first of whom was Edigu (1395–1419).

The years of Edigu's rule saw the end of the Horde as a unified state, partly as a result of the problems created by Timur's victory over Toqtamish. The latter had managed to escape, and in August 1399, having made an alliance with Lithuania, attempted to regain control over the Horde; but he was, again, soundly defeated, this time by the forces of the Horde itself. Once the problem of Toqtamish's ambitions was eliminated, a new problem arose in the form of Russian dissension. Remembering their victory at the Kulikovo and having seen the weaknesses of the Horde at the time of Timur's attack, the Russians again attempted to rid themselves of the "Tartar" yoke. Even though Edigu was able to keep the overall situation under control, it was becoming clear that the Horde as a unified force was on its way out. The partition process began shortly after Edigu's death.

What external pressures and attacks had failed to accomplish was to be realized by internal dissension and the absence of strong leadership: the Mongols were eliminated from the area and from world politics as a major force. The process was a slow and gradual one. It was not until the reign of Kuchuk Mehmed (1435–1465) that the Golden Horde broke up into the three khanates of the Crimea, Kazan, and Astrakhan. Rivalries between these khanates continued for several centuries, and it appears that none of them fully realized that the reign of the Horde, and with it that of the Mongols, had come to an end. The formal end of the Golden Horde came in 1502, the year Mengli Giray (1478–1515), the ruler of the Crimean khanate, attacked and destroyed Sarai, once the Horde's capital.

The power of the Golden Horde had withered away slowly and almost imperceptibly during the middle decades of the fifteenth century under the conflicting interests and aspirations of its components. The name of the Golden Horde and its Chingizid association continued for a long time thereafter. It is, however, doubtful that one can still speak of a "Mongol domain" after the reign of Toqtamish, and especially after the reign of Edigu. The Mongols of the Golden Horde, like those of the Chaghatai Khanate, had undergone a complete Turkicization, which slowly but inexorably moved it away from the Chingizid traditions. The internal tensions within the Horde inevitably led to the creation of three new states, though each claimed to be the continuation of the old one.

The new khanates belong to Mongol history only as successor states. Of the three, the Crimean khanate survived the longest. Founded about 1440 by Hajji Giray, it did not disappear until 1783, when it was absorbed by a new force on the steppe, the Russian empire. Although the Crimean khans considered themselves the legitimate successors to the rule of Batu, their history is no longer Mongol history, even in the broadest sense of the term. It became intimately intertwined with both Russian and Ottoman history and properly belongs to Turkish history in the narrow and modern sense of Turkish. The Crimean khans, however, managed to maintain at least one tradition of the Golden Horde: the exaction of tribute from the the Russians. These payments ended only in 1681, during the reign of Peter the Great and after the khanate had become a vassal of the Ottoman empire.

The khanate of Kazan, in existence from about 1436 until 1552, was no longer a real Mongol state, politically or linguistically. The Turkish-speaking element had absorbed practically all the Mongol-speaking elements; moreover, the population included many Finno-Ugric groups, such as, for example, the Cheremis and the Mordvin.[52] Relations between Kazan, the Crimean khanate, and the Ottoman empire were relatively good; eventually, Kazan recognized the Ottoman emperor as its suzerain. Though on good terms with the Crimean and Ottoman rulers, Kazan's basic orientation was towards Moscow. The Muscovy state was becoming the most important of the Russian principalities and, as such, sought to eliminate Kazan as the most visible symbol of "Mongol" oppression. After several unsuccessful attempts, Tsar Ivan the Terrible was able, on 15 October 1552, to invest Kazan and thus bring to an end the last remnant of Mongol power in that part of the steppe. The fall of Kazan opened the way to Russian penetration of the Central Asian steppe, a penetration that brought the Russians all the way to the Pacific Ocean.[53]

The third successor state, the khanate of Astrakhan, so called because it was centered near the city of that name, was founded in or around 1466 and was the smallest of the three khanates. Beset by numerous problems, including constant attacks by the Crimean khanate, it began to look for allies. It sought the assistance of the emerging Russian empire, and the latter, seeing an opening to the Caspian, readily acceded to Astrakhan's request. Shortly after the fall of Kazan, in 1554, Russia gave up the pretense that Astrakhan was an independent state. The tsar appointed a puppet ruler, and Astrakhan became part of the Russian empire. After that, the Mongols were present in significant numbers only in their original homeland and on the Chinese border.

Unlike those of the other subdivisions of the Mongol empire, the decline and fall of the Golden Horde was almost imperceptible. There was no sudden halt or change, only a very slow transition from one state to another. This makes periodization of the Horde's history difficult. A threefold division seems to be the most practical. The first is the Mongol period proper, which can be dated from the beginning of the reign of Batu in 1237 to the death of Janibeg in 1357. The second, the Turco-Mongol period, covers the reigns of Toqtamish and Edigu, that is, 1377 to 1419, when descendants of Mongol princely houses still played a role in a more or less unified Horde but the Mongol traditions were fading into the background. The third is the period of transition that led to the creation of three separate and essentially Turkish khanates. In the periodization of the Horde's history, the main problem is to choose a date for its formal end, and whatever approach is used, the selection is and has to be arbitrary. The traditional final date is that of the fall of Kazan, 1552, because it opened Central Asia to Russian penetration and ended, for all practical purposes, Mongol influence on Russia. Choosing this date, however, implies that Kazan was the real and only successor state to the Horde. It seems preferable to choose the year 1502, the year of the destruction of Sarai, as the end of the Golden Horde. With the destruction of the Horde's capital, the last symbol of its independence disappeared.

A Periodization
of the Chingizid Empire

The separate study of each of the subdivisions of the Chingizid empire is a practical and useful approach, but it tends to obscure, if not prevent, an adequate assessment of the empire as a whole. An evaluation of the conditions within the Chingizid empire involves the difficult task of periodization, which is rendered especially difficult by its enormous size, its great complexity, and its remarkable diversity. Historical conditions and events only rarely lend themselves to precise temporal definition, and historical change rarely, if ever, occurs at a specific time and place. Periodization is, nevertheless, a task every historian must attempt. It appears that the Chingizid empire as a whole—that is, from the Urals to the Chinese coast—can be divided into three major periods. The first is the period of creation and consolidation; the second is the imperial period; and the third is the decline and fall.

The only period that presents no serious dating difficulties is the first. The most convenient event for dating its beginning is the 1206 *quriltai,* at which the leader of the newly created nomadic confederation, Temujin, assumed the title of Chinggis-khan. Although he was already the most powerful leader on the steppe at that time, the *quriltai* confirmed his authority and witnessed the submission to that authority of all the other leaders on the steppe. The formal end of this period came in 1264, when Ariq-buqa surrendered to Qubilai. The real end, however, was the death of Mongke in 1258: by that time, Mongol authority was firmly established throughout the then-known world; Qaraqorum had become the real capital of the empire; and the campaigns, with the exception of the one against the Southern Sung, had virtually come to an end. The years between 1258 and 1264 saw the transition to the second, or imperial, period.

The imperial period formally begins with the *quriltai* during which Qubilai assumed the title of emperor. It ends with the final surrender of Qaidu's allies to the House of Tolui and thus covers the period from 1260 to 1303. Because of the nature of its events, the first period in Mongol history is quite self-evident, but the second requires more justification. Indeed, the imperial period is the time when the empire was divided into four distinct geographical parts. Tradition treats these parts as independent entities without really considering whether the facts justify such a treatment. It has become customary, because it is easy to look at the differences between them rather than at their similarities.

In each of the subdivisions, the Mongol rulers had to take into consideration local conditions, but throughout the empire they remained guided by Mongol traditions in their decision-making processes. Moreover, there is some evidence, although it is not abundant, that most Mongols considered Qubilai the Great Khan even though he had moved the capital from Qaraqorum to Peking; it should not be forgotten that, at that time, and certainly for the Mongols, China was the world's political and cultural center. The Qaidu war of restoration, too, supports the theory of a conceptual unity of the empire: Qaidu wanted to restore the nomadic nature of the empire and return its center to the steppe. His refusal to recognize Qubilai, as well as the fact that only the Chaghatai Khanate supported him, and then only half-heartedly, indicates that most Mongols preferred the situation as it was. The heaviest fighting and expenditures in the Qaidu war were borne by the Yüan but affected, in multiple ways, the Il-khans, the Golden Horde, and the Chaghatai Khanate. When Qaidu was killed and his allies surrendered two years later, there is evidence that there was a sense of rediscovered unity throughout the empire and that peace negotiations were conducted between all the subdivisions of the Chingizid empire. This rediscovered unity did not last long. Shortly after the events of 1303 each of the subdivisions went its own way.

To have the second period end and the third period begin in 1303 is purely arbitrary, but the surrender of Qaidu's last allies was an event welcomed by all the subdivisions of the empire and therefore seems the most appropriate dividing line. The third period is characterized by the progressive decline and collapse of the empire. It is a difficult, if not impossible, task to find a precise closing date for this period; it seems, though, that the decade between 1350 and 1360 is appropriate, and so for convenience sake one can adopt the year 1355. By that time, the Chaghatai Khanate had ceased to exist, having split into two new and separate states. The Golden Horde was about to enter the period of civil war that ended some twenty years later when the House of Batu lost control over the Horde. The Il-khanid empire had been broken up into several successor states. A few remnants of Mongol rule remained, but new and more vigorous forces had made their appearance. In China, the Yüan rulers had become unable, and perhaps unwilling, to stem the tide of events that led to the establishment of the Chinese Ming dynasty less than fifteen years later. After 1368 the only surviving subdivision of the Chingizid empire was the Golden Horde. Whether or not it was still a "Mongol" state is open to debate.

This tentative periodization of the Chingizid empire permits a better evaluation of the causes of the decline and fall of the world's largest continuous empire. Among the numerous factors that led to the collapse of the immense empire built by Chinggis-khan and his successors, two stand out: the centrifugal tendencies inherent in a nomadic empire, and the consequences of the Qaidu war of restoration.

In traditional nomadic empires, the centrifugal forces usually found their clearest expression in personality clashes within the ruling clan. The impact of this phenomenon on the rises and falls of these empires is evident, as was shown in earlier chapters, in the history of the Turkic empire. Even the Manchu, China's last dynasty, was subject to this phenomenon. The founder of a nomadic empire was of necessity a strong and charismatic personality, but then so were his generals and advisors, and when the occasion arose, one of them might attempt to usurp power. The nomadic nature of these empires prevented adequate control by the ruler over subordinates outside his immediate circle, and consequently ruthlessness became a characteristic of a nomadic empire. No leader would hesitate to execute all potential contenders for the throne, even infants, for whenever such a potential contender managed to survive, either through luck or through intrigue, the empire was eventually faced with serious political and military problems: witness the case of Qaidu, and, to some extent, that of Chinggis-khan himself. The inherent tensions of a nomadic empire led to short reigns for the founder's successors and, eventually, to the collapse of the empire itself.

Although Qaidu's career and the war of restoration have never been studied in detail, it is clear that they had a major role in the collapse of the Chingizid empire. The nature of the war and the fact that it lasted well over a quarter of a century indicate that a substantial portion of the Mongols had rejected the existing institutions. The decision to recreate a nomadic empire shook the foundations of the Chingizid empire and led to a bitter struggle between what can be called the nomadic conservative wing, headed by Qaidu, and the rest of the Mongol world. The war placed a serious burden on the resources of the empire, but its most important consequence was that, after the defeat of Qaidu and the surrender of his allies, it became clear that the conceptual unity of the empire had been broken. For a few years afterwards, the fiction of imperial unity was maintained, but eventually each subdivision discovered that it had little common ground with the others except for origin and language. The subdivisions increasingly turned inward and away from the others. Under these various pressures, the Chingizid empire, like previous nomadic empires, collapsed. Political and military turmoil again characterized steppe politics. This turmoil, a consequence of the Mongols' repeated attempts to recreate their lost empire, ended when the steppe was incorporated into the Chinese and Russian empires.

10

The Successor States

The collapse of the Yüan dynasty, the disintegration of the Il-khanid state, and the partition of the steppe meant the end of the Mongols as a world power, and, in the long run, the end of the nomadic horseman as a threat to sedentary states. The collapse of the vast empire created by Chinggis-khan did not mean that the Mongols disappeared as a political force. Although the steppe's influence on the surrounding sedentary states drastically declined, the steppe itself remained a region in turmoil, a turmoil that regularly had repercussions in the sedentary states. Until well into the seventeenth century, the Mongols were a latent threat to the security of the states they had once occupied. New steppe confederations arose regularly and attempted to recreate, at least in part, the lost Chingizid empire. These efforts were unsuccessful, not because the Mongols had lost their vigor, but because social, political, and economic conditions had changed. When the Chingizid empire collapsed, the sedentary states gained the strategic edge, and they were never to lose it.

The actual causes of the decline of the steppe within a few decades of the collapse of the Mongol domains in the sedentary areas are not clearly known. Agriculture had begun to encroach on the steppe from every direction, reducing the amount of pasture land available to the Mongols. At the same time, the number of mounts available to the nomadic warrior diminished considerably, although it is not known whether there was a cause-effect relationship between the two phenomena. Innovations in weaponry, especially in firearms, gave the sedentary states the technological advantage that until that time had been on the side of the nomadic horseman. The use of firearms facilitated the defense of the border areas and drastically reduced the efficacy of nomadic cavalry attacks.

Nevertheless, on several occasions the Mongols were able to seize the initiative. In the middle of the fifteenth century, and again during the early eighteenth century, they came close to re-establishing a large and independent empire. On the eastern and western borders of the steppe, however, two new empires arose during the seventeenth century and began to expand into the Central Asian steppe, the Mongol homelands. In time, Russia and Manchu China divided the steppe between them. The Mongols were forcibly subdued and lost their independence, some to the Russians, the majority to the Manchus. It was not until the twentieth century, when Chinese influence in Central Asia was at its lowest and the Russian October Revolution had created a new power structure, that some Mongols, with Russian help, were able to set up a new independent state, the Mongolian People's Republic.

The Resurgence of the Sedentary States

Under the Mongol empire, the Central Asian nomad had not only gained complete control over the principal sedentary areas surrounding the steppe but had occupied several of these areas, principally Persia and China. In order to rule their vast domain, however, the Mongols had to abandon the traditional practices of the steppe and adopt, albeit in a modified form, the governmental techniques of the sedentary states. Because of their numerical inferiority, the Mongols had to accept into their political structure an educated native elite, which constituted a serious break with their tradition and presented a danger to the preservation of Mongol ethnicity. The most serious threat to Mongol authority, however, was that the use of a native elite and sedentary administrative practices could lead to a resurgence of the sedentary states. Although the process was slow and almost imperceptible, that is precisely what happened. The resurgence occurred in all the subdivisions, but it affected the Yüan dynasty and the Golden Horde most seriously.

In China, the Mongols began to lose control after the 1328 coup d'état. The process was a slow one, and the dominance of Confucian traditions and politics was not clearly evident until the demise of Bayan the Merkid. Several leading members of the Mongol elite recognized the threat increased Confucianization presented to the survival of the Yüan dynasty and attempted to change the course of events. The most prominent of these was Toghto, who twice was prime minister, from 1340 to 1344, and from 1349 to 1355. During his tenure Toghto initiated a series of reforms that, although ostensibly aimed at helping the population at large, had as their real purpose the survival of the dynasty. His reforms were aimed not only at restoring the dynasty's economy, but also at the pacification of the rebellions that had erupted in South China. One of the principal rebels whom Toghto sought to eliminate was Chang Shih-ch'eng (1312–1367),[1] who, in June 1353, had seized the city of Kao-yu on the Grand Canal, a vital link between North and South China. In the fall of 1354, Toghto launched a massive assault on Kao-yu. Chang Shih-ch'eng's forces were no match for the army assembled by Toghto, but suddenly, as Kao-yu was about to fall, the Mongol forces stopped and withdrew. Toghto had been cashiered by the emperor, recalled, and exiled. Hie died early in 1355 on his way to Yünnan, poisoned by his opponents.[2]

As was shown in the previous chapter, Toghto's dismissal virtually marked the end of the Yüan dynasty. Many of the troops who had been loyal to him, and thus, by extension, to the Yüan dynasty, defected to the rebels. The latter, noting that no serious reaction was now to be expected from Peking, began to concentrate upon fighting each other, all vying to become the dominant group. The reasons behind Toghto's sudden dismissal still are not clear, and his loyalty, or disloyalty, to the Yüan dynasty is still debated among Chinese historians. Toghto's radical policies unquestionably had created enemies for him both at the court and in the provinces, especially since he had sought to restrict the power of other officials. Furthermore, he had antagonized the second empress when he failed to endorse her son Ayushiridara as the heir apparent. He was reluctant to do so, however, not from political motives, but because the principal empress had given birth to a son, thus complicating the legitimation as heir apparent of Toghon Temur's oldest son.[3] In the political struggles at the court, Toghto was the loser, and his sudden acceptance of the emperor's orders can possibly be explained by the fact that it was the second time he had had to face a cabal. Probably he felt that, in the words of John W. Dardess, whatever his enemies did, it "would make no difference, for the inheritance of Chinggis-khan and Qubilai was at an end; the Yüan was, in all essential respects, finished."[4]

In the years that followed Toghto's dismissal, China witnessed a drastic increase not only in the number of rebellions that broke out, but also in regionalism: local officials recognized the emperor but acted as *de facto* rulers. The rebellions were primarily located in Central China. Regionalism was most manifest in North China, where it was spearheaded by Mongols themselves, the two principal leaders being Chaghan Temur and his nephew Kökö Temur.[5] Chaghan Temur had begun to establish his independent fief shortly after Toghto's dismissal. By the middle of 1358, he controlled substantial portions of Shensi, Shansi, and Hunan provinces. Although the Yüan tried various approaches, peaceful and military, to regain control, it failed to do so, primarily because of its own bungling policies. When Chaghan Temur was assassinated, he was succeeded by Kökö Temur, whom the Yüan court had to recognize as a legitimate official. By 1365 he had become the kingpin in North China and Mongol court politics. The Yüan court was not able to curb Kökö Temur's power, and neither was the future emperor of the Ming dynasty, Chu Yüan-chang. The latter came into contact with Kökö Temur in 1363, when it appeared that an alliance between the two was a possibility. That alliance never came about, but Chu Yüan-chang continued his attempts to form one until after the establishment of the Ming dynasty. In 1369 his forces were able to drive Kökö Temur out of his stronghold in the former Tangut territory, and the latter threw in his lot with the Mongols on the steppe. Nevertheless, he continued to threaten the Ming dynasty until his death near Qaraqorum in 1375.

Most of the rebellions in Central China had broken out in the early 1350s. After Toghto's demise, the nature of these rebellions changed, and they assumed more importance. Their main purpose at first had been self-protection from the exactions of officials, Mongol and Chinese alike; they were aimed at the dynasty as such, without ethnic considerations. Confronted with the court's manifest impotence, made all the clearer by the events at Kao-yu, the rebellions took on the character of a Chinese civil war and acquired an ideology. In the beginning many rebels sought their immediate victims among the landlord and scholar-official class that oppressed them; in the latter part of the 1350s the rebels actively sought the support of that class. To all rebel leaders it was clear that the days of the Yüan were numbered. The outcome of the rebellion would be the creation of a new dynasty, which was to be founded by the victor in the Chinese civil war. To establish a dynasty and legitimate it in Confucian terms, the support of the scholar-official class was a necessity.[6]

The victor in the civil war was Chu Yüan-chang, a native from Hao-chou (modern Feng-yang in Anhwei province), where he grew up in poverty. On 23 January 1368, with his major rivals eliminated but the Yüan still controlling Peking, Chu Yüan-chang proclaimed himself emperor, adopted the dynastic name *Ming* ("bright, enlightened") and the personal reign title *Hung-wu* ("grand military achievement"). Thus began a new era in Chinese history; for only the second time, a commoner had become emperor.[7] His first task was to drive the remnants of the Yüan dynasty from China. This task was accomplished when his forces took Peking on 14 September 1368, but it was not until 1377 that Chu Yüan-chang controlled the whole of China. The fact that the Mongols had left China, however, did not mean that they had suddenly ceased to be a potential threat to the sedentary nation. Those who had followed Toghon Temur to the steppe clearly cherished the hope of returning to a China which they felt was theirs. But many Mongols had been unable or unwilling to leave China.

The Mongols who remained did so either because they were born in China, and a return to the ancestral steppe and the harshness of nomadic life did not appeal to them, or because they had been cut off from the routes that led to the steppe by the forces of Chu Yüan-chang. These Mongols had to accommodate themselves to the loss of their prominent position to a native Chinese elite, and most of them undoubtedly accepted this situation. The changeover was facilitated by the fact that many Mongols had joined the Chinese rebels.[8] As has been pointed out on several occasions, at no time did these rebellions have racial overtones: from the beginning the leaders of the rebellions assumed that many Mongols would and could remain in China. When Chu Yüan-chang became the emperor of the new, and last, native Chinese dynasty, the policies he adopted towards the Mongols were based on that premise. Mongols, as well as other foreigners in China at that time, were allowed to keep the civil and military posts they occupied if they formally recognized the new emperor. The essence of the Ming policies was the assimilation of the foreign element, and it seems that as far as the Mongols in China proper were concerned, the assimilation was a smooth process, practically completed within a decade of the founding of the Ming dynasty. Just as there is no evidence that many Mongols objected to this policy, there is no evidence of Chinese protests, either.[9]

If the Mongols in China did not create any particular problems for the Ming dynasty, the same cannot be said of the Mongols on China's frontiers. When the Mongols left China, they viewed their departure as a strategic withdrawal that would enable them to regroup and reconquer China. The Ming emperor and his officials were well aware of these intentions and therefore began to develop specific defensive policies. On the surface, the situation resembled that of pre-Mongol days—the nomad on the steppe threatened the sedentary area—but having occupied the sedentary areas for more than a century, the nomadic people had undergone important changes, as had the sedentary people. As soon as the Ming government was solidly established, it took the offensive, militarily and diplomatically, in order to prevent the formation of a strong, new confederation on the steppe. It also attempted, successfully, to create a buffer zone between itself and the steppe proper. The buffer zone, populated by Chinese and Mongols, supported a mixture of pastoral nomadism and agriculture and slowly encroached on the steppe regions. Like Qubilai, Chu Yüan-chang promoted agriculture on the frontier, but as a means of neutralizing the Mongols.

Although the Mongol threat was a serious one, problems within China itself kept Chu Yüan-chang from concentrating his efforts on the frontier. Thus, throughout the first decade of his reign, the defense of the Ming was essentially a passive one. Expeditions were sent into the frontier regions, but without any overall military plan; their primary purpose was to keep Ming territory under control, and whenever necessary to stage punitive raids. This limited policy was, in fact, all the Ming economy could bear during those years. The most important of these expeditions were those of Hsu Ta against Kökö Temur.[10] The first campaign took place in 1370 and forced Kökö Temur to withdraw to the steppe. In 1371 another massive expedition against Kökö Temur was launched, but in May of that year, the Chinese forces suffered a serious defeat, and after that, caution was the order of the day. The military expeditions were relatively successful; their success, however, was primarily due to dissension among the Mongols themselves. In contrast, the Ming's political measures, which exploited Mongol dissensions, were more successful. Many Mongols were lured into Chinese service both on the frontiers and in the interior.[11] Although assimilation of these Mongols was a slow process, most of them remained loyal to the Chinese side.

Throughout the early period of Chu Yüan-chang's reign, the principal guideline for the military was to avoid battle with a superior Mongol force. After 1385 the situation changed drastically. The Ming's passive defense had permitted the Mongols to regroup, and it was clear to all concerned that the only way to deal with the problem was to attack the Mongols, rather than simply to defend against them by establishing military colonies on the frontier, the traditional Chinese defense since the early Han dynasty. The Ming adopted an offensive defense based on cavalry warfare. Whereas the Mongols had dismounted to rule the peasants, the Ming dynasty took to the saddle to control the nomads.

The active frontier policy developed after 1385 was to remain a feature of the Ming's policy towards the Mongols, although static defenses like walled fortifications were not neglected. By 1395 the Ming dynasty had reached its maximum size. The change to an active policy had two major consequences for the dynasty itself: an increase in horse trading and horse breeding and, eventually, the relocation of the Ming capital from Nanking to Peking.[12] The supply of horses had always been a major problem for Chinese governments. In the past, it frequently had had to rely on its enemy, the Central Asian nomad, to obtain horses; the Ming policy was created to reduce substantially, and if possible to eliminate, this unhealthy reliance by increasing trade with submitted Mongol tribes, a policy that formed part of the overall policy of Sinicization of foreign elements, and by developing the Imperial Stud. The main effort to increase horse production began in 1397 and was largely successful, even though the Chinese remained at a disadvantage.[13]

The transfer of the Ming capital to the north, closer to the scene of Mongol-Chinese conflicts, was completed during the reign of Chu Ti (1360–1424), better known as the Yung-lo emperor. Strategy dictated the northward move: location in Peking permitted faster control of border incidents and substantially shortened the communication lines between the court and the field army during a campaign. It was from Peking, the Northern Capital, that the Yung-lo emperor and his successors dealt with the new Mongol empires established on the eastern steppe.[14]

In Eastern Asia, the resurgence of the sedentary state came after the Mongols had returned to the steppe. In the western domains of the Mongol empire, the sedentary states reasserted their importance while the Golden Horde was still in existence. In fact, it could be argued that there was a relationship between the rise of Russia, especially the Muscovite state, and the decline of the Golden Horde. The increasing power of the sedentary states in Eastern Europe was a direct result of the fact that the Mongols of the Golden Horde did not actually occupy these territories. Furthermore, the fact that the Golden Horde was not actively involved in the collection of taxes (it used the local nobility for that) and the fact that it allowed the princes and the churches of the area to form financial agreements encouraged the development of the Eastern European states.

The resurgence of the sedentary areas in the West began after the final defeat of Toqtamish by the forces of Edigu. The principal beneficiary of Toqtamish's defeat was the emerging Muscovite state, which, for nearly a decade afterwards, was free from major incursions by the forces of the Golden Horde. The rise of Muscovy was facilitated by the Golden Horde's support and encouragement of the activities of the Russian Great Prince Vassili, who used the freedom of action accorded to him to strengthen his control over the surrounding areas in an early attempt to unify the Russian princely states. The Horde, however, was still quite powerful and soon began to view Vassili as a potential threat to their own authority. Edigu, during the first decade of his rule, began a campaign to reassert the Horde's authority over Russia, and, in the fall of 1408, he invaded Russia, entering Moscow on 5 December. To regain control over Moscow, however, Edigu had to enlist Lithuania's support, and hence to allow Lithuania to continue to assert its independence from the Golden Horde. When Witold, Lithuania's ruler, declined Edigu's proposal for an alliance, the emir was not in a position to react against his refusal. When Edigu died in 1419, he had been unable to check the growth of Muscovite autonomy. Lithuania had fallen outside the sphere of influence of the Golden Horde and assumed an independent history.[15]

With the death of Edigu a prolonged period of disorder began for the Golden Horde, which ended with the division of the Horde into three successor states. The disorder permitted Lithuania to consolidate its independence and Moscow to assume an independent status, although it was not until much later that it was able to break its tributary relations with the Horde's successor states. The Grand Duke Ivan III's accession to the throne of Moscow in 1462 marked the beginning of an active foreign policy aimed at assuming as much independence as possible. Full independence, however, proved impossible, and Ivan had to find an accommodation with the Crimean khanate. Through careful manipulation of political rivalries in the khanate of Kazan, Ivan was able to assume the title of Kazan in 1469.[16] In 1480, aided by a severe winter, Ivan repulsed the Crimean khanate's forces, enabling him almost to sever relations with them. When Ivan died in 1505, active control over Russia by the Horde's successor states had ceased, even though tribute was still being paid. His actions, however, permitted his successor, Ivan IV or Ivan the Terrible, to begin Russia's expansion into Central Asia, which eventually led to Russian dominance over nearly the whole of Central Asia.[17]

In the Il-khanid domain, as in the Chaghatai Khanate, no rise of sedentary traditions and structures occurred after the collapse of the Mongol empire; no major changes occurred in Iran until the advent of the Safavid dynasty around 1500. The collapse of the Il-khanid dynasty meant only that Mongol control had ceased. The Chaghatai Khanate, which had split into two successor states, was forcibly reunited by the Mongol ruler of the Ili region, Tughluq Temur. It was from the former Chaghatai Khanate that a serious attempt was made to restore the Chingizid empire in the name of a Mongol ruler by a member of a Turkic family and an advisor to Tughluq Temur: Timur-i-leng or Tamerlane.

Timur and
the Timurids

By the middle of the fourteenth century, the former Chaghatai Khanate remained an ill-defined state in which both sedentary and nomadic traditions vied for dominance. The former, together with Islam, dominated Transoxiana. The nominal ruling elite were families of Mongol origin, but real power was held by an elite of Turkic origin. It was into one of these families that, in 1336, was born Timur, who was to become the founder of a new dynasty. He became known to history as Timur-i-leng, "Timur the Lame," a name which was transformed by Westerners into "Tamerlane." The family with which Timur was associated was that of the Barlas, who held sway over the area of Kech, to the south of Samarqand. At the time of Tughluq Temur's invasion of Transoxiana, the ruler of Kech was Hajji Barlas, allegedly an uncle of Timur. In 1360, Hajji Barlas was forced to abandon resistance against Tughluq Temur and fled from Kech to seek asylum in Khurassan.[18]

Little is known about Timur's youth except that he was ambitious. Tughluq Temur's conquest of Transoxiana gave him a legitimate excuse to replace Hajji Barlas as the ruler of Kech. He pledged allegiance to the new Mongol ruler, and the latter immediately confirmed him as the ruler of Kech. Timur's loyalties, other than to his own interests, are doubtful. When Hajji Barlas staged a comeback and defeated Timur's forces, the latter immediately recognized him as his overlord. In 1361, however, Tughluq Temur firmly established his authority over Transoxiana, and Hajji Barlas was murdered while attempting to regain Khurassan, Tughluq Temur appointed his son as viceroy over Transoxiana, and Timur became the latter's emir, with no intention of remaining Tughluq Temur's loyal servant. He broke with him and allied himself with Mir Hussein, the ruler of Balkh. Together they attacked Tughluq Temur's son and, in 1364, were able to drive him out of Transoxiana. They found a remote descendant of the Chaghatai ruler Du'a, made him the ruler of the new domain, and pledged allegiance to him. Throughout his reign, Timur maintained the myth that he was a mere emir of the legitimate Chaghatai ruler.

The alliance between Mir Hussein and Timur was of short duration. Soon after their victory, war broke out between them, and Timur was forced to withdraw to Khurassan. For the next several years, Timur led the life of a swashbuckling adventurer. When the Mongols of the Ili region again threatened to invade Transoxiana, Mir Hussein, in name of Islam, made peace with Timur. The reconciliation gave Timur the opportunity that had long evaded him. The exact nature of the political intrigues that followed the reconciliation are not known, for the sources serve only to justify the actions of Timur, the eventual victor in the contest. It appears, however, that he was able to exert his authority over Transoxiana, while Mir Hussein withdrew into present-day Afghanistan, to the city of Balkh. Suddenly, without the slightest pretext, Timur crossed the Oxus, invaded Badakshan, and appeared at the gates of Balkh, taking Mir Hussein by complete surprise. Mir Hussein had no alternative but surrender, and Timur became the uncontested ruler of Transoxiana. Although Mir Hussein was pardoned by Timur, he was murdered by Timur's advisors. Balkh underwent the fate of many of the cities Timur was to conquer later: because of its support of Mir Hussein, its ruler, many of its inhabitants were put to the sword.[19]

On 10 April 1370, having conquered Balkh, Timur formally became the new emir of Transoxiana and proclaimed himself the successor of Chinggiskhan. His avowed aim was the reconstruction of the Chingizid empire, and soon he began the conquests to achieve that aim. Although he was the uncontested ruler over Transoxiana, Timur could not claim descent from a Mongol ruling house, and this problem of Chingizid legitimacy appears to have weighed heavily on his mind. Throughout his reign, he maintained a series of puppet rulers whose only qualification was that they were legitimate, although remote, descendants of a Chingizid house; Timur justified all his actions in their name. Furthermore, he never assumed the title *khan*; it was only in 1388 that he began to use the Islamic title *sultan,* without abandoning the fictional supremacy of his appointed Mongol khan. There was, however, a major difference between the empire created by Chinggiskhan and the one created by Timur. Chinggis-khan's empire was essentially homogeneous and had a solid foundation that Timur's empire never enjoyed. The latter's basic weakness, transcended only by Timur's personality and that of his immediate successor, was its heterogeneity. Its culture belonged to a Turkic-Persian tradition, its legal structure had a Turkic-Chingizid foundation, and its political-religious structure was a mixture of Mongol and Islamic traditions. Moreover, it had no dynamic center, no imperial tradition; hence, within a few years of Timur's death, the empire disappeared.[20]

After consolidating his control over what had been the Chaghatai Khanate, a process completed around 1380, Timur began to plan the reconquest of the Chingizid domains. The first victim of the Timurid onslaught was to be

Eastern Persia, in particular the territory of Khurassan. Persia was politically a weak state, but it was more important in Timur's eyes that it represented a major part of the Chingizid empire. The first invasion began in 1381 with a march on Herat. Herat was then under the Kart dynasty headed by Ghiyath al-Din, who, shortly before Timur's invasion, had conquered the city of Nishapur. Ghiyath al-Din's plans to resist the invader were thwarted when his army surrendered to Timur and the population of Herat, in whose memory the last sacking by the Mongols must still have been quite vivid, refused to participate in the city's defense. Ghiyath al-Din surrendered and was banished to Timur's capital, Samarqand, and the walls of Herat were torn down. A year later, a rebellion in the city was severely repressed. Towers were built with the skulls of the massacred population, and Ghiyath al-Din was ordered to commit suicide. Thus ended the Kart dynasty. The conquest of Herat was followed by the conquests of Khurassan and Mazandaran; by 1384 Timur was in control over all of Eastern Persia.

The conquest of Western Persia, then under the rule of the Jalayir dynasty, began in earnest in 1386. The campaign lasted two years; and in the process the cities of Isfahan and Hamadan were laid waste. Timur, however, was forced to return to Samarqand when Toqtamish, the ruler of the Golden Horde, began to threaten the security of his domains. The campaign against Toqtamish ended in disaster for the latter. However, Timur made no serious attempt to conquer the entire Qipcaq steppe, even though it had once belonged, and in fact still belonged, to the descendants of Chinggis-khan, but contented himself punishing Toqtamish severely. In 1392 he resumed the conquest of Western Persia. The second campaign lasted five years and gave Timur control over Shiraz, among other cities. After the fall of Shiraz in April 1393, he proceeded to Hamadan and from there to Baghdad, arriving at its gates in October. Timur entered the city, and after a three-month rest, he brought the war north to Armenia, Georgia, and the southern Qipcaq steppe. These wars took place during the years 1394 and 1395. Timur's absence from Iraq permitted the ruler of Baghdad, who was assisted by Egyptian Mamluks, to return to his city. In 1401, however, Timur reclaimed the city and ordered a general massacre, which apparently involved a hundred thousand victims. Henceforth Baghdad remained under Timurid control until a short time after Timur's death.[22]

Timur's interests, however, were not limited to the territories that had once been under Mongol control. In August 1398 he launched a campaign against the Delhi sultanate on the slim pretext that its Islamic leaders were too lenient with the infidel Hindus. The real reasons for Timur's attack, other than his territorial ambitions, were the enormous loot that could be gathered from this wealthy area and the fact that the once-powerful sultanate had entered a period of decline, its internal dissensions sapping its military strength. Timur's forces left from Kabul in present-day Afghanistan and crossed the Indus River in September 1398. In a trail of blood (for no other image describes the carnage) Timur's forces proceeded towards Delhi and arrived at the city gates in December 1398. Before he began his attack, Timur ordered some one hundred thousand Hindu prisoners of war executed so that they would not hinder the movement of his troops. On 17 December the Timurid troops defeated the sultanate's forces on the banks of the Jamnu; the elephants thrown into battle by the Indians did not affect the outcome. Although Timur had promised to spare the citizens of Delhi, their resistance made Timur issue an order for the complete sack of the city and the massacre of its inhabitants. On 1 January 1399, he left Delhi to return to Samarqand loaded with loot. On his return journey, he ordered Hindus skinned alive in fulfillment of the vow of a holy war he had made before the invasion. In March 1399 Timur again crossed the Indus River, having inflicted on India, in the words of Sir Wolseley Haigh, "more misery than had ever before been inflicted by any conqueror in a single invasion."[23]

In 1400 Timur again turned his attention to the west, this time campaigning against the Mamluk empire's presence in Syria and against the emerging Ottoman empire. In quick succession, Timur took the cities of Aleppo, Hama, and Homs; in the winter of 1400, his forces were at the gates of Damascus. Negotiations to avoid the sack of the city were held, and Timur agreed not to sack it in return for the payment of a heavy ransom.[24] Once inside the city walls, however, he increased his ransom demand tenfold. As the population resisted this exorbitant demand, he ordered the city ransacked and its citizens massacred: each Timurid soldier was to present him with at least one head. When, subsequently, Timur intervened in Anatolian affairs, a conflict broke out with the emerging Ottoman empire, then under the leadership of Bayezid I. In July 1402 the antagonists met in battle near present-day Ankara. Bayezid was defeated and taken prisoner, and he died in captivity. His defeat marked the zenith of Timur's territorial expansion. However, in 1406 Timur had begun planning the final campaign of his career: the conquest of China; it was an ambitious undertaking for the seventy-year-old conqueror. He died on his way to China, in the city of Otrar, on 19 February 1405.[25]

When Timur's power was near its zenith, at the beginning of the fifteenth century, the European powers considered making an alliance with him against the rising Ottoman empire. The initiative came from Charles VI of France and Henry III of Castile. It appears that they had in mind an alliance similar to the proposed alliance against the Mamluks of the Mongols and the papacy. As with earlier negotiations, no results were obtained, but as a consequence of these contacts several Western accounts of Timur's court have survived. The most important one is that of Henry's ambassador, Ruy Gonzáles de Clavijo. An equally important, although unofficial, account is that of the German Johan Schiltberger, who had been a prisoner of Bayezid I, and after the Ottoman ruler's defeat, a prisoner of Timur. Regrettably, these accounts have not been submitted to the same scrutiny as the accounts of earlier Western travellers to the Mongol court.[26]

Two characteristics distinguish Timur's conquests, aimed at restoring the

Chingizid empire, from the Mongol conquests. First of all, unlike the Mongols, Timur never consolidated his rule over a conquered area; he was thus forced to return to the same area several times. The failure to consolidate was an essential weakness and led to the quick disintegration of the empire. The second characteristic was the gratuitous violence of the campaigns. Timur's name had during his lifetime already become a synonym for wanton destruction and cruelty. Prisoners were rarely taken; cities and villages were plundered and their populations massacred, all on the slightest of pretexts, and for no apparent purpose. This is in stark contrast to the Mongol conquests. Although they were by no means a gentle people, the destruction inflicted by the Mongols nearly always served a specific political or military purpose.

The Timurid empire never reached the size of the Mongol empire, and the reason lay in its foundation. Chinggis-khan inherited and built on a Central Asian imperial tradition that dated back to the time of the Hsiung-nu, two centuries before the Christian era. It was an empire of the steppe, and its ethnic and social traditions were common to Türks and Mongols. Its dynamic center was, and basically remained, the steppe. Timur's empire was the result of circumstances and of his indisputable military talents. Although the Mongol empire had within it strong centrifugal tendencies, it was long subjected to a central bureaucratic administration, and, after the end of Qaraqorum as its center, to a conceptual unity. In Timur's empire, the state belonged to the clan as a whole, and the various princes were, for all practical purposes, independent rulers within their fiefs. This state of affairs did not develop in the Mongol empire until almost its final disintegration; in contrast, Timur's empire collapsed as suddenly as it came about. Timur's empire was the last attempt to recreate a Chingizid world empire. Strangely, this attempt was undertaken, not by a Mongol, but by a Turk, who through the appointment of descendants of Chaghatai maintained a facade of Chingizid legitimacy; the nominal Mongol rulers of Timur's empire were Soyurghatmish (1370–1388) and his son Mahmud (1388–1402).

Although Timur had adopted Chinggis-khan as a model, there was a remarkable difference between the two men. V. V. Barthold's description of Chinggis-khan as a mere robber-chieftain unable to see the difference "between the qualifications of the chief of a band of ten men and those of the ruler of an empire,"[27] is not only inaccurate but also unfair, but it applies to Timur. It cannot be denied that Timur was extensively educated, but this did not make him a better ruler, even though his military talents cannot be denied. In recreating the Chingizid empire, Timur could have had the benefit of hindsight, but he did not. The only quality he had in common with Chinggis-khan, other than his military talent, was boundless ambition. The French historian René Grousset gives a telling description of Timur's personality. "Tamerlane was entirely in the tradition of classical tragedy. That which dominated in him was a long-term machiavellianism, sustained hypocrisy identified with reasons of state. A Napoleon who had the mind of Fouché, a Philip II descended from Attila. Serious and somber, enemy of gaiety, like the man of the Escurial, devout like him, but a soldier full of ardor, as well as an experienced and prudent captain, while simultaneously a friend of artists and writers, enjoying poetry like a man from Shiraz; that was the man whose seizure of Balkh finally made him the ruler of Central Asia."[28]

Like Chinggis-khan, Timur had designated his successor. In an empire that was viewed as the private domain of its ruler and whose cohesion depended on the ruler's personality, it was inevitable that the succession would lead to political strife. Timur's empire proved no exception. It was his fourth son, Shahrukh, who emerged as the victor in the succession struggle. His reign, from 1407 to 1447, marked the beginning of a long period of relative peace. Shahrukh achieved in Herat what Timur had hoped to accomplish in Samarqand. The new capital became the cultural center of the empire and one of the most important cities in the Middle East. Shahrukh did not continue any of the conquests begun by his father, but devoted all his time to cultural pursuits and the education of the Timurid princes. While Shahrukh personally ruled Khurassan, his son Ulugh-beg ruled over Transoxiana. In theory, he ruled in the name of his father; in practice he was an independent ruler.[29]

When Shahrukh died in 1447, Ulugh-beg assumed the regency. He did not, however, possess the political and administrative talents of his father, and, moreover, was a rather mediocre general. Shahrukh's death marked the beginning of a civil war that ended two years later with the death of Ulugh-beg. The new ruler was a great-grandson of Timur, Abu Sa'id. First he ruled the empire from Samarqand, then from Herat, but he was unable to assert his authority permanently throughout the Timurid domain. In February 1469 he was assassinated, and with him disappeared the last of the great Timurids.[30] Khurassan and Transoxiana were ruled by local potentates who no longer laid any claim to the empire of Chinggis-khan or, for that matter, to that of Timur. Towards the end of the fifteenth century, new forces had arisen on the borders of the former Chaghatai Khanate. The expansion of the Ottoman empire, the rise of Persia under Shah Ismail I, the founder of the Safavid dynasty, and the resurgence of India under the Great Moghuls combined with technological innovations in warfare to prevent the creation of a new empire within the Khanate's domains. The task of recreating a Chingizid empire reverted to the Mongols and to the central steppe.

Before concluding this section on the Timurids, brief mention of their relations with Ming China should be made. The initiative to establish relations came from Chu Yüan-chang, and in 1394 the Ming emperor received a letter of submission allegedly written by Timur. The description of its contents given in the Chinese annals is pure fiction. In 1395 Timur received a Chinese mission and was insulted at being treated as a vassal of China.

Plans were made for war, and in the meantime the Chinese mission was held captive. Under Shahrukh and the Yung-lo emperor, relations between the empires improved and were conducted on a more realistic basis. The Yung-lo emperor maintained the fiction of the submission of the Timurid state, but only for internal consumption. Relations were strictly commercial, and they ceased in 1424 after Yung-lo's son, Chu Kao-chih,[31] acceded to the throne. During his reign, Ming China gave up its claim to all the territory of the Mongol empire.[32]

The Mongols on the Eastern Steppe

When the Mongols left China under the leadership of the last Yüan emperor, Toghon Temur, they did not abandon their claim to control over it. For the next two decades they maintained the Northern Yüan dynasty, whose primary aim was the reconquest of the former Yüan dynasties. Toghon Temur died in 1370 in Ying-ch'ang, in northwestern Jehol, and the restoration attempt was carried on by his son Ayusiridara and grandson Toghus Temur. Although Ayusiridara was the ruler of the Northern Yüan, effective control was exerted by Kökö Temur. In 1370, less than a month after he had assumed the throne, the Chinese attacked and recaptured Ying-ch'ang, forcing Ayusiridara to flee farther into the steppe. With the fall of the town, the Northern Yüan lost its foothold in China. Four years later, Kökö Temur died, and his death seriously weakened the military capabilities of the Mongols. The prudence of Chu Yüan-chang, however, prevented China from taking full advantage of this situation, and for the remainder of Ayusiridara's reign, China remained on the defensive.

Chinese policy at the time was aimed at attracting Mongols into the Chinese cultural realm, and thus absorbing them. This policy met with a certain degree of success, as many Mongols, especially those near the border, were dissatisfied with Northern Yüan rule. Deeper in the steppe Chinese influence was also felt, and manifested itself in a sympathy for Chinese customs among leading Mongols. The official policy, however, was aimed at eliminating this influence, and was, probably, the reason why Ayusiridara's oldest son, Maidiribala, was denied the throne in favor of Toghus Temur.[34] During Toghus Temur's reign, China abandoned its passive defense policy for an active one. With Kökö Temur's death, the only serious Mongol military leader left was Naghachu, who was primarily in control of the Liaotung area.[35] He was defeated by the Ming forces in January 1387 and surrendered to the Chinese emperor. Immediately after his surrender, the Chinese army undertook a daring march through the Gobi Desert to strike at the heart of the Northern Yüan. In November 1387 the Chinese forces surprised the Mongols in the vicinity of Lake Buyur. The entire Mongol force was wiped out, and most of the Northern Yüan officials were taken prisoner. Toghus Temur managed to escape, but he was murdered a year later near Qaraqorum. With his death, the Northern Yüan had ceased to exist, and the steppe was plunged into anarchy.

The defeat at Lake Buyur, coupled with the ineptitude of the Northern Yüan administration, totally discredited the House of Qubilai. In the political vacuum created by Toghus Temur's defeat and death, other Mongol tribes attempted to establish themselves as the dominant group. The Chinese court actively promoted dissension among the Mongol clans, for it meant that there was little likelihood that a new, strong confederation could be formed. In 1399 the Qubilaid dynasty came to a formal end when its last ruler was assassinated by the chieftain of the Qirghiz.[36] Qirghiz supremacy was short-lived for they, in turn, were attacked by Arughtai, a chieftain of the Eastern Mongols, and by Mahmud, the chieftain of the Oirat tribes.

The rise to power of these two chieftains presented the first serious threat to Chinese security since the accession to the throne of Emperor Chu Ti. Arughtai clearly intended to restore the Qubilaid house and the dominance of the Chingizid tradition when he appointed as nominal ruler over the Eastern Mongols Bunyasiri, a descendant of Qubilai who resided in Uighur territory. The ambitions of Arughtai and Mahmud clashed, and the former was forced to move his encampments. The Yung-lo emperor, to take advantage of Arughtai's apparent weakness, sent an army into the steppe to eliminate him, only to be resoundingly defeated. Yung-lo thereupon decided to lead the campaign himself, and in 1410 he inflicted a serious defeat on the forces of Arughtai and Bunyasiri. For a while, relations between Arughtai and the Chinese court were peaceful, permitting Yung-lo to concentrate his efforts on the budding Oirat empire under Mahmud's leadership. Then, in 1422, Arughtai staged a major raid into China, which led to the Yung-lo emperor's third and most massive campaign into Mongolia. This campaign had only a mixed success, for Chu Ti was not able to eliminate Arughtai, but only to force him to cease to harass China. Arughtai's position had become precarious, for the power of the Oirats was on the increase. In 1434 he was killed by the Oirats, and his sons submitted to the Chinese. The first attempt at restoring the House of Qubilai had failed.[37]

The first serious attempt at recreating a Mongol empire on the steppe came under the direction of the Oirat, a tribe that had not had a major role in the Chingizid empire. Little is known about Mahmud, their chieftain at this time. After briefly supporting Arughtai, he allied himself with the Yung-lo emperor against the Eastern Mongols and began to lay the basis for the first Oirat empire. The friendly relations between Mahmud and the Chinese court, however, were short-lived, for Mahmud perceived the true nature of Chinese policy towards the Mongols: China applied the rule of "divide and conquer" and switched its alliances accordingly. Mahmud kept his distance from the Chinese, who then began to support Arughtai. A war, in which the Ming forces intervened, broke out between the two Mongol chieftains, and Mahmud was killed in battle. He was succeeded by his son Toghon, who re-established friendly relations with the Chinese. Mahmud's death, however, did not mean the end of Oirat ambitions; Toghon set out to avenge his father and killed Arughtai.

Arughtai's death meant the end of obstacles to the plans of the Oirat. From 1436 until 1439, the year of his death, Toghon began a systematic campaign to gain control over the other Mongol tribes on the eastern steppe. He was successful, and his increasing power became a source of concern to the Chinese court, which began defense preparations. Toghon's death provided no relief to the Chinese. He was succeeded by his son Esen,[38] who proclaimed himself emperor, made a marital alliance with a Chingizid family, and obtained the submission of all the northern tribes. With these actions, the first Oirat empire had come into being.

Esen's reign marked the zenith of the first Oirat empire's power. Initially the Chinese court was pleased with this development on the steppe, for it appeared that with the creation of an Oirat empire, the threat of a Chingizid restoration had been eliminated. This proved to be an illusion. Esen was able to establish his authority over the Ili region and enter the Chingizid house there by marrying the elder sister of the young khan of the Eastern Mongols, Toghto-buqa. For the next several years, Esen campaigned throughout the steppe and established his authority over other Mongol tribes, which was not always accepted voluntarily. The Chinese, preoccupied with the territorial expansion of Esen's domain, resumed their old policy of divide and conquer, bestowing favors and gifts upon Toghto-buqa, and failing to realize that he was a ruler in name only.

Relations between Esen and the Chinese court quickly took a hostile turn. Esen complained about the encroachment of Chinese peasants on Mongol territory, the dishonesty of the traders and border officials, and the rude and demeaning receptions granted his tributary missions to the Chinese court. The Chinese, on the other hand, complained about Esen's territorial encroachment, his interception of trade and tribute missions, and the unruliness and enormous size of the missions he sent to Peking, sometimes as many as three thousand men.[39] Mutual recriminations were such that only the flimsiest excuse was needed for the political antagonism to be transformed into armed conflict. In July 1449, Esen invaded China. The Oirat forces had the advantage, and the Chinese suffered a serious defeat at Yang-ho, opening the road to Tatung and thus threatening the Chinese capital itself. The eunuch Wang Chen convinced the emperor, Chu Ch'i-chen, to lead the campaign against Esen personally. This proved to be a major error. The Chinese army was defeated, Wang Chen was killed, and the emperor was taken prisoner and led into captivity. The situation was ominous for the Chinese, for now the road to Peking was open and essentially undefended. For an unexplained reason, Esen did not press forward. Holding the Chinese emperor proved useless as a bargaining tool, for the Chinese court appointed a new emperor, Chu Ch'i-yü, in September 1449.[40]

Failing to take Peking when he had the opportunity proved to be a critical mistake for Esen. When he made another incursion into Chinese territory, just one year later, he met with very serious resistance and was forced to withdraw. By that time, too, he appears to have lost substantial support among the Eastern Mongols. A rift had developed between him and his nominal ruler, Toghto-buqa, who favored peaceful relations with China. Armed conflict broke out, and Toghto-buqa was killed. This action eroded Esen's power base. With the nominal Chingizid ruler of the Oirat empire eliminated, Esen proclaimed himself khan. In doing so, however, he lost all claim to legitimacy, for that title was by custom reserved for a descendant of the Chingizid dynasty. A civil war broke out, and Esen was assassinated in 1455, thus bringing to an end the first Oirat empire. The steppe reverted to anarchy.

The years following Esen's death saw several smaller Mongol confederations vying for control, but it was not until nearly a decade later that a new force was able to consolidate itself. The leader of the new confederation, primarily made up of Eastern Mongols, was Batu-Mongke, better known under his royal title *Dayan Khan*.[41] Very little is known about his early career, and he appears with the royal title in 1482, when, in a manner reminiscent of Chinggis-khan, he organized the Eastern Mongols into a new and powerful confederation. Dayan Khan claimed a Chingizid descent and placed his empire-building effort in the Chingizid tradition. His efforts, however, were not unchallenged. The most serious challenge came from Ibrahim, a Mongol whose ancestry and tribal affiliation are not known but who probably belonged to a branch of the Oirat. The first open conflict between Dayan Khan and Ibrahim occurred in 1495, and the latter was forced to seek refuge in China, in Northern Shensi. From there, Ibrahim continued to raid both Chinese territory and Dayan Khan's camps. In 1509 the Chinese general Ma Ang pushed him back into the steppe, where, the next year, he was defeated by Dayan Khan's forces and had to seek refuge in the Kokonor area. There Ibrahim was able to create a small empire that exerted a certain amount of control over the tea and horse markets. He was finally eliminated in 1533 by Dayan Khan's grandson Qutughtai Sechen.[42]

With the disappearance of Ibrahim, Dayan Khan became the undisputed leader of Eastern Mongolia. He then began to expand his domain at the expense of the Chinese. The conflict reached its high point in an epic battle in the vicinity of Peking. The battle, which took place in the winter of 1517, lasted forty-eight hours and saw the Chinese emperor personally directing the military operation, albeit from some distance from the front. Dayan Khan's forces were defeated and forced to withdraw into the steppe. For the next decade, relations between the Mongols and the Chinese were peaceful, primarily on account of the dissension among the Mongols themselves that threatened Dayan Khan's authority. Hostilities resumed in 1528 and ended in 1532, when Dayan Khan was decisively defeated; the cause

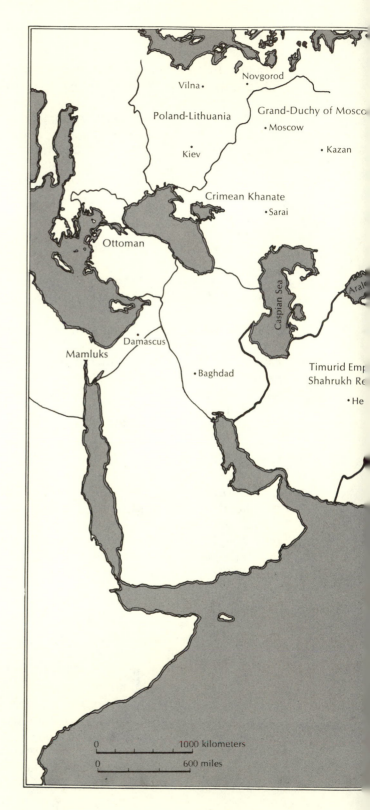

Map 4
*Mongol Domains
in the Sixteenth Century*

Vilna •

Novgorod
•

Poland-Lithuania

Grand-Duchy of Mosco

• Moscow

Kiev
•

• Kazan

Crimean Khanate

• Sarai

Ottoman

Caspian Sea

Aral

Damascus

Mamluks

Timurid Emp
Shahrukh Re

• Baghdad

• He

1000 kilometers
0

0   600 miles

276

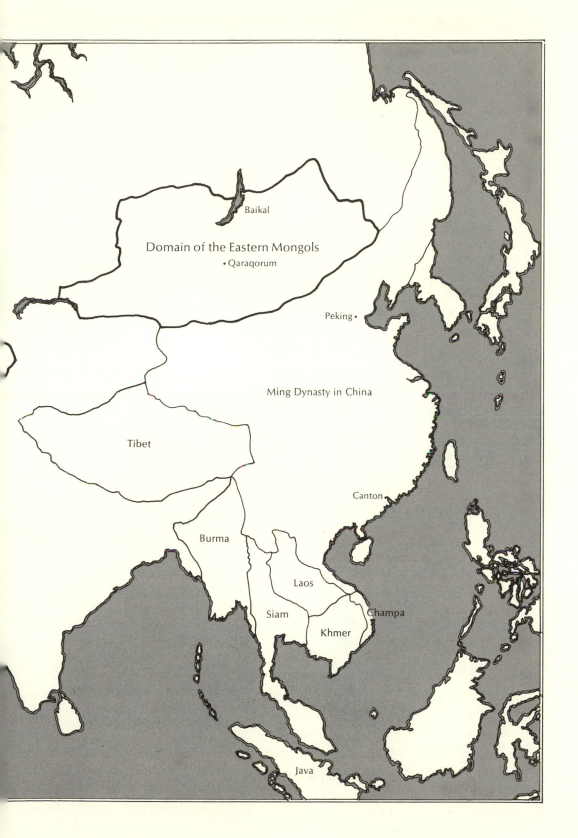

Baikal

Domain of the Eastern Mongols

• Qaraqorum

Peking •

Ming Dynasty in China

Tibet

Canton

Burma

Laos

Champa

Siam

Khmer

Java

of the war, ironically, had been the Chinese refusal to make peace with Dayan Khan. It was during this war that sources first mention the Mongols' next and most powerful ruler, Altan Khan.[43]

Altan Khan was born in 1507 and was a grandson of Dayan Khan. In 1533, when his father, Bars Bolod, died, his elder brother, Qutughtai Sechen, inherited the Mongols of the Ordos region, while Altan Khan assumed control over the Mongols known as the Twelve Tümed, located to the north of the Shensi border. This was the only group he ever actually ruled. The two brothers resumed the traditional raiding of the Chinese border areas, and they openly laid claim to the traditions of the Yüan dynasty by proclaiming themselves its successor. Altan Khan became the *de facto* leader of the new confederation, and after he inflicted a serious defeat upon the Chinese in 1542, his authority was unchallenged. Under his rule, the Eastern Mongol confederation reached the high point of its power and was able to reclaim the old Mongol capital of Qaraqorum.[44]

Although attacks on the Chinese border were by now a tradition, the attacks of the sixteenth century were no longer aimed at reconquering the territories once held by the Yüan dynasty, but at forcing the Chinese to trade with the Mongols. The Chinese refusal to trade was the work of officials at the court whose unrealistic view of the situation at the border persisted even after border officials had advised the court in favor of trade in light of the fact that the Mongols were willing to handle the matter within China's tributary framework of foreign relations.[45] (This situation is reminiscent of the one that existed at the time of the Turkic empire, nearly a thousand years earlier.) Unable to satisfy their economic needs peacefully, the Mongols did so violently, continually inflicting defeats upon the Chinese border forces. Rather than admit that the court's policies were wrong, blame was placed on the bearers of bad tidings, the border commanders.[46]

From the beginning of his career, Altan Khan attempted to place Mongol-Chinese relations on a rational, peaceful basis. Confronted with the Ming court's obstinacy, he was forced to continue the traditional nomadic raiding parties; unquestionably, one of the factors in his strategy was the relative weakness of nomadic warfare methods when confronted with firearms. The situation changed abruptly in 1570. The court in Peking was dominated by two very capable, and realistic, officials, Kao Kung and Chang Chü-cheng, and the Chinese governor-general who normally dealt with Mongol affairs, Wang Ch'ung-ku, was equally capable and was, moreover, a friend of the officials just mentioned. In Mongolia, Altan Khan was preoccupied with Tibetan affairs. His grandson, Badgachi, suddenly defected to the Chinese.[47] Using Altan Khan's concern for Badgachi as a lever, a treaty was negotiated between China and Altan Khan and formally approved on 21 April 1571. The first presentation of "tribute" occurred three months later, and from then on, it took place at the annual trading fairs at the border. Peace did not come immediately, but Altan Khan's forceful actions, among them depriving Mongol princes who violated the agreement of their trading privileges, and China's efforts to control its border officials finally brought about the peace the Mongols had sought since 1542. The peace brought about by Altan Khan and Wang Ch'ung-ku lasted almost until the end of the Ming dynasty.[48]

The Sedentary
Penetration of the Steppe

Altan Khan's reign witnessed not only the renascence of Mongol power and wealth, but also the massive conversion of the Mongols to Tibetan Buddhism. This is often called the second conversion of the Mongols by those who accept the authenticity of a Mongol conversion at the time of Chinggis-khan and his successors. As was shown earlier, the history of the Mongols during the imperial period does not provide any evidence even remotely suggesting that the Mongols converted in large numbers to Tibetan Buddhism. This religion was present at the Yüan court in a form commonly known as the Red Hat sect, or the unreformed sect. In reaction against the sect's decadence, a reform movement started towards the end of the fourteenth century under the leadership of a monk from Amdo, Tsong-kha-pa. The sect he created became known as the Yellow Hat sect, and in less than half a century, it had become the dominant sect and transformed Tibet into a truly theocratic state. The state, eventually headed by the Dalai Lamas, existed until 1958, the year of the Dalai Lama's exile to India. One of the political aims of the new sect was the recreation of the Tibetan empire as it had existed at the time of the T'ang dynasty. Instead of military conquest, the new state was based on active proselytizing.[49]

The creation of the new Tibetan power, whose political history has remained virtually unexamined, coincided to a large degree with the reigns of Dayan Khan and Altan Khan. From the beginning of the sixteenth century, the Ming government expressed a serious interest in inviting the leader of the new power, bSod-nams-rgya-mtsho (1542–1588),[50] to the Chinese court. Chinese interest in meeting the Tibetan hierarch and incorporating Tibet within the traditional Chinese tribute system was viewed by Altan Khan as a disguised attempt to interfere in the affairs of the Kokonor area. Relations between Altan Khan and bSod-nams-rgya-mtsho began in 1574, when the Tibetan hierarch refused to come personally to Altan Khan's court and sent one of his deputies to begin diplomatic negotiations. The next year, bSod-nams-rgya-mtsho did go to Altan Khan's court. His mission had a twofold purpose: first, to come to an agreement with the powerful Mongols with regard to their border raids, and, second, to expand Tibetan religious as well as political control outside of Tibet's borders.

Neither the Mongols nor the Tibetans had forgotten the history of the Yüan dynasty, especially the relationship between Qubilai and the 'Phags-pa Lama. The Tibetan hierarch saw the chance to use history to promote the interests of his church; Altan Khan perceived that if he established a relationship with the Tibetan hierarch, the prestige attached to Qubilai's name could be used for propaganda among his unruly subjects. Who took the initiative is essentially irrelevant. The interests of both leaders coincided, and they met in the Kokonor area. On that occasion, Altan Khan adopted Tibetan Buddhism, and bSod-nams-rgya-mtsho declared him a reincarnation of Qubilai. Since bSod-nams-rgya-mtsho viewed himself as the reincarnation of the 'Phags-pa Lama, the politically important connection with the Yüan dynasty was established. The relationship between the Mongol ruler and the Tibetan hierarch was covered by the so-called "Dual Order Doctrine," the patron-lama relationship that was alleged to have existed between Qubilai and the 'Phags-pa Lama. The doctrine was also used to represent Tibetan Buddhist institutions as the legitimate continuation of Chingizid traditions.[51] At the end of the ceremony, Altan Khan bestowed upon the Tibetan hierarch the title *Dalai Lama,* or "the Universal Lama." It is under this title that bSod-nams-rgya-mtsho's successors, as well as his two predecessors, became known to history. After this initial contact between the two leaders, the Tibetans began an active missionary campaign that brought Mongol life under the complete domination of Tibetan cultural traditions.

The most spectacular coup staged by the Tibetans occurred after the death of bSod-nams-rgya-mtsho in 1588. In conformity with their traditions, the leaders of the Tibetan church began their search for his reincarnation and "discovered" him among the descendants of Altan Khan. The new Dalai Lama, Yon-tan-rgya-mtsho, was the son of Altan Khan's grandson Sümir Daicing. Yon-tan-rgya-mtsho, still an infant, left Mongolia for Tibet; from which he ruled the church in both countries.[52] A direct result of the discovery of the new Dalai Lama among the Mongols was that an important part of Mongol political authority came to rest with the Tibetans in distant Lhasa. The Dalai Lama, and his representative in Mongolia, the rJe-btsun dam-pa Qutuqtu, had become the most important political power on the steppe. Control over Lhasa automatically resulted in control over Mongolia. The massive conversion to Tibetan Buddhism in the years that followed probably contributed to the decline of Mongol military strength. What outside attacks and internal factional warfare had failed to accomplish, Tibetan Buddhism did in less than two centuries. By the middle of the eighteenth century, the Mongols were no longer a serious political and military threat to their neighbors.[53]

The death of Altan Khan resulted in a resurgence of the traditional centrifugal tendencies, all the more strongly since, during his reign, Mongol unity had been based entirely on his personal charisma. The civil wars that followed his death, although they did not permit Chinese recovery of lost territory or the establishment of actual Chinese control, shifted the emphasis of Mongol power away from Inner Mongolia and towards the Kokonor area and the territory of the Qalqa Mongols, roughly the present-day Mongolian People's Republic.

Nearly simultaneously with the Tibetanization of the Mongol tribes, two new sedentary empires on opposite ends of the steppe began their ascendancy: the Russian and the Manchu. Almost from their inception, these empires expanded into the steppe. This expansion, Mongol internal dissension, and advances in military technology were soon to preclude any resurgence of Chingizid ambitions among the nomadic horsemen. An attempt was made by the Jungars, an Oirat confederation, but it was short-lived, and after its collapse the Mongols played no role on the steppe until the second quarter of the twentieth century, when the Qalqa Mongols were able to reassert their independence. They did so, however, in the spirit of the Russian October Revolution, not within the Chingizid tradition.[54]

The Russian expansion into the steppe began during the reign of Ivan the Terrible, after the fall of Kazan and the subsequent submission of the Astrakhan khanate to Muscovite authority. In 1554, after he had obtained the submission of the Siberian tribes, Ivan assumed the title "Lord of all Sibir," an act by which he symbolically laid claim to the vast unexplored territory beyond the Urals. It was, however, not until almost twenty years later, and then on private initiative, that the first successful crossing of the Urals was made. The crossing, made by the rich and influential Stroganoff family, was directly related to the Russian fur trade. Under the leadership of the commander of their private army, Vasili Timofeiev, alias Yermak the Cossack, the Stroganoff family penetrated Siberia, taking Sibir, the capital of the Tatar Khan Kumchuk, and thus formally opening the area to Russian penetration.

Yermak's penetration, in the form of major raids, took place between 1579 and 1584, and it was in 1582 that he took the city of Sibir. His efforts were followed by waves of Russian immigration into Central Asia: first into Siberia, then into Mongol territories proper. It took the Russians, who more often than not acted without their government's approval, a mere sixty years to reach the Pacific Ocean. In 1604 the town of Tomsk on the Ob River was founded, followed by the towns of Yakutsk and Okhotsk, respectively in 1632 and 1638, and in 1648 Kamchatka, the first Russian town on the Pacific coast, was created. After reaching the shores of the Pacific, Russian immigration turned south. In 1651 the new immigrants founded the town of Irkutsk near Lake Baikal in Mongol territory, and in 1666 the town of Albazin on the Amur River, in Manchu territory.[55]

The impulse behind the Russian march to the Pacific was financial and economic, rather than political, in nature. Three groups of people participated in what is often called the Russian conquest of Siberia.[56] The first group was the *promyshleniki*, a type of military force that acted a a buffer, although not a neutral one, between the natives and the second group, the *torgovye liudi*, or traders. The third group, the *sluzhylie liudi*, represented the state and comprised both civil administrators and military officials. The penetration had followed the east-west confluents of the Siberian rivers, and it was on these confluents that the first settlements, the *ostrogs*, were established. These were often no more than a few log cabins, whose residents were involved in trade, trapping, and minimal agriculture. The *ostrogs* served as the central gathering point for the collection of the *yasak*, or tribute, an institution imposed by the new immigrants which resembled the *dan* in European Russia. Official claim to the newly settled territories came with the appointment to the *ostrogs* of *voevodas,* a sort of governor-cum-tax-collector. Although warfare between the Russian settlers and the local population erupted regularly, the Russian penetration of the steppe does not resemble the Anglo-Saxon penetration of the American West, to which it is often compared. The natives intermingled with the Russians, inter-marriage was common, and social prejudice seems to have played only a limited role. The harshness of Russian central administration was felt by the native and the Russian settler alike.[57]

At about the time the Russians reached the Ob River, a new force was coming into existence in Northern China. The region bounded to the north by the Amur was inhabited by tribes of Jürchen origins and had been in a state of anarchy since the Yüan dynasty. These tribes were sedentary and had been subjected to a high degree of Sinicization since Ming times.[58] Around 1580 a new coalition of Jürchen tribes was formed through the efforts of Nurhaci, the founder of the Manchu empire. He had all the characteristics commonly attributed to a steppe ruler, but the state he created was sedentary and had heavy Chinese overtones. He conceived of his empire as a continuation of the Jürchen Chin dynasty, for he called it *Ta Chin,* "the Great Chin." The name "Man-chou" was adopted by his successor, Abahai, at the same time (that is, on 15 May 1639) that he adopted a new and symbolic title, *Ch'ing,* meaning "pure," for his dynasty. Nurhaci quickly consolidated his control over the Jürchen tribes, and by 1613 he was, for all practical purposes, in full control. Three years later, he proclaimed his empire and began to exert pressure on the Chinese. He established his capital near Mukden, but his southward movement met with serious Chinese resistance in 1621. The campaign was continued by Abahai and culminated, in 1644, under Abahai's successor, in the Manchu conquest of China. Once again, the entire Middle Kingdom was under "barbarian" rule.[59]

From the beginning of their rise to power, the Manchus were in contact with the Mongols, especially those living in Inner Mongolia. Nurhaci's policy from the start was to incorporate these Mongols into his empire as a separate political entity, of almost equal status with the Manchus them-selves. He also had friendly relations with the Qalqa confederation on the central steppe. Recognition of Nurhaci's authority came in 1607, when the Mongols accepted him as their *qaghan* and proclaimed him *Kündelen qaghan,* "the respected emperor." After 1616 Nurhaci referred to himself by the Manchu form of this title, *Sure Kundulen Han.*[60] Mongol influence in the early Manchu empire was substantial: Nurhaci adopted many Mongol legal and tax terms and in 1599 ordered the development of a Manchu script based on the Mongol script. Although the Qalqa Mongols supported Nurhaci, they remained outside of his domains. In contrast, the Inner Mon-gols, like the Tümed and the Chahar, joined the Manchu as independent units within the Manchu banner armies. The first Mongol banner unit was created in 1621, and by 1635 there were eight. The incorporation of Inner Mongols continued during Abahai's reign. At the same time, it became necessary to develop a policy dealing with the Mongols as a whole, for even the Manchus realized the potential threat in a revival of Chingizid ambitions. To deal with this problem, and with Central Asians in general, Abahai created around 1638 a special office called the *Li-fan Yüan*, the "Board of Barbarian Rites." This was not a foreign ministry; foreign affairs were handled by the traditional Chinese Board of Rites. It did, however, treat the Mongols, and later the Tibetans, as a political entity distinct from the Chinese.[61]

Manchu control over the Eastern and Southern Mongols was firmly established by 1644, the year the Manchus established their control over China. It was, however, equally necessary to establish control over the Qalqa Mongols, for if they united with the Oirats on the western steppe, a powerful steppe confederation could be created, and some of the Qalqa princes were in favor of such an alliance. Initiatives in this matter came from both the Manchu and the Mongol sides. The Manchu K'ang-hsi emperor began by exerting control over the principal Tibetan religious representative in Urga, present-day Ulan-bator. This was accomplished at a *quriltai* of Qalqa princes at Küreng Belchir, to the north of present-day Bayan-chingor Aimak, in 1686. The principal Qalqa prince, the Tusiyetu Khan, and the religious head of the Mongols, the rJe-btsun dam-pa Qutuqtu, were opposed to an alliance with the Oirats and favored submission to the Manchus. The formal submission took place during a *quriltai* held in the spring of 1691 on the Dolonnor.[62] With this submission, the Qalqa Mongols were incorporated into the Manchu banner system, and, with few exceptions, remained loyal subjects of the Manchu emperor. After Dolonnor, the Manchus developed a religious policy aimed at keeping the Mongols under control, a policy formulated in Peking but exerted on the Mongols from Lhasa.[63]

The simultaneous expansion of both the Russian and the Manchu empires onto the steppe inevitably was to lead to conflict between the two powers. Their differences came to a head during the last quarter of the seventeenth century, and they settled them, at least temporarily, in a treaty negotiated and signed at Nerchinsk at the end of the summer of 1689. This treaty defined the specific spheres of influence on the central and northern steppe, leaving the status of the southern and western steppe in doubt. The treaty of Nerchinsk, together with the Dolonnor *quriltai,* placed the majority of the Mongols firmly under Manchu rule, a situation that persisted until the end of the Manchu dynasty in 1907. At the time of the Nerchinsk treaty, a new Mongol empire—the Oirat Jungar empire—had arisen in the west. Its history does not properly belong to the subject matter of this book. The Jungar empire was the last hurrah of the nomadic horsemen. They were defeated, never to rise again, by the Manchu Ch'ien-lung emperor in the middle of the eighteenth century.[64]

11

Postscript

The reasons commonly advanced for the decline of the steppe, such as the influence of Buddhism or the use of firearms, are a reflection of the evenemental approach to the steppe's history and hence fail to take into consideration that history's totality. The major defect in the historiographical techniques used up to the present is their basic assumption that there was no autochthonous historical tradition on the central steppe. Series of events have been studied, but without reference to earlier events or causal or modal explanations. The common technique has been to study the rise of a charismatic personality, such as Chinggis-khan, and the events associated with him; thus, the history of the steppe has been arbitrarily divided into a succession of personalities and a series of outstanding events, which are studied as if no relationship existed between them, as if they had occurred in a vacuum. This evenemental approach, although it is convenient, does not permit one to elaborate an explanation of recurrent events on the steppe, such as the frequency of war between tribes.

Explanations of the decline of the steppe have also reflected the short-comings of the source materials available, and this is true of Central Asian history generally. Although the Central Asian nomads, in particular the Türks, the Uighurs, and the Mongols, left written records, a study of their history still involves the extensive use of Chinese materials. This has led to a historiographical phenomemon, peculiar to Central Asian history, best described as the "Sinitic syndrome." First, the Chinese sources are accepted at face value, although it is acknowledged that they reflect Chinese hostilities and biases against the "barbarians." Second, the available material is given a predominantly Confucian interpretation.[2] Finally, the material is neatly categorized, first into a Chinese dynastic framework, and then into separate subject areas (such as politics, economics, social structures, and the like). The dynastic categorization obviously ignores temporal continuity, while the subject categories are approached as if no relationship existed between them.

However, the failure of modern researchers to bring together evidence from various disciplines extends beyond the uncritical use of Chinese materials in studying Central Asian nomads. Whenever the history of nomadic societies is examined, the social sciences, particularly economics, are rarely taken into consideration, even though the source materials refer directly and indirectly to economic affairs. On the other hand, the study of contemporary nomadic societies, such as the Yomut and the Basseri in Iran, emphasizes anthropological and economic aspects, without reference to historical framework. Often the conclusions thus reached are simply extrapolated into the past, implying that nomadic societies are not subject to historical change.

A better understanding of the decline of the Central Asian steppe—in fact, of its entire history—can be obtained when the emphasis is shifted away from events to a broader framework. The French historiographical school known as the *Annales* school, founded by Lucien Febvre and Marc Bloch and brought to its present dominance of French historical scholarship by Fernand Braudel,[3] provides a methodology that is ideally suited to this endeavor. The essence of the school is its harmonious combination of history with the social sciences. It sees history not as the study of a narrow series of events, but as the study of time periods of medium and long duration, known respectively as "conjunctures" and "structures."[4] The study of many factors—political, economic, and social among them—thus leads to the interpretation of an area's development over a fairly long duration. In the examination of the Turkic empire, for example, it leads to the conclusion that there was a single Imperial Period, which underwent four stages in its development, rather than that there were four distinct periods, as the traditional division suggests. The elaborated "conjuncture" clearly shows the economic conditioning of the Turkic empire, and also that all four of its stages had common characteristics and requirements.

When the history of Central Asia is examined within the framework of "event-conjuncture-structure," the conclusion imposes itself that the steppe had a historical tradition of its own that began with the Hsiung-nu and culminated in the formation of the Mongol world empire. The theme of this tradition can be seen to be in the intimate relationship between economics and politics. The violence that characterized almost every aspect of the steppe's history was not of a wanton nature, but occurred as a consequence of the tribe's economic requirements. The ecology of the steppe could support only small groups, and this was an important factor in the formation of the steppe's traditional form of political organization, the tribal confederation. These confederations provided the individual tribes with political and economic protection. Trade with the sedentary states was an equally important factor in a steppe confederation's survival; the sedentary states, on the other hand, had but a limited use for steppe products. Hence, the steppe people resorted to warfare to force trade upon the sedentary states. It is possible to see an increasing sedentarization and urbanization of the steppe nomad throughout the period from the Hsiung-nu to the Mongols; however, the greatest transition from a nomadic to a sedentary lifestyle occurred during the Mongol empire.

The long-term interrelationship of political, economic, and social factors must again be scrutinized to explain why, precisely upon reaching the apogee of power under the Mongols, the steppe declined so precipitously and was never again able to pose a threat to the surrounding sedentary states. The fact is that Mongol political control over the sedentary regions and the steppe marked the end of the nomads' economic insecurity: the resources of the sedentary world became readily available, without their having to engage in warfare. Many nomads simply settled in the sedentary areas; it was easier to raise horses under the conditions that prevailed in the fertile sedentary areas, with imperial stables and imperial grazing lands, than through nomadizing on the steppe's arid expanse.[5] The remaining migratory patterns were reduced in geographical scope and began to focus on the market town, where the products of the sedentary world could be traded readily. The greater availability of agricultural products diminished the importance of the hunt, and thus the nomads' opportunity for military training, which had always been associated with it. Over a period of several generations, sedentarization became progressively more pervasive.[6] Although there is not much evidence available, it appears that during this same period the economic base of the steppe was neglected.

The causes for the decline and collapse of the Mongol world empire have been detailed elsewhere and do not need to be repeated. However, in the context of the present discussion, it must be pointed out that when pressing military and political problems forced the Mongols to return to the steppe, many of them lacked the skills needed for economic survival there. Indeed, the withdrawal from the sedentary areas was seen as temporary. The Mongols were never able to return to the sedentary lands, but neither did they truly reintegrate themselves into the ecology of the steppe world.

The sedentarization and urbanization of the steppe's population thus continued following the Mongol collapse, and so did the neglect of the economic base of the steppe, resulting from continued warfare among the various tribes for political hegemony and possibly from the impact of the Timurid expansion. It appears, moreover, that a series of natural disasters affected the size of the herds, reducing them by more than half. The economy of the steppe, which remained on a pastoral-nomadic basis in spite of sedentarization, could therefore not produce enough to satisfy the needs of the people living there.

These trends were made irreversible by the wholesale conversion to Buddhism during the reign of Altan Khan. Monastic institutions became the centers of political and economic activity, and their needs came to dominate migratory patterns. The economic requirements of the monastic institutions, however, were those of a sedentarized world, only minimally adapted to the productive ability of the steppe's economy. Consequently, the majority of the steppe's population became indebted not only to the monasteries, but also to the traders from the sedentary regions, especially the Chinese, for the necessities they could not produce.

By the end of the sixteenth century, at the very latest, the steppe found itself in the throes of an economic recession. This situation could have been reversed only by a thorough reorganization of the steppe's economy, an undertaking that created serious difficulties even in the twentieth century, when it was attempted for the first time. Until the twentieth century, however, no economic theory was available to the Central Asian nomads to enable them to attempt such a reform, or even to conceive of it. Furthermore, it was clearly in the interests of the sedentary world, whether in the East or the West, to prevent an economic recovery on the steppe, as economic strength traditionally meant military strength, and hence a threat to the security of the sedentary world. Further investigations, made difficult by the scarcity of reliable economic source materials, are needed before a final evaluation can be given.

An examination of the history of the Central Asian steppe empires, following the methodology of the *Annales* school, shows that it is an integral and important part of world history, and that for several centuries Central Asia exerted a major influence on the historical development of the sedentary states. It also reveals that the steppe was not an amalgam of heteroclitic and anarchic nomadic tribes, but a highly structured society, and that the steppe nomad had a distinct historical tradition. It was the existence of this tradition, combined with the societal structure, that permitted the nomads to create empires, to become Imperial Nomads. Because of their decline in power after the collapse of the Mongol empire, they were relegated to an obscure historical position, one that completely masked the imperial tradition that had once been their eminent domain.

Appendix 1   Guide to Pronunciation

Chinese

The best-known romanization of the Chinese characters is the Wade-Giles system. A conventional transcription of Chinese, it frequently fails to reflect accurately the Chinese sounds; hence, a few explanations are in order. Throughout the book, the Wade-Giles system has been used, except for well-known variant spellings of personal names, place names, and the like; for example *Peking* is used instead of *Pei-ching*.

Vowels

a	as in English father		u	as in pole; following a double consonant, it is pronounced as a barely audible e
e	as in English but			
i	as in English reel		ü	There is no equivalent sound in English; it is pronounced like the French *u* in bulle, or the German *ü* in *über*
ih	a hint of an *r* after ee			
o	pronounced as *aw*			

Diphthongs

ai	as *i* in nice		ua	as *wah* as in suaveness
ui	as *ay* in bay		ie	as ea in yea
ei	as *ay* in bay		iu	as *ou* in you
ao	as *ow* in bow		ou	as oe in Joe
uo	as *wa* in walk		ieh	as ea in yea with a hint of aspiration
ia	as *ya* in yard			

Consonants

The consonants *l, m, n, ng, r, s, sh,* and *w* are pronounced as their English equivalents. Aspirated consonants *ch', k', p', ts',* and *tz'* are pronounced as the English *ch, k, p, t, ts,* and *tz*. The unaspirated consonants *ch, k, p, t, ts,* and *tz* are pronounced as the English *j, g, b, d, ds,* and *dz*.

Miscellaneous

e	muttered, barely audible		en	as *on* in honor
j	as *r* in run		eng	as *ung* in hunger
hs	as *sh* in short		ien	as the English *yen*
sh	as *sh* in short, slightly heavier than hs		ung	as *ong* in the English song

Mongol and Turkic

The letters used for the transcription of Mongol and Turkic are pronounced essentially like their English equivalents. Exceptions:

jh	as *j* in the English *judge*		ö	as in the German Löwenzahn
q	as *kh* in the English *khaki*, with a slightly more pronounced aspiration		ü	as in the German über

A Chronology of the Steppe Empires

		300	200	100	B.C. A.D.

200 B.C.– 400 A.D.   The Formative Era

    210 B.C.–48 A.D.   The Hsiung-nu Empire

        48–155   The Northern Hsiung-nu

        155–400   The Hsien-pi Dynasties

400–600   The Early Empires

        386–534   The Tabghach (Northern Wei)

        380–555   The Juan-juan

        484–567   The Hephtalites

600–800   The Turkic Empire

        552–583   Formation and Apogee

        583–630   Division of the Empire

        630–683   Chinese Domination

        683–734   Restoration

800–1200   The Uighur Empires

        745–840   The Orkhon Empire

        840–1028   The Kan-chou Kingdom

        840–1209   The Qocho Kingdom

900–1200   The Chinese Border Empires

        907–1124   The Ch'i-tan

        990–1227   The Tangut

        1115–1234   The Jürchen

1000–1200   The Turkic Middle Eastern Empires

        922–1211   The Qaraqanids

        977–1186   The Ghaznavids

        1038–1194   The Saljuqs

        1077–1231   The Qwarezmshahs

1200–1400   The Mongol World Empire

        1206–1258   The Early Empire

        1260–1368   The Yüan

        1256–1335   The Ilkhans

        1237–1502   The Golden Horde

        1227–1334   The Chaghatai Khanate

A Chronology of Chinese Dynasties

B.C. 2200   2100   2000

B.C. 2205?–1766?	Hsia Dynasty (Unverified)
1766?–1122?	Shang Dynasty
1122?–256	Chou Dynasty
221–207	Ch'in Dynasty
B.C. 206–220 A.D.	Han Dynasty
A.D. 220–280	The Three Kingdoms
	220–266	Wei
	221–263	Shu Han
	222–280	Wu
266–316	Western Chin Dynasty
316–589	Era of North-South Division

301–439   Sixteen Kingdoms

304–329	Han/Chao (Hsiung-nu)
319–352	Later Chao (Hsiung-nu)
352–410	Ch'in (Tibetan?)
384–417	Later Ch'in (Tibetan?)
407–431	Hsia (Hsiung-nu)
385–431	Western Ch'in (Hsien-pi)
301–347	Ch'eng Han (Tibetan?)
348–370	Former Yen (Hsien-pi)
383–409	Later Yen (Hsien-pi)
398–410	Southern Yen (Hsien-pi)
409–436	Northern Yen
313–376	Liang
397–414	Southern Liang (Hsien-pi)
386–403	Later Liang (Tibetan?)
400–421	Western Liang
397–439	Northern Liang (Hsiung-nu)

317–589   Northern and Southern Dynasties

Northern:

386–534	Northern Wei (Tabghach)
534–550	Eastern Wei (Tabghach)
534–557	Western Wei
550–577	Northern Ch'i
557–581	Northern Chou

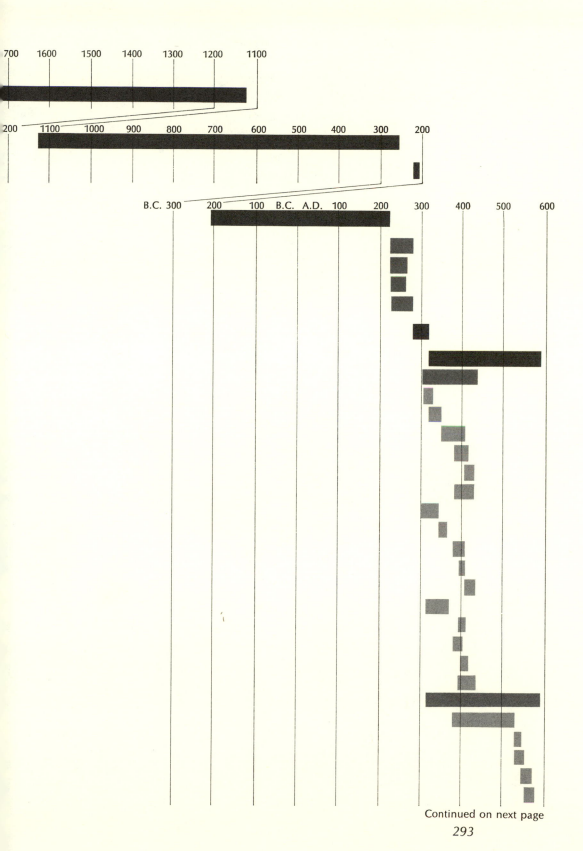

Continued on next page

A Chronology of Chinese Dynasties

Period overlaps graph on previous page

A.D. 300   400   5•

317–589	Northern and Southern Dynasties (continued)
Southern:	317–420 Eastern Chin
	420–479 Liu Sung
	479–502 Southern Ch'i
	502–557 Liang
	557–589 Ch'en

581–618   Sui Dynasty

618–907   T'ang Dynasty

907–960   Five Dynasties Period

Five Dynasties:

907–923	Later Liang
923–936	Later T'ang
936–947	Later Chin
947–951	Later Han
951–960	Later Chou

Ten Kingdoms:

907–925	Former Shu
934–965	Later Shu
907–963	Nan-p'ing
927–956	Ch'u
902–937	Wu
937–975	Southern T'ang
907–978	Wu-Yüeh
907–946	Min
907–971	Southern Han
951–979	Northern Han

960–1279   Sung Dynasty

    960–1127   Northern Sung

    1127–1279   Southern Sung

907–1125   Liao Dynasty (Ch'i-tan)

1115–1234   Chin Dynasty (Jürchen)

1260–1368   Yüan Dynasty (Mongol)

1368–1644   Ming Dynasty

1644–1912   Ch'ing Dynasty (Manchu)

700 800 900 1000 1100 1200 1300 1400 1500 1600 1700 1800 1900 2000

Appendix 4   A Chronology of Islamic Dynasties

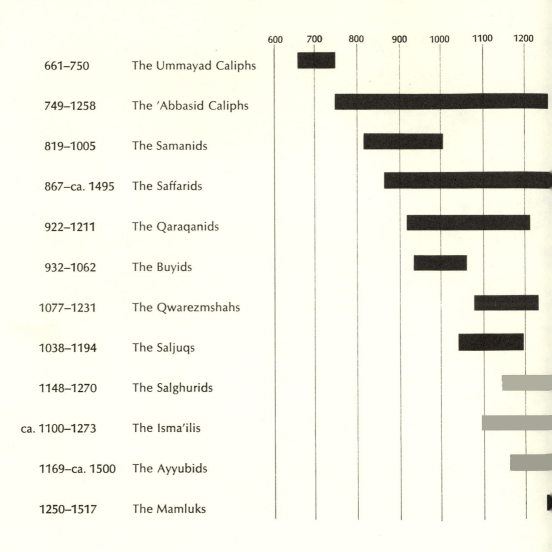

		600	700	800	900	1000	1100	1200
661–750	The Ummayad Caliphs							
749–1258	The 'Abbasid Caliphs							
819–1005	The Samanids							
867–ca. 1495	The Saffarids							
922–1211	The Qaraqanids							
932–1062	The Buyids							
1077–1231	The Qwarezmshahs							
1038–1194	The Saljuqs							
1148–1270	The Salghurids							
ca. 1100–1273	The Isma'ilis							
1169–ca. 1500	The Ayyubids							
1250–1517	The Mamluks							

Appendix 5   The Mongol Rulers

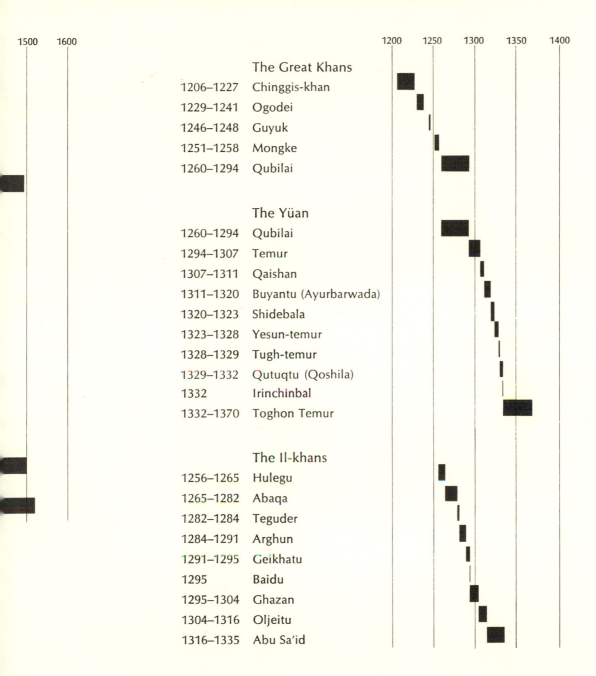

The Great Khans

1206–1227 Chinggis-khan
1229–1241 Ogodei
1246–1248 Guyuk
1251–1258 Mongke
1260–1294 Qubilai

The Yüan

1260–1294 Qubilai
1294–1307 Temur
1307–1311 Qaishan
1311–1320 Buyantu (Ayurbarwada)
1320–1323 Shidebala
1323–1328 Yesun-temur
1328–1329 Tugh-temur
1329–1332 Qutuqtu (Qoshila)
1332   Irinchinbal
1332–1370 Toghon Temur

The Il-khans

1256–1265 Hulegu
1265–1282 Abaqa
1282–1284 Teguder
1284–1291 Arghun
1291–1295 Geikhatu
1295   Baidu
1295–1304 Ghazan
1304–1316 Oljeitu
1316–1335 Abu Sa'id

Continued on next page

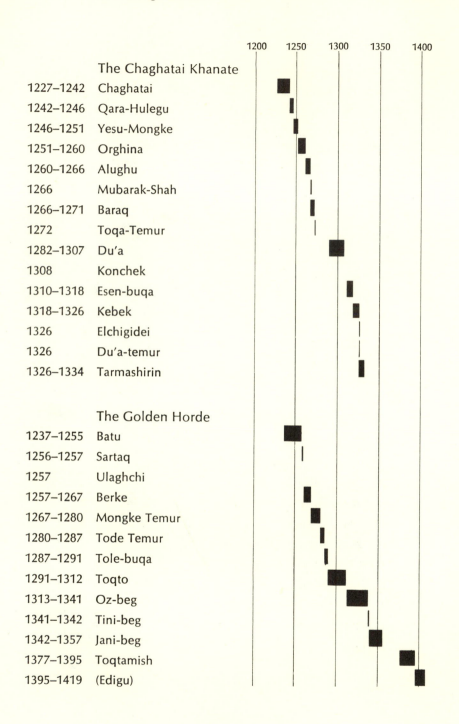

The Chaghatai Khanate

		1200	1250	1300	1350	1400
1227–1242	Chaghatai					
1242–1246	Qara-Hulegu					
1246–1251	Yesu-Mongke					
1251–1260	Orghina					
1260–1266	Alughu					
1266	Mubarak-Shah					
1266–1271	Baraq					
1272	Toqa-Temur					
1282–1307	Du'a					
1308	Konchek					
1310–1318	Esen-buqa					
1318–1326	Kebek					
1326	Elchigidei					
1326	Du'a-temur					
1326–1334	Tarmashirin					

The Golden Horde

1237–1255	Batu
1256–1257	Sartaq
1257	Ulaghchi
1257–1267	Berke
1267–1280	Mongke Temur
1280–1287	Tode Temur
1287–1291	Tole-buqa
1291–1312	Toqto
1313–1341	Oz-beg
1341–1342	Tini-beg
1342–1357	Jani-beg
1377–1395	Toqtamish
1395–1419	(Edigu)

Appendix 6   A Chronology of Important Events

B.C. 209   Accession to the throne of Mao-tun, founder of the Hsiung-nu empire

140   Reign of the Chinese emperor Han Wu-ti and establishment of Chinese control over the Tarim basin

56   First split of the Hsiung-nu empire into western and eastern branches

A.D. 25   Restoration in China of the Han Dynasty

48   Permanent division of the Hsiung-nu empire into northern and southern branches

155   End of Hsiung-nu as a major power

220   Collapse of the Han dynasty

383   Battle at the Fei River; division of China along a north-south line. In northern China, settlement and formation of foreign dynasties

386   Creation of the Tabghach–Northern Wei empire

425   First major war between the Juan-juan and the Tabghach

470   Peace between Juan-juan and Tabghach

471   Accession to the Tabghach throne of Hsiao-wen

480   Promulgation of Hsiao-wen's first Sinicization decree

484   Beginning of the reign of Hephtal III

492   Beginning of the civil war among the Juan-juan

495   Publication of the decree prohibiting the use of the Tabghach language

499   Death of Hsiao-wen

520   Reign of A-na-kuei and reunification of the Juan-juan

532   Establishment of a marital alliance between the Juan-juan and the Northern Wei

534   Split of the Northern Wei into eastern and western branches

540   Recognition by the Western Wei of Turkic autonomy

552   Turkic rebellion against the Juan-juan

552/3   Death of Bumin, the first Turkic emperor; accession to the throne of his son Muqan

555   Destruction of the Juan-juan empire

558   Last mention of the Hephtalites in the Chinese annals

567   Dismemberment of the Hephtalite empire by the Türks

567/8   Arrival of a Turkic embassy in Byzantium

570   Birth of Muhammad, founder of Islam

572   Death of Muqan

576   Accession of Tardu to the position of ruler over the Western Khanate; beginning of the decline of Turkic power

581   Reunification of China under the Sui dynasty. Death of Tsapar, third Turkic emperor; beginning of the wars of succession

603   Death of Tardu

608   Reign of Shih-pi over the Eastern Türks; reassertion of Turkic power

618   Creation of the T'ang dynasty

619   Death of Shih-pi

620   Reign of the Hsieh-li Qaghan; renewed Turkic threat against China

626   Accession to the throne of Li Shih-min, second T'ang ruler

629 Beginning of the Chinese conquest of the Tarim basin; recognition by the Chinese of the Uighurs

630 Defeat of the Hsieh-li Qaghan; China resumes control over the steppe

632 Death of Muhammad, founder of Islam

634 Death of the Hsieh-li Qaghan in the Chinese capital

648 Successful elimination by China of Turkic threat to its security

679 Failure of the anti-Chinese rebellion inspired by the Turkic A-shih-te clan

683 Successful Turkic rebellion led by Qutluq Elterish and Tonyuquq; restoration of Turkic power

691 Death of Qutluq Elterish; accession to the throne of Qapaghan; apogee of the Turkic restoration

705 Beginning of a conquest of Central Asia by Qutaiba ibn-Muslim, the Ummayad governor of Khurassan

707 First open conflict between Türks and Arabs, ending with an Arab victory near Bukhara

716 Death of Qapaghan

718 Coup by Kül-tegin and Bilge-qaghan restoring Turkic power

731 Death of Kül-tegin

734 Death of Bilge-qaghan

745 Creation of the Uighur Orkhon empire

751 Defeat of the Chinese armies on the Talas River by a combined force of Arabs, Türks, and Tibetans; end of Chinese control over Turkestan

755 Beginning of the An Lu-shan rebellion in China. Accession to the throne of Khri-srong-lde-btsan and apogee of the Tibetan empire

763 End of the An Lu-shan rebellion

789 Beginning of the succession wars in the Uighur empire

840 Destruction of the Uighur Orkhon empire by the Qirghiz

875 Beginning of the Huang Ch'ao rebellion in China

884 End of the Huang Ch'ao rebellion

907 Collapse of the T'ang dynasty and disintegration of China. Formation of the Ch'i-tan empire

922 Formation of the Turkic Qaraqanid empire in Transoxiana

924 Ch'i-tan conquest of the Orkhon region

947 Ch'i-tan adoption of a Chinese dynastic name

960 Formation of the Sung dynasty and reunification of China

970 First Ch'i-tan–Tangut war

990 Formation of the Tangut empire

994 Formation of the Turkic Ghaznavid dynasty in present-day Afghanistan

999 Destruction of the Persian Samanid dynasty by Turkic tribes

1003 Death of Li Ch'i-ch'ien, founder of the Tangut empire

1004 Ch'i-tan invasion of Sung territories

1005 Peace of Shan-yüan between Sung and Ch'i-tan

1028 Destruction of the Kan-chou kingdom by the Tanguts

1032 Accession to the throne of Li Yüan-hao; apogee of the Tangut empire

1040 Beginning of the Titular War between the Tangut and the Sung. The battle at Dandanqan, eliminating Ghaznavid control and establishing Saljuq control over Khurassan

1040 Renewed Ch'i-tan threats against the Sung; increase of Sung tribute payments to the Ch'i-tan

1044 Peace treaty between the Tangut and the Sung modeled after the Shan-yüan treaty

1048 Death of Li Yüan-hao

1063 Beginning of the reign of the Saljuq Alp-Arslan

1068 Tangut conquest of the Tibetan kingdom of bCon-kha; isolation of China from Central Asia

1072 Beginning of the reign of Malik-Shah; apogee of Saljuq power

1084 Arrival at the Ch'i-tan court of Meng-ku (Mongol?) envoys

1096 War between the Ch'i-tan and the Merkid

1114 Outbreak of the Jürchen rebellion against the Ch'i-tan

1115 Establishment of the Jürchen empire; unsuccessful Ch'i-tan peace overtures

1117 Jürchen exert complete control over the Ch'i-tan northern domains. First peace treaty between the Jürchen and the Tangut

1120 Beginning of the conflict between the Jürchen and the Sung

1123 First treaty between the Jürchen and the Sung

1124 Formation of the Qaraqitai empire in Transoxiana. Formal end of the Ch'i-tan empire. Jürchen begin their conquest of the Sung domains. Second peace treaty between Jürchen and Tangut

1127 January 9: Jürchen troops occupy the Sung capital, K'ai-feng; end of the Northern Sung

1150 Usurpation of power in the Jürchen empire by Hai-ling

1157 Death of Sanjar, the last of the Great Saljuq rulers

1161 Beginning of Jürchen repression of tribes on the steppe. Hai-ling moves his capital to K'ai-feng, former capital of the Sung

1167 Birth of Temujin, the future Chinggis-khan

1197 Beginning of the war between Chinggis-khan and Jamuqa

1203 The Baljuna Covenant

1206 The *quriltai* proclamation of Temujin as Chinggis-khan. First Mongol invasion of Tangut territory

1209 Recognition of Chinggis-khan's suzerainty by Uighur ruler of Qocho. Tangut recognition of Mongol suzerainty

1211 Mongol invasion of the Jürchen empire

1214 Mongol siege of the Jürchen capital Chung-tu, which falls on May 14

1218 Beginning of Chinggis-khan's Western campaign

1219 Mongol conquest of Otrar

1220 Mongol conquest of Bukhara, Samarqand, Tirmidh, and Gurganj. Tangut uprising against the Mongols

1221 Mongol conquest of Balkh, Merv, Herat, and Nishapur

1222 Chinggis-khan's defeat of Jalal al-Din on the banks of the Indus

1223	Death of Muqali, Mongol commander for North China. Mongol penetration into Russia as far as Novgorod
1225	Renewed Mongol attacks on the Tangut state
1227	Destruction of the Tangut state. Death of Chinggis-khan
1229	Accession to the Mongol throne of Ogodei
1230	Renewed war between the Mongols and Jalal al-Din
1231	Resumption of the Mongol conquest of the Jürchen domains
1234	*Quriltai* held to decide the conquest of the Middle East and Russia. Destruction of the Jürchen empire
1235	First Mongol–Southern Sung confrontation
1236	Fiscal reforms of Yeh-lü Ch'u-ts'ai
1237	Mongol capture of Bulghar, Veronez. Batu becomes ruler of the Golden Horde
1238	Death of Jalal al-Din. Mongol capture of Moscow, Vladimir, and Sugdaq
1240	Mongol capture of Kiev. Ogodei recalls Guyuk and Mongke from the European campaign
1241	Defeat of the Hungarians; defeat of the European knights at Leignitz. Death of Ogodei
1242	Halt of the European campaign; return of Batu to the steppe
1246	Accession to the throne of Guyuk
1248	Death of Guyuk
1251	Accession to the throne of Mongke
1255	Death of Batu. Hulegu recaptures Samarqand. First Buddhist-Taoist debate in Qaraqorum
1257	Berke assumes the throne in the Golden Horde
1258	Proclamation of Ariq-buqa as Great Khan. Hulegu captures Baghdad. Second Buddhist-Taoist debate in Qaraqorum
1259	Mongol invasion of Poland
1260	Proclamation of Qubilai as Great Khan. Hulegu captures Damascus
1262/3	First war between the Il-khans and the Golden Horde
1264	Surrender of Ariq-buqa to Qubilai, end of the war of succession
1265	Death of Hulegu; accession to the Il-khanid throne of Abaqa
1268	Resumption of Mongol attacks on the Southern Sung
1268/9	Beginning of Qaidu's war of restoration
1270	Battle of Herat; defeat of the Qaidu confederation by the Il-khan Abaqa
1271	Qubilai adopts the Chinese reign title *Yüan*
1274	Bayan of the Barin leads the final offensive against the Southern Sung
1275	Defeat of the major Sung forces
1276	February 21: formal surrender of the Sung to the Mongols
1279	Death of the last Sung pretender to the throne
1281	War between the Mongols and the Mamluks. Destruction of the Mongol fleet off the Japanese coast
1285	Major defeat of the Qaidu forces
1287	Nayan rebellion crushed by Bayan of the Barin

1292	Appointment of Bayan of the Barin as commander against Qaidu. Completion of the Forbidden City in Peking
1294	Death of Qubilai
1295	Accession of Ghazan to the Il-khanid throne. June 19: public conversion of Ghazan to Islam
1297	Ghazan adopts Islamic state symbols
1300	Reoccupation of Baghdad by the Mongols
1301	Death of Qaidu
1303	Surrender of the remaining Qaidu forces; end of the war of restoration
1304	Death of Ghazan
1327	Defeat of Tarmashirin before Delhi
1328	The Qaishan coup at the Yüan court
1334	Partition of the Chaghatai Khanate
1335	Death of Abu Sa'id, the last Il-khan
1336	Birth of Timur-i-leng
1340	Formal abolition of the Il-khanid empire
1350	Beginning of major rebellions in Southern China
1357	Death of Jani-beg, last member of the House of Jochi to rule over the Golden Horde
1368	Collapse of the Yüan; creation of the Chinese Ming dynasty
1370	Death of Toghon Temur, last Yüan emperor. Timur-i-leng conquers Balkh
1375	Death of Kökö Temur
1377	Full control over China gained by the Ming. Toqtamish, ruler of the White Horde, assumes control over the Golden Horde
1380	Mongols defeated by the Russians at Kolikovo
1382	Mongol sack of Moscow
1385	Beginning of Ming active defense against the Mongols
1388	End of the Northern Yüan. Timur-i-leng assumes the title of sultan
1393	Capture of Shiraz and Baghdad by Timur-i-leng
1395	Diplomatic exchanges between Ming China and Timur-i-leng. Toqtamish defeated by Timur-i-leng. Control over the Golden Horde passes into the hands of the Turkish emir, Edigu
1398	Timur-i-leng sacks Delhi
1400	Timur-i-leng conquers Damascus
1402	War between Timur-i-leng and the Ottoman empire
1405	Death of Timur-i-leng
1419	Death of Edigu; beginning of civil war in the Golden Horde
1436	Formation of the khanate of Kazan
1439	Accession to the position of khan over the Eastern Mongols of the Oirat Esen
1443	Formation of the Crimean khanate
1449	Esen's capture of the Chinese emperor; a new emperor is appointed in China
1455	Assassination of Esen; end of the first Oirat empire

1466   Formation of the khanate of Astrakhan
1502   Destruction of Sarai, capital of the Golden Horde
1507   Birth of Altan Khan
1528   Beginning of the wars between Dayan Khan and the Chinese
1532   First defeat of Dayan Khan
1542   Defeat of the Chinese by Altan Khan, *de facto* ruler over the Mongols
1552   Capture of Kazan by the Russians
1554   Absorption of the khanate of Astrakhan by the Russians
1558   Russian penetration of Central Asia
1571   Peace treaty between Altan Khan and the Chinese
1575   Mongol conversion to Tibetan Buddhism
1639   Formation by the Manchus of the Ch'ing dynasty
1644   Manchu control over China established
1648   Establishment of the Russian town of Kamchatka on the Pacific coast
1651   Establishment of Irkutsk
1666   Establishment of the town of Albazin on the Amur
1689   Treaty of Nerchinsk; division of Central Asia between Manchus and Russians
1691   The Dolonnor *quriltai*; Mongol recognition of the Manchu emperor

Notes

Chapter 1

1. The best bibliography is provided by Denis Sinor, *Introduction à l'Etude de l'Eurasie Centrale* (Wiesbaden, 1962). No adequate updated supplementary bibliography exists.

2. R. Grousset, *L'Empire des Steppes* (Paris, 1939), translated most recently, by Naomi Waldorf, as *The Empire of the Steppes* (New Brunswick, N.J., 1970). The translation adds to the difficulties in using the work since the translator did not transcribe all terms in the commonly accepted English romanization of Chinese, Mongol, Turkic, and Persian; some of the transcriptions are totally arbitrary, corresponding to neither a French nor an English romanization.

3. Denis Sinor, "What is Inner Asia?" in *Altaica Collecta. Berichte und Vorträge des XVII Permanent International Altaistic Conference* (Wiesbaden, 1976), pp. 250-51.

4. M. Ferenczy, "Chinese Historiographers' Views on Barbarian-Chinese Relations (14–16th C.)," *Acta Orientalia Hungaricae* 21 (1968): 353–62.

5. For a description of some of these peculiarities, see the prolegomena in Hans Bielenstein, *The Restoration of the Han Dynasty*, 3 Vols. (Stockholm, 1954–67), 1: 20–81; and Michael C. Rogers, *The Chronicle of Fu Chien. A Case of Exemplary History* (Berkeley, 1968), pp. 1–79.

6. This attitude is reflected in Western general histories of China. The most recent such work, Charles O. Hucker, *China's Imperial Past. An Introduction to Chinese History and Culture* (Stanford, 1975), devotes less than 1 percent of its pages to the so-called Conquest Dynasties. It lumps together the Ch'i-tan, the Jürchen, and the Mongols, and the Turkic impact on China receives almost no attention.

Chapter 2

1. The fact that the Tabghach kept their records in Chinese does not change this situation, for, at least with regard to the elite, it had become a thoroughly Chinese dynasty. The same applies to those Hsiung-nu and Hsien-pi tribes that created their own ephemeral dynasties in China.

2. A. Kollautz and H. Miyakawa, *Geschichte und Kultur eines völkerwanderungszeitlichen Nomadenvolkes. Die Jou-jan der Mongolei und die Awaren in Mitteleuropa*, 2 vols. (Klagenfurt, 1970); Denis Sinor, *Inner Asia. A Syllabus* (Bloomington, Ind., 1969), p. 145. It is not clear whether this referred to individuals or to households, but in either case, it reflects a small population.

3. The principal Hsiung-nu tombs were discovered in 1922. Camilla Trever, *Excavations in Northern Mongolia* (Leningrad, 1932).

4. Denis Sinor, *Introduction à l'Etude de l'Eurasie Centrale*, pp. 225–30.

5. J. Prušek, *Chinese Statelets and the Northern Barbarians in the Period 1400–300 B.C.* (Dordrecht, 1971), pp. 121–32, 222–26. The author suggests a relationship between the Hsiung-nu and the Scythians. The evidence he advances, however, is not quite convincing.

6. B. Watson, trans., *Records of the Great Historian of China. Translations from the Shih Chi by Ssu-ma Ch'ien*, 2 vols. (New York, 1961), 2: 162.

7. J. K. Fairbank, "A Preliminary Framework," in J. K. Fairbank, ed., *The Chinese World Order: Traditional China's Foreign Relations* (Cambridge, Mass., 1968), esp. pp. 4–11.

8. The best studies of the early period of Hsiung-nu history are still the trans-

lations provided by J. J. M. de Groot, *Chinesischen Urkunden zur Geschichte Asiens. I. Die Hunnen der vorchristlichen Zeit* (Berlin-Leipzig, 1921); *II. Die Westlande Chinas in der vorchristlichen Zeit* (Berlin-Leipzig, 1929).

9. On the history of this restoration, H. Bielenstein, *The Restoration of the Han Dynasty*.

10. Many of the place names mentioned in Pan Ch'ao's campaigns are only tentatively identified.

11. On the late Hsiung-nu period, W. Eberhard, "Chronologische Uebersicht über die Geschichte der Hunnen von späteren Han-Zeit," *Türk Tarih Kuruma Belletin* 4 (1940): 387–435. The best studies on the Hsien-pi are those of Gerhard Schreiber, "Das Volk der Hsien-pi zur Han-Zeit," *Monumenta Serica* 12 (1947): 145–203; "The History of the Former Yen Dynasty," Ibid. 14 (1949–55): 374–480; Ibid. 15 (1956): 1–141.

12. For the most recent summary of the state of knowledge, Otto Manchen-Helfen, *The World of the Huns. Studies in their History and Culture* (Berkeley, 1973); W. B. Henning, "The Date of the Sogdian Ancient Letters," *Bulletin of the School of Oriental and African Studies* 12 (1948): 601–15.

13. Dynasties of alleged Hsiung-nu origin were the Han (304–329), the Later Chao (319–352), and the Hsia (407–431), all located in present-day Shansi and Shensi. In Kansu province there was the Later Liang dynasty (397–439).

14. Liu Mau-tsai, *Kutscha und seine Beziehungen zu China vom 2. Jhr. bis zum 6. Jhr. n. Chr.* (Wiesbaden, 1969), esp. pp. 86–99.

15. A study of the available information is provided by O. Pritsak, "Die 24 Ta-ch'en. Studie zur Geschichte des Verwaltungsaufbaus des Hsiung-nu Reiche," *Oriens Extremus* 1 (1954): 178–202.

16. On this battle, see M. Rogers, *The Chronicle of Fu Chien.*

17. On the language of the Tabghach, L. Bazin, "Recherches sur les parlers T'o-pa (5e siècle après J.C.)," *T'oung Pao* 39 (1950): 228–329; Peter A. Boodberg, "The Language of the T'o-pa Wei," *Harvard Journal of Asiatic Studies* 1 (1936): 167–85. On the use of Tabghach as a name for China, Paul Pelliot, "L'origine du nom de la Chine," *T'oung Pao* 13 (1912): 727–42.

18. W. Eberhard, *Das Toba-Reich Nordchinas. Eine soziologische Untersuchung* (Leiden, 1949), pp. 10, 88.

19. Ibid., pp. 106–9.

20. Ibid., pp. 113–22.

21. A study of Lo-yang during the Later Han is provided by Hans Bielenstein, "Lo-yang in Later Han Times," *Bulletin of the Museum of Far Eastern Antiquities,* no. 48 (1976): 1–144.

22. W. Eberhard, *Das Toba-Reich Nordchinas*, pp. 224–27; H. Maspero and E. Balaźs, *Histoire et Institutions de la Chine Ancienne* (Paris, 1967), pp. 119–21.

23. The basic study for Buddhism during this period is E. Zürcher, *The Buddhist Conquest of China*, 2 vols. (Leiden, 1959). Taoism also had an important role during this period. J. R. Ware, trans., *Alchemy, Medicine, Religion in China in A.D. 320* (Cambridge, Mass., 1966).

24. E. Chavannes, *Mission archéologique dans la Chine septentrionale,* 3 vols. (Paris, 1913–15). See also the monumental work by S. Mizuno and T. Nagahiro, *Yün-kang Caves,* 32 vols. (Kyoto, 1952–56). (In Japanese and English.)

25. On Yang Chien and his efforts to consolidate and reunify China, A. F. Wright, "The Formation of Sui Ideology, 581–604," in J. K. Fairbank, ed., *Chinese Thought and Institutions* (Chicago, 1967), pp. 71–104.

26. Very few studies have been done on the Juan-juan. For the state of the field,

P. Olbricht, "Uchida's Prolegomena zu einer Geschichte der Jou-jan," *Ural-Altaische Jahrbücher* 26 (1954): 90–100.

27. In the year 534, the Northern Wei was divided formally into two new states: the Eastern Wei (534–550) and the Western Wei (534–551).

28. There is uncertainty as to the date of this incident. D. Sinor, *Inner Asia. A Syllabus,* p. 99, places it in the year 544. This appears to be much too early, for it leaves a period of nearly eight years between the incident and the Turkic rebellion against the Juan-juan, a rebellion allegedly caused by the incident. The primary sources are contradictory in this matter, but it seems that since the rebellion broke out in 552, the most plausible date would be between 550 and 551.

29. Denis Sinor in his *Introduction à l'Etude de l'Eurasie Centrale* gives no indication that Indo-European languages were present in Central Asia.

30. R. Ghirshman, *Les Chionites-Hephtalites* (Cairo, 1948), esp. pp. 61–67. For a contrary opinion see in particular K. V. Treven, "Kusany, Khioniti i Eftality po armjanskim istočnikam IV–VII vv." *Sovetskaja Arkheologiya* 21 (1954): 131–47; H. W. Haussig, "Awaren, Shuan-shuan und Hephtaliten," in *Handbuch der Orientalistik. Geschichte Mittelasiens* (Leiden-Köln, 1966), pp. 107–22, is without value.

31. This account of Hephtalite history is based primarily on R. Ghirshman, *Les Chionites-Hephtalites,* pp. 69–114.

32. Kollautz and Miyakawa, *Geschichte und Kultur eines Nomadenvolkes,* 1: 138–47. H. W. Haussig, "Awaren, Shaun-shaun und Hephtaliten," equates the Avars with the Hephtalites. Like Kollautz's, his statement is *ex cathedra.*

33. The best two studies on the T'u-yü-hun are Thomas D. Carroll, *Account of the T'u-yü-hun in the History of the Chin Dynasty* (Berkeley, 1953); and Gabriella Molè, *The T'u-yü-hun from the Northern Wei to the Time of the Five Dynasties* (Rome, 1970). The present account is based on the author's unpublished research notes.

34. Denis Sinor, "Autour d'une migration de peuples au Vè siècle," *Journal Asiatique* (1946–47): 1–77.

35. J. Moravcsik, "Zur Geschichte der Onoguren," *Ural-Altaische Jahrbücher* 10 (1930): 53–90.

36. A. Kollautz, "Die Awaren. Die Schichtung in einer Nomaden-Herrschaft," *Saeculum* 5 (1954): 129–78.

37. Kollautz and Miyakawa, *Geschichte und Kultur eines Nomadenvolkes,* 1: 221–38; A. Kollavtz, "Awaren, Franken und Slaven in Karantanien und Niederpannonien und die fränkische und byzantinische Mission," *Carnthia I* 156 (1966).

38. D. Sinor, *Inner Asia. A Syllabus,* pp. 148–49; W. Grumel, "La défense maritime de Constantinople du côté de la Corne d'Or et le siège des Avares," *Byzantoslavica* 25 (1964): 217–33. H. Koller, "Die Awarenkriege Karls des Grossen," in *Mitteilungen des Oesterreichische Arbeitgemeinschaft für die Ur- und Frühgeschichte,* Vol. 15 (Vienna, 1964), pp. 1–12.

Chapter 3

1. No relationship has ever been established between the two, nor is any suggested here.

2. A. von Gabain, "Buddhistische Türkenmission," in *Asiatica: Festchrift Friedrich Weller* (Leipzig, 1954), p. 164.

3. Quoted from D. Sinor, *Inner Asia. A Syllabus,* p. 103 (italics mine). The original is contained in V. Thomsen, *Inscriptions de l'Orkhon déchiffrées* (Helsinki, 1896); W. Radloff, *Die alttürkischen Inschriften der Mongolei* (St. Petersburg, 1897–99).

4. For example, B. Spuler, "Geschichte Mittelasiens seit dem Auftreten der Türken," in *Handbuch der Orientalistik,* vol. 5, pt. 5 (Leiden-Köln, 1966), pp. 122–35, 136–45.

5. Quoted from Talat Tekin, *A Grammar of Orkhon Turkic* (Bloomington, Ind., 1968), pp. 261–63; Larry W. Moses, "T'ang Tribute Relations with the Inner Asian Barbarians," in J. C. Perry and B. L. Smith, eds., *Essays on T'ang Society* (Leiden, 1976), pp. 83–85.

6. Ch'en Yin-k'o, "Lun T'ang Kao-tsu ch'eng-ch'en yü T'u-chüeh shih," *Ling-nan Hsüeh-pao* 11 (1951): 1–9; Hsiang Ta, *T'ang-tai Ch'ang-an yü Hsi-yü wen-ming,* reprint ed. (Peking, 1933, 1957).

7. This account is based upon the versions contained in the chapters on the Türks in the official Chinese annals. An acceptable translation is provided by Liu Mau-tsai, *Die chinesischen Nachrichten zur Geschichte der Ost-Türken (T'u-küe)* (Wiesbaden, 1958).

8. K. Jettmar, "The Altai Before the Türks," *Bulletin of the Museum of Far Eastern Antiquities* 23 (1951): 208–10 especially.

9. L. W. Moses, "T'ang Tribute Relations," p. 64.

10. This is sometimes called the Northern domain, an appellation which geographically is more correct. It is the one commonly used by French sinologists.

11. According to the Chinese sources, his original name was Ssu-chin. Upon his accession he assumed the name of Mu-han/Muqan Qaghan. Liu Mau-tsai, *Kutscha und seine Beziehungen zu China,* pp. 493–94, nn. 35–36.

12. This took place in 567 after some protracted negotiations. For a partial translation of her biography in the *Chou shu,* Liu Mau-tsai, *Kutscha und seine Beziehungen zu China,* pp. 19–20.

13. This occurred in a letter sent in 598 to the Emperor Maurice, quoted by Theophylactus Simocattes, *Historiae,* book VII: 7–9. E. Chavannes, *Documents sur les Tou-kiue (Turcs) Occidentaux* (St. Petersburg, 1903), pp. 245–49.

14. Liu Mau-tsai, *Kutscha und seine Beziehungen zu China,* pp. 48–49.

15. It appears, however, that Li Yüan played a much more important role in the founding of the T'ang dynasty. Howard J. Wechsler, *Mirror to the Son of Heaven. Wei Cheng at the Court of T'ang T'ai-tsung* (New Haven, 1974), pp. 8–32.

16. E. Chavannes, "Notes additionnelles sur les Tou-kiue (Turcs) Occidentaux," in *Documents sur les Tou-kiue,* pp. 5–18; Ts'en Chung-mien, *Hsi T'u-chüeh shih-liao po-ch'üeh chi k'ao-cheng* (Shanghai, 1958). On T'ang relations with regions beyond the Tarim basin, see the delightful E. A. Shafer, *The Golden Peaches of Samarkand: A Study of T'ang Exotics* (Berkeley, 1963).

17. On the dates of Kül-tegin's and Bilge-qaghan's deaths, Liu Mau-tsai, *Kutscha und seine Beziehungen zu China,* p. 620, nn. 994, 998.

18. E. Chavannes, *Documents sur les Tou-kiue,* pp. 233–42; K. Hannestad, "Les relations de Byzance avec la Transcaucasie et l'Asie Centrale aux 5è et 6è siècles," *Byzantion* 25/27 (1955–57): 423–56.

19. The Turkic empire existed from 552 to 734 A.D. During the 183 years of its existence, there were recorded 139 major raids and wars, an average of nearly one per year. If to this figure are added the total number of recorded minor border raids and incidents, the average comes close to 2.5 armed conflicts per year.

20. The following account is based upon the author's unpublished research and upon L. W. Moses, "T'ang Tribute Relations," as well as Hilda Ecsedy, "Trade and War Relations between the Turks and China in the Second Half of the 6th Century," *Acta Orientalia Hungaricae* 21 (1968): 131–80.

21. On the formation of this theory, Yü Ying-shih, *Trade and Expansion in Han China: A Study in the Structure of Sino-Barbarian Relations* (Berkeley, 1967).

22. H. Ecsedy, "Trade and War Relations between the Turks and China," p. 143, quoting from the *Ts'e-fu yüan-kuei*.

23. Ibid., p. 135.

24. Ibid., p. 137.

25. Hilda Ecsedy, "Tribe and Tribal Society in the 6th Century Turk Empire," *Acta Orientalia Hungaricae* 25 (1972): 245–46.

26. Ibid., pp. 250–51.

27. Ibid., p. 252.

28. K. Czegledy, "Coghaq-qazi, Qara-qum, Kök öng," *Acta Orientalia Hungaricae* 15 (1962): 63–68.

29. According to these sources, there were six outer prime ministers and three inner prime ministers, each defined as *Tsai-hsiang*. The definition given for these functions within the Turkic empire is identical with their function within the Chinese empire as defined in the *Chih-kuan fen-chi* (Ssu-k'u ed.), 3: 1a–55b.

30. Liu Mau-tsai, *Kutscha und seine Beziehungen zu China*, pp. 430–31.

31. Lao Ching-yüan, "T'ang che-chung fu k'ao," in *Erh-shih-wu shih pu-pien*, reprint ed. (Peking, 1957), 6: 7593–7629; T'ang Ch'ang-ju, *T'ang-shu ping-chih chien-cheng* (Peking, 1962); R. des Rotours, "Les grands fonctionnaires des provinces en Chine sous la dynastie des T'ang," *T'oung Pao* 25 (1927): 219–332; R. des Rotours, *Traité des fonctionnaires et traité de l'armée*, 2 vols. (Leiden, 1947).

32. E. G. Pulleyblank, "The An Lu-shan Rebellion and the Origins of Chronic Militarism in Late T'ang China," in Perry and Smith, *Essays on T'ang Society*, pp. 39–40.

33. *I-wei lei-tsü*, 76: 11b.

34. A. von Gabain, "Buddhistische Türkenmission," pp. 165–66. On Hsüan-tsang, S. Beal, *Si-yu-ki. Buddhist Records of the Western World, I-II* (London, 1884); A. Stein, "La traversée du désert par Hiuan-tsang en 630 ap. J.C.," *T'oung Pao* 20 (1921): 332–54.

35. Liu Mau-tsai, *Kutscha und seine Beziehungen zu China*, pp. 172–73.

36. For a detailed history, R. N. Frye, ed., *The Cambridge History of Iran*, vol. 4: *The Period from the Arab Invasions to the Saljuqs* (Cambridge, 1975).

37. R. Grousset, *L'empire des Steppes*, reprint ed. (Paris, 1965), p. 167.

Chapter 4

1. J. R. Hamilton, "Toquz-Oghuz et On Uyghur," *Journal Asiatique* (1962): 27–29.

2. After 774 the Uighur ruler adopted the title of the Besmil ruler: *Iduq-qut*, "the Holy Ruler."

3. J. R. Hamilton, *Les Ouighours à l'époque des Cinq Dynasties* (Paris, 1955), p. 139.

4. I-ti-chien was the second son of Mo-yen-cho (747–59), who was K'o-li-pei-lo's son. I-ti-chien's reign title was *tängridä qut balmish il tutmish alp külüg bilge qaghan*.

5. On the conversion of the Uighurs to Manicheism, G. Schlegel, *Die chinesische Inschrift auf dem uigurischen Denkmal in Kara Balgasun*, Mémoires de la Société Finno-Ougrienne, vol. 9 (1896), reviewed and retranslated by E. Chavannes; P. Pelliot, *Un traité manichéien retrouvé en Chine* (Paris, 1913).

6. For a list of studies on the Qirghiz, Denis Sinor, *Introduction à l'Etude de l'Eurasie Centrale,* pp. 246–48.

7. B. Spuler, *Handbuch der Orientalistik,* pp. 162–64.

8. *Chiu wu-t'ai shih* (SPPY ed.), 138: 5a; *Wu-tai shih-chi,* 74: 10a. Translations are provided by J. R. Hamilton, *Les Ouighours,* pp. 81–93.

9. On this, P. Demiéville, *Le Concile de Lhasa* (Paris, 1952).

10. The official annals of the Sung dynasty devote separate reports to the Sha-chou and the Kan-chou. The latter, however, are given the title of Uighur. *Sung shih* (SPPY ed.), 490: 7a–9a, 12a–12b.

11. E. Pinks, *Die Uiguren von Kan-chou in den frühen Sung-Zeit (960–1028)* (Wiesbaden, 1968), pp. 91–98.

12. L. Kwanten, "China and Tibet During the Northern Sung," *Oriens Extremus* 22 (1975): 161–67; L. Kwanten, "Chio-ssu-lo (997–1065). A Tibetan Ally of the Northern Sung," *Rocznik Orientalistyczny* 39 (1977): 97–106.

13. Larry V. Clark, "Introduction to the Uyghur Civil Documents of East Turkistan" (Ph.D. diss., Indiana University, 1975), pp. 51–63.

14. Mongol literature developed much later, in fact, after the collapse of the Mongol world empire. W. Heissig, *Die Familien- und Kirchengeschichtsschreibung der Mongolen* (Wiesbaden, 1959), pp. 11–49.

15. R. Grousset, *L'empire des Steppes* (1965 ed.), p. 178.

16. Many of the frescoes were brought to European museums and exist now only in photographic form, the originals having been destroyed during World War II. For an example of this art, see, in particular, A. von le Coq, *Die buddhistische Spätantike in Mittelasien* (Berlin, 1922).

17. For a detailed description of Uighur material culture as reflected in its art, A. von Gabain, *Das Leben im uigurischen Königreich von Qocho (850–1250)* (Wiesbaden, 1973).

18. See note 13 and the bibliography there mentioned.

19. On Qarluq-Tibetan relations, H. Hoffman, "Die Qarluqen in der tibetischen Literatur," *Oriens* 3 (1950): 190–208. The Chinese sources for a history of the Qarluq, although relatively abundant, have not yet been examined.

20. B. Spuler, *Handbuch der Orientalistik,* p. 170.

21. No special studies dealing exclusively with the Samanids are as yet available. The best information can be gathered from R. N. Frye, "The Samanids: A Little-known Dynasty," *Muslim World* 34 (1944): 40–45; R. N. Frye, *The History of Bukhara* (Cambridge, Mass., 1954).

22. B. Spuler, *Handbuch der Orientalistik,* p. 174.

23. C. E. Bosworth, *The Ghaznavids: Their Empire in Afghanistan and Eastern Iran, 994–1040* (Edinburgh, 1963), pp. 35–44.

24. Translated by V. Minorsky, Gibb Memorial Series, London, 1937.

25. O. Pritsak, "Von den Karluk zu den Karachaniden," *Zeitschrift des Deutschen Morgenlandischen Gesellschaft* 101 (1951): 270–300.

26. Spuler, *Handbuch der Orientalistik,* p. 185.

27. This account of Saljuq history is based primarily on C. E. Bosworth, "The Political and Dynastic History of the Iranian World (A.D. 1000–1217)," *Cambridge History of Iran,* 5: 1–202; C. E. Bosworth, *The Islamic Dynasties, A Chronological and Genealogical Survey* (Edinburgh, 1967); Claude Cahen, *La Syrie du Nord à l'époque des Croisades et la principauté franque d'Antioche* (Paris, 1940); Claude Cahen, "Les tribus turques de l'Asie Occidentale pendant la période Seljukide," *Wiener Zeitschrift für die Kunde des Morgenlandes* 51 (1948–52): 178–87.

28. The two principal studies still are M. Th. Houtsma, "Die Ghuzenstämme,"

Wiener Zeitschrift für die Kunde des Morgenlandes 2 (1888): 219–33; O. Pritsak, "Der Untergang des Reiches des Oghuzischen Yabghu," in *Fuad Köprülü Armagani* (Constantinople, 1953), pp. 397–410.

29. C. E. Bosworth, "Political and Dynastic History," pp. 18–41.

30. Ibid., p. 58.

31. Ibid., p. 56. The *Siyasat-nama* is available in translation by H. Drake, *The Book of Government, or Rules for Kings* (London, 1960).

32. C. E. Bosworth, "Political and Dynastic History," pp. 135–57; P. Pelliot, *Notes sur l'Histoire de la Horde d'Or* (Paris, 1950), pp. 176–80.

33. A history of the Ghurids is provided by Juzjani, *Tabaqat-i-Nasiri,* trans. H. G. Raverty, 2 vols. (London, 1881, 1899).

34. The best summary of Qaraqitai history is provided by K. H. Menges, "Qara-Khitay," in Karl A. Wittfogel and Feng Chia-sheng, *History of Chinese Society. Liao (907–1125)* (Philadelphia, 1949), pp. 619–74.

35. C. E. Bosworth, "Political and Dynastic History," pp. 142–46.

36. The Qwarezmian empire still awaits its historian. Most of our knowledge is derived from sources for Mongol history.

Chapter 5

1. Respectively from 960 to 1279, 1368 to 1644, 1644 to 1912.

2. H. Serruys, *Sino-Jürčed Relations During the Yung-lo Period, 1403–1424* (Wiesbaden, 1955); Ejima Hisao, "Mindai Jochoku no uma," *Shien* 62 (1954): 93–115; "Mindai Jochoku chōkō bōeki no gaikan," *Shien* 77 (1958): 1–25.

3. On chapter 3, see H. Franke, "Chinese Texts on the Jürchen. A translation of the Jürchen Monograph in the San-ch'ao pei-meng hui-pien," *Zentralasiatische Studien* 9 (1975): 119–86; M. V. Vorob'ev, *Chzhurchzheni i gosudarstvo tszin'* (Moscow, 1975), pp. 19–30; "Chzhurchzhenej gosudartsvo tszin' i Central'naja Azija, po tszin'skim istochnikam," *Strany i narody Vostoka* 9 (1971): 31–42.

4. C. O. Hucker, *China's Imperial Past,* p. 281 n., states that *chin* was chosen for its symbolic meaning. There is, however, no evidence for such a statement. The first dynasty to adopt a title with a strictly symbolic meaning were the Mongols, who adopted *yüan* or "primordial."

5. P. Ratchnevsky, "Les Che-wei étaient-ils des Mongols?" in *Mélanges sinologiques offerts à Monsieur Paul Demiéville* (Paris, 1966), p. 235; P. Pelliot, *Notes on Marco Polo,* 2 vols. (Paris, 1959), 1: 386.

6. Otagi Matsuo, *Kittan Kodai shi no Kenkyū* (Kyoto, 1959).

7. On the legends, R. Stein, "Leao Tche," *T'oung Pao* 35 (1939): 1–154.

8. The Tungusic affiliation is suggested by Karl H. Menges, "Tungusen und Ljao," *Abhandlungen für die Kunde des Morgenlandes* 38, pt. 1 (1968). A recent Russian study provides the first scientific approach to a language that still awaits deciphering but does not provide any answers. V. S. Starikov, et al., *Materialy po deshifrovke kidan'skogo pis'ma* (Moscow, 1970).

9. R. Dankoff, "Three Turkic Verse Cycles Relating to Inner Asian Warfare" (Unpublished MS., 1976).

10. L. Kwanten, "New Directions in Tangut (Hsi Hsia) Philological Research," *Sung Studies Newsletter,* no. 11–12 (1977): 50–53; *The Analysis of the Tangut (Hsi Hsia) Language: Sino-Tibetan or Altaic?* (Bloomington, Ind., 1977); on the controversy regarding Sino-Tibetan, R. A. Miller, "Sino-Tibetan: Inspection of a Conspectus," *Journal of the American Oriental Society* 94 (1974): 195–209; "Review of R. Shafer: *Introduction to Sino-Tibetan,*" *Monumenta Serica* 27 (1968): 398–435.

11. L. Kwanten, "China and Tibet," pp. 161–67; "Chio-ssu-lo," pp. 103–6.

12. On the *chieh-tu-shih,* R. des Rotours, *Traité des fonctionnaires;* "Les grands fonctionnaires des provinces," pp. 219–30.

13. Pulleyblank, "The An Lu-shan Rebellion," pp. 32–60.

14. A biography of An Lu-shan is provided by Howard S. Levy, *Biography of An Lu-shan* (Berkeley, 1961); a chronicle of the rebellion by R. des Rotours, *Histoire de Ngan Lou-chan* (Paris, 1962).

15. For the events leading up to the rebellion, E. G. Pulleyblank, *The Background of the Rebellion of An Lu-shan* (London, 1955).

16. R. Magnenoz, "La Passion de Yang Kouei-fei: Une histoire d'amour en Chinese au VIIIe siècle," *Bulletin de la Société Indochinoises de Saigon* (1960); Howard S. Levy, trans., *Lament Everlasting: The Death of Yang Kuei-fei* (Tokyo, 1962).

17. R. des Rotours, *Histoire de Ngan Lou-chan,* pp. 319–20.

18. Wang Shou-nan, *T'ang-tai fan-chen yü chung-yang kuan-hsi chih yen-chiu* (Taipei, 1969); D. C. Twitchett, "Varied Patterns of Provincial Autonomy in the T'ang Dynasty," in Perry and Smith, *Essays on T'ang Society,* pp. 90–109.

19. Howard S. Levy, *Biography of Huang Ch'ao* (Berkeley, 1955); Wang Gungwu, "The Middle Yangtse in T'ang Politics," in A. F. Wright and D. Twitchett, eds., *Perspectives on the T'ang* (New Haven, 1973), esp. pp. 221–24.

20. Of the ten dynasties that were not recognized as official, nine were in the south, one in the north. The two most important were the Northern Han (951–979) and Wu-Yüeh (907–978), respectively in present-day Shansi and Chekiang.

21. C. O. Hucker, *China's Imperial Past,* pp. 273ff.

22. Very little research has been done on this subject. The examination of contemporary sources reveals the importance of these events. Li Tao, *Hsü Tzu-chih-t'ung-chien ch'ang-pien* (Chekiang shu-chü, 1881); Chang Fang-p'ing, *Lo-ch'üan-chi* (Ssu-ku ed.).

23. L. Kwanten, "The Uneasy Alliance. Eastern Tibet Between Hsi Hsia and the Northern Sung, 998–1068" (Paper presented at the University Seminar on Traditional China, Columbia University, February 1976); J. R. Levenson, "T'ien-hsia and Kuo and the Transvaluation of Values," *Far Eastern Quarterly* 11 (1952): 447–51.

24. *Liao shih* (SPPY ed.), 1: 2b.

25. Wittfogel and Feng, *History of Chinese Society,* pp. 87–111.

26. *Liao shih,* 2: 4b–5a; Wittfogel and Feng, *History of Chinese Society,* p. 243 n. 25.

27. The official history of the Ch'i-tan was compiled during the Yüan dynasty; there is no indication that the Jürchen intended to compile one. Feng Chia-sheng, *Liao shih yüan-liu k'ao yü Liao shih ch'u chiao,* Yenching Hsüeh-pao, Monograph series, no. 5 (Peiping, 1933).

28. Precious little is known about the Northern Han. Research on it should start with Li Tao, *Hsü Tzu-chih-t'ung-chien ch'ang-pien.*

29. See the memorials on Champa in Chang Fang-p'ing, *Lo-ch'üan-chi.*

30. The memorial is found in Li Tao, *Hsü Tzu-chih-t'ung-chien ch'ang-pien,* 57: 15b–16a.

31. For a detailed study, see Ch. Schwarz-Schilling, *Die Friede von Shan-yüan (1005 n. Chr.). Ein Beitrag zur Geschichte der chinesischen Diplomatie* (Wiesbaden, 1959), pp. 100–154, translations of the documents dealing with the treaty. See also Nieh Ch'ung-ch'i, "Sung Liao chiao-p'ing k'ao," *Yenching Hsüeh-pao* 27 (1940): 1–51.

32. No satisfactory explanation has been given for this sudden collapse. The

Ch'i-tan repression of non-Chinese people like the Jürchen is well documented. Contributing to the Jürchen success, however, was the large-scale defection of Ch'i-tan military units. These defections cannot yet be explained.

33. H. Franke, "Chinese Texts on the Jürchen," p. 171.

34. *Chin shih* (SPPY ed.), chapters 1 and 2; R. Stein, "Leao Tche," pp. 95–102; H. Franke, "Chinese Texts on the Jürchen," pp. 156–60.

35. By this is meant the Jürchen who were not under direct, permanent Ch'i-tan control.

36. H. Franke, "Chinese Texts on the Jürchen," pp. 153–54; *Liao shih,* 27: 4a. Hsiao Fang-hsien was executed in 1122 on a charge of treason; his biography is in *Liao shih,* 102: 1a–1b.

37. *Chin shih,* 2: 7a–8a; *Liao shih,* 28: 3b–4a. Regrettably, all these documents appear to have been lost.

38. *Chin shih,* 2: 9b–11b; *Liao shih,* 29: 1b–3b.

39. The details of these negotiations are given in Dagmar Thiele, *Der Abschluss eines Vertrages: Diplomatie zwischen Sung- und Chin-Dynastie, 1117–1123* (Wiesbaden, 1971).

40. *Hsi Hsia shu-shih,* 33: 5b–6a; *Sung Shih* (SPPY ed.), 22: 1b–2a, 486: 8b–9a.

41. D. Thiele, *Abschluss eines Vertrages,* pp. 74–80; *Chin shih,* 2: 8b; *Liao shih,* 28: 4b.

42. A survey of these treaties is given by H. Franke, "Treaties Between Sung and Chin," in Françoise Aubin, ed., *Etudes Song/Sung Studies* (Paris, 1970), pp. 55–84; a detailed study is in D. Thiele, *Abschluss eines Vertrages,* pp. 133–45.

43. On Li Kang's efforts, J. W. Haeger, "1126–27: Political Crisis and Integrity of Culture," in J. W. Haeger, ed., *Crisis and Prosperity in Sung China* (Tucson, 1975), pp. 143–61.

44. H. Franke, "Treaties between Sung and Chin," pp. 69–74.

45. O. Franke, *Geschichte des chinesischen Reiches,* 5 vols. (Berlin, 1948–54), 4: 246–49.

46. On Sung revanchism, Winston Wan Lo, *The Life and Thought of Yeh Shih* (Hong Kong, 1974); R. Trauzettel, "Sung Patriotism as a First Step toward Chinese Nationalism," in Haeger, *Crisis and Prosperity in Sung China,* pp. 199–213.

47. H. Levy, *The Biography of Huang Ch'ao,* p. 32; *Sung shih,* 485: 1b; Ssu-ma Kuang, *Tzu-chih t'ung-chien,* 254: 10a–14b.

48. *Sung shih,* 485: 5a; L. Kwanten, "Chio-ssu-lo," p. 97.

49. L. Kwanten, "China and Tibet," pp. 161–67; "Chio-ssu-lo," pp. 99–101.

50. On the Uighurs prior to Li Yüan-hao, E. Pinks, *Die Uiguren von Kan-chou*; on Li Yüan-hao, L. Kwanten, "The Uneasy Alliance."

51. *Sung shih,* 485: 8b–9a. The Ch'i-tan never adopted the title.

52. L. Kwanten, "Chio-ssu-lo," pp. 102–4.

53. *Sung shih,* 486: 8b–9a; *Chin shih,* 134: 1a.

54. L. Kwanten, "The Career of Muqali: A Reassessment," *Sung Studies Newsletter,* no. 13 (1978), forthcoming.

55. Very few studies are available on Tangut history, and research is still in its beginning stages. The best work is E. I. Kychanov, *Ocherk Istorii Tangutskogo Gosudarstva* (Moscow, 1968); see also L. Kwanten, "The Role of the Tangut in China's Relations with Inner Asia," *Acta Orientalia* 38 (1978), forthcoming.

56. See note 8.

57. H. J. Wechsler, *Mirror to the Son of Heaven,* pp. 79–105; Harada Tanashige, *Jōkan seiyō teikon* (Tokyo, 1962).

58. R. Stein, "Leao Tche," pp. 110–47.

59. Wittfogel and Feng, *History of Chinese Society,* pp. 508–17.

60. R. Stein, "Leao Tche," pp. 54–55.

61. Wittfogel and Feng, *History of Chinese Society,* p. 572.

62. These are the so-called Sixteen Prefectures. Chao T'ieh-han, "Yen Yün shih-lui-chou ti ti-lu fen-hsi," in *Sung Liao Chin shih yen-chiu lun-chi* (Taipei, 1960), pp. 53–62.

63. R. Stein, "Leao Tche," pp. 27–32.

64. Wittfogel and Feng, *History of Chinese Society."* pp. 202–6; R. Stein, "Leao Tche," pp. 27–41.

65. Wittfogel and Feng, *History of Chinese Society,* pp. 194–99.

66. Wittfogel and Feng, *History of Chinese Society,* pp. 465–66.

67. R. Stein, "Leao Tche," pp. 41–49.

68. Since the Uighur possessed a syllabic script, this is very doubtful.

69. There is evidence that some Sung officials at least knew Ch'i-tan. H. Franke, "Two Chinese Macaronic Poems," in *Tractata Altaica* (Wiesbaden, 1976), pp. 175–80.

70. L. Kwanten, "Chinggis-khan's Conquest of Tibet, Myth or Reality?" *Journal of Asian History* 8 (1974): 8–9.

71. L. Kwanten, "Tangut Miscellanea. I. On the Inventor of the Tangut Script," *Journal of the American Oriental Society* 97 (1977): 333–35.

72. K. T. Wu, "Chinese Printing under Four Alien Dynasties," *Harvard Journal of Asiatic Studies* 13 (1950): 447–523; Nishida Tatsuo, *Seikagu no kenkyū,* 2 vols. (Tokyo, 1964–66), 1: 289–94.

73. L. Kwanten, "New Directions in Tangut (Hsi Hsia) Philological Research," pp. 50–53.

74. *San-ch'ao pei-meng hui-pien,* 3: 2a, 4: 12a, 4: 14a, 224: 8a.

75. Tao Jing-shen, *The Jürchen in Twelfth Century China. A Study of Sinicization* (Seattle, 1976), pp. 6–9, 10.

76. H. Franke, "Chinese Texts on the Jürchen," pp. 130–31.

77. Tsugio Mikami, *Kinshi kenkyu* (Tokyo, 1970), 2: 73–132.

78. *Chin shih,* 44: 2a–2b.

79. The Ch'i-tan *muke* was substantially smaller than the Jürchen; it consisted of 130 households. Dispersing them among the Jürchen reduced the chance of uprisings. *Chin shih,* 44: 2b–3a.

80. It is not clear whether or not this figure includes Chinese and Po-hai *muke.* Although they were abolished in 1124, they had come into existence before, and there is no indication that the older *muke* were disbanded. The figure does include the Ch'i-tan. Ho Ping-ti, "An Estimate of the Total Population of Sung-Chin China," in Aubin, *Etudes Song/Sung Studies,* pp. 33–53.

81. Tao Jing-shen, *The Jürchen in Twelfth Century China,* esp. chapter 3; "The Political Recruitment in the Chin Dynasty," *Journal of the American Oriental Society* 94 (1974): 25, states that 50 percent of the positions were held by imperial clansmen; 14 percent by other Jürchen; 28 percent by Chinese; and 8 percent by others. By 1175 the Chinese held 50 percent of the positions; the Jürchen as a whole, 42 percent; but the imperial clansmen, only 19 percent.

82. This system was later followed by the Mongols. The Chinese military colonies, *t'un-t'ien,* were in essence a T'ang creation. Tao Hsi-sheng, "Chin-tai men-an mou-k'e ti t'u-ti wen-ti," *Shih-huo pan-yüeh-k'an* 1 (1935): 345–52.

83. Tao Jing-shen, *The Jürchen in Twelfth Century China,* p. 60, states that in 1193 there were 11,499 officials—4,705 Jürchen and 6,794 Chinese.

84. In his study on the Jürchen, Tao Jing-shen fails to show the repressive and

cruel nature of Hai-ling's reign. He emphasizes solely his efforts to introduce Chinese forms.

85. Tao Jing-shen, *The Jürchen in Twelfth Century China,* pp. 68–83.

86. The most recent study of the script, Gisaburo N. Kiyose, *A Study of the Jürchen Language and Script in the Hua-i i-yü with Special Reference to the Problem of its Decipherment* (Kyoto, 1977), does not contribute anything new to the field; it is merely a repetition, and not a well-acknowledged one at that, of work done several years ago by Lo Fu-ch'eng, *Ju-chen i-yü* (Dairen, 1934); and especially the work of Hiroaki Yamaji, *A Juchen-Japanese-English Glossary* (privately published, Tokyo, 1956); D. S. Watanabe, *Memorials to the Throne of Ming from Nüchen* (Osaka, 1933); and Yamamoto Mamora, "Joshin yakugo no kenkyū," *Kobe Gaidai Ronso* 2 (1951): 64–79; all works which are not readily available.

87. For example, P. Pelliot, *La Haute-Asie* (Paris, 1931), pp. 22–33; and see the treatment of conquest dynasties in C. O. Hucker, *China's Imperial Past.*

88. Robert Redfield, Ralph Linton, M. J. Herskovitz, "A Memorandum for the Study of Acculturation," *American Anthropologist* 38 (1936): 149–52; M. J. Herskovitz, *Acculturation. The Study of Culture Contact* (New York, 1938).

89. Stanislav Andreski, *Military Organization and Society,* 2d ed. (Berkeley, 1968), pp. 20–38.

90. John W. Dardess, *Conquerors and Confucians. Aspects of Political Change in Late Yüan China* (New York, 1973), p. 3.

91. Claudine Lombard-Sulman, *Un exemple d'acculturation chinoise. La province de Gui zhou au XVIIIe siècle* (Paris, 1972); Robert B. Oxnam, *Ruling from Horseback. Manchu Politics in the Oboi Regency, 1661–1669* (Chicago, 1975) are the most recent examples.

92. Wittfogel and Feng, *History of Chinese Society,* pp. 5–16.

93. J. W. Dardess, *Conquerors and Confucians.*

94. The most recent study is Tao Jing-shen, *The Jürchen in Twelfth Century China.* This is not the place for a book review (see the author's forthcoming review in the *Journal of the American Oriental Society*). Although the work is a welcome contribution to the field, it suffers from several serious methodological faults. The primary one is that it starts from the premise that the Jürchen were Sinicized and then sets out to prove it. It never makes the process clear, nor does it give any indication of Chinese reactions, in spite of the fact that the bibliography clearly indicates that the author is familiar with other studies. Regrettably, however, he does not appear to be familiar with David H. Fischer, *Historians' Fallacies. Toward a Logic of Historical Thought* (New York, 1970).

Chapter 6

1. Gareth Jenkins, "A Note on Climatic Cycles and the Rise of Chinggis Khan," *Central Asiatic Journal* 18 (1974): 217–26.

2. G. Vernadsky, *The Mongols and Russia* (New Haven, 1953), p. 5.

3. See A. von Gabain, *Das Leben im uigurischen Königreich von Qocho.*

4. The records of the various states first mention the Mongols only after they have undergone the first attack.

5. W. Weiers, "Bemerkungen zu den Nachrichten über die Tsu-pu zur Liao-Zeit (907–1125)," *Zentralasiatische Studien* 7 (1973): 545–65.

6. *Liao shih,* 24:3b. The entry is dated the first day of the second month, i.e., 9 March 1089. A second mission arrived during the third month.

7. These are the *Secret History of the Mongols,* in Mongol but written in Chinese

characters; *History of the Campaigns of Chinggis-khan,* a Chinese translation of a Mongol text now long lost; two Persian works, *History of the World-Conqueror* by Juvaini, and *The Compendium of Histories* by Rashid al-Din. For a brief description of each, L. Kwanten, "Fuentes para el estudio de la historia de Mongolia," *Estudios de Asia y Africa* 12 (1977): 37–66.

8. On the history of the work, W. Hung, "The Transmission of the Book Known as the Secret History of the Mongols," *Harvard Journal of Asiatic Studies* 14 (1951): 432–92. For an extreme viewpoint, and not a well-documented one at that, H Okada, "The Secret History of the Mongols. A Pseudo-Historical Novel," *Proceedings: Third East Asian Altaistic Conference* (Taipei, 1969), pp. 61–67.

9. Several translations of this work exist. E. Haenisch, *Die Geheime Geschichte der Mongolen* (Leipzig, 1941); P. Pelliot, *L'Histoire secrète des Mongols* (Paris, 1949), which contains a translation of chapters 1 through 6 only. An English translation, without critical notes, is I. de Rachewiltz, "The Secret History of the Mongols," *Papers on Far Eastern History,* 1971 ff. An excellent translation by Professor Francis W. Cleaves of Harvard University is in press.

10. *Secret History,* paragraphs 54–56.

11. *Secret History,* para. 116; P. Pelliot and L. Hambis, *Histoire des Campagnes de Genghis Khan* (Leiden, 1951), 1: 230–32; for the term *anda,* B. I. Vladimirtsov, *Le régime social des Mongols. Le féodalisme nomade* (Paris, 1948), pp. 76–77.

12. *Secret History,* paras. 105–9.

13. *Secret History,* para. 110. Sometime after she was freed, Börte gave birth to Jochi. There are some hints that Chinggis-khan might not have been his father. The story is substantially different in Rashid al-Din, *The Successors of Chinggis-khan,* trans. J. A. Boyle (New York, 1971), pp. 97–98.

14. *Secret History,* para. 118; Pelliot and Hambis, *Campagnes de Genghis Khan,* pp. 25–26.

15. The name *Wang-khan* is a combination of the Chinese and Mongol terms for king. In the *Secret History,* he is also known as Ong-khan, *Ong* being the Mongolized version of *Wang.*

16. F. W. Cleaves, "The Historicity of the Baljuna Covenant," *Harvard Journal of Asiatic Studies* 18 (1955): 357–421.

17. In the biography of Muqali, *Yüan Shih* (SPPY ed.), 119: 1b, it is stated that the campaign was undertaken because of the evil character of the Jürchen ruler.

18. The Tangut allegedly refused him food and drink. Pelliot and Hambis, *Campagnes de Genghis Khan,* p. 231.

19. L. Kwanten, "Chinggis-khan's Conquest of Tibet," pp. 1–22; "The Nature of Tibetan-Mongol Relations. A Critique of the Caghan Teüke," *Journal of the American Oriental Society* (forthcoming).

20. *Yüan shih,* 149: 10b; I. de Rachewiltz, "Personnel and Personalities in North China During the Early Mongol Period," *Journal of the Economic and Social History of the Orient* 9 (1966): 98.

21. *Yüan shih,* 1:9b; *Chin shih,* 14: 2b.

22. *Yüan shih,* 1: 10a; *Chin shih,* 14: 4b–5a.

23. Charles Peterson, "First Sung Reactions to the Mongol Invasion of the North," in Haeger, *Crisis and Prosperity in Sung China,* pp. 241–48.

24. I. de Rachewiltz, "Muqali, Bol, Tas and An-t'ung," *Papers on Far Eastern History,* no. 15 (1977): 50.

25. This and the following paragraphs are based on research for a biographical study of Muqali, part of a detailed re-examination of Chinggis-khan's career. Some preliminary results are presented in L. Kwanten, "The Career of Muqali." The

standard work still is H. Desmond Martin, *The Rise of Chingis-khan and His Conquest of North China* (Baltimore, 1950).

26. *Yüan shih,* 119: 2b.

27. *Yüan shih,* 119: 3a.

28. *Yüan shih,* 1: 11a–11b, 119: 3b–4a; *Chin shih,* 16: 3ff.

29. *Yüan shih,* 1: 12a, 119: 4b.

30. I. de Rachewiltz, "Personnel and Personalities," pp. 99ff.

31. J. A. Boyle, trans., *The History of the World-Conqueror by 'Ala ad-din 'Ata-Malik Juvaini* (Manchester, 1950), p. 79.

32. Ibid., pp. 142–49.

33. Ibid., p. 177.

34. Ibid., pp. 132–36.

35. I. de Rachewiltz, "Yeh-lü Ch'u-ts'ai (1189–1243): Buddhist Idealist and Confucian Statesman," in A. F. Wright and D. Twitchett, eds., *Confucian Personalities* (Stanford, 1962), p. 195; *Kuo-ch'ao wen-lei* (STPK ed.), 57: 11b–12a.

36. J. A. Boyle, *History of the World-Conqueror,* p. 149.

37. This has been admirably translated by A. Waley, *Travels of an Alchemist* (London, 1931).

38. For a study and a translation, I. de Rachewiltz, "The Hsi-yu lu by Yeh-lü Ch'u-ts'ai," *Monumenta Serica* 21 (1962): 1–128.

39. Sometimes it is stated that the tomb is located in the Ordos area. This, however, is an error. Mongol tradition does not permit worship of deceased persons on the actual place of burial. In the Ordos region is located the Chinggis-khan cult, not his tomb. J. van Oost, *Au Pays des Ortos (Mongolie)* (Paris, 1933), pp. 82–90; Klaus Sagaster, *Die Weisse Geschichte. Eine mongolische Quelle zur Lehre von den Beiden Ordnungen Religion und Staat in Tibet und der Mongolei* (Wiesbaden, 1976), pp. 204–21.

40. J. A. Boyle, *The Successors of Genghis Khan,* p. 18.

41. *Yüan shih,* 2: 1b, 85: 1b–2a. This took place in the eighth month, i.e., 9 September–7 October 1230.

42. *Yüan shih,* 85: 1a–1b.

43. J. A. Boyle, *The Successors of Genghis Khan,* pp. 76–93.

44. *Yüan shih,* 2: 1a; *Chin shih,* 17: 4b.

45. *Yüan shih,* 2: 1a; *Chin shih,* 17: 5a, indicates the failure of the Jürchen mission.

46. *Yüan shih,* 2: 1b.

47. *Yüan shih,* 2: 2a. Tolui died in the ninth month, i.e., 16 September–15 October 1232.

48. *Yüan shih,* 2: 2b–3a; *Chin shih,* 19: 5b–6b; Hok-lam Chan, "Prolegomena to the Ju-nan i-shih. A Memoir of the Last Chin Court under the Mongol Siege of 1234," *Sung Studies Newsletter,* no. 10 (1974): 2–19.

49. J. A. Boyle, *History of the World-Conqueror,* p. 459; *The Successors of Genghis Khan,* pp. 48–50.

50. J. A. Boyle, *The Successors of Genghis Khan,* p. 52.

51. *Yüan shih,* 2: 2b–3a; Boyle, *The Successors of Genghis Khan,* pp. 54–56.

52. (1195–1246). His biography is in *Sung shih,* 412: 1a–8a. See also *Sung-jen ch'uan-chi tzu-liao so-yin,* pp. 1300–1301.

53. J. A. Boyle, *The Successors of Genghis Khan,* pp. 59–60; B. Spuler, *Die Goldene Horde. Die Mongolen in Russland, 1223–1502.* 2d ed. (Wiesbaden, 1962), pp. 10–32.

54. Denis Sinor, "Les relations entre les Mongols et l'Europe jusqu'à la mort

d'Arghoun et de Béla IV," *Cahiers d'histoire Mondiale* 3 (1956): 45; B. Spuler, *Die Goldene Horde,* pp. 21–22.

55. *Yüan shih,* 2: 4a; J. A. Boyle, *The Successors of Genghis Khan,* p. 201.

56. *Yüan shih,* 2: 4b; Rashid al-Din specifies the cause of Ogodei's death. J. A. Boyle, *The Successors of Genghis Khan,* pp. 65–66.

57. B. Spuler, *Die Goldene Horde,* pp. 29–31.

58. J. A. Boyle, *The Successors of Genghis Khan,* p. 185.

59. The *Yüan shih* is silent about this. J. A. Boyle, *The Successors of Genghis Khan,* p. 143.

60. J. A. Boyle, *The Successors of Genghis Khan,* pp. 177, 183.

Chapter 7

1. This alludes to a statement in the official history of the Han dynasty when Lu Chiu gave the emperor advice on how to govern. The emperor, Han Kao-tsu, had acceded to the throne after a long civil war. *Han shu,* 13: 6b.

2. "After us, the flood," a statement attributed to Louis XIV of France.

3. On steppe feudalism, B. I. Vladimirtsov, *Le régime social des Mongols.* As to European feudalism, the author follows the definitions given by L. Ganshof van der Meersch, *Qu'est-ce que la féodalité* (Brussels, 1950).

4. J. A. Boyle, *The Successors of Genghis Khan,* pp. 207–13.

5. On this, L. Olschki, *Guillaume Boucher* (Baltimore, 1946).

6. J. A. Boyle, *The Successors of Genghis Khan,* p. 247, states that he suffered from gout.

7. On this problem, D. Schlegel, "Koexistenz oder Annexionskrieg? Kublai Khans Politik gegenüber dem Sung Reiches, 1256–1257," *Saeculum* 19 (1968): 390–405; "Hao Ching (1222–1275), ein chinesischer Berater des Kaiser Kublai Khan" (Habilitationsschrift, Munich, 1966).

8. J. A. Boyle, *The Successors of Genghis Khan,* p. 255.

9. Su T'ien-chüeh, *Kuo-ch'ao wen-lei.* This work, contemporary with Qubilai's reign, contains the texts of the memorials submitted to Qubilai before he became emperor. This very important source for the history of the Mongols has not yet been fully exploited.

10. On these distances, J. W. Dardess, "From Mongol Empire to Yüan Dynasty: Changing Forms of Imperial Rule in Mongolia and Central Asia," *Monumenta Serica* 30 (1972–73): 122–25.

11. On Nayan's lineage, L. Hambis, *Le Chapitre CVII du Yuan Che* (Leiden, 1954), pp. 110ff. A study, in Dutch, of his rebellion is given by E. P. J. Mullie, *De Mongoolse Prins Nayan* (Brussels, 1964).

12. On Bayan's career, F. W. Cleaves, "The Biography of Bayan of the Barin in the Yüan Shih," *Harvard Journal of Asiatic Studies* 19 (1956): 185–303. The appointment is described on pp. 266ff.

13. H. Franke, "Chia Ssu-tao, Last Bad Prime Minister?" in Wright and Twitchett, *Confucian Personalities,* pp. 217–34.

14. F. W. Cleaves, *Bayan the Barin,* pp. 227–28.

15. *Yüan shih,* 7: 13b. On the *Book of Changes, I-ching* in Chinese, see R. Wilhelm, *The I-ching, or Book of Changes* (New York, 1950). The literal meaning of the word *yüan* is "head, chief, first"; in the *I-ching* it has the meaning of "the primal force, the origin of the universe." The Mongols were the first dynasty to adopt a philosophical term as a dynastic name. In this they were followed by the

two succeeding dynasties, the Ming and the Ch'ing. The name was adopted by Qubilai upon the recommendation of his Chinese advisors. Initially, he planned to name the dynasty the "Great Mongol Empire" (*Ta Meng-ku*). *Kuo-ch'ao wen-lei,* 40: 4b.

16. There is agreement among all historians that Qubilai was a legitimate emperor of China, even within Chinese legal concepts. Argument still exists as to when to date the beginning of the Yüan. The dates range from 1260, the year of Qubilai's accession to the throne, to 1282, the date when Sung loyalists ceased using Sung reign titles. There are two intermediate dates: 1271, the year of the proclamation of the Yüan, and 1279, the year of the death of the last Sung throne pretender. In the light of the fact that Qubilai conceived of himself as the Great Khan, apparently was recognized as such by other Mongols, and regarded China as merely another province of the Mongol empire, maybe the date of Chinggis-khan's *quriltai,* 1206, should be considered as its starting date.

17. Vietnamese resistance was led by Tran Quoc Tuan, better known as Tran Hung Dao. He wrote a book on defense tactics against the Mongols entitled *Binh-thu yeu-luoc* ("Resumé of Military Tactics"). It is surprising that this work is still gathering dust on library shelves.

18. It is estimated that there were at most one million to one and a half million Mongols in the strict sense of the word.

19. On these matters, C. Shirokauer, "Neo-Confucians under Attack: The Condemnation of Wei-hsüeh," in Haeger, *Crisis and Prosperity in Sung China,* pp. 163–98; James T. C. Liu, "How Did a Neo-Confucian School Become a State Orthodoxy?" *Philosophy East and West* 23 (1973): 483–505; J. W. Haeger, "The Intellectual Context of Neo-Confucian Syncretism," *Journal of Asian Studies* 31 (1972): 499–513.

20. Hok-lam Chan, "Liu Ping-chung (1216–1274). A Buddhist-Taoist Statesman at the Court of Khubilai Khan," *T'oung Pao* 53 (1967): 98–146. Other Confucians seem to have had an important influence on Qubilai, in particular Kuo Shou-ching (1231–1316), a man of Tangut origins. His biography is in *Yüan shih,* 164: 3b–7b.

21. Based on Hok-lam Chan, "Liu Ping-chung," pp. 120–21.

22. *Yüan shih,* 87: 1b–2b; 93: 2b11. A description of its contents is given by H. F. Schurmann, *The Economic Structure of the Yüan Dynasty* (Cambridge, Mass., 1956), p. 57 n. 4.

23. J. W. Dardess, "From Mongol Empire to Yüan Dynasty," pp. 137–39.

24. The Mongol Han-lin Academy is described in *Yüan shih,* 87: 3a–3b. As yet, no study has been devoted to it.

25. L. Kwanten, "Tibetan-Mongol Relations During the Yüan Dynasty, 1206–1368," Ph.D. diss., University of South Carolina, 1972; "The Nature of Tibetan-Mongol Relations." A recent article stresses the religious nature of these relations. It is based primarily on Tibetan materials, and for information on the Yüan, and the Mongols in general, uses the highly inadequate, and inaccurate, study of H. H. Howorth, *History of the Mongols from the 9th to the 19th Century* (London, 1876–1927). The article suffers from the same methodological mistakes as nearly all previous studies of Tibetan-Mongol relations. T. V. Wylie, "The First Mongol Conquest of Tibet Reinterpreted," *Harvard Journal of Asiatic Studies* 37 (1977): 103–33.

26. The best resumé of 'Phags-pa linguistics is given by Miyoko Nakano, *A Phonological Study of the 'Phags-pa Script and the Meng-ku tzu-yün* (Canberra, 1971). The brief biography of the 'Phags-pa Lama, however, is best omitted (pp. 24–38). His biography remains to be written.

27. Hok-lam Chan, *Liu Ping-chung*, pp. 132–33.

28. O. Franke, *Geschichte des chinesischen Reiches*, 4: 491.

29. Karl Jahn, *Ta'rīh-i-Mubarak-i Ġazānī des Rāšīd al-Dīn. Geschichte der Ilḫane Abāgā bis Ġaihātū* (The Hague, 1957), p. 11.

30. Ibid., pp. 38–39; J. A. Boyle, *The Successors of Genghis Khan*, p. 273; Rashid al-Din, *Sbornik Letopisi*, trans. L. K. Khetagurov et al. (Moscow, 1952), p. 187. The second part of his name indicates a *Chinese* title.

31. Initially, Berke supported Ariq-buqa, whose name appears on coins of the Golden Horde. Afterwards, when Ariq-buqa had surrendered to Qubilai, Berke apparently supported the latter. It should be pointed out, however, that Qubilai's name does not appear on the coins of the Golden Horde.

32. B. Spuler, *Die Goldene Horde*, p. 252; J. A. Boyle, *The Successors of Genghis Khan*, p. 265.

33. This theory is clearly expressed by J. W. Dardess, "From Mongol Empire to Yüan Dynasty."

34. On the events leading up to this coup and the coup itself, J. W. Dardess, *Conquerors and Confucians*.

35. J. A. Boyle, *The Successors of Genghis Khan*, p. 218, lists the following areas under Arghun Aqa's authority: Khurassan, Mazandaran, Iraq, Fars, Kirman, Adherbaidjan, Georgia, Lur, Arran, Armenia, Diyarbakr, Rum, Mosul, and Aleppo. On these regions, G. Le Strange, *Mesopotamia and Persia under the Mongols in the Fourteenth Century A.D. from the Nuzhat al-Qulub of Hamd Allah Mustaufi* (London, 1903).

36. Arghun Aqa remained associated with the area's government until the reign of Abaqa, during which he held the function of vizier. He died in June 1275 near Tus. K. Jahn, *Ta'rīh-i-Mubārak-i Ġazānī*, p. 21.

37. J. A. Boyle, "The Death of the Last 'Abbasid Caliph: a Contemporary Muslim Account," *Journal of Semitic Studies* 6 (1961): 145–61; J. Kritzeck, "Ibn al-Tiqtaqa and the Fall of Baghdad," in J. Kritzeck and R. B. Winder, eds., *The World of Islam: Studies in Honour of Philip K. Hitti* (New York, 1959), pp. 159–84.

38. The Mamluk forces received unexpected assistance from the Crusader states. Although the latter viewed the Mongols as potential allies against the Mamluks, they adopted a neutral, but pro-Mamluk, attitude, providing the Mamluks with needed supplies. This policy was adopted in the mistaken belief that the Mamluks would be grateful for the assistance given them and that, consequently, they would not attack the Crusader states.

39. Spuler, *Die Goldene Horde*, pp. 38–39.

40. Although Berke was a Muslim, there is no indication that the war broke out on account of Hulagu's execution of the 'Abbasid caliph, as is often suggested. The war was primarily inspired by territorial and economic claims. On Mamluk–Golden Horde relations, A. N. Poliak, "Le caractère colonial de l'état mamlouk dans ses rapports avec la Horde d'Or," *Revue d'Etudes Islamiques* 9 (1935): 231–48.

41. K. Jahn, *Ta'rīh-i-Mubārak-i Ġazānī*, p. 20.

42. Ibid., p. 31; Klaus Lech, *Das mongolische Weltreich. al-'Umarī's Darstellung der mongolischen Reiche in seinem Werk Masālik al-abṣār fi mamālik al-amṣār* (Wiesbaden, 1968), p. 323 n. 13.

43. On the reign of Ahmad or Teguder, B. Spuler, *Die Mongolen in Jran. Politik, Verwaltung und Kultur der Ilchanen-Zeit*, 1220–1350 (Berlin, 1955), pp. 77–81; K. Lech, *Das mongolische Weltreich*, p. 333 n. 79.

44. K. Jahn, *Ta'rīh-i-Mubārak-i Ġazānī*, p. 39

45. Ibid., p. 45.

46. Quoted from J. A. Boyle, "Dynastic and Political History of the Il-khans," *Cambridge History of Iran,* 5: 374.

47. K. Jahn, *Ta'rīḫ-i-Mubārak-i Ġāzānī,* p. 50; B. Spuler, *Die Mongolen in Iran,* pp. 86–89; Karl Jahn, "Das iranische Papiergeld," *Archiv Orientalni* 10 (1938): 308–40.

48. Once his rule was firmly established, although Islam remained the only accepted religion, it appears that Ghazan reverted to the religious tolerance of his forebears. On the sources for Ghazan's conversion, L. Kwanten, "Fuentes para el estudio de la historia de Mongolia," pp. 61–62.

49. One aspect of Il-khanid history which has not yet been examined is the nature of the relations between the Il-khans and the Mamluks. Defections from one side to another were rather common, and these defectors were often given positions of high responsibility, in one case, that of Il-khanid governor for Damascus.

50. Oljeitu's original name was "Ass-herd," a name given to him in accordance with the tradition by which Chinggis-khan received the name of his father's enemy. *Khuda-banda* meant "Slave of God," a name in accordance with Oljeitu's Islamic faith. His full title was *Ghiyath al-Din Muhammad Khuda-Banda Oljeitu Sultan.*

51. B. Spuler, *Die Goldene Horde,* p. 83; A. Mostaert and F. W. Cleaves, eds., *Les Lettres de 1289 et 1305 des Ilkhans Arghun et Oljeitu à Philippe le Bel* (Cambridge, Mass., 1962); E. Haenisch, "Zu den Briefen der mongolischen Il-khane Argun und "Öljeitü an den König Philipp den Schönen von Frankreich (1289 und 1305)," *Oriens* 2 (1948): 216–35.

52. K. Lech, *Das mongolische Weltreich,* p. 147, p. 325 n. 26; p. 350 n. 192; p. 334 n. 85; B. Spuler, *Die Mongolen in Iran,* p. 108.

53. B. Spuler, *Die Goldene Horde,* pp. 31–32, 266–69; F. Balodis, "Alt-Sarai und Neu-Sarai, die Hauptstadt der goldenen Horde," *Latvijas Universitatas Raksti* 13 (1926): 3–82.

54. P. Pelliot, *Notes sur l'Histoire de la Horde d'Or,* pp. 28–29; on Sartaq, p. 34; on Ulagchi, pp. 34–44; on Berke, pp. 47–51; B. Spuler, *Die Goldene Horde,* pp. 33–52.

55. B. Spuler, *Die Goldene Horde,* pp. 35–37; on the role of Nevskii, A. M. Ammann, *Kirchenpolitische Wandlungen im Ostbaltikum bis zum Tode Alexander Nevskis* (Rome, 1936); on the invasion of Poland, Iwamura Shinobu, "Mongol Invasions of Poland in the Thirteenth Century," *Memoirs of the Research Department of the Toyo Bunko* 10 (1938): 103–57; B. Szczesniak, "Hagiographical Documentation on the Mongol Invasion of Poland in the Thirteenth Century. I. The Preaching Friars," *Memoirs of the Research Department of the Toyo Bunko* 17 (1957): 167–95.

56. Very little research on Mongol-Byzantine relations has been done. One has to rely on works such as A. Graf, "Die Tartaren im Spiegel der byzantinische Literatur," in *Jubilee Volume in Honour of Professor Bernhard Heller* (Budapest, 1941), pp. 77–85; C. Chapman, *Michel Paléologue. Restaurateur de l'empire byzantin (1261–1282)* (Paris, 1926); G. Ostrogorsky, *Geschichte des byzantinischen staates* (Munich, 1940).

57. B. Spuler, *Die Goldene Horde,* pp. 52–62; P. Pelliot, *Notes sur l'Histoire de la Horde d'Or,* pp. 58–62.

58. B. Spuler, *Die Goldene Horde,* p. 57; W. de Tiesenhausen, *Recueil de matériaux relatifs à l'histoire de la Horde d'Or* (St. Petersburg, 1884), 1: 354.

59. He was the son of Tatar, the first son of Boghal, the seventh son of Jochi. Rashid al-Din places the death of Mongke-Temur in 1282. J. A. Boyle, *The Successors of Genghis Khan,* pp. 113, 124.

60. The influence of Nogai and his descendants on the southern steppe remained

substantial. In time, it led to the identification of these people as the Nogai Türks, descendants of the Mongols but speaking a particular Turkic dialect. On this language and its culture, N. A. Baskakov, *Nogajsko-russkij slovar'* (Moscow, 1963); V. M. Zirmanskij, "Epicheskie skazanija o nogajskikh bogatyrjakh v sveta istorishcheshikh istochnikov," *Tjurksij gervicheskij epos* (1974): 389–516.

61. P. Pelliot, *Notes sur l'Histoire de la Horde d'Or*, pp. 92–94.

62. K. Lech, *Das mongolische Weltreich*, pp. 262–63.

63. Located to the northwest of present-day Kuldja, *Encyclopédie de l'Islam*, Nouvelle édition (Leiden, 1960–   ), 1: 430–31, 2: 1193–94.

64. R. Grousset, *L'Empire des Steppes*, pp. 398–99.

65. J. A. Boyle, *The Successors of Genghis Khan*, p. 142.

66. Ibid., pp. 326–29.

67. The khanate was divided along religious lines; the northern areas were Buddhist, the southern areas, Islamic.

68. The best study presently available is G. A. Bezzola, *Die Mongolen in abendländischer Sicht. (1220–1270): ein Beitrag zur Frage der Völkerbegegnungen* (Bern, 1974).

69. R. Röhricht, "Analekten. I. Briefe des Jacobus de Vitriaco (1216–21)," *Zeitschrift für Kirchengeschichte* 16 (1896): 92–93 (in Latin).

70. D. Sinor, "Les relations entre les Mongols et l'Europe"; N. Pfeiffer, *Die ungarische Dominikanerprovinz von ihre Gründung bis zur Tartarenverwüstung, 1241–1242* (Zurich, 1913).

71. G. A. Bezzola, *Die Mongolen in abendländischer Sicht*, p. 113: (1) Where did the Mongols come from? (2) What do they believe in? (3) What are their religious representations and customs? (4) How do they live? (5) What is their strength? (6) How numerous are they? (7) What plans do they harbour? (8) How do they consider agreements? (9) How do they treat envoys?

72. B. R. Phaire, "Papal Motivations for an Asian Apostolate (1245–1254). An Analysis" (Ph.D. diss., New York University, 1972). This work analyzes the papal bulls on these missions without regard to their context. It starts from a predetermined conclusion that the missions had no political nature.

73. The pope's letter urged the Mongols to adhere to Christian teaching, to follow his example, and to cease plundering and massacring Christians in Europe and the Orient.

74. Many studies have been devoted to it. There is, however, no good English translation available. The best translation is J. Becquet and L. Hambis, *Jean de Plan Carpin: Histoire des Mongols* (Paris, 1965).

75. It has often been claimed that prior to this report no reliable information was available and that no missions had been sent into Mongol-controlled territory. Although Denis Sinor demonstrated more than two decades ago that such a statement is erroneous, it still finds common acceptance. In fact, Hungarian missions had preceded them, and it was on the basis of information gathered by them that the later missions proceeded. Denis Sinor, "Un Voyageur du treizième siècle: Le Dominicain Julien de Hongrie," *Bulletin of the School of Oriental and African Studies* 16 (1952): 589–602.

76. P. Pelliot, *Les Mongols et la Papauté* (Paris, 1924), pp. 66–139.

77. Ibid., pp. 141–222.

78. For a translation of his work, C. Dawson, *The Mongol Missions* (London, 1955). A new, more accurate, and better-annotated translation is urgently needed.

79. J. A. Boyle, "The Journey of He'tum I, King of Little Armenia to the Court of the Great Khan Möngke," *Central Asiatic Journal* 9 (1964): 175–89.

80. On the decline of European interest, G. A. Bezzola, *Die Mongolen in abendländischer Sicht,* especially part 4.

Chapter 8

1. Stanislav Andreski, *Military Organization and Society,* pp. 137ff.

2. This account is based primarily on B. I. Vladimirtsov, *Le régime social des Mongols.*

3. Contrary to some popular studies on Chinggis-khan, he never carried the title of *qaghan*. According to Pelliot and Hambis, *Campagnes de Genghis Khan,* p. 15, the title was first used by Ogodei and was used, retrospectively, by Chinese historians for all Mongol rulers, including Chinggis-khan and his ancestors. The title is of Turkic origin. G. Doerfer, *Türkische und Mongolische Elemente in Neupersischen* (Wiesbaden, 1965), 2: 141–79.

4. The Borjigid was the clan of Chinggis-khan; the Qonggirad, the clan of his wife. The Borjigid remained the principal Mongol clan until the twentieth century. A genealogy of this clan, in Manchu, was published in 1732, and a Chinese and Mongol translation in 1839. A French translation was published by L. Hambis, *Documents sur l'histoire des Mongols à l'époque des Ming* (Paris, 1969), pp. 153–237. The Chinese and Mongol texts are made available by W. Heissig and C. R. Bawden, eds., *Mongghol borjigid obogh-un teüke von Lomi (1732). Meng-ku shih-hsi-pu* (Wiesbaden, 1957).

5. The author follows the definitions of L. Ganshof van der Meersch, *Qu'est-ce que la féodalite?* and M. Bloch, *La société féodale* (Paris, 1939–40).

6. B. I. Vladimirtsov, *Le régime social des Mongols,* pp. 123–50.

7. J. A. Boyle, *History of the World-Conqueror,* pp. 42–43.

8. B. Spuler, *Die Goldene Horde,* pp. 274–80. The clearest case of centifugal tendencies is the *de facto* usurpation of power by Noqai.

9. K. Lech, *Das mongolische Weltreich,* pp. 148–49.

10. L. Hambis, *Le Chapitre CVIII du Yuan Che.*

11. Stanislav Andreski, *Military Organization and Society,* pp. 122–23, 148–55. These neologisms are defined as follows on pp. 232–33—*neferic*: military organization characterized by a high military participation ratio, high subordination, and high cohesion; *tallenic*: military organization with a high military participation ratio, low subordination, and low cohesion; *ritterian*: a military organization with a low military participation ratio, low subordination, and low cohesion.

12. A description of this is given by John of Plano Carpini. Another terrifying account is given by Grigor of Akanc'; see R. N. Frye and R. P. Blake, eds. and trans., "History of the Nation of Archers (the Mongols)," *Harvard Journal of Asiatic Studies* 12 (1949): 269–399.

13. J. A. Boyle, *History of the World-Conqueror,* pp. 23–34; K. Lech, *Das mongolische Weltreich,* pp. 97–99; G. V. Vernadsky, "The Scope and Contents of Chinggis-khan's Yasa," *Harvard Journal of Asiatic Studies* 3 (1938): 337–60.

14. G. Mangold, *Das Militärwesen in China unter der Mongolen-Herrschaft* (Bamberg, 1971), pp. 16–20.

15. One of the least studied aspects of warfare in both Central and East Asia is the gathering of intelligence. Spying is frequently mentioned in Li Tao, *Hsü Tzu-chih-t'ung-chien ch'ang-pien.*

16. A detailed study of the Yüan military structure is provided by Hsiao Ch'i-ch'ing, *The Military Establishment of the Yüan Dynasty* (Cambridge, Mass., in press) and G. Mangold, *Das Militärwesen in China.*

17. *Yüan shih,* 77: 9b–11b.

18. This is best evidenced by the struggle between Bayan the Merkid and the Chinese bureaucracy. J. W. Dardess, *Conquerors and Confucians,* in particular chapter 3. Furthermore, it appears that many Mongols never even learned Chinese, while many Chinese did learn Mongol.

19. Stanislav Andreski, *Military Organization and Society,* pp. 184–85.

20. K. Sagaster, *Die Weisse Geschichte.*

21. For a critique of K. Sagaster's study and the *caghan teüke,* see L. Kwanten, "The Nature of Tibetan-Mongol Relations."

22. *Yüan shih,* 85: 1a.

23. P. Ratchnevsky, *Un Code des Yüan* (Paris, 1937), p. 54.

24. P. Pelliot, *Notes on Marco Polo,* 1: 167; J. A. Boyle, *The Successors of Genghis Khan,* pp. 61–65.

25. F. W. Cleaves, "The Sino-Mongolian Inscription of 1362 in Memory of Prince Hindu," *Harvard Journal of Asiatic Studies* 12 (1949): 1–133; "Darugha and Gerege," Ibid. 16 (1953): 237–59.

26. See the appointments made by Muqali, *Yüan shih,* 119: 1a–5a.

27. *Yüan shih,* 85: 1a.

28. B. I. Vladimirtsov, *Le régime social des Mongols,* pp. 110ff.

29. *Yüan shih,* 2: 1b; 85: 1b–2a.

30. A description of these reforms is given in J. A. Boyle, *The Successors of Genghis Khan,* pp. 218–22. Information can also be derived from *Yüan shih,* 3: 1a–6b.

31. E. Balaźs, "Chinesische Geschichtswerke als Wegweiser zum Praxis der Bürokratie," *Saeculum* 8 (1957): 210–23.

32. Legge, pp. 249–50 (author's translation).

33. The familiarity which Qubilai had with Confucianism from the start of his career is somewhat suspicious. Indeed, he appears to be a nearly perfect Confucian in many of his statements, which would lead one to suspect that the records of Qubilai's career were doctored after he became emperor.

34. Several of these memorials, which could adequately be titled "Blueprints for Government," are contained in Su T'ien-chüeh, *Kuo-ch'ao wen-lei,* chapters 13, 14, and 15.

35. Hsü's Heng's biography is in *Yüan shih,* 158: 4b–11b; and his proposal is in *Kuo-ch'ao wen-lei,* 13: 1a–17a. Shih T'ien-tse's biography is in *Yüan shih,* 155: 5a–9a, and Liu Ping-chung's in *Yüan shih,* 157: 1a–5a. The latter has been the subject of a study by Hok-lam Chan, "Liu Ping-chung."

36. H. J. Wechsler, *Mirror to the Son of Heaven,* especially chapters 6 and 7. Tsukiyama Chisaburō, *Tōdai seiji sedio no kenkyū* (Osaka, 1967).

37. Charles O. Hucker, *The Censorial System of Ming China* (Stanford, 1966), pp. 25–29.

38. *Yüan shih,* 87: 4b–9a.

39. A great deal of confusion exists with regards to this title during the Yüan dynasty. The definitions given by P. Pelliot, however, apply. P. Pelliot, "Les Kouo che ou les maîtres du royaume dans le bouddhisme chinois," *T'oung Pao* 12 (1911): 671–76.

40. For example, see the entries on Buddhism in the *Yüan-tien-chang,* in particular chapter 33.

41. *Yüan shih,* 87: 4a–4b. The exact function of this office and the difference between it and its Sung homonym have not been subjected to study. For the Sung dynasty, J. H. Winkelman, *The Imperial Library in Southern Sung China, 1127–1279* (Philadelphia, 1974).

42. *Yüan shih,* 87: 1b–2b; the Ssu-nung-ssu was created early in 1270. In the twelfth month of that year (13 January–10 February 1271), it was renamed Ta-ssu-nung. Matsumoto Yoshimi, "Gendai ni okero shusei no sōritsu," *Tōhō Gakuhō* 2 (1940): 328–37; H. F. Schurmann, *Economic Structure of the Yüan Dynasty,* pp. 43–48.

43. J. W. Dardess, *Conquerors and Confucians,* p. 161, states that the Mongols and the Central Asians constituted 3 percent of all registered households in China but had legal claim to 50 percent of all examination degrees.

44. On Mongol rites, *Yüan shih,* 77: 9b–11b; on the Mongol Han-lin Academy, 87: 3a–3b. Yamamoto Takayoshi, "Gendai ni okeru kanrin ni tsuite," *Tōhō Gakuhō* II (1955): 81–89.

45. J. W. Dardess, *Conquerors and Confucians,* esp. chapter 5.

46. G. Mangold, *Das Militärwesen in China,* pp. 20, 28, 37–43; J. W. Dardess, *Conquerors and Confucians,* p. 62.

47. *Handwörterbuch der Islam* (Leiden, 1941), pp. 673ff.

48. H. Horst, *Die Staatsverwaltung der Grossseljuqen und Horazmshahs* (Wiesbaden, 1964), p. 92.

49. This description is based primarily on H. Horst, *Die Staatsverwaltung der Grossseljuqen und Horazmshahs.*

50. H. Horst, *Die Staatsverwaltung der Grossseljuqen und Horazmshahs,* p. 62; Claude Cahen, "L' évolution de l'iqta' du IXe au XIIIe siècle," *Annales: Economies, Sociétés, Civilisations* 8 (1953): 25–52.

51. That the system was appealing to the Mongols is evidenced by the fact that after the demise of Yeh-lü Ch'u-ts'ai, Ogodei appointed 'Abd al-Rahman as governor and an attempt was made to introduce the Islamic tax-farm system.

52. L. Petech, "Les marchands italiens dans l'empire Mongol," *Journal Asiatique* (1962): 549–74.

53. F. Balodis, "Alt-Sarai und Neu-Sarai"; Spuler, *Die Goldene Horde,* pp. 264–70.

54. B. Spuler, *Die Goldene Horde,* pp. 320–30.

55. K. Lech, *Das mongolische Weltreich,* pp. 117–19.

56. P. Olbricht, *Das Postwesen in China unter der Mongolenherrschaft im 13. und 14. Jahrhundert* (Wiesbaden, 1954); B. Spuler, *Die Mongolen in Iran,* pp. 422–26; B. Spuler, *Die Goldene Horde,* pp. 404–15.

57. L. W. Moses, "Tang Tribute Relations," pp. 61–89.

58. For two differing interpretations of nomadic taxation practices, H. F. Schurmann, "Mongolian Tributary Practices of the Thirteenth Century," *Harvard Journal of Asiatic Studies* 19 (1956): 304–89; J. M. Smith, Jr., "Mongol and Nomadic Taxation," *Ibid.* 30 (1970): 46–85.

59. D. Twitchett, *Financial Administration under the T'ang Dynasty* (Cambridge, 1963); Sudō Yoshiyuki, *Sō-dai keizai-shi kenkyū* (Tokyo, 1962).

60. H. F. Schurmann, *Economic Structure of the Yüan Dynasty,* p. 131.

61. The best study on this subject is H. Franke, *Geld und Wirtschaft in China unter der Mongolherrschaft* (Leipzig, 1949).

62. H. F. Schurmann, *Economic Structure of the Yüan Dynasty,* pp. 222–36; E. H. Schafer, "A Fourteenth Century Gazetteer of Canton," in *Oriente Poliano* (Rome, 1957), pp. 67–93.

63. An excellent study of the mechanism of the salt monopoly during the Sung dynasty is provided by Edmund H. Worthy, "Regional Control in the Southern Sung Salt Administration," in J. W. Haeger, *Crisis and Prosperity in Sung China,* pp. 101–42; for a general study, Tseng Yang-feng, *Chung-kuo yen-cheng shih* (Taipei, 1966); a translation of the relevant chapter of the *Yüan shih* is provided by H. F. Schurmann, *Economic Structure of the Yüan Dynasty,* pp. 166 ff.

64. The following account is based on I. P. Petrushevsky, *Zemledelie i agrarnie otnosheniya v Irane XII–XIV vekov* (Leningrad, 1960); "The Socio-Economic Condition of Iran under the Il-khans," *Cambridge History of Iran,* 5: 483–582.

65. I. P. Petrushevsky, "Socio-Economic Condition," p. 497.

66. I. P. Petrushevsky, *Zemledelie,* pp. 96–100; I. P. Petrushevsky, "Socio-Economic Condition," p. 498, gives tables based on Hamd Allah Qazvini's *Nuzhat al-qūlūb.* The total taxes collected by the divan in the pre-Mongol period in the Il-khanid regions amounted to 100,580,000 dinars, versus 19,203,800 dinars during the 1335–40 period.

67. To what degree Ghazan might have been inspired by Qubilai is a matter of speculation. It must be noted, however, that contacts between the Yüan and the Il-khans existed and that one of Ghazan's principal advisors was Bolod Cingsang, an envoy from Qubilai to the Il-khanid court.

68. I. P. Petrushevsky, "Socio-Economic Condition," pp. 494–500.

69. B. Spuler, *Die Goldene Horde,* pp. 420–23.

70. K. Lech, *Das mongolische Weltreich,* p. 138; on the size of the taxes, B. Spuler, *Die Goldene Horde,* pp. 316–20.

71. B. Spuler, *Die Goldene Horde,* pp. 388–409; also P. P. Panaitescue, "La route commerciale de la Pologne à la Mer Noire au Moyen-Age," *Revista Istorica Romana* 3 (1933): 192–93; A. J. Jakubovskij, *Feodal'noe obshchestvo Srednei Azii i ego torgovolja s vostochnoj evropoi v X–XV vv* (Leningrad, 1933).

72. Because very little information is available on the economic situation in the Chaghatai Khanate, it has not been discussed here.

73. J. P. Roux, "Tängri. Essai sur le ciel-dieu des peuples altaiques," *Revue de l'histoire des religions* 149 (1956): 49–82, 197–220; Ibid. 150 (1956): 27–54, 173–212; "Notes additionelles à Tängri. Le ciel-dieu des peuples altaiques," Ibid. 154 (1958): 32–66.

74. P. Ratchnevsky, "Die mongolische Grosskhane und die buddhistische Kirche," in *Asiatica: Festschrift Friedrich Weller* (Leipzig, 1954), pp. 490–91.

75. His biography is in *Yüan shih,* 125: 6a–7a.

76. This was reported by Wilhelm van Ruysbroeck, in A. van den Wijngaert, ed., *Sinica Franciscana. I. Itinera et Relationes Fratrum Minorum Saeculi XIII–XIV* (Quarracchi, 1929), pp. 297–98. The *Pien-wei-lu,* a thirteenth-century work compiled by Buddhists and dealing with the controversy, adds that Mongke gave priority to Buddhism.

77. The account of the dispute is based on J. Thiel, "Der Streit der Buddhisten und Taoisten zur Mongolenzeit," *Monumenta Serica* 20 (1961): 1–81.

78. P. Pelliot, "La secte du lotus blanc et la secte du nuage blanc," *Bulletin de l'Ecole Française de Extrême Orient* 3 (1903): 304–17; Ibid. 4 (1904): 436–40.

79. E. Haenisch, *Steuergerechtsame der chinesischen Kloster unter der Mongolen-Herrschaft* (Leipzig, 1940).

80. J. W. Dardess, *Conquerors and Confucians,* p. 51. For a history of Islam in China, Tazaka Kōdō, *Chūgoku ni okeru kaikyō no denrai to sono kōtsū* (Tokyo, 1964).

81. One of the most important of these advisors was the philosopher-astronomer Nasir al-Din Tusi, a protégé of Hulagu and a Shi'i theologian. J. A. Boyle, "The Longer Introduction to the Zij-i-ilkani of Nasir al-Din Tusi," *Journal of Semitic Studies* 8 (1963): 244–54.

82. J. A. Boyle, "Dynastic and Political History," pp. 369–70.

83. Quoted from A. Bausani, "Religion under the Mongols," *Cambridge History of Iran,* 5: 542.

84. The impression that Persia was a unified Shi'i state is not entirely correct. Up to the time of Oljeitu, cities like Baghdad and Shiraz remained bastions of Sunni doctrine. It was not until the Safavids, some two centuries later, and after the merging of the Shi'i and Sufi that it became the major form of Islamic thought in Persia. The credit, or the blame, for this change must be given to the Mongols.

85. B. Spuler, *Die Goldene Horde,* pp. 217–19.

86. K. Lech, *Das mongolische Weltreich,* pp. 117–18.

87. See the relevant chapters in the magisterial opus of J. Needham, *Science and Civilization in China,* 7 vols. (Cambridge, 1954–); a magnificent study of mathematics in China, with comparisons to Europe, was recently published by U. Libbrecht, *Chinese Mathematics in the Thirteenth Century. The Shu-shu chiu-chang of Ch'in Chiu-shao* (Cambridge, Mass., 1973).

88. H. Franke, "Could the Mongol Emperors Read or Write Chinese?" *Asia Major* 3 (1952): 28–41.

89. Ch'en Yüan, *Western and Central Asians in China under the Mongols,* trans. Ch'ien Hsing-hui and L. Carrington Goodrich (Los Angeles, 1966).

90. C. T. Hsia, *The Classical Chinese Novel. A Critical Introduction* (New York, 1968), pp. 34–114.

91. B. W. Robinson, *Persian Miniature Paintings* (London, 1967).

Chapter 9

1. J. W. Dardess, *Conquerors and Confucians;* "The Transformation of Messianic Rebellion and the Founding of the Ming Dynasty," *Journal of Asian Studies* 29 (1970): 539–58.

2. L. Kwanten, "Fuentes para el Estudio de la Historia de Mongolia," pp. 51–52.

3. Even on a temporal basis this division is incorrect. The Golden Horde functioned as a semi-autonomous state about thirty years before the Yüan and the Il-khans.

4. The Tatar domination came to an end when the Kereyit and the Jürchen united against them.

5. Rashid al-Din describes as Turkish the following tribes: Jalair, Tatar, Onggud, Kereyit, Naiman, and, intriguingly, the Tangut. His statement, however, needs further investigation. L. A. Khetagurov, *Sbornik Letopisi,* 1: 102–3.

6. B. I. Vladimirtsov, *Genghis Khan* (Paris, 1948), pp. 36 ff.

7. The best example of this is the raid of Jebe and Subudei. Their principal task was to pursue the ruler of Qwarezm.

8. In East Asian politics, regionalism is defined as assuming a political course independent from the central government, without an outright rejection of it, i.e., the emperor. The best description of regionalism and its role in Chinese history can

be found in Stanley Spector, *Li Hung-chang and the Huai Army. A Study in Nine-teenth Century Regionalism* (Seattle, 1963).

9. For an illustration of this, see the conflict between Chormaghan, Chin-temur and Körgüz in Persia, J. A. Boyle, *The Successors of Genghis Khan,* pp. 51–53.

10. The *Yüan shih,* 2: 4a–4b, states that Ogodei recalled Guyuk but does not give the reasons.

11. B. Spuler, *Die Goldene Horde,* p. 31.

12. J. A. Boyle, *The Successors of Genghis Khan,* pp. 207–17.

13. Little is known about the early career of Qubilai. It is clear, however, that he did not participate in the European campaign. He is first mentioned during the Buddhist-Taoist debates. J. Thiel, "Streit der Buddhisten und Taoisten." With regard to the campaign against the Southern Sung, Qubilai seems to have been involved more in strategy than in actual campaigning.

14. J. A. Boyle, "The Death of the Last 'Abbasid Caliph: a Contemporary Muslim Account," pp. 145–61.

15. On Qaidu, J. A. Boyle, *The Successors of Genghis Khan,* pp. 139–42, 298–99; J. W. Dardess, "From Mongol Empire to Yüan Dynasty," pp. 117–65.

16. J. W. Dardess, "From Mongol Empire to Yüan Dynasty," p. 133; Abe Takeo, *Nishi Uiguru kokushi no kenkyū* (Tokyo, 1954), pp. 84–85.

17. J. A. Boyle, *The Successors of Genghis Khan,* pp. 266–69; L. Hambis, *Le Chapitre CVII du Yuan Che,* p. 115 n. 6; Tu Ch'i, *Meng-wu-erh shih-chi,* 76: 8a–10a.

18. *Yüan shih,* 8:8a, 9:20b; J. A. Boyle, *The Successors of Genghis Khan,* pp. 266, 323; Abe Takeo, *Nishi Uiguru Kokushi no Kenkyū,* pp. 80–84; J. W. Dardess, "From Mongol Empire to Yüan Dynasty," pp. 133–37.

19. J. W. Dardess, "From Mongol Empire to Yüan Dynasty," pp. 138–39.

20. L. Kwanten, "Chio-ssu-lo; The Role of the Tangut."

21. L. Kwanten, "Tibetan-Mongol Relations," pp. 124–32.

22. E. P. J. Mullie, "De Mongoolse Prins Nayan," *Mededelingen van de Konin-klijke Akademie der Wetenschappen* 26 (1964): 3–53.

23. F. W. Cleaves, "The Biography of Bayan of the Barin," pp. 185–301.

24. J. A. Boyle, *The Successors of Genghis Khan,* p. 329.

25. Ibid., pp. 139–41.

26. Su T'ien-chüeh, *Kuo-ch'ao ming-ch'en shih-lüeh,* 3: 9a.

27. Mostaert and Cleaves, *Les Lettres de 1289 et 1305*; E. Haenisch, "Zu den Briefen der mongolischen Il-khane Argun und Oljeitu," pp. 216–35.

28. J. W. Dardess, *Conquerors and Confucians,* p. 3, defines it as follows: "it must be noted that 'Confucianization'—the adoption by outsiders, even Chinese outsiders, of a certain system of ethical and political behavior—was as a process distinct from 'Sinicization,' which involved not only the loss of national and linguistic identity, but also a most un-Confucian denial of the facts of ancestry. . . ."

29. J. W. Dardess, *Conquerors and Confucians,* pp. 52–74; L. Hambis, "Note préliminaire à une biographie de Bayan le Märkit," *Journal Asiatique* 241 (1953): 215–48.

30. Those scholars who followed the teachings of the Sung scholar Chu Hsi. James T. C. Liu, "How did a Neo-Confucian School Become a State Orthodoxy?" pp. 483–505.

31. J. W. Dardess, *Conquerors and Confucians,* pp. 75 ff.

32. This was Kökö Temur, whose Chinese name was Wang Pao-pao (d.1375). John W. Dardess, "Kökö Temur," in L. Carrington Goodrich and Chaoying Fang, eds., *Dictionary of Ming Biography, 1368–1644.* 2 vols. (New York, 1976), pp. 724–28; J. W. Dardess, *Conquerors and Confucians,* pp. 148–56.

33. A. F. Wright, "Sui Yang-ti: Personality and Stereotype," in A. F. Wright, ed., *The Confucian Persuasion* (Stanford, 1960).

34. F. W. Mote, "Kao Chi," *Dictionary of Ming Biography,* p. 698, states that the period of compilation was from February to mid-September 1369. The most important feature is that the *Yüan shih* does not contain Confucian commentaries.

35. See, for example, C. O. Hucker, *China's Imperial Past.*

36. Based on A. Mostaert, *Textes Oraux Ordos* (Pei-p'ing, 1937), p. 133.

37. H. Serruys, *The Mongols in China During the Hung-wu Period* (Brussels, 1956–59); H. Serruys, *The Tribute System and Diplomatic Missions* (Brussels, 1967).

38. Ch'en Yüan, *Western and Central Asians in China under the Mongols.*

39. H. Franke, *Geld und Wirtschaft in China.*

40. Ever since the Han dynasty (206 B.C.–220 A.D.) China had been governed by a professional bureaucratic body whose income was derived not from personal wealth, but from salaries usually paid in both cash and kind. During the Yüan, cash payments were the standard practice.

41. Hok-lam Chan, "The Rise of Ming T'ai-tsu (1368–88): Facts and Fiction in Early Ming Historiography," *Journal of the American Oriental Society* 95 (1975) 679–715.

42. *Dictionary of Ming Biography,* pp. 381–92.

43. R. Grousset, *L'empire des steppes,* pp. 356ff., considers them as successors to the Il-khans.

44. The successor states to the Il-khans have been the subject of little research. The most recent study, and one of the very few, is J. M. Smith, Jr., *The History of the Sarbardar Dynasty, 1336–1381 A.D. and its Sources* (The Hague, 1970).

45. L. Ganshof van der Meersch, *Qu'est-ce que la féodalité?;* L. Krader, "Feudalism and Tatar Policy of the Middle Ages," *Comparative Studies in History and Society* 1 (1958): 74–94; A. N. Poliak, "La féodalité islamique," *Revue d'Etudes Islamiques* 12 (1938): 247–65.

46. *Encyclopédie de l'Islam,* 3: 43–44.

47. I. P. Petrushevsky, "Socio-Economic Condition," pp. 483–84.

48. F. Balodis, "Alt-Sarai und Neu-Sarai"; B. Spuler, *Die Goldene Horde,* pp. 264–69.

49. B. Spuler, *Die Goldene Horde,* pp. 121–35.

50. Ibid., pp. 126–27.

51. Ibid., pp. 136–59.

52. On the Cheremis and the Mordvin, D. Sinor, *Introduction,* pp. 21–26.

53. M. Mancall, *Russia and China. Their Diplomatic Relations to 1728* (Cambridge, Mass., 1971), pp. 9–31.

Chapter 10

1. *Dictionary of Ming Biography,* pp. 99–103.

2. J. W. Dardess, *Conquerors and Confucians,* pp. 121–22.

3. *Dictionary of Ming Biography,* pp. 15–17.

4. J. W. Dardess, *Conquerors and Confucians,* p. 127.

5. J. W. Dardess, "The Transformation of Messianic Rebellion," pp. 538–58; The importance of the scholar-official class in the creation of new dynasties is well illustrated by James B. Parsons, *The Peasant Rebellions of the Late Ming Dynasty* (Tucson, 1970).

7. *Dictionary of Ming Biography,* pp. 381–92; Wu Han, *Chu Yüan-chang* (Peking, 1949); for a critique of the sources, Hok-lam Chan, "The Rise of Ming T'ai-tsu."

8. H. Serruys, *The Mongols in China,* pp. 34–46.

9. Ibid., pp. 54–64; W. Fuchs, "Mongolen in Mittel- und Süd-China um 1388," *Oriens Extremus* 2 (1955): 175–203.

10. *Dictionary of Ming Biography,* pp. 602–8.

11. H. Serruys, *The Mongols in China,* pp. 89–119; Edward L. Farmer, *Early Ming Government. The Evolution of Two Capitals* (Cambridge, Mass., 1976), pp. 57–70.

12. These two terms, respectively, mean "the Southern Capital" and "the Northern Capital."

13. Inaba Iwakichi, "Mindai Ryoto no bashi," *Shigaku Zasshi* 24 (1913): 45–63, 77–89; H. Serruys, "Sino-Mongol Trade During the Ming Dynasty," *Journal of Asian History* 9 (1975): 34–56; Sechen Jagchid, *Pei-ya yu-mu min-tsu yü Chung-yüan nung-yeh min-tsu chien-ti ho-p'ing chan-cheng yü mao-i chih kuan-hsi* (Taipei, 1972).

14. The best study on the Ming dual capital system is the work by Edward L. Farmer already cited. On Chu Ti, *Dictionary of Ming Biography,* pp. 355–65.

15. B. Spuler, *Die Goldene Horde,* pp. 143–54; M. Zdan, "Stosunki litwesko-tatarskie za czasów Witolda w.ks. Litevy," *Ateneum Wileńskie* 3 (1930): 529–601; J. Pfitzner, *Grossfürst Witold von Litauen als Staatsman* (Brünn, 1930).

16. B. Spuler, *Die Goldene Horde,* p. 175.

17. B. Barthold, *Istoriya izucheniya vostoka v Evrope i Rossii,* Leningrad, 1925; Kapterev, N. F., *Kharakter otnosheniye Rossii k pravoslavnomu Vostoka,* Moscow, 1914.

18. Elias Ney, ed., and Denison Ross, trans., *A History of the Moghuls of Central Asia, Being the "Tarikh-i Rashidi" of Mirza Muhammad Haidar Dughlat* (London, 1898), p. 15.

19. Petis de la Croix, trans., *Histoire de Timur-Bec, connu sous le nom du Grand Tamerlan, Empereur des Mogols et Tartares* (Delft, 1723), 1: 175–94.

20. R. Grousset, *L'Empire des Steppes,* p. 497.

21. Petis de la Croix, *Histoire de Timur-Bec,* 1: 359, 361.

22. Ibid., 3: 363–71; 4: 93–97.

23. *The Cambridge History of India,* 3: 200. True to the Chingizid tradition, Timur ordered that artisans be spared and that they be sent to his capital, Samarqand, where they were to put their skills to use for the city's embellishment. On the Indian campaign, see also A. A. Semenov, *Gijasaddin Ali: Dnevnik pohoda Timura v Indija* (Moscow, 1958).

24. Walter J. Fishel, *Ibn Khaldun and Tamerlane: Their Historic Meeting in Damascus, 1401 A.D. (803 A.H.)* (Berkeley, 1952).

25. Tag as-Salmani, *Shams al-Husn. Eine Chronik vom Tode Timurs bis zum Jahre 1409,* trans. H. R. Roemer (Wiesbaden, 1956), pp. 26–28.

26. Ruy Gonzáles Clavijo, *Embajada a Tamerlan. Estudio y edición de un manuscrito del siglo XV,* ed. F. L. Estrada (Madrid, 1943); K. F. Neumann, *Reisen des Johannes Schiltberger* (Munich, 1859). On the relations between Timur and Charles VI, see Silvestre de Sacy, "Mémoire sur une correspondance inédite de Tamerlan avec Charles VI," *Mémoires de l'Académie des Inscriptions* 6 (1822): 470–522.

27. V. V. Barthold, *Four Studies on the History of Central Asia, Vol. 2, Ulugh Beg* (Leiden, 1958), p. 38.

28. R. Grousset, *L'Empire des Steppes,* p. 492, my translation.

29. According to the numismatic evidence for the area, the political structure of the Timurid state is a complicated matter. During Timur's reign, it was already a custom to strike currency in the name of the nominal Mongol ruler, even after his

death. Although Transoxiana was ruled by Ulugh-beg, coins were struck in the name of Shahrukh.

30. On this, see the works of Tag as-Salmani and V. V. Barthold referred to above. On the Timurid Abu Sa'id, see M. Quatremère, *Notice de l'ouvrage persan qui a pour titre "Matla-assadin" ou "madjma albahrein," et qui contient l'histoire des deux sultans Schah-rokh et Abou Said* (Paris, 1843).

31. *Dictionary of Ming Biography*, pp. 338–40.

32. J. F. Fletcher, "China and Central Asia, 1368–1884," in Fairbank, *The Chinese World Order*, pp. 209–17.

33. For their biographical notices, *Dictionary of Ming Biography*, pp. 15–17, 1290–93, 1293–94.

34. Maidiribala's allegiance was doubtful, for he had spent four years in China (1370–1374) as a prisoner. When he was released, he tried to negotiate a treaty between his father and the Chinese.

35. *Dictionary of Ming Biography*, pp. 1083–85.

36. L. Hambis, *Documents sur l'histoire des Mongols*, p. 18.

37. W. Franke, "Yung-lo's *Mongolei-Feldzüge*," *Sinologische Arbeiten* 3 (1945): 1–54; W. Franke, "Chinesische Feldzüge durch die Mongolei im frühen 15. Jahrhundert," *Sinologica* 3 (1951–53): 81–88; L. Hambis, *Documents sur l'histoire des Mongols*, pp. 94–97.

38. *Dictionary of Ming Biography*, pp. 416–20.

39. L. Hambis, *Documents sur l'histoire des Mongols*, p. 99.

40. Ibid., pp. 100–101; *Dictionary of Ming Biography*, pp. 289–94, 294–97, 1347–48.

41. H. Serruys, *Genealogical Tables of the Descendants of Dayan-qan* (The Hague, 1958); Wada Sei, "A Study of Dayan Khan," *Memoirs of the Research Department of the Toyo Bunko* 19 (1960): 1–42.

42. *Dictionary of Ming Biography*, pp. 683–85.

43. L. Hambis, *Documents sur l'histoire des Mongols*, pp. 47–52.

44. Ibid., pp. 54–55.

45. Yang Lien-sheng, "Historical Notes on the Chinese World Order," in Fairbank, *The Chinese World Order*, pp. 20–33.

46. L. Hambis, *Documents sur l'histoire des Mongols*, pp. 59–60; *Dictionary of Ming Biography*, pp. 252–55, 1503–5.

47. *Dictionary of Ming Biography*, pp. 53–61, 1369–74.

48. H. Serruys, *The Tribute System and Diplomatic Missions*; H. Serruys, "Four Documents Relating to the Sino-Mongol Peace of 1570–1571," *Monumenta Serica* 19 (1960): 1–66; L. Hambis, *Documents sur l'histoire des Mongols*, pp. 64–73, where the date is given as 1570.

49. R. Kaschewsky, *Das Leben des lamaistischen Heiligen Tsonghkapa bLo-bzan-grags-pa (1357–1419)* (Wiesbaden, 1971); H. Hoffmann, *Die Religionen Tibets. Bon und Lamaismus in ihres geschichtlichen Entwicklung* (Freiburg/München, 1956).

50. *Dictionary of Ming Biography*, pp. 22–23.

51. See Chapter 8, pp. 201–2.

52. W. Heissig, "Zur geistige Leitung der neubekehrten Mongolen des späten 16. und frühen 17. Jahrhunderts," *Ural-Altaische Jahrbücher* 26 (1954): 101ff.; Sh. Bira, *Mongolian Historical Literature of the XVII–XIX Centuries Written in Tibetan*, trans. Stanley N. Frye (Bloomington, Ind., 1970).

53. R. J. Miller, *Monasteries and Culture Change in Inner Mongolia* (Wiesbaden, 1959), pp. 1–10, 24–31.

54. This did not prevent the Mongolian People's Republic from making Chinggis-khan one of its national heroes.

55. George V. Lantzeff, *Siberia in the Seventeenth Century: A Study of the Colonial Administration* (Berkeley, 1943); Raymond M. Fischer, *The Russian Fur Trade, 1550–1700* (Berkeley, 1943); V. I. Shemkov, *Ocherki po istorii kolonizatii Sibiri v. XVII–nachale XVIII v.v.* (Moscow, 1946).

56. The term *conquest* has to be given a very broad definition, as no organized military campaign was undertaken.

57. M. Mancall, *Russia and China,* pp. 11–20.

58. H. Serruys, *Sino-Jürced Relations During the Yung-lo Period,* pp. 64–66.

59. R. Oxnam, *Ruling From Horseback,* pp. 15–37; Arthur W. Hummel, ed., *Eminent Chinese of the Ch'ing Period* (Washington, D.C., 1943), pp. 1–3, 594–99.

60. His original title had been *Sure Beile,* "the wise prince." His new title means "the wise, respected emperor." *Ta-ch'ing man-chou shih-lu,* pp. 123–24.

61. On the banner system, Robert H. G. Lee, *The Manchurian Frontier in Ch'ing History* (Cambridge, Mass., 1970), pp. 24–40. On the *Li-fan yüan,* M. Mancall, "The Ch'ing Tribute System: An Interpretative Essay," in Fairbank, *The Chinese World Order,* pp. 72–75. Although the *Li-fan yüan* was an important Manchu institution, it has not yet been subjected to serious inquiry, even though its collected statutes, the *Ch'in-ting Li-fan yüan tse-li* and the *Ch'in-ting Li-fan yüan pu tse-li,* are still in existence.

62. On these matters, and for an appropriate bibliography, see K. Sagaster, *Subud Erike. "Ein Rosenkranz aus Perlen," Die Biographie des I. Pekinger Lcan-skya Khu-tukhtu Nag dban blo bzan c'os ldan* (Wiesbaden, 1967), pp. 83–136.

63. S. Jagchid, "The Manchu Ch'ing Policy Towards Mongolian Religion," in W. Heissig et al., eds., *Tractata Altaica. Denis Sinor sexagenario optime de rebus altaicis merito dedicata* (Wiesbaden, 1976), pp. 301–20.

64. On this, W. Fuchs, "Galdanica. Miszellen zum Kriege Kanghsi's gegen Galdan," *Monumenta Serica* 9 (1944): 174–98; and especially I. Ya. Zlatkin, *Istoria dzhungarskogo khanstva (1635–1758)* (Moscow, 1964).

Chapter 11

1. L. W. Moses, "T'ang Tribute Relations," pp. 61–64.

2. See the author's forthcoming review of Tao Jing-shen, *The Jürchen in Twelfth Century China,* in the *Journal of the American Oriental Society.*

3. The name of the school is derived from its periodical, *Annales: Economies, Sociétés, Civilisations,* which was founded in 1929. The dominant work of this school is the famous work by F. Braudel, *La Méditerranée et le monde méditerranéen à l'époque de Philip II,* 2 vols., rev. ed. (Paris, 1966); trans. Siân Reynolds, *The Mediterranean and The Mediterranean in the Age of Philip II* (New York, 1972–73).

4. For a study of the principles of the school and F. Braudel's historical thought in particular, see J. H. Hexter, "Fernand Braudel and Le Monde Braudellien . . ." *Journal of Modern History* 44 (1972): 480–539.

5. Probably the perennial wars between the Golden Horde and the Il-khans over the grazing lands of Arran and Adherbaidjan, and the wars between the Il-khans and the Chaghatai Khanate over the Badghis Meadows in Khurassan have to be examined in this light.

6. On the assumption that a generation lasted forty years on the average, three generations of Mongols had been subjected to the sedentarization trends.

Selected Bibliography

Books

Ammann, A. M. *Kirchenpolitische Wandlungen im Ostbaltikum bis zum Tode Alexander Nevskis*. Rome, 1936.

Andreski, Stanislav. *Military Organization and Society*. 2d. edition. Berkeley, 1968.

Aubin, Françoise, ed. *Etudes Song/Sung Studies*. Paris, 1970.

Barthold, W. *Turkestan Down to the Mongol Invasion*. Oxford, 1928.

Baskakov, N. A. *Nogajsko-russkij slovar'*. Moscow, 1963.

Becquet, J., and L. Hambis. *Jean de Plan Carpin: Histoire des Mongols*. Paris, 1965.

Bezzola, G. A. *Die Mongolen in abendländisches Sicht. (1220–1270): ein Beitrag zum Frage der Völkerbegegnungen*. Bern, 1974.

Bielenstein, H. *The Restoration of the Han Dynasty*. 3 vols. Stockholm, 1954, 1959, 1967.

Bosworth, C. E. *The Ghaznavids: Their Empire in Afghanistan and Eastern Iran, 994–1040*. Edinburgh, 1963.

———. *The Islamic Dynasties. A Chronological and Genealogical Survey*. Edinburgh, 1967.

———. *The Later Ghaznavids, Splendor and Decay*. New York, 1977.

Boyle, J. A., trans. *The History of the World-Conqueror by 'Ala al-Din 'Ata-Malik Juvaini*. 2 vols. Manchester, 1950.

———. *The Successors of Genghis Khan*. New York, 1971.

Brand, Charles M., trans. *Deeds of John and Manuel Comnenus*. New York, 1976.

Braudel, Fernand. *La Méditerranée et le monde méditerranéen à l'époque de Philip II*. 2 vols. Paris, 1966.

Cahen, Claude. *La Syrie du Nord à l'époque des Croisades et la principauté franque d'Antioche*. Paris, 1940.

Carroll, Thomas D. *Account of the T'u-yü-hun in the History of the Chin Dynasty*. Berkeley, 1953.

Chang Pi-ta et al., eds. *Sung-jen ch'üan-chi tzu-liao so-yin*. 6 vols. Taipei, 1975–76.

Chapman, C. *Michel Paléologue. Restaurateur de l'empire byzantin (1261–1282)*. Paris, 1926.

Chavannes, E. *Mission archéologique dans la Chine septentrionale*. 3 vols. Paris, 1913–15.

Ch'en Yüan. *Western and Central Asians in China under the Mongols*. Translated by Ch'ien Hsing-hai and L. Carrington Goodrich. Los Angeles, 1966.

Clark, Larry V. "Introduction to the Uyghur Civil Documents of East Turkestan." Ph.D. dissertation, Indiana University, 1975.

Dardess, John W. *Conquerors and Confucians. Aspects of Political Change in Late Yüan China*. New York, 1973.

Dawson, C. *The Mongol Missions*. London, 1955.

De Groot, J. J. M. *Chinesische Urkunden zur Geschichte Asiens. I. Die Hunnen der vorchristlichen Zeit. II. Die Westlande Chinas in der vorchristlichen Zeit*. Berlin-Leipzig, 1921, 1929.

Demiéville, P. *Le Concile de Lhasa*. Paris, 1952.

Des Rotours, R. *Histoire de Ngan Lou-chan*. Paris, 1962.

———. *Traité des fonctionnaires et traité de l'armée*. 2 vols. Leiden, 1947.

Drake, H., trans. *The Book of Government, or Rules for Kings*. London, 1960.

Eberhard, W. *Das Toba-Reich Nordchinas. Eine soziologische Untersuchung*. Leiden, 1949.

Eckman, J. *Chaghatay Manual*. Bloomington, Ind., 1966.

Fairbank, J. K., ed. *The Chinese World Order: Traditional China's Foreign Relations*. Cambridge, Mass., 1968.

Farmer, Edward L. *Early Ming Government. The Evolution of Two Capitals*. Cambridge, Mass., 1976.

Feng Chia-sheng. *Liao shih yüan-liu k'o yö Liao shih ch'u chiao*. Yenching Hsüeh-pao. Monograph Series, no. 5. Pei-p'ing, 1933.

Fischer, David H. *Historians' Fallacies. Toward a Logic of Historical Thought*. New York, 1970.

Fishel, Walter J. *Ibn Khaldun and Tamerlane: Their Historic Meeting in Damascus, 1401 A.D. (803 A.H.)*. Berkeley, 1952.

Franke, H. *Geld und Wirtschaft in China unter der Mongolenherrschaft*. Leipzig, 1949.

Franke, O. *Geschichte des chinesischen Reiches*. 5 vols. Berlin, 1948–54.

Gabain, A. von. *Das Leben im uigurischen Königreich von Qocho (850–1250)*. Wiesbaden, 1973.

Ghirshman, R. *Les Chionites-Hephtalites*. Cairo, 1948.

Goodrich, L. Carrington, and Chaoying Fang, eds. *Dictionary of Ming Biography, 1368–1644*. 2 vols. New York, 1976.

Gottschalk, H. L. *Al-Malik al-Kamil von Egypten und seine Zeit. Ein Studie zur Geschichte Vorderasiens und Egypten in der ersten Hälfte des 7/13 Jahrhunderts*. Wiesbaden, 1958.

Grousset, R. *L'Empire des Steppes*. 3d ed. Paris, 1965.

Haeger, J. W., ed. *Crisis and Prosperity in Sung China*. Tucson, 1975.

Haenisch, E. *Die Geheime Geschichte der Mongolen*. Leipzig, 1941.

―――. *Steuergerechtsame der chinesischen Kloster unter der Mongolen-Herrschaft*. Leipzig, 1940.

Hambis, L. *Le Chapitre CVII du Yuan Che*. Leiden, 1954.

―――. *Documents sur l'histoire des Mongols à l'époque des Ming*. Paris, 1969.

Hamilton, J. R. *Les Ouighours à l'époque des Cinq Dynasties*. Paris, 1955.

Harada Tanashige. *Jōkan seiyō teikan*. Tokyo, 1962.

Henthorn, W. E. *Korea : The Mongol Invasions*. Leiden, 1963.

Herskovitz, M. J. *Acculturation. The Study of Culture Contact*. New York, 1938.

Hiroaki Yamaji. *A Juchen-Japanese-English Glossary*. Tokyo, 1956.

Hodgson, G. S. *The Order of the Assassins. The Struggle of the Early Nizari Isma'ili's against the Islamic World*. The Hague, 1955.

Horst, H. *Die Staatsverwaltung der Grossseljuqen und Horazmshahs*. Wiesbaden, 1964.

Hsiang Ta. *T'ang-tai Ch'ang-an yü Hsi-yü wen-ming*. Peking, 1933.

Hsiao Ch'i-ch'ing. *The Military Establishment of the Yüan Dynasty*. Cambridge, Mass., in press.

Hucker, Charles O. *China's Imperial Past. An Introduction to Chinese History and Culture*. Stanford, 1975.

Irons, William, and N. Dyson-Hudson, eds. *Perspectives on Nomadism*. Leiden, 1972.

Ise Suntarō. *Chūgoku seiichi keieishi kenkyū*. Tokyo, 1968.

Jahn, Karl. *Ta'rīḫ-i-Mubārak-i Ġāzāni des Rašid al-Din. Geschichte der Ilḫāne Abāgā bis Gāihatū* (The Hague, 1957).

Khetagurov, L. A., et al., trans. *Rashid al-Din. Sbornik Letopisi*. Moscow-Leningrad, 1946–60.

Kiyose Gisaburo. *A Study of the Jürchen Language and Script in the Hua-i i-yü with Special Reference to the Problem of its Decipherment*. Kyoto, 1977.

Kollautz, A., and Hisayuki Miyakawa. *Geschichte und Kultur eines völkerwanderungs-*

zeitlichen Nomadenvolkes. Die Jou-jan der Mongolei und die Awaren in Mitteleuropa. 2 vols. Klagenfurt, 1970.

Kritzeck, J., and R. B. Winder, eds. *The World of Islam: Studies in Honour of Philip K. Nitti.* New York, 1959.

Kwanten, L. *The Analysis of the Tangut (Hsi Hsia) Language: Sino-Tibetan or Altaic?* Bloomington, Ind., 1977.

———. "Tibetan-Mongol Relations During the Yüan-Dynasty, 1206–1368." Ph.D. Dissertation, University of South Carolina, 1972.

Kychanov, E. I. *Ocherk Istorii Tangutskogo Gosudarstva.* Moscow, 1968.

Le Strange, G. *Mesopotamia and Persia under the Mongols in the Fourteenth Century A.D. From the Nuzhat al-Qulub of Hamd Allah Mustaufi.* London, 1903.

Lee, Robert H. G. *The Manchurian Frontier in Ch'ing History.* Cambridge, Mass., 1970.

Lech, Klaus. *Das mongolische Weltreich. al-'Umari's Darstellung der mongolischen Reiche in seinem Werk Masālik al-abṣār fī mamālik al-amṣar.* Wiesbaden, 1968.

Levy, Howard S. *Biography of An Lu-shan.* Berkeley, 1961.

———. *Biography of Huang Ch'ao.* Berkeley, 1955.

Li Shu-t'ung. *T'ang-shih k'ao-pien.* Taipei, 1965.

Li Tao. *Hsü Tzu-chih-t'ung-chien ch'ang-pien.* Chekiang shu-chü, 1881.

Liu Mau-tsai. *Die chinesischen Nachrichten zur Geschichte der Ost-Türken (T'u-küe).* Wiesbaden, 1958.

———. *Kutscha und seine Beziehungen zu China von 2. Jhr. bis zum 6. Jhr. n. Chr.* Wiesbaden, 1969.

Lo Fu-ch'eng. *Ju-chen i-yü.* Dairen, 1934.

Lombard-Sulman, Claudine. *Un exemple d'acculturation chinoise. La province de Gui zhou au XVIIIe siècle.* Paris, 1972.

Mancall, M. *Russia and China. Their Diplomatic Relations to 1728.* Cambridge, Mass., 1971.

Manchen-Helfen, O. *The World of the Huns. Studies in Their History and Culture.* Berkeley, 1973.

Mangold, G. *Das Militärwesen in China unter der Mongolen-Herrschaft.* Bamberg, 1971.

Martin, H. Desmond. *The Rise of Chingis-khan and His Conquest of North China.* Baltimore, 1950.

Maspero, H., and E. Balaźs. *Histoire et Institutions de la Chine Ancienne.* Paris, 1967.

Mirsky, J. *Sir Aurel Stein, Archeological Explorer.* Chicago, 1977.

Molè, Gabriella. *The T'u-yü-hun from the Northern Wei to the Time of the Five Dynasties.* Rome, 1970.

Mostaert, A., and F. W. Cleaves, eds. *Les Lettres de 1289 et 1305 des Ilkhans Arghun et Oljeitu à Philippe le Bel.* Cambridge, Mass., 1962.

Mullie, E. P. J. *De Mongoolse Prins Nayan.* Brussels, 1964.

Nakano, Miyoko. *A Phonological Study of the 'Phags-pa Script and the Meng-ku tzu-yün.* Canberra, 1971.

Nishida Tatsuo. *Seikagu no kenkyū.* 2 vols. Tokyo, 1964–66.

Olbricht, P. *Das Postwesen in China unter der Mongolenherrschaft im 13. und 14. Jahrhundert.* Wiesbaden, 1954.

Olschki, L. *Guillaume Boucher.* Baltimore, 1946.

Ostrogorsky, G. *Geschichte des byzantinischen Staates.* Munich, 1940.

Otagi Matsuo. *Kittan Kodai shi no kenkyū*. Kyoto, 1959.

Oxnam, Robert B. *Ruling from Horseback. Manchu Politics in the Oboi Regency, 1661–1669*. Chicago, 1975.

Pelliot, P. *L'Histoire secrète des Mongols*. Paris, 1949.

―――. *Les Mongols et la Papauté*. Paris, 1933.

―――. *Notes on Marco Polo*. 2 vols. Paris, 1959.

―――. *Notes sur l'histoire de la Horde d'Or*. Paris, 1950.

――― and L. Hambis. *Histoire des Campagnes de Genghis Khan*. vol. 1. Leiden, 1951.

Perry, J. C., and B. L. Smith, eds. *Essays on T'ang Society*. Leiden, 1976.

Petrushevsky, I. P. *Zemledelie i agrarnie otnosheniya v Irana XII–XIV vekov*. Leningrad, 1960.

Pfeiffer, N. *Die ungarische Dominikaerprovinz von ihre Gründung bis zum Tartarenverwüstung, 1241–1242*. Zürich, 1913.

Phaire, B. R. "Papal Motivations for an Asian Apostolate (1245–1254), An Analysis." Ph.D. dissertation, New York University, 1972.

Pinks, E. *Die Uiguren von Kan-chou in den frühen Sung-Zeit (960–1028)*. Wiesbaden, 1968.

Prušek, J. *Chinese Statelets and the Northern Barbarians in the Period 1400–300 B.C.* Dordrecht, 1971.

Pulleyblank, E. G. *The Background of the Rebellion of An Lu-shan*. London, 1955.

Raverty, H. G., trans. *The Tabaqat-i Nasiri by Juzjani*. 2 vols. London, 1881, 1899.

Rogers, Michael C. *The Chronicle of Fu Chien. A Case of Exemplary History*. Berkeley, 1968.

Sagaster, K. *Subud Erike. "Ein Rosenkranz aus Perlen," Die Biographie des I. Pekinger Lcan-skya Khutukhtu Nag dban blo bzan c'os ldan*. Wiesbaden, 1967.

―――. *Die Weisse Geschichte. Eine mongolische Quelle zur Lehre von den Beiden Ordnungen Religion und Staat in Tibet und der Mongolei*. Wiesbaden, 1976.

Schlegel, D. "Hao Ching (1222–1275), ein chinesischen Berater des Kaisers Kublai Khan." Habilitationsschrift, Munich, 1966.

Schurmann, H. F. *Economic Structure of the Yüan Dynasty*. Cambridge, Mass., 1956.

Schwarz-Schilling, Ch. *Die Friede von Shan-yüan (1005 n. Chr.). Ein Beitrag zur Geschichte der chinesischen Diplomatie*. Wiesbaden, 1959.

Serruys, H. *The Mongols in China During the Hung-wu Period*. Brussels, 1956–59.

―――. *Sino-Jürčed Relations During the Yung-lo Period 1403–1424*. Wiesbaden, 1955.

―――. *The Tribute System and Diplomatic Missions*. Brussels, 1967.

Sinor, D. *Inner Asia. A Syllabus*. Bloomington, Ind. 1969.

―――. *Introduction à l'Etude de l'Eurasie Centrale*. Wiesbaden, 1963.

Smith, J. M., Jr. *The History of the Sarbardar Dynasty, 1336–1381 A.D. and its Sources*. The Hague, 1970.

Spector, Stanley. *Li Hung-chang and the Huai Army. A Study in Nineteenth Century Regionalism*. Seattle, 1963.

Spuler, B. *Die Goldene Horde. Die Mongolen in Russland, 1223–1502*. 2d. ed. Wiesbaden, 1965.

―――. *Die Mongolen in Iran. Politik, Verwaltung und Kultur der Ilchanen-Zeit, 1220–1350*. Berlin, 1955.

―――, ed. *History of the Mongols. Based on Eastern and Western Accounts of the Thirteenth and Fourteenth Centuries*. Berkeley, 1972.

Starikov, V. S., et al. *Materialy po deshifrovke kidan'skogo pis'ma*. Moscow, 1970.

Sudo Yoshiyuki. *Sō-dai keizai-shi kenkyū*. Tokyo, 1962.

Tag as-Salmani. *Shams al-Husn. Eine Chronik von Tode Timurs bis zum Jahre 1409.* Translated by H. R. Roemer. Wiesbaden, 1956.

T'ang Ch'ang-ju. *T'ang-shu ping-chih chien-cheng.* Peking, 1962.

Tao Jing-shen. *The Jürchen in Twelfth Century China. A Study of Sinicization.* Seattle, 1976.

Thiele, D. *Der Abschluss eines Vertrages. Diplomatie zwischen Sung- und Chin-Dynastie, 1117–1123.* Wiesbaden, 1971.

Tiesenhausen, W. de. *Recueil des matériaux relatifs à l'histoire de la Horde d'Or.* Vol. 1, *Extraits des ouvrages arabes.* St. Petersburg, 1884.

Trever, C. *Excavations in Northern Mongolia.* Leningrad, 1932.

Ts'en Chung-mien. *Hsi T'u-chüeh shih-liao po-ch'üeh chi k'ao-cheng.* Shanghai, 1958.

Tseng Yang-feng. *Chung-kuo yen-cheng shih.* Taipei, 1966.

Tsukamoto, Z. *Wei Shou. Treatise on Buddhism and Taoism.* Translated by L. Hurvitz. Kyoto, 1956.

Twitchett, D. *Financial Administration under the T'ang Dynasty.* Cambridge, 1963.

Van Oost, J. *Au Pays des Ortos (Mongolie).* Paris, 1933.

Vernadsky, G. *The Mongols and Russia.* New Haven, 1953.

Vladimirtsov, B. I. *Genghis-khan.* Paris, 1948.

―――. *Le régime social des Mongols. Le féodalisme nomade.* Paris, 1948.

Vorob'ev, M. V. *Chzhurchzheni i gosudarstvo tszin'.* Moscow, 1975.

Waley, A. *Travels of an Alchemist.* London, 1931.

Wan Lo, Winston. *The Life and Thought of Yeh Shih.* Hong Kong, 1974.

Wang Shou-nan. *T'ang-tai fan-chen yü chung-yang kuan-hsi chih yen-chiu.* Taipei, 1969.

Ware, J. R., trans. *Alchemy, Medicine, Religion in China in A.D. 320.* Cambridge, Mass., 1966.

Watson, B., trans. *Records of the Great Historian of China. Translations from the Shih Chi by Ssu-ma Ch'ien.* 2 vols. New York, 1961.

Wechsler, H. J. *Mirror to the Son of Heaven. Wei Cheng at the Court of T'ang T'ai-tsung.* New Haven, 1974.

Wilhelm, R. *The I-ching, or Book of Changes.* New York, 1950.

Wittfogel, K. A., and Feng Chia-sheng. *History of Chinese Society. Liao (907–1125).* Philadelphia, 1949.

Wright, A. F., and D. C. Twitchett, eds. *Perspectives on the T'ang.* New Haven, 1973.

Yakubovskii, A. Y. *Zolotaya Ordo i cye podenie.* Moscow, 1950.

Yü Ying-shih. *Trade and Expansion in Han China: A Study in the Structure of Sino-Barbarian Relations.* Berkeley, 1967.

Zlatkin, I. Ya. *Istoria dzhungarskogo khanstva (1635–1758).* Moscow, 1964.

Zürcher, E. *The Buddhist Conquest of China.* 2 vols. Leiden, 1959.

Articles

Balazs, E. "Chinesische Geschichtswerke als Wegweiser zum Praxis der Bürokratie." *Saeculum* 8 (1957): 210–23.

Balodis, F. "Alt-Sarai und Neu-Sarai, die Hauptstadt der goldenen Horde." *Latvijas Universitates Raksti* 13 (1926): 3–82.

Bausani, A. "Religion under the Mongols." In *The Cambridge History of Iran,* 5: 538–49.

Bazin, L. "Recherches sur les parlers T'o-pa (5e siècle après J.C.)." *T'oung Pao* 39 (1950): 228–329.

Blake, R. P., and R. N. Frye. "History of the Nation of Archers (The Mongols) by Grigor of Akanc'." *Harvard Journal of Asiatic Studies* 12 (1949): 269–399.

Boodberg, P. A. "The Language of the T'o-pa Wei," *Harvard Journal of Asiatic Studies* 1 (1936): 167–85.

Bosworth, C. E. "The Political and Dynastic History of the Iranian World (A.D. 1000–1217)." In *Cambridge History of Iran*, 5: 1–202.

Boyle, J. A. "The Death of the last 'Abbasid Caliph: a Contemporary Muslim Account." *Journal of Semitic Studies* 6 (1961): 145–61.

———. "Dynastic and Political History of the Il-khans." In *Cambridge History of Iran*, 5: 303–421.

———. "The Journey of He'tum I, King of Little Armenia, to the Court of the Great Khan Möngke." *Central Asiatic Studies* 9 (1964): 175–89.

Cahen, C. "L'évolution de l'iqtā' du IXe au XIIIe siècle." *Annales: Economies, Sociétés, Civilisations* 8 (1953).

———. "Les tribus turques de l'Asie Occidentale pendant la période Seljukide." *Wiener Zeitschrift für die Kunde des Morgenlandes* 51 (1948–52): 178–87.

Chan Hok-lam. "Liu Ping-chung (1216–1274). A Buddhist-Taoist Statesman at the Court of Qubilai Khan." *T'oung Pao* 53 (1967): 96–146.

———. "Prolegomena to the Ju-nan i-shih. A Memoir of the Last Chin Court under the Mongol Siege of 1234." *Sung Studies Newsletter*, no. 10 (1974): 2–19.

———. "The Rise of Ming T'ai-tsu (1368–88): Facts and Fiction in Early Ming Historiography." *Journal of the American Oriental Society* 95 (1975): 679–715.

Ch'en Yin-k'o. "Lun T'ang Kao-tsu ch'eng-ch'en yü T'u-chüeh shih." *Ling-nan Hsüeh-pao* 11 (1951): 1–9.

Cleaves, F. W. "The Biography of Bayan of the Barin in the Yüan Shih." *Harvard Journal of Asiatic Studies* 19 (1956): 185–303.

———. "The Boy and his Elephant." *Harvard Journal of Asiatic Studies* 35 (1975): 14–59.

———. "A Chinese Source Bearing on Marco Polo's Departure from China and a Persian Source on his Arrival in Persia." *Harvard Journal of Asiatic Studies* 36 (1976): 181–203.

———. "Darugha and Gerege." *Harvard Journal of Asiatic Studies* 16 (1953): 237–59.

———. "The Historicity of the Baljuna Covenant." *Harvard Journal of Asiatic Studies* 18 (1955): 357–421.

———. "The Sino-Mongolian Inscription of 1362 in Memory of Prince Hindu." *Harvard Journal of Asiatic Studies* 12 (1949): 1–133.

Dardess, J. W. "From Mongol Empire to Yüan Dynasty: Changing Forms of Imperial Rule in Mongolia and Central Asia." *Monumenta Serica* 30 (1972–73): 117–65.

———. "The Transformation of Messianic Rebellion and the Founding of the Ming Dynasty." *Journal of Asian Studies* 29 (1970): 539-58.

Des Rotours, R. "Les grands fonctionnaires des provinces en Chine sous la dynastie des T'ang." *T'oung Pao* 25 (1927): 219–332.

Eberhard, W. "Chronologische Uebersicht über die Geschichte der Hunnen von späteren Han-Zeit." *Türk Tarih Kuruma Belleten* 4 (1940): 387–435.

Ecsedy, H. "Trade and War Relations Between the Turks and China in the Second Half of the 6th Century." *Acta Orientalia Hungaricae* 21 (1968): 131–80.

———. "Tribe and Tribal Society in the 6th Century Turk Empire." *Acta Orientalia Hungaricae* 25 (1972): 245–62.

Ejima Hisao. "Mindai Jochoku chōkō bōeki no gaikan." *Shien* 77 (1958): 1–12.

———. "Mindai Jochoku no uma." *Shien* 62 (1954): 93–115.

Esin, E. "Tarkhan Nizak or Tarkhan Tirek? An Enquiry Concerning the Prince of

Badhghis who in A.H.91/A.D.709–710 Opposed the 'Ommayyad Conquest of Central Asia." *Journal of the American Oriental Society* 97 (1977): 323–32.

Ferenczy, M. "Chinese Historiographers' Views on Barbarian-Chinese Relations (14–16th C.)." *Acta Orientalia Hungaricae* 21 (1968): 353–62.

Franke, H. "Chinese Texts on the Jürchen. A Translation of the Jürchen Monograph in the San-ch'ao pei-meng hui-pien." *Zentralasiatische Studien* 9 (1975): 119–86.

———. "Treaties Between Sung and Chin." In F. Aubin, ed., *Etudes Song/Sung Studies*. Pp. 55–84.

Fuchs, W. "Galdanica. Miszellen zum Kriege Kanghsi's gegen Galdan." *Monumenta Serica* 9 (1944): 174–98.

———. "Mongolen in Mittel- und Süd-China um 1388." *Oriens Extremus* 2 (1955): 175–203.

Frye, R. N. "Notes on the History of Transoxiana." *Harvard Journal of Asiatic Studies* 19 (1956): 106–25.

Graf, A. "Die Tartaren im Spiegel der byzantinische Literatur." In *Jubilee Volume in Honour of Professor Bernhard Heller* (Budapest, 1941). Pp. 77–85.

Grumel, W. "La défense maritime de Constantinople du côté de la Corne d'Or et le siège des Avares." *Byzantoslavica* 25 (1964): 217–33.

Haeger, J. W. "1126–27: Political Crisis and Integrity of Culture." In J. W. Haeger, ed., *Crisis and Prosperity in Sung China*. Pp. 143–61.

———. "The Intellectual Context of Neo-Confucian Syncretism." *Journal of Asian Studies* 31 (1972): 499–513.

Haenisch, E. "Zu den Briefen der mongolischen Il-khane Argun und Öljeitü an den König Philipp den Schönen von Frankreich (1289 und 1305)." *Oriens* 2 (1948): 216–35.

Halperin, C. J. "A Chingissid Saint of the Russian Orthodox Church: 'The Life of Peter, *Tsarevitch* of the Horde.'" *Canadian-American Slavic Studies* 9 (1975): 324–35.

Hambis, L. "Note préliminaire à une biographie de Bayan le Märkit." *Journal Asiatique* 249 (1953): 215–48.

Hamilton, J. R. "Toquz-Oghuz et On-Uyghur" *Journal Asiatique* (1962): 23–63.

Hannestad, K. "Les relations de Byzance avec la Transcaucasie et l'Asie Centrale aux 5è et 6è siècles." *Byzantion* 25/27 (1955–57): 423–56.

Henning, W. B. "The Date of the Sogdian Ancient Letters." *Bulletin of the School of Oriental and African Studies* 12 (1948): 601–15.

Hexter, J. H. "Fernand Braudel and Le Monde Braudellien . . ." *Journal of Modern History* 44 (1972): 480–539.

Ho Ping-ti. "An Estimate of the Total Population of Sung-Chin China." In F. Aubin, ed., *Etudes Song/Sung Studies*. Pp. 33–53.

Horst, H. "Eine Gesandschaft des Mamluken al-Malik an-Nasir an Il-han-Hof in Persien." In W. Hauerbach, ed., *Orient in der Forschung. Das Festschrift für Otto Spies*. Wiesbaden, 1967. Pp. 348–70.

Houtsma, M. Th. "Die Ghuzenstämme." *Wiener Zeitschrift für die Kunde des Morgenlandes* 2 (1888): 219–33.

Hung, W. "The Transmission of the Book Known as the Secret History of the Mongols." *Harvard Journal of Asiatic Studies* 14 (1951): 432–92.

Jahn, K. "Das iranische Papiergeld." *Archiv Orientalni* 10 (1938): 308–40.

Jenkins, G. "A Note on Climatic Cycles and the Rise of Chinggis Khan." *Central Asiatic Journal* 18 (1974): 217–26.

Kiyoshi Yabuuchi. "Gen-min rehikō shih." *Tōhō Gakuhō* 14 (1944):

Kollautz, A. "Die Awaren. Die Schichtung in einer Nomaden-Herrschaft." *Saeculum* 5 (1954): 129–78.

———. "Awaren, Franken und Slaven in Karantanien und Niederpannonien und die fränkische und byzantinische Mission." *Carinthia I* 156 (1966).

Krader, L. "Feudalism and Tatar Policy of the Middle Ages." *Comparative Studies in History and Society* 1 (1958): 74–94.

Kwanten, L. "The Career of Muqali: A Reassessment." *Sung Studies Newsletter*, no. 13 (1978), forthcoming.

———. "China and Tibet During the Northern Sung." *Oriens Extremus* 22 (1975): 161–67.

———. "Chinggis-khan's Conquest of Tibet. Myth or Reality?" *Journal of Asian History* 8 (1974): 1–22.

———. "Chio-ssu-lo (997–1068). A Tibetan Ally of the Northern Sung" *Rocznik Orientalistyczny* 39 (1977): 92–106.

———. "Fuentes para el estudio de la historia de Mongolia." *Estudios de Asia y Africa* 12 (1977): 37–66.

———. "The Nature of Tibetan-Mongol Relations. A Critique of the Caghan Teüke." *Journal of the American Oriental Society* (forthcoming).

———. "New Directions in Tangut (Hsi Hsia) Philological Research." *Sung Studies Newsletter*, no. 11–12 (1977): 50–53.

———. "Tangut Miscellanea. I. On the Inventor of the Tangut Script." *Journal of the American Oriental Society* 97 (1977): 333–35.

Kychanov, E. I. "Les guerres entre les Sung du Nord et le Hsi Hsia." In F. Aubin, ed., *Etudes Song/Sung Studies*. Pp. 103–18.

Levenson, J. R. "T'ien-hsia and Kuo and the Transvaluation of Values." *Far Eastern Quarterly* 11 (1952): 447–51.

Liu, J. T. C. "How Did a Neo-Confucian School Become a State Orthodoxy?" *Philosophy East and West* 23 (1973): 483–505.

Matsumoto Yoshimi. "Gendai ni okeru shusei no sōritsu." *Tōhō Gakuhō* 2 (1940): 328–37.

Menges, K. H. "Tungusen und Ljao." *Abhandlungen für die Kunde des Morgenlandes* 38, pt. 1 (1968): 1–60.

Miller, R. A. "Review of R. Shafer: *Introduction to Sino-Tibetan*." *Monumenta Serica* 27 (1968): 398–435.

———. "Sino-Tibetan: Inspection of a Conspectus." *Journal of the American Oriental Society* 94 (1974): 195–209.

Moravcsik, J. "Zur Geschichte der Onoguren." *Ural-Altaische Jahrbücher* 10 (1930): 53–90.

Moses, L. W. "T'ang Tribute Relations with the Inner Asian Barbarians." In J. C. Perry and B. L. Smith, eds., *Essays on T'ang Society*. Pp. 61–89.

Nieh Ch'ung-ch'i. "Sung Liao chiao-p'ing k'ao." *Yenching Hsüeh-pao* 27 (1940): 1–51.

Okada, H. "The Secret History of the Mongols. A Pseudo-Historical Novel." In *Proceedings. Third East Asian Altaistic Conference*. Taipei, 1969. Pp. 61–68.

Olbricht, P. "Uchida's Prolegomena zu einer Geschichte der Jou-jan." *Ural-Altaische Jahrbücher* 26 (1954): 90–100.

Panaitescu, P. P. "La route commerciale de la Pologne à la Mer Noire au Moyen-Age." *Revista Istorica Romana* 3 (1933): 172–93.

Pelliot, P. "L'origine du nom de la Chine." *T'oung Pao* 13 (1912): 727–42.

Petech, L. "Les marchands italiens dans l'empire mongol." *Journal Asiatique* (1962): 549–74.

Peterson, C. "First Sung Reactions to the Mongol Invasions of the North." In J. W. Haeger, ed., *Crisis and Prosperity in Sung China*. Pp. 241–48.

Petrushevsky, I. P. "The Socio-Economic Condition of Iran under the Il-khans." In *Cambridge History of Iran*, 5: 483–582.

Poliak, A. N. "Le caractère colonial de l'état mamlouk dans ses rapports avec la Horde d'Or." *Revue d'Etudes Islamiques* 9 (1935): 231–48.

———. "La féodalité islamique." *Revue d'Etudes Islamiques* 12 (1938): 247–65.

Pritsak, O. "Der Untergang des Reiches des Oghuzischen Yabghu." In *Fuad Köprülü Armagani*. Constantinople, 1953. Pp. 397–410.

———. "Die 24 Ta-ch'en. Studie zur Geschichte des Verwaltungsaufbaus des Hsiung-nu Reiche." *Oriens Extremus* 1 (1954): 178–202.

———. "Von den Karluk zu den Karachaniden." *Zeitschrift des Deutschen Morgenlandischen Gesellschaft* 101 (1951): 270–300.

Pulleyblank, E. G. "The An Lu-shan Rebellion and the Origins of Chronic Militarism in Late T'ang China." In J. C. Perry and B. L. Smith, eds., *Essays on T'ang Society*. Pp. 32–60.

Rachewiltz, I. de. "The Hsi-yu lu by Yeh-lü Ch'u-ts'ai" *Monumenta Serica* 21 (1962): 1–128.

———. "Muqali, Bol, Tas and An-t'ung." *Papers on Far Eastern History*, no. 15 (1977): 45–62.

———. "Personnel and Personalities in North China During the Early Mongol Period." *Journal of the Economic and Social History of the Orient* (1966): 88–144.

———. "Yeh-Lü Ch'u-ts'ai (1189–1243): Buddhist Idealist and Confucian Statesman." In A. F. Wright and D. Twitchett, eds., *Confucian Personalities*. Stanford, 1962. Pp. 189–216.

Ratchnevsky, P. "Les Che-wei étaient-ils des Mongols?" In *Mélanges sinologiques offerts à Monsieur Paul Demiéville*. Vol. 1. Paris, 1966. Pp. 225–51.

Redfield, R., R. Linton, and M. J. Herskovitz. "A Memorandum for the Study of Acculturation." *American Anthropologist* 38 (1936): 149–51.

Röhricht, R. "Analekten. I. Briefe des Jacobus de Vitriaco (1216–21)." *Zeitschrift für Kirchengeschichte* 16 (1896): 72–113.

Roux, J. P. "Notes additionnelles à Tängri. Le ciel-dieu des peuples altaiques." *Revue de l'histoire des religions*, no. 154 (1958): 32–66.

———. "Tängri. Essai sur le ciel-dieu des peuples altaiques." *Revue de l'histoire des religions*, no. 149 (1956): 49–82, 197–220; no. 150 (1956): 27–54, 173–212.

Schafer, E. H. "A Fourteenth Century Gazetteer of Canton." In *Oriente Poliano*. Rome, 1957. Pp. 67–93.

Schlegel, D. "Koexistenz oder Annexionskrieg? Kublai Khans Politik gegenüber dem Sung Reiches, 1256–1276." *Saeculum* 19 (1968): 390–405.

Schreiber, G. "The History of the Former Yen Dynasty." *Monumenta Serica* 14 (1949–55): 374–480; 15 (1956): 1–141.

———. "Das Volk der Hsien-pi zur Han-Zeit." *Monumenta Serica* 12 (1947): 145–203.

Schurmann, H. F. "Mongolian Tributary Practices of the Thirteenth Century." *Harvard Journal of Asiatic Studies* 19 (1956): 304–89.

Shinobu Iwamura. "Mongol Invasions of Poland in the Thirteenth Century." *Memoirs of the Research Department of the Toyo Bunko* 10 (1938): 103–57.

Shirokauer, C. "Neo-Confucians under Attack: The Condemnation of Wei-hsüeh." In J. W. Haeger, ed., *Crisis and Prosperity in Sung China*. Pp. 163–98.

Sinor, D. "Autour d'une migration de peuples au Ve siècle." *Journal Asiatique* (1946–47): 1–77.

———. "Les relations entre les Mongols et l'Europe jusqu'à la mort d'Arghoun et de Béla IV." *Cahiers d'histoire mondiale* 3 (1956): 39–62.

———. "Un Voyageur du treizième siècle: Le Dominicain Julien de Hongrie." *Bulletin of the School of Oriental and African Studies* 16 (1952): 589–602.

———. "What is Inner Asia?" In *Altaica Collecta. Berichte und Vorträge des XVII Permanent International Altaistic Conference*. Wiesbaden, 1976. Pp. 245–58.

Smith, J. M., Jr. "Mongol and Nomadic Taxation." *Harvard Journal of Asiatic Studies* 30 (1970): 46–85.

———. "Mongol Manpower and Persian Population." *Journal of the Economic and Social History of the Orient* 18 (1975): 271–99.

Spuler, B. "Mittelasien seit dem Auftreten der Türken." In *Handbuch der Orientalistik*. Vol. 5, Pt. 5. Leiden, 1966. Pp. 123–310.

Stein, R. "Leao Tche," *T'oung Pao* 35 (1939): 1–154.

Tao Hsi-sheng. "Chin-tai meng-an mou-k'e ti t'u-ti wen-ti." *Shih-huo pan-yüeh-kan* 1 (1935): 345–52.

Tao Jing-shen. "The Political Recruitment in the Chin Dynasty." *Journal of the American Oriental Society* 94 (1974): 24–34.

Thiel, J. "Der Streit der Buddhisten und Taoisten zur Mongolenzeit." *Monumenta Serica* 20 (1961): 1–81.

Trauzettel, R. "Sung Patriotism as a First Step Toward Chinese Nationalism." In J. W. Haeger, ed., *Crisis and Prosperity in Sung China*. Pp. 199–213.

Treven, K. V. "Kusany, Khioniti i Eftality po armjanskim istočnikam IV–VII vv." *Sovetskaja Arkheologiya* 21 (1954): 131–47.

Twitchett, D. "Varied Patterns of Provincial Autonomy in the T'ang Dynasty." In J. C. Perry and B. L. Smith, eds., *Essays on T'ang Society*. Pp. 90–109.

Vernadsky, G. "The Scope and Contents of Chinggis-khan's Yasa." *Harvard Journal of Asiatic Studies* 3 (1938): 337–60.

Vorob'ev, M. V. "Chzhurchzhenej gosudarstvo tszin' i Central'naja Azija po tszin'-skim istochnikam." *Strany i narody vostoka* 9 (1971): 31–42.

———. "Xojzjajstvo i byt chzhurchzhenej do obrazovanija dinastii tszin'." *Geograficheskoe obshchestvo SSSR, Doklady po etnografia (Leningrad)* 1 (1965): 3–27.

Wang Gungwu "The Middle Yangtse in T'ang Politics." In A. F. Wright and D. Twitchett, *Perspectives on the T'ang*. Pp. 193–235.

Weiers, W. "Bemerkungen zu den Nachrichten über die Tsu-pu zur Liao-Zeit (905–1125)." *Zentralasiatische Studien* 7 (1973): 545–65.

Worthy, E. "Regional Control in the Southern Sung Salt Administration." In J. W. Haeger, ed., *Crisis and Prosperity in Sung China*. Pp. 101–42.

Wu, K. T. "Chinese Printing under Four Alien Dynasties." *Harvard Journal of Asiatic Studies* 13 (1950): 447–523.

Wylie, T. V. "The First Mongol Conquest of Tibet Reinterpreted." *Harvard Journal of Asiatic Studies* 37 (1977): 103–34.

Yamamoto Mamora. "Joshin yakugo no kenkyū." *Kobe Gaidai Ronsō* 2 (1951): 64–79.

Yamamoto Takayoshi. "Gendai ni okeru kanrin ni tsuite." *Tōhō Gakuhō* 11 (1955): 81–99.

Index